Health is the New Wealth

Living Above the Affliction Zone

By
Rich Travis

www.richtravisbooks.com
Health is the New Wealth, 20710 Amber Ct, Bend, OR 97701

USD $24.95 | ISBN 978-0-9700549-6-8

Publisher: Klein Graphics LLC, Concord,
Distributed through Amazon KNP

Contents

ORIENTATION—
Getting the Most From This Book 5

CHAPTER 1.
Overview—At The Crossroads ... 9

CHAPTER 2.
Problem One—How Does Our "Healthcare" System Really Work? 27

Who decided that those who profit off disease should be in charge of healthcare, anyway?

CHAPTER 3.
Problem Two—How Do We Promote "Chronic Wellness"? 75

What are the key dynamics of chronic disease, and how do they tie in with the medical-pharmaceutical machine?

CHAPTER 4.
Solution One—Health is the New Wealth 119

Let's review the last section.

CHAPTER 5.
Solution Two—Living Beyond the Affliction Zone 187

CHAPTER 6.
Establishing an Effective Medical Approach 217

PRELUDE TO CHAPTER 7.
Re-Orientation—Getting The Most From The Rest of This Book 259

CHAPTER 7.
Influences of the American Medical System on Adulthood and Aging, Part 1: The Dilemma 263

CHAPTER 8.
Influences of the American Medical System on Adulthood and Aging, Part 2: The Solution 325

CHAPTER NOTES 415

BIBLIOGRAPHY 439

APPENDIX

Appendix A:
Recommended Websites 443
Appendix B:
Overview And Contrast Of Two Competing Medical Approaches 445
Appendix C:
Drugs Impair Various Organs And Systems Within The Body 451
Appendix D:
A Systematic Approach To Gradual Drug Reduction 453
Appendix E:
Diet For Life 461
Appendix F:
4 Simple Rules To Shape Up Your Brain 463
Appendix G:
Getting Started 469
Appendix H:
Premise and Supporting Evidence: A Healthy Lifestyle
Decreases Hospital Utilization and Medical Costs 473

Orientation—
Getting the Most From This Book

When I wrote this book, I held two audiences in mind: those affected by chronic disease (either their own or that of someone they love), and those with the responsibility of treating the chronically ill, either on the front lines of direct patient care or in healthcare management, policy, and reform. Every healthcare professional has a responsibility to be his/her patient's advocate. If they are not committed to that first and foremost, they are in the wrong business.

Both audiences also have a personal responsibility. The first audience has a responsibility to overcome chronic disease by living in a way that is consistent with their recovery. Their only other alternative is to live in a way that is inconsistent with their recovery, which is to encourage their own decline. The second has a responsibility to provide treatment that is consistent with the "goal of payment," which I contend is for patients to get well and not simply to have the symptoms of their progressive decline treated and/or medicated.

The first group consists of people who are chronically ill, their family, and their friends. They've been told that their salvation lies in prescription drugs and surgical procedures, and there are strong reasons to believe that this is not so—that these products of the American medical-pharmaceutical machine actually prolong the underlying illness by treating symptoms instead of addressing causes. Members of this group need hope that health and wellness are actually possible, and they also need a specific "framework of help" to make that possibility into their personal experience.

The second group consists of all healthcare professionals, doctors, nurses, therapists, as well as healthcare managers, administrators, and healthcare policymakers and healthcare reformers —men and women involved with legislative groups and non-profit leadership, with granting foundations and advocacy agencies. Members of this group need to examine their mission, and if it is to improve the health of their patients, then they need to lead their patients, practice, and the industry in the direction that will most effectively fulfill that mission. That is, they have a moral mandate to promote the type of healthcare that the best evidence supports.

Both of these groups need to grasp that our healthcare crisis is largely the result of an unwillingness to do the "real work". Real solutions require time and hard work whereas consumers, corporations and social systems seem fixated on short term gratification. Perhaps that is why we are so caught up with providing (or accepting) "solutions" that only treat the effects instead of examining and rooting out the causes. It takes a great deal more time and dogged determination to dig beneath the surface and unearth the real problems and discover where the real solutions lie. Throughout the book I examine threads of connection, some for better and many for worse between the people, processes, products, and politics of medicine.

At the Crossroads ... overviews key themes, challenges, conflicts, and appeals recurring throughout the book.

Problem One addresses medical system issues in contemporary America: people, processes, products, and politics. This includes a look at groups and organizations such as chronically ill patients, hospitals, treatments, and research and political entities. All of these are expressions of what I like to refer to as the American Medical Approach. This book also explores what kinds of key connections exist among these players in the processes of illness and wellness, who benefits (or doesn't) from the current model and why, and offers some core recommendations for spurring the system to be more ethical and economical. This leads to political and economic proposals for constructive system change, which are detailed in *Solution One—Health is the New Wealth.*

Problem Two focuses on "prescriptive practices" for preventing illness through promoting wellness. It examines 1) human nature's propensity toward sweetness and ease and its subsequent attraction of chronic disease, and 2) modern medicine's complicity in "business with disease" because of its financial reward system based on "fees for disease". This results in its focus on the treatment of symptoms versus the removal of causes, because the entire system is entrenched in a "disease-for-profit" medical model. This leads to personal practices for optimizing health and wellness which are detailed in *Solution Two—Living Beyond the Affliction Zone.*

Establishing an Effective Medical Approach draws together the proposals and practices from this book into the form of concise and practical plans for implementation.

The *Bibliography* and *Appendices* provide additional resources and in-depth topical information that support and defend the concepts presented in this book.

It's okay to read an essay or two, put the book down, steep on it or sleep on it, and go back to the book again later. In fact, I suspect that's how most people will get the most out of this book.

Finally, I have two specific suggestions for getting the most out of this material. First, do not try to ingest too much of the information at once. This content should provide plenty of material for discussion and meditation. Each Problem and Solution section is divided into relatively short segments, so that the concepts, questions, and evidence could be viewed in smaller bites, and so that each part could be investigated more thoroughly with references and resources. Second, read slowly and deeply and reflect on this book's implications for personal transformation. I hope its content will help you realize that *to improve your health is to acquire great wealth* and that wealth is largely yours for the taking. I hope its content *also* inspires personal and professional advocacy for the chronically ill and stimulates the transformation of our medical care delivery system into one that is truly evidence-based and actually delivers on its promises.

That said, I wish you and your loved ones success in the disciplines that lead to wellness.

Rich Travis, RN, BSN

CHAPTER 1.
OVERVIEW—AT THE CROSSROADS ...

At the Crossroads ... gives an overview of key themes, challenges, conflicts and appeals recurring throughout this book.

Every day at work as a registered nurse, I see the physical results of people's apathy and vulnerability. I work in a sub-acute cardiac monitoring unit of a hospital. This environment is filled with patients who, as a result of many years of self-neglect and self-indulgence, are now confined to the most limiting, powerless, and vulnerable existences imaginable—not just while in the hospital, but every day. Their symptoms make life a veritable nightmare: excessive weight, weakness, shortness of breath, joint pain, chest pain, running bowels, near-fainting spells, clouds of confusion—the list goes on.

Now, they probably don't see their life in such dire terms because they're comparing their today with their yesterday. But, if they were to compare their *debilitated* today to a *healthy* person's today, they would be aghast, absolutely *appalled* at how far they had slipped from a vitally alive state.

However, I see it, and it grieves my heart every day. I wouldn't admit it on the floor, but I will bare all here. I care about my patients, and it grieves my heart to see so much pain. Their condition, which I will call a state of abject health poverty, is very different from the world I step out of every day as I enter into their world.

In my personal world, I am surrounded on a daily basis by friends and athletes who live with robust recreational venues, happy hearts, and vibrant energy. They lead active lives which sustain their health. In fact, it actually "gives them life" and keeps them "topped off" and running smoothly. As the old adage goes, "Healthy is as healthy does!"

But then I come back to work and pour through my patients' charts to analyze their prior history and current condition so as to understand how I might help their current need. It is easy to see that it all started with one diagnosis of something small and seemingly innocuous: high blood pressure, elevated blood sugar, or shortness of breath some 10, 15, 20 years ago. Then we step through the progression of their medical history and are brought to their today. Here we find a list of diseases and co-morbidities that could fill a page, and behind that is the list of past and current medications, medical interventions, diagnostic tests, prior hospitalizations, and current crisis and presenting symptoms. It alarms me that all these chronicles of progressive physical decline began 10, 15, 20 years ago with a simple diagnosis. I think, *Could all of this have been prevented? Where did it all go wrong?*

Applying my medical training, I review the patient's condition, including:

1] Medical history
2] Diagnosis
3] Symptoms
4] Medical orders
5] Nursing interventions
6] Patient teaching to be performed

I review their Plan of Care: blood draws at 6 AM. Fleet Enema in the early morning, followed by barium studies later in the morning. Medications at 6—9—12—5—9. Juggling all of these priorities is a challenge as this is only one of my four patients. I also have patients with diarrhea in Room 2 and chest pain in Room 3, and the patient with dementia in Room 4 pulled out his IV. Another day of racing among competing priorities, trying desperately not to drop the ball and let someone get hurt, or worse—actually causing someone to get hurt by making a mistake.

Here I am, working on the floor, trying to keep up with all my nursing responsibilities and the patients' medication schedules. I understand the rationale for all the medications we are giving and the tests we are conducting and the interventions we are performing. But there is still something missing! When I look beneath the surface of the symptoms we are medicating and the diagnosis we are treating, I see that the *underlying causes* of their condition are largely unaddressed.

Despite all the best intents and treatments and lifesaving interventions provided by the medical system, the real problems are often not even addressed. People with chronic diseases are getting through their hospital stays and surviving for yet another day of struggle, but they are not coming away any different or better equipped to prevent a relapse. I mean, sure, we get them through their immediate crisis and we stabilize their profound physiological compromise. But overall, they leave just about the way they arrived: sick, just no longer unto death. They came here leading sedentary, unhealthy, inactive lives, which actually promoted their underlying disease's progression. And they go home to resume the exact same life and lifestyle that led to their being hospitalized in the first place.

I care deeply about my patients. I keep wondering: "What if?" What if someone had gotten a hold of them when they developed their earliest set of "concerning" symptoms and received their first significant diagnosis, and sat down with them and told them what I am going to tell you? Maybe, just maybe, things could have been a whole lot different…

America is at the crossroads with our medical system; the system needs to decide between patients or profits, and between ethics or abuses.

I contend that the real needs of the chronically ill for lifestyle reform are being sidestepped for the financial gain associated with the treatment of their progressive decline, and that the medical system has a financial responsibility to not simply treat the symptoms of decline, but proactively support their prevention.

It is the fiduciary responsibility of medical care systems to provide the type of care that patients want to receive—the result of which is to get well and prosper—and not simply have the symptoms of their progressive decline medicated. It is the duty of medical care systems to provide the best evidence-based approaches to their patient's recovery from disease and the best evidence-based approaches to the diseases' reversal whenever possible.

Healthcare corporations claim that they "care about our health." Their messages sound genuine, sincere, and convincing—but in reality, I believe their actions fall short of their claims.

This sad phenomenon should (and could) end. Patients could (and should) be strongly supported in a return to chronic wellness. But it will take medicine attending to patients' *real needs for health*, instead of focusing on the industry's need for profit derived from the treatment of the symptoms of their progressive decline.

But does the current medical system really care? The proof of this system's devotion to patients will be demonstrated in the creation of large Lifestyle Transformation Centers equipped with all the necessary coaching and supports to move chronic disease-aholics through a 12-step path to freedom from disease. Those who attract chronic disease to themselves cannot or will not be able to make the lifestyle changes necessary to reverse their chronic diseases; they need the prescriptive support of a mandated lifestyle revision program to make their adjustment to a healthy lifestyle not only a possibility but a strong probability.

The medical system must decide whether to support its paying patients through transition to a healthy lifestyle, or to simply continue to profit from their going under. Medicine is at the crossroads of opportunity to promote a pathway of breakthrough to all those patients who don't realize that living above their chronic disease is just a lifestyle away. The burden of responsibility for mandating and facilitating lifestyle transition depends almost entirely upon the medical system, as patients have not the wherewithal to rise out of the miry clay.

For modern medicine to simply bring the effect of toxic pills to bear against the tide of a self-undermining lifestyle is akin to simply rearranging the chairs on the deck of the Titanic as it approaches a very clearly identified and foreknown iceberg. Modern medicine needs to consider its complicit role in allowing millions to live with and be defeated by chronic disease that is entirely manageable. They have the wherewithal from their astronomical earnings to provide the facilities, coaching, and 12-step support system necessary to persuade, encourage, and immerse the chronically ill in the demonstrated lifestyle habits that produce consistently good health. They need to take that more principled path.

> **Patients with chronic illness are likewise at a crossroads. They need to decide between taking personal responsibility that leads back to wellness, and passive recidivism that yields continued physical decline, repeated hospital visits, and worsening or new symptoms.**

The healthcare system can set the stage, but there are other actors in this play who also need to revise their roles in the plot at hand. The sad state of affairs I see daily in my hospital work can end if chronically ill people themselves would take a hard look at their existence, take personal responsibility for their health, and adopt the behaviors of people who have taken good care of their bodies. They would then gradually return to the experience of vitality, power, confidence, compliments, independence, self-fulfillment, and joyful living.

This isn't rocket science. People have bodies, and those bodies end up where their behavior takes them. If you don't like where you are, reverse the steps that took you there. Your feet represent your behavior, and your health flows out of your behavior. Adding pills filled with toxic chemicals to the behavioral steps that got you to your current unpleasant place will not transport you; only your feet will take you away from where your feet have brought you. Only healthy behavior will take you to a place of healthy consequences.

Such radical changes take motivation and a degree of discomfort, but they will yield hope and a future. To remain the same will involve progressively deeper levels of discomfort, humiliation, and losses of strength and independence. Do you wish to become a progressive burden to yourself and your loved ones, or do you wish to be a source of continuing support and strength?

Would you rather make the effort to swim and walk regularly, drink carrot juice, and eat a diet high in fruits, salads, and vegetables, or would you prefer to make a great effort to get out of bed and get dressed? Both groups of people experience exertion. Which group do you want to be a part of? In this life, exertion isn't an option: either you'll be exerting yourself in the effort to get and stay well, or you'll be exerting yourself through the daily pains and ailments that result from letting your body go to hell.

> **It is increasingly scientifically evident that healthy lifestyle management of chronic disease is superior in every way to chemical management. This scientific evidence demands an ethical medical response. But three things present significant challenges: corporate greed, human apathy, and vulnerability to discouragement.The latter two have bankrolled the former.**

We have billions of dollars at work within the medical system. In the case of chronic disease, the chief beneficiaries of that vast wealth are the pharmaceutical and medical industries, not patients. I believe that aggressive lifestyle management and fitness programs introduced directly into the lives of the one to five percent most chronically ill would cost one-fifth of the cost of our current medical model's crisis intervention and emergency hospitalization of patients for the treatment of largely preventable declines.

> *"However, if we look at the other end of the cost continuum, opportunities abound. A mere 1 percent of the insured are consuming 30 percent of total costs, and the top 5 percent account for as much as two-thirds of all costs. Herein lies the problem--as well as the massive potential for what we might call a "5 percent solution." That solution lies in identifying the specific chronic and acute conditions that move people into that high-cost 5*

percent bracket and then systematically and consistently bringing to bear strategic, targeted, consistent, high-leverage interventions to keep those people from migrating to the high-cost end of the curve. When people are in crisis, we need to provide best care. But we also need to stop large numbers of people from progressing into that crisis."[1]
- George Halvorsen: The 5% Solution

I'm fully convinced that chronic disease management through aggressive lifestyle reconstruction will yield for the chronically ill the skills, confidence, and inspiration necessary for successful, low-cost, healthy management of their conditions.

HEALTHY LIFESTYLE KEY TO CONTROLLING COSTS

First, our health care system does not spend its finite resources efficiently. Instead of focusing on preserving and enhancing Americans' health, our system encourages treatment only after a "crisis" has occurred.

Given this orientation, it's not surprising that we spend the vast majority of our health care dollars on treatment of patients with one or more chronic diseases such as diabetes or heart disease. Treatment of patients with chronic illnesses accounts for 75 cents of every health care dollar, or $1.65 trillion in 2007. . . Second, while these direct health care costs are astounding, they are dwarfed by the economic cost of lost productivity. Our economic prosperity depends on having a healthy work force.... If left unchecked, chronic diseases will cost our economy $4.1 trillion by 2023, mostly because of lost productivity, according to Milken Institute estimates.[2] - www.politico.com

> "What do the campaign platforms of Sens. Hillary Clinton, John McCain, and Barack Obama have in common? Preventive medicine, and the belief that prevention saves money. But does it?
>
> "Our "health-care system" is primarily a disease-care system. Last year, $2.1 trillion was spent in this country on medical care, or 16.5 percent of the gross national product. And 95 cents of every medical-care dollar went to treat disease after it had already occurred. At least 75 percent of these costs were spent on treating chronic diseases such as heart disease and diabetes that are preventable

or even reversible. A RAND study projected nearly $81 billion in annual national health expenditure savings due to prevention and disease-management programs.

"Incentives are often perverse. For example, insurance companies pay more than $30,000 to amputate a diabetic foot even though most amputations are preventable by scrupulous foot care, which is usually not covered by insurance. When I lecture, I often begin by showing a slide of doctors busily mopping up the floor around an overflowing sink, but no one is turning off the faucet. Similarly, Dr. Denis Burkitt (who discovered Burkitt's lymphoma) once said that raising money to pay for ambulances and a hospital at the base of a cliff is not as smart as building a fence at the top to keep cars from falling off.

"It's important to treat not only the problem but also its underlying causes. Otherwise, the same problem often recurs (for example, bypass grafts or angioplastied arteries often clog up again), a new set of problems may occur (such as side effects from medications), or there may be painful choices.

"Our research at the Preventive Medicine Research Institute (PMRI), as well as the studies of other investigators, have shown that your body often has a remarkable capacity to begin healing itself, and much more quickly than had once been realized, when the underlying causes of illness are addressed. For many people, the choices we make each day in what we eat and in how we live are among the most important underlying causes. Hillary Clinton's health plan calls for a "focus on prevention: wellness not sickness.... Insurers must cover high priority preventive services that experts agree are proven and effective. This focus on prevention will improve health and lower costs in the long run." John McCain states on his campaign Web site that "We can improve health and spend less, while promoting competition on the cost and quality of care, taking better care of our citizens with chronic illness, and promoting prevention that will keep millions of others from ever developing deadly and debilitating disease." Barack Obama's health plan states, "This nation is facing a true epidemic of chronic disease. An increasing number of Americans are suffering and dying needlessly from diseases such as obesity, diabetes, heart disease, asthma and HIV/AIDS, all of which can be delayed in onset if not prevented entirely." Also, Sen. Ron Wyden has sponsored the Healthy Americans Act, which emphasizes prevention and has bipartisan support. Given this consensus, many people were surprised by some recent articles questioning the value of prevention. As David Brown wrote earlier this month in The Washington Post, "Studies show it's often cheaper to let people get sick ... Even when prevention greatly reduces future cases of a particular illness, overall cost to the health-care system typically goes up when lots of disease-preventing strategies are put into practice." For example, he questioned the value of taking cholesterol-lowering drugs.

"Even if this analysis were true--and there are several fallacies in his calculations--it ignores the fact that most people can significantly lower their cholesterol levels and blood pressure by making comprehensive lifestyle changes that are free rather than by taking a lifetime of drugs that are costly. In our research, we found that improved nutrition, moderate exercise, stress-management techniques and social support caused a 40 percent average reduction in harmful LDL-cholesterol levels in men and women during the course of a year without drugs. Last year, more than $20 billion was spent in this country on cholesterol-lowering drugs, so the potential cost savings would be significant if more people made comprehensive lifestyle changes in lieu of drugs.

"A similar but somewhat more balanced perspective was published two months ago in The New England Journal of Medicine. The authors wrote, "Sweeping statements about the cost-saving potential of prevention, however, are overreaching. Studies have concluded that preventing illness can in some cases save money but in other cases can add to health care costs ... In general, whether a particular preventive measure represents good value or poor value depends on factors such as the population targeted, with measures targeting higher-risk populations typically being the most efficient."

"I agree that cost savings can be greatest and can be seen most quickly in those who are at highest risk or who have chronic diseases. For example, my colleagues and I at the nonprofit PMRI conducted a demonstration project in collaboration with eight hospitals to determine if comprehensive lifestyle changes could be a safe and effective alternative to bypass surgery or angioplasty in those who were eligible to receive it. After one year, almost 80 percent of people were able to safely avoid heart surgery or angioplasty, and Mutual of Omaha calculated saving almost $30,000 per patient in the first year."[3]

EXECUTIVE SUMMARY

Expenditures for health care in the United States continue to rise and are estimated to reach $1.66 trillion in 2003. Much of these costs can be attributed to the diagnosis and treatment of chronic diseases and conditions such as diabetes, obesity, cardiovascular disease and asthma.

- Approximately 129 million U.S. adults are overweight or obese which costs this Nation anywhere from $69 billion to $117 billion per year.
- In 2000, an estimated 17 million people (6.2 percent of the population) had diabetes, costing the U.S. approximately $132 billion. People with diabetes lost more than 8 days per year from work, accounting for 14 million disability days.
- Heart disease and stroke are the first and third leading causes of death in the United States. In 2003 alone, 1.1 million Americans will have a heart attack. Cardiovascular diseases cost the Nation more than $300 billion each year.
- Approximately 23 million adults and 9 million children have been diagnosed with asthma at some point within their lifetime, with costs near $14 billion per year.

A much smaller amount is spent on preventing these conditions. There is accumulating evidence that much of the morbidity and mortality associated with these chronic diseases may be preventable.

For many Americans, individual behavior and lifestyle choices influence the development and course of these chronic conditions. Unhealthy behaviors, such as a poor diet, lack of physical activity, and tobacco use are risk factors for many chronic conditions and diseases. A high calorie diet and sedentary lifestyle commonly result in excessive weight gain. Overweight and obesity are risk factors for a large number of chronic diseases, most significantly, type 2 diabetes, congestive heart failure, stroke, and hypertension. Encouraging individuals to adopt healthy habits and practices may reduce the burden of chronic disease in communities throughout the United States.

Recently, public and private efforts and programs are increasingly designed to promote healthy behaviors. Employers are becoming more aware that overweight and obesity, lack of physical activity, and tobacco use are adversely affecting the health and productivity of their employees and ultimately, the businesses' bottom line. As a result, innovative employers are providing their employees with a variety of work-site-based health promotion and disease prevention programs. These programs have been shown to improve employee health, increase productivity and yield a significant return on investment for the employer. For example, a recent review of health promotion and disease management programs found a significant return on investment for these programs, with benefit-to-cost ratios, ranging from $1.49 to $4.91 (median of $3.14) in benefits for every dollar spent on the program. Several major companies with award-winning cost-saving health promotion disease prevention programs are profiled in this report and include:

- Motorola's wellness program, which states the company spent $3.93 for every $1 invested.
- Northeast Utilities WellAware Program, which in its first 24 months reduced lifestyle and behavioral claims by $1,400,000.
- Caterpillar's Healthy Balance program, which is projected to result in long term savings of $700 million by 2015.
- Johnson & Johnson's Health and Wellness Program, which has produced average annual health care savings of $224.66 per employee.
- By changing the way they live, individual Americans could change their personal health status and the health landscape of the Nation dramatically.[4]

EFFECTS OF EXERCISE AND DIET ON CHRONIC DISEASE

by Christian K. Roberts and R. James Barnard

Overwhelming evidence from a variety of sources, including epidemiological, prospective cohort, and intervention studies, links most chronic diseases seen in the world today to physical inactivity and inappropriate diet consumption. . . .

> Chronic diseases present an enormous burden to society by increasing medical costs and human suffering.
>
> Physical activity and diet are effective interventions, for what Booth and coworkers have coined "the war on chronic disease." Clearly, there is overwhelming evidence linking most chronic diseases seen in the world today to physical inactivity and inappropriate diet consumption.
>
> A concerted effort to increase primary prevention of chronic disease through the translation of research data on the value of exercise and diet to the general public and legislation to urge implementation of primary prevention strategies as opposed to opportunistic care are essential.[5]
>
> In general, whether a particular preventive measure represents good value or poor value depends on factors such as the population targeted, with measures targeting higher-risk populations typically being the most efficient.[6]

I am asking the medical care system to act with compassion and provide patients with the tools for self-recovery, instead of milking the consequences of poor lifestyle for every penny.

To the medical professionals on the front lines who are attempting to help patients in the best way with limited resources, I have no beef. Their hearts are in the right place and they're doing their best to keep up with the incredible demands of a mechanized medical system. But medical corporations which have little purpose other than profit have entered the arena of the human condition. They withhold a preventive medical approach, one with clear evidence of superior patient outcomes, in order to profit from the symptoms of patients' ongoing decay. They financially harvest the chronically ill for dollars. The situation is absolutely damnable; in the arena of medicine, withholding preventive principles in order to profit from the treatment of ongoing conditions is an idea inspired by the devil and fueled daily by the idolatry of greed.

We have two major issues to content with:

1] Corporate Greed: corporations' pathological pursuit of profits.

2] Human Ignorance/Apathy

People with chronic health problems need to own up to how they have contributed to their own health equation and take positive steps to end the nightmare that has become their physical existence.

I am appealing to patients who appear to be the happy and passive victims of their chronic disease. I say *happy* because if they weren't content (at some level) in their downwardly spiraling predicament, they probably would fight hard to procure a different outcome. I am appealing to them to *give living well a chance.* Every cell in the human body has amazing recuperative powers. If people trodden down by chronic disease start living in ways that are good for them, the body will respond thankfully, and immediately begin reversing the consequences of self-abuse and physical neglect. As people have decreasing pain, improving function, and restoration of vitality, they begin to enjoy living healthfully. They grasp the value and deep reward of being truly good to themselves, and they begin to understand and habituate their new life patterns.

From a growing body of scientifically verified evidence, we know people who lead genuinely healthy lives have healthy bodies and experience relatively no chronic disease. We also know that those who have been officially diagnosed with chronic conditions, but resolutely adopt genuinely healthy activities, dramatically decrease, if not entirely eliminate, those conditions. We already know this. A great deal of evidence is already available.[7]

We need to examine the evidence we already have, and design transformational programs that implement the most effective strategies, approaches, and practices. It is time for a paradigm shift in medicine. We know the shortest distance between chronic disease and physical recovery is through behavior modification, so we need to stop ignoring reality—especially out of devotion to higher profit margins. The reason a "for profit" corporation exists is for profit. A corporation will only pursue socially responsible behavior when public opinion, specifically the appearance of being environmentally or socially responsible, will improve that corporation's image, and therefore possibly increase their profits.

> **Profit in itself is not bad for guiding corporate decision making; however, since corporations are deemed "persons," then as persons they should be held responsible and accountable for their impact upon society.**

Currently, corporations will kick a few bones in the direction of causes they feel will best boost their corporate image, but that's as deep as it goes. The real decisions about corporate goals and directions, agendas and methods, protocols and procedures, products and services, and the treatment of employees and the environment are all focused upon the bottom line. Highest profit is the idol that corporations bow to, and these corporations are progressively blatant in demanding that all employees, citizens, societies, economies, and environments bow as well.

What if we could figure out ways for medical or insurance corporations to profit from people being *well*? What if we could funnel the greatest monetary gains to corporations whose means and methods benefited the water, air, animals, and society? Imagine corporations serving mankind and encouraging the environment instead of enslaving mankind and destroying the environment. Of course this is, by current corporate ideals, ridiculous, but I wanted to at least present the idea of an ideal federal government that would listen to the needs of its constituents, and serve and protect those constituents with fierce love. Such a government would perform its responsibilities with integrity and financially punish corporate methods, practices, processes, products, and byproducts found to be detrimental to people, the economy, and the environment. We need a living, dynamic, evolving document with the authority of the law to outline and define the moral, ethical, and functional responsibilities that the government owes to its governed.

It is against the law for individuals to enslave and destroy. Isn't it time that corporations be severely punished for destructive behavior? Corporations are fined for abuses of society and the environment, but evidently not with enough frequency or sting to make the attempts unprofitable. I believe corporations committing illegal and destructive acts against people and the environment know that the fines for doing wrong are simply a reasonable cost of running a successful business. Economically speaking, it wouldn't make sense to do it any other way. I say it's time to make damaging the world's people and environment hurt the medical industry's bottom line enough so that it is truly discouraged.

So, if a $3 million fine didn't discourage wrongdoing, maybe a $30 million fine would. And if not, probably a $300 million fine, or more, would finally begin to get their attention. It's time that violations be addressed forcibly, lest they continue ad infinitum.

But for this to take place, people need a united voice, and that voice would be the words of this living document, which enumerates the people's ideas of the moral, ethical, and functional responsibilities it requires of its government. It must declare the general will of the majority to which the government shall be held accountable. It is to the good of society as a whole that the government and all its citizens must be held accountable. The government must serve its people and not the other way around.

IS ETHICAL MEDICINE EVEN POSSIBLE?

Consider the intelligence-gathering capabilities of a medical system whose government financially rewarded corporations for improvements in patient health, and decreased financial rewards to corporations when patients experienced a decline in their health.

Think of the potential benefit to our society (given corporations' voracious appetite for profit) if medical profits hinged upon decreasing the prevalence of disease amongst its patients. Consider an overarching insurance corporation that would not receive any more money for treating a sick patient versus treating a well patient. Its responsibility is for the medical care of its members whether they are sick or well, and so it would behoove them to keep their members well, since treating the well person costs far less. That particular institution's profits would increase as its patients remain well, and decrease as their patients' health declines. Imagine this group-agency-organization receiving insurance premiums monthly or government payments monthly and it could *keep all the money in profits if people needed no medical care.* On a large scale, this would have huge financial power—billions of dollars. What huge incentive that greedy organization would have to see all its members live well and prosper! This then makes sense as an ideal model for the promotion of ethical medicine.

Consider the importance of that institution doing its own medical research to discover the most efficient ways to restore health and well-being. Suppose these corporations conducted considerable studies to examine the cost of proactively facilitating and promoting client wellness. Suppose they determined through those studies that it costs *considerably less* to keep someone well, or to restore chronic conditions to wellness, than to continually treat ongoing conditions that are worsening. And just suppose this corporation were then willing to make the huge paradigm shift in medical care and begin to profoundly promote wellness. Suppose they elect to create Lifestyle Transformation Centers and invest heavily in senior-friendly YMCAs in America. Suppose they even exert influence upon the health and wellness industry to promote its rise in power. You would then have a health-promoting medical system to replace the disease-cultivating medical system.

Imagine with me the huge savings that would be realized if clients could be convinced, through being virtually required by policy and protocol, to maintain a healthy existence, and then given access to every necessary support needed to assure it. Imagine if participation in health-promoting activities among the chronically ill population was closely monitored and supported, and if the chronically ill began to exhibit signs and symptoms of declining health, their behavioral support would be increased.

WHERE WOULD THE MONEY FOR LIFESTYLE TRANSFORMATION CENTERS COME FROM?

Consider the cost of one average-length stay in a hospital for a chronic condition is as much as a fully-paid membership at a senior-friendly YMCA for approximately *33 years*. Consider a medical science that pursues prevention of disease instead of profit from disease. Consider a new medical paradigm whose power lies in reducing the cost of insurance and premiums rather than expanding products and services. Consider a "triple threat" approach to medical care that is preventative and cost-effective: (1) doctor-prescribed health programs, (2) nutritional education, lifestyle guidance, and 12 step support, and (3) provision of uncompromisingly healthy foods and organic juices. This approach would shift the locus of power away from the delivery of medical products and services and towards the delivery of improved patient outcomes. In this way, we would usher in a healthcare revolution which has the ability within 20 years to dramatically reduce obesity, chronic disease, and human suffering.

The only thing standing in our way is that the old guard's locus of power is seated within the camp of the disease-for-profit medical model. Through their broad and powerful influence, the American Medical Association (AMA) and pharmaceutical and medical corporations dictate control over the course and direction of American medicine from the top down. They control the selection of medical textbooks for medical and nursing students, the approval of scientific research and research facilities, the choice of best practices in hospitals and outpatient clinics, and monopolization of the types of medical products and services that are covered by insurance.

This medical model is in heated competition with the preventative model I am promoting. Medical insurance will cover many operations, procedures, and drugs for deepening disease states, but if you have any inkling of staying well, you are almost entirely on your own to finance it. Some insurance and medical corporations have wellness and thrive campaigns going on (to attract already healthy citizens into their patient risk pool). But have you ever seen a health and fitness center customized to the needs of the chronically ill attached to a hospital? Do you ever see comprehensive health and fitness programs, with 12-step support for the chronically ill, being prescribed to those with a clinical history of attracting illness to themselves?

Thousands of people lead illness-prone lives that are devoid of healthy behaviors, and these people frequent our hospitals and clinics, fill them to overflowing, come back time and time again with the same conditions—

and yet have you ever once seen any kind of comprehensive health and fitness center attached to a hospital or clinic? Of course not. Profit comes from the treatment of ongoing disease, not the promotion of deepening wellness.

However, the *appearance* of a socially responsible medical system improves public opinion, and that is good for the bottom line. So we continually see medical corporations claiming that "we are rooting for you." We need the medical corporations to get honest and start supporting us, too—not with mere health education classes for the already-motivated and well-equipped, but with Lifestyle Transformation Centers for the overwhelmed who have given up.

> **Medical science is funded almost entirely by the pharmaceutical industry. In this sense, it is more closely akin to product research and development. Medical science is a tool to discover new drugs: Profits from older drugs diminish as they become available in generic versions. It's not about curing the disease—it's about keeping the chemical profits high. This must change.**

The current dominant model of disease treatment is in contrast and opposition to a prevention model of medicine that profits when people are well, but loses capital when clients fall ill and require drugs and medical services. This medical model, in contrast to our current one, would seek above all else for patients to be healthy and drug-free. This medical model would be very willing to invest in true prevention—that is, in economical wholesale comprehensive health promotion programs for the chronically ill—on the front end, in order to avoid the astronomical costs associated with acute care re-hospitalizations on the tail end.

We are told that medical science is serving mankind, but I propose that science serves its highest bidders, which are its financiers. It "discovers" what it is told to discover, that is, what it is funded to search for. Scientists are not given money to discover the *causes* of and most effective treatments for disease; they are most frequently employed by pharmaceutical corporations to formulate molecular compounds (chemicals) that counteract the *symptoms* of disease for the purpose of patent and profit.

Take for example cardiovascular disease—the #1 killer in America. Researchers are not paid to discover the cause and cure for cardiovascular disease. They are paid to discover new interventions and chemicals to treat the symptoms of ongoing and progressive declines.

Or, take the issue of high blood pressure: medical scientists are funded by drug companies to research and formulate chemical compounds that cause your blood pressure to go lower, by making the walls of your blood vessels dilate, or by making your kidneys pull more fluid out of your blood. This is simply introducing a chemical into the body to produce an effect that is opposite of the effect of the symptom upon the cardiovascular system. They are not curing the cause of the patient's high blood pressure; they are simply counteracting the symptom (rising blood pressure) which the body has put in place as a warning of an underlying malfunction or abnormality. The drug simply takes that symptom and makes it go away.

And so it goes with most drugs. In most cases nothing is done about the underlying problem responsible for causing the symptom. What is lacking is a search for the underlying causes, and their removal. When we address a symptom by removing its cause, the problem is gone. When we address a problem by merely counteracting its symptom, the problem inevitably expresses itself again and again, though sometimes in different ways. The only possible conclusion of this process is progressive rifts of failure.

Here's an analogy: I have a car that I don't care very much about. I don't take very good care of it because it's not a priority. Last summer the "check engine" light started coming on whenever I'd drive it and that made me a bit uncomfortable. I'm not very mechanical and know even less about my car's electrical system, so I took my car to a mechanic. He asked what the problem was and I told him whenever I turned the car on the "check engine" light came on, and that was bothering me, and I wanted it turned off.

He looked at me kind of strange and said, "Don't you want to find out *why* the check engine light is coming on?"

I said, "Hey, my life is very busy right now. I just want the 'check engine light' to go away."

Friends, the check engine light is like a symptom; the honest mechanic (honest medicine) finds the real problem and helps me fix it; the unethical mechanic (unethical medicine) just turns off the light (the symptom).

When our bodies are healthy, we exhibit health. When something is out of whack, we exhibit a symptom that something is wrong: pain, stiffness, nausea, dizziness, weakness, rising or lowering blood pressure, increasing heart rate, shortness of breath, etc. These indicators alert us to underlying internal disorders and imbalances (systemic problems). Taking a drug to counteract the symptom often actually *encourages* further neglect of the *real* problem. Given the pharmaceutical company agenda, the real problem won't be corrected, but will simply re-manifest later as deepening cascades of decline, and they will have other medications for these symptoms.

If only more medical scientists were funded to search for the most effective cures and treatments, wherever they were to be found! Instead, pharmaceutical corporations pay medical scientists to research according to very strict guidelines as to where it is thought that a patentable and marketable "discovery" will be found. In my mind, this is "product development," and falls far short of real medical research. It is science used as a tool for corporate profit, a prostitute of corporate greed instead of a guide to breakthroughs for the benefit of mankind.

In the following pages, I propose various approaches to the challenge of changing our medical paradigm and ourselves. I outline specific details about the kind of behavioral modification programs and lifestyle transformation centers which I suggest are crucial to this challenge. Read, consider, and respond. This book is designed for you to interact with it, and it gives many prompts for further reading and investigation.

Most importantly: Think for yourself. Draw your own conclusions and then take strategic action. I urge you to join with me in becoming part of the solution. Our health, our children's health, and our nation's future and economy depend upon it. We cannot change a system which profits from "disease by design." We must form a new system that profits only from the wellness of its clients—that system alone will strive for its own wealth through the prosperity of its clients.

Chapter 2.
Problem One—How Does Our "Healthcare" System Really Work?

WHO DECIDED THAT THOSE WHO PROFIT OFF DISEASE SHOULD BE IN CHARGE OF HEALTHCARE, ANYWAY?

Problem One addresses medical system issues in contemporary America: people, processes, products, and politics. This includes a look at groups and organizations such as chronically ill patients, hospitals, treatments, research, political entities, and the current "medical-pharmaceutical machine" in America. It also explores what kinds of key connections exist among these players in the processes of illness and wellness, who benefits (or doesn't) from the current paradigm model and why, and some core recommendations for spurring the system to be more ethical and economical. This leads to political and economic proposals for constructive system change which are detailed in the section on *Solution One—Health is the New Wealth.*

1-1. CORPORATE MEDICINE'S CHIEF AND OVER-RIDING CONCERN IS THE BOTTOM LINE—PROFIT, NOT PEOPLE.

We as a nation are experiencing three phenomena simultaneously:

1] Exploding profits for the pharmaceutical and medical industries.

2] A massive undermining and erosion of the United States economy.

3] And, not least, unchecked and untold misery as modern medicine cashes in on our poor health.

I wish it were clear how deeply money controls medicine. Quite simply, the course of medicine in America is defined by a calculated pursuit of profits by the wealthiest principals of the medical system. I am talking about the medical power brokers at the very top who control the direction of the overall industry. These are profit-minded businesspeople, and as diligently as top athletes strive for their goals, these power brokers strive for the highest profits and highest financial rewards. These corporate entrepreneurs and executives have proven profit-making ability. They are paid handsome salaries to garner increasing profits for the corporate stockholders.

The professionals in the highest ranks of corporate medicine are there for the right reasons: because they can make the highest incomes for the corporation. These are the profit seekers, and they are a perfect fit for their positions. They seek profit personally, and they gain it by conferring increased profits upon their employers. It's a match made in . . . well, somewhere. Out of the closed-door meetings of the corporate elite we receive directions in medical care that have little to do with patient outcomes and everything to do with financial outcomes. These are corporate patriots committed to the company's prosperity. They do it for the money.

I want to camp out and explore this formula for success that has become our corporate legal structure. Corporations are publicly-owned entities, owned by the investors who purchase stock. Corporations are so structured that the leaders are working on behalf of a disinterested and unknowing body of investors. It creates the appearance of good, as if the movers and shakers are not pursuing personal gain but rather the benefit of all the investors corporately. And the investors appear good because they are never informed of the details of just how their profit is secured. So everyone is a good guy.

In this way, acts of heinous corporate greed can be conducted, and no one can be pointed to as personally at fault and, more importantly, no one can be held personally financially accountable. This is the big one because this game was designed for the money. It's all about the money.

Remember, corporations are not in business to serve the needs of mankind—they are in business to make a profit. Corporations which fund modern medical research and perform modern medical care are profit-seeking machines. They have no moral conscience attuned to benefiting mankind.

Profit is the first, last, and virtually exclusive consideration in every decision. Profit is the beginning and the end of all that they need to know or care to be concerned about. Any other pursuit or consideration would be an irresponsible—and in fact *illegal*—handling of their investors' capital.

Corporate interest is not in saving the world. Corporate interest is in profit. This is *corporatism*—that is, capitalism without a conscience. It is amoral, pathological self-interest. Authentic capitalism responds to free market forces; corporatism seeks to control market forces and to limit market choices to that which powerful corporate interests deem profitable.

Now, profit incentive is natural and healthy when controlled by integrity. However, when corporations place profit above principle and wealth above integrity what we witness is pathological greed, which uses manipulation and deceit to achieve its ends. It is usually considered a criminal offense when an individual in society desecrates or harms the environment or harms another individual in pursuit of personal advantage or gain. However, when a corporation desecrates or harms the environment or another individual in their pursuit of corporate advantage or gain it is considered "externalizing costs." What is morally unconscionable in individuals and *controlled* by laws is considered "efficiency" when performed by corporations and *protected* by law. This is not ethical. However, it is currently legal. For corporations to place profits above the principle of decreasing human suffering is quite simply evil, but that is exactly what the legal structure of these corporations actually requires them to pursue. The "suffering" are simply the "externalized collateral damage" resulting from these corporations' pathological pursuit of profit.[8]

Capitalism, then, breaks down when bullies take over and force their will upon weaker parties. There must be a system of checks and balances to ensure that stronger parties do not exact their profit at a weaker party's expense. Until power and control of American medicine is in the hands of corporations which profit from patients getting *well,* we will not see reductions in chronic disease. Currently, the corporate powers controlling medical research and treatments profit from disease, not health. We, the American people, stand as safely as sheep whose shepherds are wolves.

1-2. I CONTEND THAT LARGE CORPORATIONS, AGENCIES, AND GOVERNMENT DO NOT HAVE A RIGHT TO FEED UPON THE FAILING HEALTH OF THE WEAK, ESPECIALLY FOR THE SAKE OF EXCESSIVE PROFITS. IT IS DETRIMENTAL TO SOCIETY AS A WHOLE, IS DAMAGING TO THE AMERICAN ECONOMY, AND PROMOTES WEAKNESS AND DEPENDENCY WITHIN THE AMERICAN PEOPLE.

I believe that a "survival of the fittest" mandate has been taken up by the corporate "person." The corporation's survival depends upon their becoming the most fit financially, and many medical corporations become financially strong by profiting off the self-destruction that results from the behavioral weaknesses of *others*.

Is it alarming to you to consider that there are huge and extremely powerful medical corporations that profit from growing rates of obesity and chronic disease? Does it comfort you to consider that the chief legal responsibility of these medical corporations is to *pursue the profit* associated with obesity and chronic disease?

Does it comfort you as a consumer to know that the medical treatment chosen for you has been chosen because it will bring the greatest profit to the pharmaceutical and hospital industries providing your care? Or to know that unnecessary medical tests and procedures (which often cause more harm than good) are performed purely to reduce risks of malpractice suits?

Don't you realize that if medical corporations focused their great wealth, power and resources on identifying and eliminating the precursors of chronic disease, they would thus undermine their profits? It is simply unconscionable, not to mention illegal, for them to even consider so ruthlessly jeopardizing the investments and wealth of their shareholders.

No intelligent corporate self-interest will undermine its own prosperity. No intelligent corporation defeats its own self-interest by removing its consumers' need for its products. Those products and services are, of course, the very ones that bring the greatest profits to the corporate employer.

From a corporate pharmaceutical perspective, humans can be viewed as "orifices of opportunity." The orifices of opportunity are the "portals of entry" into the human body through which drugs (chemicals of profit) can be administered. These orifices can be defined as the human's potential portals of profit. Humans can be viewed as financially viable units of harvest, each possessing several potential portals through which to profit.

But it is the ethical responsibility of any business receiving our money (our medical insurance premiums) each month to spend it in ways that serve our needs and interests, not just their own. In a free market economy, corporate profit is supposed to be the result of providing a product of such value to the public that it attracts market share. Profits are supposed to be a reflection of the public's satisfaction with the company's product or service.

In a free market system, the consumer decides which products best meet his or her needs. Business cannot make those decisions for the consumer. And yet, that is exactly what is taking place in medicine: the modern pharmaceutical-medical industrial complex (in league with health insurers) has defined and limited insured medical services to the chemical/surgical solutions of highest profit to the industry.

And what is it that makes these corporations the most profit? The increase and progression of highly preventable physical decline.

1-3. MODERN MEDICINE MAKES THE MOST MONEY WHEN PEOPLE ARE CHRONICALLY ILL (BUT NOT DEAD!).

These medical corporations are simply making an accurate observation when they acknowledge that *good health is bad for business*. Just sit with this for a moment. A society's dramatically improved health would be very bad for business for very many corporations that are very large and very powerful.

The shocking reality underlying corporate medicine is that the success of the medical corporations that control the direction, emphasis, and focus of American medicine depends not only upon the *presence* of chronic disease but its *increasing prevalence*. That, simply put, is why prevention plays such an insignificant role in current treatment protocols for chronic disease. Preventive health care and positive health maintenance reduce both the presence and prevalence of chronic disease.

The livelihood of medical corporations relies upon the presence of the weak, frail and dependent. There's no financial reward in patients becoming or remaining well; it is only through consumption of medical products and services that the corporate controllers of modern medicine make their profit.

The reasoning, whether understood or blatantly acknowledged or not, sounds like this: "We profit from treating ongoing disease and we do not perform services or sell products if people are well." Let me expand upon that a bit, *speaking as if I were in their shoes*. This script shows the underlying agenda of these disease-as-profit corporations:

"Treat the symptoms, but don't remove the origins of disease—they are our path to colossal wealth! Mow the weeds but don't pull them out. We dare not turn people onto the path of health, lest pain (the greatest incentive to purchase our pretty powders) dry up. Healthy, aware people require hardly any medical goods and services; it's only the ill ones we can count on to make us wealthy."

"*Therefore:* We need to cultivate a culture of drug dependency through a million ads which misdirect the public. We need to turn people's eyes *away* from a search for the causes of disease, and *toward* our array of bottled solutions (and sprays and drips and pills and powders). We need people to be fascinated with our answers, not looking for the causes of their problems. In this way they get treated on the surface but continue to decay at the root, which assures us continuing and greater profits in the future. As long as we can keep them buffaloed as to the causes of physical decline and mesmerized with the newest, fanciest and prettiest designer drugs and diagnostics, we will be astronomically rich!"

"We need to build five-billion dollar hospitals, and keep people passing by the five-million dollar YMCAs. We must continue to reflect our utter dismay at the growing rates of obesity, cardiovascular disease, and cancer among kids and adults. We must let it be known how hard we are working at solving these alarming problems. When we say that we aim at decreasing these chronic conditions, we want it to be believed, believed, believed. But in reality, the fees from their disease is our wealth, gained through treating, treating, treating."

So, to summarize, the current system thinking goes like this: "A healthy populace is not a drug-dependent populace. We must present an alternative to healthy behavior, so that people will not get well and therefore will continue to be dependent upon our drugs. If people were aware of their powerful internal resources for recovery, healing, wellness, and independence, they would depend upon our chemical and surgical interventions less and less. Knowledge of the truth will set people free, and it is this knowledge we must steer very clear of. The truth is our greatest threat."

1-4. THE GREATEST FEAR OF THE PROFIT-THROUGH-ILLNESS INDUSTRIES IS THAT SOCIETY MIGHT REALIZE THE ECONOMIC INTELLIGENCE OF FOCUSING ON DISEASE PREVENTION.

Why is the medical industry prescribing treatments that clearly do not restore health? The reason is that even though the treatments don't restore health, they certainly "bring home the bacon."

At the highest levels of corporate medicine, humans are viewed as viable organisms to be targeted for financial harvesting. Healthy people and dead people consume very few pharmaceutical, diagnostic, and surgical products and services; only living sick ones are financially viable units of harvest. Billions of dollars a year are squeezed out of the bodies of the chronically ill by treating the symptoms of their unhealthy lifestyles.

There are incredibly huge amounts of money in "the medical system" to care for the chronically ill; but it is the system that profits from this huge amount of money, *not* the chronically ill.

While the executives of the medical system say they wish us to live well and prosper, it is also an undeniable financial reality that their highest paying customers—that is, their "preferred" clientele—are their sickest, most unhealthy patients. *If only everyone would disregard those executives' admonitions to live well and prosper, their companies could reap an even larger harvest off the diseases they knowingly fail to prevent!*

You see, what we experience currently is a pharmaceutically-driven and pharmaceutically-calculating medical system that ruthlessly demonstrates the principle of "survival of the fittest": Those who take good care of themselves remain above the affliction zone, and those who don't will bring their symptoms to a parasitic medical system which profits off chemically treating the continually worsening symptoms. Fundamentally, it boils down to corporations making huge profits off of patients' poor behavioral choices.

In a sense, this is a fascinating demonstration of the "law of the jungle," wherein pharmaceutical and medical industries become stronger and more financially fit by preying upon the weak who fail to take proper care of themselves. I say it is a calculated "hunt" because the course correction of behavioral modification into healthier lifestyles is not vehemently promoted, mandated, and prescribed by these "health" industries. Instead, they validate the weak in their current behavior, comfort them with a treatment of their symptoms, and thereby encourage their health-destroying habits. And so the weak get weaker, have more symptoms, undergo additional treatments and additional pills, and thereby yield increased profits to the strong. Meanwhile, the fitter members of society remain above the disease-attracting behaviors, and above any indoctrination into the chemically-compliant life.

1-5. OUR AMERICAN MEDICAL SYSTEM HAS BEEN DESIGNED IN A WAY THAT MAXIMIZES THE SALES OF PHARMACEUTICAL AGENTS.

The corporate medical elite who largely determine the direction of medical care in America, and who also strongly influence what is defined as "best medical practices," recognize *there is a clear inverse relationship between pharmaceutical sales and consumers' health.* People who take good care of themselves and maintain a health promoting lifestyle consume very few pharmaceuticals, while those who are indolent and demonstrate an aversion to the behaviors that would improve their health consume large quantities of pharmaceuticals. The pharmaceutical industry wants its products and services to be consumed with increasing frequency by as many patients as possible, in ever-increasing quantities, for as many years as possible.[9]

I talk of a corporate medical system that suppresses the prevention of chronic diseases and promotes the drugging of Americans. Surely you have seen the obvious rise in drug advertisements on TV and radio. This amounts to nothing less than the pharmaceutical industry's attempt to formulate and groom a psychological dependence upon drugs. The same is witnessed in magazine ads and many a radio slot. This medical system's message is, "Just say yes to drugs."

The financial impact of health regeneration among the chronically ill would be devastating to the pharmaceutical and medical industries. It is clearly understood that drugs, not health promotion, must remain the central focus of modern medicine if the pharmaceutical and medical industries are to continue to profit.

All the millions of dollars that could be spent building healthy lifestyle transition centers with all the necessary staff and group support to help people through the difficult transition to a truly healthy self-rejuvenating set of habits and lifestyle are being smartly diverted into the discovery of the next generation of pills to treat the symptoms of your ever-deepening progression of physical deterioration. A very, very profitable plan indeed.

Corporations cannot create a patent for a self-enabling, self-preserving healthy lifestyle, so there is little profit incentive for the mass merchandizing of health and wellness. Nor is conducting lifestyle modification programs (as a for-profit endeavor) lucrative enough to be of any interest to the major medical conglomerates, especially compared to the mega-profits resulting from hospitalizations, surgeries, and sales of drug products. Lifestyle modification programs are highly capable of producing dramatic improvements in patient outcomes, but are not even marginally lucrative.

For example, there *is* profit in appropriating large research grants from government organizations for the purpose of *finding* a solution to the growing epidemic of obesity. But there's almost no profit from implementing the *known* solution. The solution to obesity holds no financial incentive to these medical corporations, ah, but the treatment of the *symptoms* of obesity promises to yield a very lucrative harvest. So, instead of preventing or reversing the disease process, medical corporations are quite content to sit back and bring in, that is, *reap* the huge financial rewards of treating its symptoms. There is nothing left to do but observe the windfall of fortunes generated from treating the myriads of disease which are spawned, incubated, and cultivated for harvest in the rich, fertile soils of obesity.

The large medical conglomerates and pharmaceutical corporations claim to be working hard to maintain your health and prevent your chronic physical decline. But I see very little definitive evidence of it among those already chronically ill. Prevention of disease is a different industry; for them to claim it is part of their industry is inherently deceitful.

We must realize that corporate medicine does not convey the foundational principle of "survival of the fittest" to its consumers. *That* message is reserved for its own corporate heart and its own financial fitness. These take precedence over its proclaimed socially responsible medical mission of providing effective medical care for society. Were medicine to define itself as illness care, then it would at least be forthright about where its financial loyalties lie. But because it has purported to be a "health care" system it has intentionally deceived the public into believing that our good as a society is their corporate objective. Corporations profit from increasing prevalence of disease in society. It is impossible for these corporations to be honestly defined as healthcare companies.

1-6. THE ONLY HONEST AND FORTHRIGHT STANCE FOR MODERN MEDICINE TO TAKE IS TO CALL ITSELF BY WHAT IT IS: DISEASE CARE.

This industry profits off the treatment of disease. A fit society will render obsolete an opportunistic and exploitative medical machine that profits from disease just as a life-sucking parasite nourishes itself from the slow dying of its host.

Chronic disease is a behaviorally-induced condition. As long as it is treated chemically instead of behaviorally, we can clearly see that medicine's interest is purely financial and not curative.

I am all for profit, but let it be profit derived from instilling good habits instead of from feeding upon the ill effects of poor health habits. I am all for profit, but let it be a profit redirected to corporations which foster health, corporations which make money as the chronically ill are released from decay. Let profit be pulled away from corporations whose business is with disease, whose profits rise as peoples' health falls. Needless to say, this transition will be difficult and met with stiff resistance.

As long as a disease-for-profit system is in control of American medicine, chronic disease and obesity will continue to flourish. Any other course would be less lucrative—indeed, illegal—according to the charters of this system, which mandate acting in the best *financial* interests of its *shareholders,* not the highest ethical interests of its customers

Highly effective healing modalities and treatments that don't produce profits for these medical and pharmaceutical corporations are not only irrelevant to them, but in fact *counterproductive* to their profit-making. If patients were actually healed effectively, they would require less of the medical products and services of the corporations.

For corporations whose profits come from treating diseases with chemicals, it would be financially irresponsible to invest in research for disease prevention. It would jeopardize their profits! If they found effective methods of disease prevention, the public might expect those preventive measures to be implemented. Instead of pursuing prevention, billions of dollars go into discovering new chemical treatments for the symptoms. Furthermore, when their exclusive patents for effective chemicals expire and the corresponding excessive profit margins decrease, they simply pursue the next generation of pills.

These corporations eat, sleep, and breathe a "for profit" agenda that meditates exclusively upon increasing the distribution of their products and services unto an ever larger segment of the population. Any federal research funding granted to them will be employed to such ends.

Does it alarm you to consider that the medical corporations in charge of your medical care profit most when you consume *more* drugs, *more* diagnostics, and *more* invasive procedures? Does it alarm you to consider that what they define as consumer loyalty is really a progressively sicker, more drug-dependent society? They tout chronic disease as a nearly epidemic problem that is getting worse, but they fail to mention that it is also the greatest source of their burgeoning profits. The increasing prevalence of chronic disease in our country may seem like a problem to some, but the glowing health of Americans would spell the financial ruin of a great many medical corporations, and severely cut resources for ongoing medical "research."

The pursuit of profit has made medicine into a parasite that feeds upon self-imposed consequences of human behavior, rather than the promoter of healthier ways of being. If medicine professes to serve the patient, it must strive to deliver what is good for the client, not patiently wait for the ill effects of the client's self-neglecting, self-destabilizing behaviors. *Isn't the omission of doing a good tantamount to the commission of doing a wrong?* Medicine has power to do good and yet does not do it. It allows personal harms to be sustained so as to profit from those harms. Is this not malevolent and a form of parasitic pirateering on patients?

If it is not the act of an outright predator, then at a minimum it's the act of a calculating, opportunistic disease monger. Even in the classical Hippocratic Oath, the foundation of Western medicine, practitioners swear to "prescribe regimens for the good of my patients" and "never do harm to anyone." However, non-prevention of a known preventable is to premeditate and approve detrimental patient outcomes for profit. That does inflict harm—and that is utterly reprehensible.

A medical system that does not give first and utmost attention to restoring vibrant health is placing its profits above its patients' interests. Until medicine's emphasis is on the recovery of health through the re-introduction of a healthy lifestyle, medicine will continue to be opportunistic—poised to profit from human weakness, instead of compassionately poised to return people to a behavior pattern that enriches their lives. Until nature's gracious endowment of the ability to positively adapt to healthy physical challenges is brought to bear against nature's equally powerful propensity to conserve energy (that is, its enervation and atrophy of unchallenged systems)—the health of sedentary humans will *continually degenerate* as is predicated by the law of entropy. Similarly, this can be seen in the laws of motion: An object in motion tends to remain in motion and an object at rest tends to remain at rest. These are powerful laws of nature and nature is not capricious; chance and happenstance happens to us all but for the far larger part, whatever man sows—this shall he also reap.

"A rolling stone gathers no moss."

And people who exercise gather far fewer diseases. Nonetheless, the pharmaceutical and medical sciences will continue to search for ways to profit off of the people's *reluctance* to live healthfully and responsibly. Actually, given the nightmarish consequences of chronic disease, *reluctance* to live healthfully is not a strong enough word. These corporations will continue to profit off the people's *repulsion* to healthy, responsible, self-controlled, self-empowering behavior.

The purposes of a benevolent and socially-ordered corporate medical model are diametrically opposed to the purposes of a predatory corporate medical model whose prosperity is predicated upon the ongoing availability, indoctrination and dependence of the chronically ill. America can no longer afford to take her medical guidance from an industry that profits from her physical degeneration! And how does the industry profit from our physical degeneration? By avoiding prevention, and by treating only symptoms, never causes.

1-7. SPECIFICALLY IN REGARD TO CHRONIC DISEASE, MODERN MEDICINE APPEARS TO ONLY BE INTERESTED IN TREATING SYMPTOMS, AND NOT ELIMINATING CAUSES.

Modern medicine, operating largely outside the context of medical ideals, treats symptoms without addressing their underlying causes (i.e., ailment-attracting lifestyles). By ignoring the underlying causes of the symptoms it so devoutly services, it thereby promotes human debility, mental and physical misery, and the erosion of the U.S. economy.

There are several definitions of the word entropy, but the one I am particularly interested in is a law of nature that states that everything in the universe tends toward disorder, degeneration, decay and death. Picture a newly constructed and freshly painted red barn standing in a golden field of wheat. Given enough time (without additional organizational input) that barn will fall down and rot to nothing. That is the natural order of things, and is a law of nature.

Modern medicine's prescriptive recommendation for people whose behavior encourages personal entropy is to take their pills as directed and call again when conditions worsen. These chronically ill people assist the universe's work of entropy by clinging to a lifestyle that accelerates their personal decay. This alliance and collaboration with universal entropy creates a powerful synergy of self-disorganization. Pharmaceutical corporations step into this vortex of self-dissolution and have the audacity to suggest that their pills (infused, swallowed, or injected) can overthrow this powerful collusion, halt decline, and reorganize the body. *They have the audacity to claim they can stop people from experiencing the effects of their causes.* A chronically ill person is swimming downstream with a strong stroke in the midst of a wide river, and these pharmaceutical magicians claim that this person can, merely by swallowing pills, reverse their direction.

So the question arises: Why are medical power brokers (who govern the direction of modern medicine) treating poor health choices that produce poor health outcomes with drugs, since we know that good health follows good habits?

Lifestyle Habits Of The Chronically Well

Those who stay chronically healthy actively promote the daily regeneration of their health through the following types of activities, which the unhealthy consistently neglect and thus actively promote the daily degeneration of their health

1] Drinking freshly juiced/blended vegetables and smoothies.

2] Engaging in aerobic activity.

3] Engaging in resistance exercise and/or strength training

4] Consuming a predominantly alkaline diet with large amounts of fruits, salads, and lightly cooked vegetables.

5] Consuming almost entirely whole foods, i.e. whole grains, nuts, seeds, legumes, vegetables, lean meats, and fish.

6] Supplementing an optimal diet with nutrient dense (whole food) supplements rich in vitamins/minerals, trace elements, and phytonutrients (i.e., plant-derived compounds with healthful benefits).

7] Practicing yoga, tai chi, dancing/rhythm, Zumba, combination cardio/resistance, stretching and other activities that improve flexibility, coordination and muscle strength.

8] Practicing periodic fasting and use of heat therapies (Jacuzzi, steam & dry sauna) for detoxification through sweating.

9] Taking extended walks in nature to get lots of fresh air and sunshine.

10] Meditating, Journaling, Praying, Sabbath Rest, and Spiritual Discipline.

11] Engaging in outdoor recreation amidst the wind, surf, sun, sea, mountain air, crystal clear pools, trickling brooks, and powerful waves.

12] Engaging in self expression through music and the arts.

13] Remaining socially engaged in the community.

1-8. WE KNOW IT'S PROFITABLE TO TREAT THE ILL INSTEAD OF SUSTAINING THE HEALTHY, BUT IS THIS APPROACH ETHICAL?

It is true that for some conditions, medications perform a great deal of the necessary work and thus are very important, but in a large number of cases, especially for chronic health conditions, medication simply cannot correct the root causes of deteriorating health.

This is of course where the entire pharmaceutical panacea steps in with empty promises of relief from chronic conditions which only vigilant self-reorganization can satisfactorily address. But whose satisfaction are we seeking here? The satisfaction of pharmaceutical profits, or the satisfaction of lives made whole?

Here's an illustration that applies primarily to chronic disease: Picture life as a lake and people as boats floating upon it. As people age they develop holes in their health, largely along and proportional to their nutritional and behavioral habits, as well as some genetic propensities. These "holes" in the integrity of their health are like "holes" in a boat. Modern medicine's response to our "holes" is to step up to the lakeshore, survey the situation, and, shrewd businessmen that they are, open a water pump rental business.

You may ask, Why rent water pumps to these boaters out on the lake of life, when repairing the holes would be far more economical, effective, and permanent? The reason modern medicine does not repair the holes (that is, shore up and eliminate the underlying causes of the decline) is that it is far more profitable to rent water pumps to desperate people in sinking boats. It's simply a matter of economics.

1-9. HERE AGAIN, I REPEAT THE MEDICAL SYSTEM'S SELF-SERVING SCRIPT:

"Treat the symptoms, but don't remove the origins of disease—they are our path to colossal wealth! Mow the weeds but don't pull them out. We dare not turn people onto the path of health, lest pain (the greatest incentive to purchase our pretty powders) dry up. Healthy, aware people require hardly any medical goods and services; it's only the ill ones we can count on to make us wealthy."

"Therefore: We need to cultivate a culture of drug dependency through a million ads which misdirect the public. We need to turn people's eyes *away* from a search for the causes of disease, and *toward* our array of bottled solutions (and sprays and drips and pills and powders). We need people to be fascinated with our answers, not looking for the causes of their problems. In this way, they get treated on the surface but continue to decay at the root, which assures us continuing and greater profits in the future. As long as we can keep them buffaloed as to the causes of physical decline and mesmerized with the newest and fanciest and prettiest designer drugs and diagnostics, we will be astronomically rich!"

"We need to build five-billion dollar hospitals, and keep people passing by the five-million dollar YMCAs. It is a wonderful, wonderful business indeed. We must continue to reflect our utter dismay at the growing rates of obesity, cardiovascular disease, and cancer among kids and adults. We must let it be known how hard we are working at solving these alarming problems. When we propose that we aim at decreasing these chronic conditions, we want it to be believed, believed, believed. But in reality, their disease is our wealth, gained through treating, treating, treating."

The pharmaceutical-medical corporation's only logical course of action is to treat symptoms without eliminating causes, which will assure a current and continuing consumer base, and ongoing and increasing consumption. It's simply economically essential that they treat symptoms without eliminating causes.

The purpose for taking most medications is to treat the symptoms of the ongoing physical degeneration of the patient who is being harvested for pharmaceutical profits. The patient's condition is being milked for the medical system's profit. It is not reversed or eliminated, either for the patient's welfare or for the welfare of the nation.

Chemical products that alter symptoms of degenerating health while neglecting the *causes* of degenerating health actually cultivate a dependence upon those chemical products, and indirectly increase the likelihood of those symptoms becoming worse. Without educating, actively prescribing, and mandating the lifestyle reformation that is needed to produce effective and permanent improvements in health, the medical system indirectly supports that which oppresses patients and compels them to seek medical support.

Prevention of chronic disease is given next to zero attention, zero focus, zero facilities, and zero support. But when it comes to precipitous declines in the patient's health, the medical system springs into action to feed upon (provide services for) the patient.

1-10. THE CHRONICALLY ILL "ATTRACT DISEASES" TO THEMSELVES, EVEN THOUGH THESE DISEASES ARE QUITE OFTEN ENTIRELY PREVENTABLE. SO, WHY DOESN'T CONVENTIONAL MEDICINE SEEK TO STOP THIS CYCLE?

"We are still standing at the bank of the river, rescuing people who are drowning. We have not gone to the head of the river to keep them from falling in. That is the 21st Century Task."
- Gloria Steinem

The chronically ill have profound propensities to attracting chronic disease unto themselves, and modern medicine does not so much as begin to address these tendencies. For instance, the medical system treats only the symptoms of diabetes, and never pays more than lip service to the revolution in lifestyle that would *eliminate* the precursors and underlying causes of that chronic disease.

The solution to obesity, also, holds no financial incentive to these medical corporations, but the treatment of the *symptoms* of obesity promises to yield a very lucrative harvest, as long as the problem of obesity is not brought into check. With obesity and its myriad of accompanying afflictions quickly becoming the number one *preventable* cause of death,[10] modern medicine continues to treat symptoms (the results of obesity), making little attempt to identify, grapple with, and modify the underlying causes found in human behavior.

Modern medicine is cognizant of the scientific evidence and knowledge surrounding the unquestionably valuable, life-restoring, life-enhancing, health-imbuing, spiritually uplifting, stress-reducing, nutritionally fortifying, immune system strengthening benefits of a truly healthy lifestyle. Yet they fail to inform and, more importantly, they fail to encourage, mandate, prescribe, instruct, enforce, support, facilitate, and foster these well-proven healing practices.

Modern medicine claims to "see" through a scientific lens, yet refrains from revealing the complete truth, that is, the scientific evidence about the dismal failure of chemicals to *correct* the problems of the chronically ill.[11] It also refrains from revealing the scientific evidence that "healthy is as healthy does," and that "chemicals cannot erase what behavior hath begot." In this, they clearly demonstrate a complicit conflict of interest. So, they are thereby implicated in the untold woe resulting from predictable and preventable health declines.

Why does the conventional medical system apply the authoritative verb "prescribe" in relationship to medicine and apply the more diminutive verb "recommend" in relationship to lifestyle modification? Why does modern medicine virtually demand, forcefully supply, and rapidly facilitate the use of its chemicals, products, and services, while it weakly recommends behavioral modification?

Let's revisit why patients come to the medical system. Is it to have their health restored or is it merely to have the symptoms of their progressive deterioration treated? If the medical industry's objectives were consistent with the chronically ill patients' objectives (resolution of their health problems), they would virtually demand, forcefully supply, and rapidly facilitate healthy lifestyle revision. Why don't they? The incriminating answer is, there's no financial reward in patients becoming or remaining well; it is only through consumption of medical products and services that the corporate controllers of modern medicine make their profit.

While hospital corporations are busily building new hospitals and expanding existing ones to take advantage of the looming harvest of the advancing diseases of the aging Baby Boomers, there is little to no effort being made to decrease the prevalence of the chronic diseases afflicting those patients. Those chronic diseases are highly preventable and/or dramatically reducible, but it is evident that the emphasis is rather to process and harvest those diseases—and that requires more processing plants (hospitals). If this is not true, why are widely-known, scientifically-verified findings about ways to eliminate or significantly reduce chronic disease being overtly ignored, while billions of dollars are poured into building and expanding hospitals?

1-11. IS IT REALLY AN ADVANCEMENT IN MEDICINE TO MANUFACTURE YET ANOTHER CHEMICAL TREATMENT FOR SYMPTOMS OF A DISEASE THAT IS PREVENTABLE BY MEANS OF A HEALTHY LIFESTYLE?

Many conditions are largely avoidable through prescribing a healthy lifestyle, combined with supervision and group support. So, what is really gained by patients having better treatment for conditions they need not have? The American Medical Approach simply adds drugs to the predominantly sedentary self-degenerating lifestyle responsible for the chronic disease. No wonder it has historically failed in producing wellness for the chronically ill.

But, you may ask, what about all the wonderful uplifting advertisements of our medical providers proclaiming that they "want to be with us for life," and the multi-billion dollar hospital building campaigns that they say are "building a healthy future for us?"

Well, I agree that they want to be with us for life all right, but the idea that more hospitals, medical clinics, diagnostic equipment, tests, or drugs build a healthy future for us is confusing to me. Their concern for us comes into play only when we experience a precipitous decline in health. If our medical providers were actually investing heavily in our *health*, we wouldn't *be* in a health crisis at the hospital or clinic. We wouldn't need a new drug or diagnostic testing device if they were spending billions toward our healthiness.

If you find yourself going down the "slippery slope" of chronic disease, modern medicine will be there ... just be sure to have your checkbook or medical policy number in hand. But if you want to climb out, that is, avoid progressive deterioration from chronic conditions—which usually start with relatively minor symptoms—be warned that you are virtually entirely on your own to find competent, preventive advice. Sure, they have a drug for your every symptom. But the causes continue unchecked and, in fact, gain steam for another eruption elsewhere through a different symptomatic expression. On and on the whirlpool spins downward as accumulated toxins overwhelm our immune system, a lack of wholesome nutrition starves our natural defenses, and a decrease in healthy activity shrivels our physical vitality, thus gradually disabling our own capacity for self-healing.

You do not want to become one of the many chronically ill who, at around age 50, enter into the medical system with their first diagnosis and their first set of designer-colored drugs. The medical system appears to not want to scare or upset patients with admonitions about the long-range consequences of health-free living, and certainly does very little to disrupt the lifestyle that brought them through the golden arches of fast "fix" medicine for their first "genuine diagnosis" and their very own customized assortment of drugs. From that time forth these "loyal clients" will be groomed for harvest and have their symptoms emolliated (softened and soothed) while the underlying cause of their "developing" condition is gingerly avoided. Of course, with the underlying cause undisturbed, the symptoms continue to express themselves as the clients utilize a gradually growing array of products, diagnostic tests, and surgical procedures. This group forms a highly profitable consumer base. These are the "frequent flyers."

The chemical objective is to identify the effect (symptom) resulting from a deterioration of a physiological system within the body—usually the result of the presence of unhealthy habits and the absence of healthy habits—and then to chemically oppose that effect. Let me spell it out in a ditty:

Health is won
Disease is spun
It is up to us
Which course we run

1-12. THE DEGENERATION OF PHYSIOLOGICAL SYSTEMS WITHIN THE BODY (BASICALLY POOR HEALTH) HAS BEEN REDEFINED AS "DISEASE"—THAT IS, A MYSTERY—INSTEAD OF IDENTIFIED AS A CLEAR "CAUSE-AND-EFFECT CONSEQUENCE" OF POOR HEALTH HABITS.

The natural consequence of poor health habits is physical deterioration, but that consequence has been redefined as a "symptom." Now, rather than "warning signs" of the body signaling deterioration—usually easily enough corrected if caught (and re-taught) early—the patient instead has a mysterious *disease,* with accompanying mysterious *symptoms.* The implication is that these are things that only medical experts with pills or procedures are able to handle. And thus the chemical and medical dependency begins.

"Just as nature gives us physical pain to guide us to doing or not doing things in the physical realm, nature gives us emotional pain to guide us toward doing or not doing things in the emotional or mental realm. The wonderful thing is that you're constructed so that if you simply listen carefully to yourself—to your mind, your body and your emotions—and follow the guidance you're given, you can dramatically enhance the quality of your life."

\- Brian Tracy[12]

Actively facilitating health promotion to the chronically ill will never be a recommendation of conventional medical research. Continual and progressively more complex treatments, yes—but prevention and/or reduction of disease through the facilitated recovery of health, *never.*

Modern medicine's domain of expertise and profit is the chemical, diagnostic, and surgical management of the symptoms of our progressive physical degeneration. When physical problems resulting from behavioral causes are treated chemically, but not addressed behaviorally, then it very quickly becomes clear that corporate profits take precedence over patient recovery. It becomes clear that those behavioral causes *are intentionally ignored and neglected* so as to increase the profit potential of preventable diseases. This is entirely unacceptable.

1-13. MODERN MEDICINE OFFERS LIP SERVICE TO HEALTHY BEHAVIOR, BUT NO REAL SUPPORT.

"An ounce of prevention is worth a pound of cure," goes the axiom. The medical field offers lip service to this truth, on billboards and radio spots. But it hardly proactively emphasizes disease prevention, and especially not for the chronically ill, who hear *far mor*e from the medical industry about pills, procedures, and/or surgery. The compelling pharmaceutical ads and colorful medical billboards "sell" the public on taking the right pills and having the right medical coverage—and then they slip in something about eating right and exercising too.

So we constantly hear health-affirming advertising drivel about getting well and staying well from medical and pharmaceutical corporations. But when it comes to actually supporting the chronically ill in lifestyle modification, these same companies are nowhere around. If this is not true, then we should see every hospital group dedicating a meaningful percentage of its new hospital construction budget to lifestyle transition centers devoted to motivating patients to get excited and serious and committed to adopting a disease-preventing lifestyle.

Real rubber meets real road when the chronically ill are given the tools and resources to lift themselves from ruts of spiraling decline and into the liberty of self-imposed spiraling incline. So, an industry truly governed by compassion, as this one claims to be, would not hesitate to back up their talk with fully subsidized lifestyle transition centers specifically for the "at risk" and chronically diseased population.

1-14. THE "HEALTHY PEOPLE" INITIATIVE HAS THE RIGHT IDEA

"Healthy People" began in 1979 as a national health promotion and disease prevention initiative in America. Its overall goals are to increase the quality and years of healthy life. It is a statement of national health objectives designed to identify the most significant preventable threats to health and to establish national goals to reduce these threats. Since 1990, the specifics have been updated for each new decade, so we are now looking forward to the Healthy People 2020 version.

I'll use Healthy People 2010 here, since its extensive final report is available online.[13] Healthy People 2010 was designed to achieve two overarching goals:

1] *Increase Quality and Years of Healthy Life.* Help individuals of all ages increase life expectancy *and* improve their quality of life.

2] *Eliminate Health Disparities.* Eliminate health disparities among different segments of the population.

These goals sound hopeful and even inspiring; however, this is not enough. I am asking for concrete action to back it up. The need is not for lofty goals but concrete methods of implementation. I request that our government leaders go after chronic disease the way they went after Saddam Hussein. I request that they pour money into lifestyle improvement and obesity reduction like they poured money into bombing Iraq.

Now, don't get me wrong, the government has made a good beginning and stated benevolent intentions in the Healthy People 2010 initiatives. However, they have left implementation to local agencies and the conventional medical system. This is comparable to leaving the sheep to the care of the wolf.

Take diabetes: The medical system treats only the symptoms of diabetes, and pays little more than lip service to the revolution in lifestyle that would *eliminate* the precursors and underlying causes of that chronic disease.

Conventional medicine will be slow to "prevent" the milking of its cash cows. The closest conventional medicine gets to "prevention" takes the form of yearly flu vaccinations, pap smears, prostate exams, and similar billable procedures. In truth, these are only quasi–preventive "products and services" which paint the medical provider as genuinely interested in prevention. These diagnostic screenings for early detection of developing abnormalities are not bad; it's just that the medical industry is going "way shy" of the real deal, i.e. the promotion of a lifestyle that breeds a healthy, natural, drug-free resilience to common chronic conditions.

Again, *early detection is not a bad thing*. However, early detection only leads to early treatment, which, technically speaking, is not prevention at all, just forms of "interception" and "intervention." The prevention of which I speak is aggressive removal of known causes of chronic disease and thus prevention of those conditions. And yes, the pharmaceutical and medical industries will fight tooth and nail any true prevention-based approach to health, wellness, and chronic disease reversal.

1-15. … BUT WE HAVE TO CONCLUDE THAT CORPORATE MEDICINE WILL FIGHT ANY AND ALL TRUE PREVENTION-FOCUSED APPROACHES.

The concept of preventing treatable conditions is a huge threat to every medical system whose profit is dependent upon symptoms needing treatment. As it stands right now, every medical corporation dependent on the presence of disease for its continuing prosperity will be resistant to any movement that threatens to reduce its consumer base. This means that establishing institutions that specifically assist the chronically ill in becoming healthy and strong will meet tremendous opposition. The livelihood of medical corporations relies upon the presence of the weak, frail, and dependent.

Every medical movement that *deeply* threatens the prevalence of chronic disease in America will be vehemently opposed by the pharmaceutical industry. The attack will be waged from every quadrant of the pharmaceutically-subsidized medical system: from medical and pharmaceutical lobbyists in Washington to medical science and funded medical research; from medical product engineers to diagnostic equipment developers; from the formation of "evidence-based" medical protocols and medical "best practices" to medical schools and prevailing medical philosophies. Every aspect of pharmaceutically-subsidized medical delivery will be on alert to identify and vehemently oppose anything that *deeply* threatens the prevalence of chronic disease in America.

Healthy people's lifestyles stand as a direct threat to the prosperity of pharmaceutical and other related corporations that currently control medical politics and courses of treatment in America. So, lip service to changing lifestyle will be entertained, but any dramatic movement to *prevent* lifestyles that promote chronic disease will be ignored, remain unfinanced, and even attacked as quackery by the reigning pharmaceutically-subsidized conventional medical empire. Lip service to being healthy will be tolerated, but real improvements in American health will be insidiously and perniciously undermined by the corporations profiteering off disease.

1-16. SO I RAISE THE QUESTION FOR ALL AMERICANS: WHAT CAN WE DO?

The problem is not the absence of an answer. The answers to the challenges of obesity and chronic disease are discoverable, and in fact, discovered! Many are widely known and are well supported with scientific evidence.[14] The problem is the current system's resistance to a healthy revision of itself. It's the tremendous power and grip of a corporate medical system that refuses to release its control over medical delivery in America.

By their self-vested authority, this industry—which uses what I am terming the "American Medical Approach"—and its henchmen have not only minimized the number of non-drug therapies available, they have also persuaded the American people to doubt that anything but drugs can make them well. As a result, insurance coverage for most preventive therapeutic modalities not officially recognized by the American Medical Approach are not even considered. With competing medical models of care thus eliminated, the pharmaceutical/medical complex has enjoyed humongous profits from the gleanings of a very large harvest. It's truly been a wonderful run and a productive season for them.

The truth is that many forms of chronic disease are preventable and even reversible through significant behavior modification. This is the truth that modern medical science continuously drowns out in the noise of advertisements for chemicals. If this is not true, why are widely-known, scientifically-verified findings about ways to eliminate or significantly reduce chronic disease being overtly ignored, while billions of dollars are poured into building and expanding hospitals and patenting new drugs to "better treat" the symptoms of ongoing decline?

Evidence of effective modalities of healing are not being shared with the public by traditional vendors of the American Medical Approach; not by the conventional hospitals, medical clinics or pharmacies, nor by the doctors, nurses and pharmacists under their employment. Consumers must search for themselves, but considerable scientific evidence is available for those willing to make the effort. (The bibliography and later parts of this book review many of the principles and practices we need to embrace to make the paradigm shift from treating disease symptoms to creating and sustaining wellness.) Again, the truth is that many forms of chronic disease are preventable and even reversible through significant behavior modification.

Our conventional medical system has fed us a load of hogwash when it implies that health and chronic disease are different sciences, different phenomenon. They purport that health and fitness is the field of coaches, athletes, and exercise physiologists, while chronic disease falls to medical doctors and medical scientists. I propose that the experts in chronic disease are the coaches, athletes, and exercise physiologists because they know how to stay as far away as possible from self-degenerating behavior and its consequences.

Don't count on medical science to serve the interests of mankind—it's been bought off by the pharmaceutical/medical/industrial complex.

1-17. SCIENCE—AND SCIENTISTS—HAVE BEEN BOUGHT OFF, THAT IS, HAD A MAJORITY OF THEIR RESEARCH FUNDED BY PROFIT-SEEKING PHARMACEUTICALS.

We the people are in somewhat of a bind. What is beneficial for individuals, societies, and the environment is largely unprofitable for corporations. Think of the benefit that could be achieved if medical science were actually used for the sake of mankind and the welfare of the planet! But instead, science has become a prostitute turning tricks for whoever pays her the greatest tribute.

When corporations examine which research projects to fund, they analyze what the proposed end product will be. If the product is not deemed financially lucrative, the corporation will deny initial funding, or ongoing funding, regardless of its potential benefit to mankind.

So here's the barrel over which corporately financed science has people:

1] Medical science is funded largely by mega-wealthy corporations, which *will only* finance experiments that they anticipate will produce a profitable (patentable) product. It does not matter how potentially beneficial the research might be for mankind.

2] When experiments and research that are funded by other sources yield discoveries that are beneficial to mankind, the corporately-funded scientific community resists acknowledging the validity of those experiments or their discoveries. Why? Because the mainstream, corporately-financed scientific body did not supervise and oversee those experiments. Hence, they see no ethical obligation to affirm or implement those discoveries.

3] The loop repeats. Corporations will not finance scientific investigation into any line of research whose anticipated end products or therapies are not deemed to be highly profitable—and they will not support, verify or publish the findings of research funded by other financial parties. Findings that are of potentially significant benefit to society are routinely dismissed while the fevered pursuit of "products that profit" is hot and relentless.

Pharmaceutical corporations control a majority of the financial resources available for research. They guide the direction, focus, and outcomes of research, and thus they control the types of medical discoveries being made, validated, and publicized. Unfortunately, healthy lifestyles that are self-enabling and self-preserving—while profitable to the individual in profound ways—do not support corporate profit. Medical profit requires consumer dependency.

Look at what our profit-driven medical system does to the direction of medical research. The term "medical research" conjures up images of men in white lab coats, geniuses locked deep in thought behind thick-rimmed glasses, pensive furls in their brows, relentlessly probing for solutions to the maladies that have plagued mankind for centuries.

Well, sorry to burst the bubble, but it's largely about the money. The quest behind that pensive furl is how to find new chemical patents to treat the same ongoing problems. It has nothing to do with eliminating the underlying problems.

Instead, the first goal is to break down the patient's notion of personal capability and self- efficacy. The next goal is to displace personal confidence and replace it with fascination and confidence in "the experts." Third, its goal is to imply that patients are largely powerless and thus cultivate dependency.

Alchemy is the predecessor of modern-day chemistry, which in turn is the foundation of the pharmaceutical industry. One of the most famous medieval goals of alchemy was to find a way to turn baser metals into gold and to find a universal cure for disease. Alchemy evolved into chemistry and while chemistry has given up the goal of finding a universal cure for disease, chemistry has indeed found a way to turn baser compounds into gold. Actually, the price of many modern-day pharmaceuticals (by the ounce) is greater than the price of gold!

> **Moreover, the most famous alchemical pursuit, chrysopoeia (the transmutation of base metals into gold), was viewed with a mixture of greed and terror by the political authorities of the time. Such knowledge might bring enormous wealth to those who had it, but it had the ability to destroy the currency. Many countries passed laws forbidding the transmutation of metals, even as their kings secretly patronised alchemy hoping to gain an advantage over other monarchs. Alchemists, to borrow a phrase from Winston Churchill, were "to be on tap, not on top."[15]**

For corporations whose profits come from treating diseases with chemicals, it would be financially irresponsible to invest in research that yields disease prevention. It would jeopardize their profits!

So, instead of pursuing prevention, billions of dollars go into discovering new chemical treatments to replace the old chemical treatments for which the highly lucrative patent fees have run dry. In the "Twisted History Of Alchemy" the author describes how alchemists lost favor and credibility while "chymists" gained respectability and eventually chemistry was accepted into the "Academy of Sciences" but some things never change. A great majority of scientists and chemists are still held captive, "to be on tap but not on top." This is after all, all about the money; according to the corporate powers (monarchs) of our day.[16]

1-18. IT THEREFORE FOLLOWS THAT PUBLICLY FUNDED OR FEDERALLY FUNDED MEDICAL RESEARCH SHOULD NEVER BE PERFORMED BY INDIVIDUALS OR FACILITIES INFLUENCED BY THE MEDICAL-PHARMACEUTICAL MACHINE.

This restriction is not currently in place. Unfortunately, that means the great majority of federally funded medical research in this country is being used to further the profits of the medical industry, not to benefit mankind.

Now, there is nothing illegal with publicly owned medical corporations using their *own* financial resources to pursue their *own* profit. But there is no justifiable reason for the federal government to fund medical research being done by corporations whose exclusive aim is their own profit. It is illogical for the government to assume that any publicly-held medical corporation will perform medical studies of a strictly benevolent nature. These corporations eat, sleep, and breathe "for profit" agendas that focus exclusively upon increasing the distribution of their products and services unto an ever larger segment of the population. Any federal research funding granted to them will be employed to further corporate profit over social or environmental good.

Occasionally medical researchers make discoveries that are not profitable to the medical corporations—that is, they are only highly promising for mankind. *Those* discoveries are lightly esteemed and quickly glossed over, if not completely ignored, by the medical scientists on the corporate payroll.

Scientific integrity and profit incentive are incompatible when it comes to healthcare. In my opinion, creating an environment for scientists to look for solutions to chronic disease can only be conducted honestly when that research is an impartial, systematic, logical, and evidence-based search for viable, economically sound, effective healthcare solutions. There should be no motive other than a benevolent concern for elimination of the underlying causes of chronic disease and improving the human condition. Period.

I'm sure that if cats ruled the world, mouse production would become a viable industry. Both organic "free range" and conventional mouse production would increase dramatically *if* cats ruled the world.

In this metaphor, the cats stand for the pharmaceutical industry's power over the market, that is, their powerful influence over medical economics, medical education, and the media. The mice represent the priorities and pernicious incentives sought by the pharmaceutical powers over the air. Fundamentally, from a pharmaceutical corporations perspective, disease and dependency upon drugs is very good for business.

In other words, medical science isn't truly objective unless it's free of all financial constraints, and strictly and exclusively committed to the scientific process and the benevolent search for the most viable and effective solutions to the health challenges of mankind. But, if medical science continues to be funded by any industry as it is now, it is inevitable that its medical "discoveries" and solutions will profit and serve its corporate sponsors far more than any other party. Hence modern medicine's strong emphasis upon the treatment of what *becomes* ongoing and progressive decline, rather than placing a strong emphasis upon the elimination of the underlying behavioral, psychosocial, and environmental causes of disease.

1-19. I'M NOT AGAINST FREEDOM AND A CAPITALIST ECONOMY—BUT I AM AGAINST MEDICAL-PHARMACEUTICAL CORPORATIONS RUNNING A RESEARCH "GREED-CONOMY" WHERE DISEASE IS USED, THAT IS, INCUBATED FOR UNETHICAL PROFITEERING.

Product development by scientists for corporate profit is a natural outgrowth of capitalism. It's not a bad idea in general. Capitalism ideally fosters new discoveries and advancing technologies in a free market; however, when disease becomes a vulnerability to be exploited rather than a problem to be eliminated, capitalism becomes the people's enemy, as disease progression becomes the means to wealth.

I am convinced that an abusive form of capitalism controls modern medicine and has deeply reduced its ability to benefit mankind, because in America, disease equals profit. The scientific research and medical discoveries of modern medicine reflect the financial interests of their funding source, the pharmaceutical industry. It does not reflect the interest of mankind in acquiring effective solutions to disease.

Ethical medical research will limit itself to discovering the most effective, least harmful solutions to disease. At no point will its investigations be undertaken for the pursuit of profit. *Ethical medical research should be conducted to fulfill a need, not exploit one.* Medical profit should be the reward for solving medical problems. Medical problems are solved by addressing and eliminating their underlying causes, not by softening the effects (symptoms) of those causes.

Most drugs are prescribed for symptoms that can be traced back to one or more poor lifestyle habits, whether a lack of sunshine or too much salt, a lack of exercise or too much stress, a lack of self-nurturing or too much nutrition-less food. *The need is for a change in choices, not exploitation of their consequences.* Profit is not bad, but *disease for profit* is a scheme hatched in hell.

1-20. WHY HAVEN'T OUR MOST HIGHLY EDUCATED MEDICAL SCIENTISTS MADE THE CONNECTION YET BETWEEN LIFESTYLE AND ITS IMPACT ON HEALTH?

Scientists are in a unique position to investigate phenomena and distill that research into useful insights, tools, information, products, and resources for society. But the pharmaceutical and medical industries have a majority of medical scientists tied up in investigations that yield only new chemicals, diagnostic tests, and surgical procedures. So, these industries are in effect using science to further the public's dependence on chemical, diagnostic, and surgical solutions, instead of encouraging and enabling scientists to discover ways to support society in supporting itself.

With their purse strings, the medical/pharmaceutical complex is preventing science from utilizing its great strength and capacity to offer society much, much more. In this way, the medical pharmaceutical complex has become the dark enemy of the evolution and betterment of our society.

The strategy, again, is to:

- ignore existing evidence
- ignore recent research
- discourage ongoing research about disease prevention through the promotion of health
- research only chemical and surgical management of the ongoing and progressive symptoms of disease
- make a profit

So why haven't our most highly educated medical scientists made the connection yet between lifestyle and its impact on health? Because medical science has in many ways been relegated to the position of a corporate errand boy. The majority of medical scientists have little say over the types of research they explore. The priorities of their employers limit research to ways that hold strong potential for increasing corporate profits, which depend upon the disease-laden, drug-dependent consumer. But we could revolutionize American healthcare if large amounts of money were poured into finding ways to motivate people who are, by their daily choices, in a maze of declining health, and then support them as they replace those habits with health invigorating activities.

1-21. IT IS ESTIMATED THAT 75% OF ALL HEALTHCARE DOLLARS ARE SPENT UPON LARGELY PREVENTABLE CONDITIONS.[17] YET ACTUAL PREVENTION OF THESE CONDITIONS RECEIVES EXTREMELY LITTLE ATTENTION.

And this is as it should be—*from the medical-pharmaceutical corporation's point of view, that is.* Why should such a profitable phenomenon be stemmed? Why choke the goose that's laying the golden eggs? The profits are in disease, not prevention! Nothing will ever be changed by those who are profiting from the problem. They have no reason to!

Much research will be done in the name of reducing chronic disease in America, but all this research will not yield any effective solutions if the research is being funded by the industries that profit from the epidemic's continuing prevalence. No real progress will ever be made by these entities because there is so much more profit to be made in allowing these problems to run their course than there is in ending them.

Honest and intelligent medical research into the problem of obesity lands quickly in the court of lifestyle modification. But conducting lifestyle modification programs as a for-profit endeavor is simply not lucrative enough to be of any interest to the major medical conglomerates, especially compared to the mega-profits resulting from hospitalizations, diagnostics, surgeries, and the sale of drug products. Lifestyle modification programs are highly capable of producing dramatic improvements in patient outcomes, but are not even marginally profitable.

Now there *is* profit in appropriating large research grants for the purpose of finding a solution to the growing epidemic of obesity and curbing the advance of chronic disease in America—there's just no profit in actually finding a real solution. So, many solutions will be discovered but none of them will be effective or economical.

Highly effective, economical methods of reducing and even eliminating obesity are not mysteries stumping our sharpest medical research doctors and scientists. The problem is with the medical system. The problem is not the problem. The problem is the system. Specifically, the medical reimbursement system. The problem is that the current medical system, from its lofty peaks through all its sundry parts, is financially rewarded for treating illness. Fees-for-disease. So research scientists cannot focus upon preventing, slowing, or eliminating medical conditions because their employers' profits *depend upon* continued disease. And their *own jobs* depend on their employers' continued profitability.

An amazing degree of impotence will undoubtedly be exhibited by medical research efforts to find effective solutions to America's growing obesity and chronic disease epidemic. Discoveries will be vague or inconclusive, public education will be unclear, and implementation will be weak. Impotence and incompetence will mark efforts to staunch the growth of America's disease epidemic. Obesity and chronic disease will continue to expand as long as the government allows *industry* to inform public opinion, guide research, and persuade cultural trends. There is no question that obesity is very profitable to a few industries. As long as a fees-for-disease reimbursement policy remains in control, chronic disease and obesity will continue to flourish.

I find it ironic that at the core of modern medicine is modern science, and at the core of modern science is the concept that we have evolved through natural selection—a concept based on survival through adaptation, that is, the "survival of the fittest." Yet in practice, modern medicine promotes increasing weakness and the dependency of our species upon drugs, and does next to nothing to encourage the "natural" fitness of the species. So, forgive me for asking, but if medical scientists believe in evolution's "natural selection" favoring the "survival of the fittest," why do they promote the weaknesses associated with dependency upon drugs, and thus *encourage*—no that's not strong enough—why do they actually *promote* personal powerlessness?

If your lifestyle is not working, i.e. your survival is being threatened, as demonstrated by the development of high blood pressure or diabetes, or (fill in the blank _____), why adapt? Why adapt your lifestyle by eating healthier, exercising more, and taking an active interest in things that give you life, when you can just take a pill?

However, if that doesn't make sense to you, there is another course of reasoning we can follow that is consistent with the laws of nature, (and our survival): the course of self examination, self correction, and healthy adaptation. When some aspect of our lifestyle is not working, as demonstrated by our experiencing symptoms of declining health, we examine our lifestyles and amend those behaviors that are sabotaging our health and undermining our interest in surviving and thriving.

"All things are legitimate (permissible—and we are free to do anything we please), but not all things are helpful (expedient, profitable, and wholesome). All things are legitimate, but not all things are constructive (to character) *and* edifying (to spiritual life)."[17a] 1 Corinthians 10: 23 Amplified Bible

Many are called to live abundantly, but few choose an abundant life because it requires we live responsibly.

On the other hand, corporatized medicine achieves its objective of profit by treating the symptoms of poor choices and unhealthy lifestyles (which encourages poor choices and unhealthy lifestyles) and indoctrinates people into a lifestyle of passivity and chemical dependence.

1-22. WHY IS IT THAT THE WORLD'S MOST HIGHLY EDUCATED MEDICAL SCIENTISTS CAN'T SEEM TO GET A HOLD OF THE CLEAR PATH TO PHYSICAL RECOVERY?

I think it's fair to attribute their silence to the financial conflicts of interest inherent within our current medical system. When the spirit of corruption perceives a good person, "he" (the spirit of corruption) attempts to make them bad. If that fails, he just keeps them distracted with busy work, tying up their time and draining their energy with less important things than making a difference in the world; making them ineffectual in the pursuit of greater goods and services. This explains the great "hog tying" of medical scientists today.

The scientific community could explore, discover, and publish so much for the benefit of all mankind. Instead it has been all but bought off by industry in the pursuit of almighty profits.

Take for example the agricultural industry; the vast majority of agricultural scientists are not researching ways to improve the nutritional quality of food, but rather doing research on how to produce more crops. Hence, science is leading the march in how to produce higher volumes of nutrient-depleted foods, grown in nutrient-depleted soils. Why? Because more crop production yields increased crop sales. Never mind that producing *more* nutrient-*less* food produces more chronic disease because that produces more drugs sales. Unfortunately, federal agricultural policies and Food and Drug Administration (FDA) policies defend and support agricultural and pharmaceutical profits over the health of its own citizens. Similarly, fast food scientists are paid by the fast food industry to find ways to increase human compulsion to consume larger and larger amounts of nutritionally depleted, chemically altered, virtually addictive food-like substances, all with FDA approval. Science may serve industry, but unfortunately it is rarely given freedom to spread its wings, roll up its sleeves and delve into making the world a better place.

Science is so busy making money for industry that it has largely surrendered its responsibility, its voice, its high calling, and its capability to make a difference in the world. This sounds harsh, but it's true. Science is simply following the money. And when you see the huge discrepancy between the little amount invested in disease reversal and the huge amount invested in bringing new products to market for the ongoing treatment of reversible conditions, it becomes crystal clear that modern medicine is in it for the money. And that is simply to say modern medicine is harvesting humans for the profitability of the chronic diseases they intentionally choose not to prevent.

Why is there so little ethical medical research being done? Conventional medical research, funded primarily by pharmaceutical corporations, will *never* conduct truly preventive research studies. We *need* a governing body to fund such research, entirely independent of financial conflicts of interest.

And I'm sorry to say, our elected representatives are unlikely to come to our assistance, either. Many of them, too, have been handsomely bought off.[18]

Fast Food And Slow Death

The public has few options in choosing healthy fast foods. People don't want their freedoms limited, but they forget their choices are already limited. Most simply buy their fat-laden, salt-saturated fast foods because that is what the fast food scientists have determined sells the most. Fast food scientists work for the industry which promotes fast foods, whose incentive is not public health and curbing obesity in America, but attracting consumers and addicting them to their own bellies' expansion. The success of the whole operation depends upon finding ways to promote food addictions. It's a well-understood fact among these scientists that fat cells seek satiation, and so if you can get people fat, then their own fat cells will continually compel them to remain saturated.[19]

> *"Welcome to the Bulge Building King, what will you have today?"*
>
> *"Yes, I will have a fat cell accelerator as well as the fat cell saturator. I'll also have the coronary occluder, to stoke a stroke, and for dessert I'll have the Master of Disaster blood sugar blaster! I can't wait to swallow that bait! How better to satisfy the metabolic food addictions that your ever-calculating fast food scientists have cultivated within me?"*

Should these scientific advancements in "food enhancement" be monitored? Should the fast food industry be held accountable for so chemically altering nature's products as to make them addictive substances? Consider the massive grocery chains and the processed foods industries. On a scientific level, these industries are well aware that healthy foods encourage trim waistlines and the natural moderation of appetite. People just don't have a hankering to get fat on apples. But to get fat on apple pies and apple fritters makes a heaven of approaching heaven's gates, and it's only a coronary away.

THE OTHER KINDS OF RESEARCHERS

There has always been a splinter group of ethical medical pioneers who have not been completely extinguished. Included in this group are such luminaries as Dr. Max Gerson (Gerson Therapy), Nathan Pritikin (Pritikin Longevity Center), Dr. Dean Ornish (Heart Disease Reversal Program), Dr. Daniel Amen (Amen Clinics), Dr. Mehmet Oz, Dr. Mark Hyman (The Daniel Plan) and Dr. Elson Haas to name just a few. They wage a brave public education campaign about natural, non-toxic methods of healing. Natural medicine pioneers conduct their research with the purpose of discovering ways to decrease disease and the suffering it causes mankind through the effective use of nature's own therapeutic resources. They help patients bring their thoughts, diet, behavior, exercise, recreation and habits into harmony with healthy natural living.

They have conducted their medical research without the powerful financial backing of the purveyors of pharmaceuticals who have steered the great majority of mainstream medical scientists *clear* of natural preventions.

1-23. POLITICIANS HAVE BEEN BOUGHT OFF THROUGH CAMPAIGN CONTRIBUTIONS AND LOBBYING. THIS HAS SKEWED NATIONAL HEALTH POLICIES TOWARD GREED. NOT GOOD.

I contend that large corporations, agencies, and government do not have a right to feed upon the failing health of the weak, especially for the sake of excessive profits. It is detrimental to society as a whole. It damages the American economy. It promotes weakness and dependency within the American people.

It's not that the government has not had good intentions. It has defined some lofty resolutions! Here are two of the *Healthy People 2020* objectives on nutrition and physical activity:

Nutrition and Weight Status: (Healthy People 2020)

Goal

Promote health and reduce chronic disease risk through the consumption of healthful diets and achievement and maintenance of healthy body weights.

Overview

The Nutrition and Weight Status objectives for Healthy People 2020 reflect strong science supporting the health benefits of eating a healthful diet and maintaining a healthy body weight. The objectives also emphasize that efforts to change diet and weight should address individual behaviors, as well as the policies and environments that support these behaviors in settings such as schools, worksites, health care organizations, and communities.

The goal of promoting healthful diets and healthy weight encompasses increasing household food security and eliminating hunger.

Americans with a healthful diet:

- Consume a variety of nutrient-dense foods within and across the food groups, especially whole grains, fruits, vegetables, low-fat or fat-free milk or milk products, and lean meats and other protein sources.

- Limit the intake of saturated and trans fats, cholesterol, added sugars, sodium (salt), and alcohol.
- Limit caloric intake to meet caloric needs.

All Americans should avoid unhealthy weight gain, and those whose weight is too high may also need to lose weight.

Why Are Nutrition and Weight Status Important?

Diet and body weight are related to health status. Good nutrition is important to the growth and development of children. A healthful diet also helps Americans reduce their risks for many health conditions, including:

- Overweight and obesity
- Malnutrition
- Iron-deficiency anemia
- Heart disease
- High blood pressure
- Type 2 diabetes
- Osteoporosis
- Oral disease
- Constipation
- Diverticular disease
- Some cancers

Physical Activity (Healthy People 2020)

Goal

Improve health, fitness, and quality of life through daily physical activity.

Overview

Released in 2008, the Physical Activity Guidelines for Americans (PAG) is the first-ever publication of national guidelines for physical activity. The Physical Activity objectives for Healthy People 2020 reflect the strong state of the science supporting the health benefits of regular physical activity among youth and adults, as identified in the PAG. Regular physical activity includes participation in moderate and vigorous physical activities and muscle-strengthening activities.

More than 80 percent of adults do not meet the

guidelines for both aerobic and muscle-strengthening activities. Similarly, more than 80 percent of adolescents do not do enough aerobic physical activity to meet the guidelines for youth. Working together to meet Healthy People 2020 targets via a multidisciplinary approach is critical to increasing the levels of physical activity and improving health in the United States.

The Physical Activity Objectives for 2020 highlight how physical activity levels are positively affected by:

a] Structural environments, such as the availability of sidewalks, bike lanes, trails, and parks

b] Legislative policies that improve access to facilities that support physical activity

Why Is Physical Activity Important?

Regular physical activity can improve the health and quality of life of Americans of all ages, regardless of the presence of a chronic disease or disability.

Among adults and older adults, physical activity can lower the risk of:

Early death, Coronary heart disease, Stroke, High blood pressure, Type 2 diabetes, Breast and colon cancer, Falls, Depression

Among children and adolescents, physical activity can:

a] Improve bone health.

b] Improve cardiorespiratory and muscular fitness.

c] Decrease levels of body fat.

d] Reduce symptoms of depression.

For people who are inactive, even small increases in physical activity are associated with health benefits.[20]

THE PROBLEM IS . . .

Our national health initiatives (Healthy People 2020) have a goal of *decreasing* chronic disease, but our corporate medical polices have the goal of increasing profits, which only comes from an *increase* in these diseases. It is understandable that parasites feed opportunistically off their host. However, it is unethical and preposterous for government to give the parasite the "care" and control of the host.

The federal government's national health policy is noble in its intention, but blind and negligent in its execution. It is a socialistic policy, that is, a policy concerned with the "social good." And within a capitalistic nation, such an ethical, "for-benefit" policy can only be effectively carried out by giving power and authority to corporations *who profit from health and wellness*. They are the only ones powerful enough to provide a check to the "solely for-profit" medical parasites. This shift and support for an ethical medical delivery system must be fully subsidized and strongly defended by the federal government, or its noble goals are not worth the paper they're printed on.

If the government would apply to defeating chronic disease just a fraction of the resources it has applied to bombs, wars, and destruction, we would see significant improvements in a short period of time. But of course the whole political game is such a den of bribes that the people with the integrity and skill sets necessary to make effective changes are usually neither wealthy enough nor corrupt enough to receive the significant corporate and special interest backing required to run successfully for high political office.

My point is, let's be *real*. If the federal government or large medical corporations wanted to achieve the good intentions they profess to carry close to their heart, they would achieve them in short order—if these stated good intentions were anything deeper than social image posturing. But the truth is:

1] The money needed is already circulating through these failing systems, which demonstrate social injustices and/or incompetence.

2] The problems have S.M.A.R.T. (specific, measurable, attainable, realistic, timed) solutions. Rational, feasible, effective solutions are readily conceivable.

3] The problem is that third parties are profiting in some way from the systems' failure, and they currently have a fair holding and persuasion in the case. They are resisting any change that might topple their profits.

4] The core underlying problem is that disease is profitable, health is not. The system's financial success (wealth) depends upon its ineffectiveness. That is, much of the disease industry's wealth depends upon the absence of its clients' health.

1-24. WHOSE RESPONSIBILITY IS IT TO FIX THIS MESS OF A MEDICAL SYSTEM?

Is it the responsibility of a capitalistic society to support recovery from chronic disease among its less fortunate, less disciplined and more aged population? Is it the responsibility of a democratic government to work toward fulfilling the emerging needs of its own people? Someday justice will balance all accounts, but until then it will continue to be as it has always been: A powerful few will continue to take advantage of the trust and tolerance of the gentle majority. This time it's corporate characters playing out the same old script. The agenda of a few greedy corporations—with the American government in their back pocket—control the physical outcomes of an unaware majority. Corporations have taken over the role of tyrants and dictators.

"The hottest places in Hell are reserved for those who in time of moral crisis preserve their neutrality."
- Attributed to Dante Alighieri

Pharmaceutically-funded medical lobbyists have fists full of dollars to push legislation that promotes the chemical agenda of these drug lords. Numerous highly effective, natural therapeutic treatment programs that have attempted to gain a footing within the American medical market have been so successfully attacked by the American Medical-Pharmaceutical Machine Approach and Food and Drug Administration (FDA) that they were forced to close their doors and move their facilities to other countries.[21] The message is clear: American soil is the turf of these drug lords and the American people are theirs to harvest. The American public has no laissez faire "let the market decide" privilege in regards to medical treatments, because freedom imparts power, and these lords desire dominion over an enslaved, drug-dependent nation.

Freedom of speech is a centrally important right and is currently constitutionally protected; as such, corporations and the government cannot be too obvious about harassing those given to expressing the truth. However, there is no difficulty at all for corporations to flood the public with half-truths. It requires keen, nimble, sure-footed perceptiveness to see through the propaganda and myths being promulgated.

While the alliance between Big Pharma and government policy makers appears to be deepening, it is nonetheless in direct conflict with the interests and welfare of the American people. How has it come to this, that a government elected to be "a government by the people for the people" has degenerated into a government whose leaders are of a wealthy elite class, serving powerful corporate industrial interests? When will the government conscience awake to recount the injustices that they have performed against their own people?

Similar political injustices have been noted throughout time, as evidenced in historical literature:

"You hate those prophets, who go to public places and speak against evil,
"even though they teach good, simple truths.
"You take unfair taxes from the poor.
"You take loads of wheat from them.
"You build fancy houses with cut stone,
"but you will not live in them.
"You plant beautiful vineyards,
"but you will not drink the wine from them.
"This is because I know about your many sins.
"You have done some very bad things:
"You hurt people who do right,
"you accept money to do wrong,
"and you keep the poor from receiving justice in court."

- Amos 5:10-12 (Easy-to-Read version) ERV – Bible

I contend that for the government agencies which are large enough to effect social change, it is a moral imperative to represent the interests of the millions of people who pay their taxes and medical insurance premiums and have placed their trust in those government agencies and medical care providers.

And what about your doctor, nurse, and other medical care providers? The vast majority of them sincerely care and will help you the best they can, but that care will rarely involve genuine prevention.

1-25. MEDICAL CARE PROVIDERS—THE VAST MAJORITY OF THEM—ARE ONLY DOING THEIR JOB. BUT THAT RARELY INVOLVES PREVENTION.

We have been persuaded, through myriad forms of media, that medicine is humane, objective, and compassionate. The numerous advertising campaigns show us competent and compassionate doctors and nurses embracing human need and frailty with dignity and professionalism. The reality is that the professionals on the front lines are there largely for the right reasons; They feel a natural empathy and calling to treat and heal those who are ill. These are the caregivers, and the advertisements are half true.

Unfortunately, medical doctors and nurses are not paid to represent the patient. They are not paid to conduct independent study and then inform their patients what their own investigations reveal to be the best forms of treatment. Medical doctors and nurses are first and foremost employees, and they are largely obligated to limit their treatment recommendations to the products and services offered by their employer.

Those products and services are, of course, the ones that bring the greatest profits to their corporate employer. The employer is a medical/pharmaceutical corporation (whose divisions and boundaries are often confusing to decipher) whose profits largely depend upon increasing the usage of their products and services—which is, in turn, largely dependent upon the ongoing presence and increasing prevalence of disease.

Let me be clear here, I am talking about a system. I am not talking about your doctor, nurse, or pharmacist; these are hard-working employees punching the corporate clock like the rest of us. I do not talk of doctors and nurses on the front lines. I talk of a corporate medical system that suppresses the prevention of chronic diseases and promotes the drugging of Americans. Your doctor is far removed from this labyrinth of power and intrigue at the top of the medical game. He or she is simply doing his best to help patients with a very limited tool chest of available options.

Most physicians have good intentions and have earned the right to sleep well at night. Many physicians wish people would take better care of themselves and yet, knowing the entrenched unhealthy habits of their patients, have grown weary of a good intentioned attempt to change mankind one patient at a time. They have a set of products, tests, and services they can offer, and they do their best to make the right decisions to assist patients through their current health care crisis. But beyond that immediate crisis, any escape from a long spiral into physical decay is left entirely to the patient. The physician’s daily schedule is so overwhelming that changing the world toward a healthier tomorrow (though important in theory) is outside his/her dictates. Doctors are not employed to resolve the roots of chronic disease for their clients; they are employed to diagnose immediate and long-term physical problems, and to make product recommendations for the treatment of those short-term problems and ongoing chronic declines.

You must realize that when you go to a medical doctor, the entire focus of your exchange will almost always consist of discussing your physical problem and its symptoms. Is there anything wrong with this picture? Think about it a moment. The reason this is relevant and yet not very obvious is the subtleness of the transaction. The doctor has been taught to ask what is wrong, and then to test, diagnose, and prescribe in that order. This may appear very normal and something you have never questioned. But what I am presenting in this book is a very different proposition. I propose that the above scenario is a deceptive marketing ploy. It is a ploy, a ruse, a scheme because its objective is to sell chemicals, and it is deceptive because it does not clearly define this agenda.

Let me elaborate: The doctor asks you what’s wrong and what are your symptoms, and you answer, "This is ailin' me here, Doc," or, "I'm a hurtin' something fierce right here," or "This part right here, why don't it work like it used to?" or "Every time I climb stairs I feel like I'm climbin' Mt. Everest."

Then your doctor says, "Well, let me see!" He/She then performs additional tests and assessments, renders a diagnosis, and consults his authoritative resources that define best medical practices, protocols, procedures and, most prominently, what medications are appropriate for your particular condition. These recommendations have been written up by the medical and pharmaceutical powers, whose authority is conferred upon them by … well, by themselves. How? The pharmaceutical powers that subsidize medical schools, medical research, and medical literature are the same powers that "authoritatively" recommend the products, protocols, practices, and procedures which they also just so happen to have coincidently created for sale, distribution, rental, and/or service for their corporate gain.

It almost always happens that this disease starts with the patient having some seemingly insignificant symptoms, for which they receive their good doctor's prescriptions, and home they go. Such doctors offer their wares as they are employed to do, but they rarely offer comprehensive plans and tools for overcoming the deeper roots of the symptoms, because that is not what they are employed to do.

It is modern medicine's dependence upon sickness that prompts it to sidestep the relevancy of patients' desire to be well. Patients want to know the whole truth about how to get well and be fully supported in making changes that will promote their full recovery. *This cannot be given to them if the treatments being offered depend upon their continuing affliction.* This dilemma has been neatly skirted by modern medicine choosing to address disease only from its symptoms forward. Symptoms produce a pseudo need and doctors are taught to focus on and modify only the symptoms, even though the solutions to chronic health problems are quite frequently behavioral changes.

So who suffers because of this system? You, your family, your friends, the economy, and even the government and maybe even HMOs—everyone but the pharmaceutical and medical industries.

1-26. WHAT ABOUT THE PATIENTS? WHAT ABOUT PEOPLE WHO SUFFER WITH CHRONIC ILLNESS?

Consider with me the last 75 years of medicine. We have looked at the chronically ill and thrown at them:

1] Assessment (examination of the diseased state).
2] Diagnosis (definition of the diseased state).
3] Drugs (chemical modification of the diseased state).
4] Surgery (removal or modification of the affected organs within the diseased state).

And the result of this treatment model is that people are living longer in the diseased state. This is consuming larger and larger portions of the gross national product. This has been highly effective in prolonging and deepening the profits of the medical and pharmaceutical industries. But, however profitable it is for corporate medicine, it is a source of financial and emotional grief for our country.

Modern medicine has failed to convert the chronically ill to wellness. For the individual, we see two principle effects resulting from the allopathic medical treatment model:

1] *A progressive decline in physiological health.* Why would we see this? Because drugs are often many times more harmful to patients than the problems for which they're taking them. Remember, medications are toxic, poisonous, lethal substances that are prescribed in very small non-lethal doses.
2] *An increasing dependency upon and consumption of an ever-widening assortment of drug solutions.* In fact, modern medicine's message has become so deeply imbedded in the American psyche that we believe doing drugs whenever something ails us is the unquestioned and obvious first choice.

We need to be exposed to all the information available, but the primary pipeline for conveying medical information has a vested financial interest in our reaching certain specific conclusions as consumers. Thus, it highlights certain bits of information while discounting other bits, in order to move us along as one massive, gullible, and docile herd in a large, multidimensional, concerted effort to bring us into line with their greatest profit.

We are not being told the whole truth about drugs. We are not being told the whole truth about the number of deaths caused by medication errors, and human errors of medical personnel and patients. We are not being told that the leading cause of death in the United States is the American healthcare system.[22] We are not told of the deplorably poor recovery rate of drug sluggers, that is, the patients slugging down medications two, three, four times a day, year after year after year. We are not told about the dangers of taking too many medications (polypharmacopia). We are not told the evidence that medications stress the human system and actually speed up the rate of generalized physiological breakdown. We are not told the long-term damaging effects of medications upon various systems of the body. We are not told that medications are almost always merely treating the symptomatic effects of deeper health problems that stem from generalized poor health, poor habits, and poor diet. "Down" is the only direction patients are going until these problems are addressed, and there is no way that pills are going to lift them from that responsibility.

1-27. FAILURE IS OUR UNFORTUNATE LEGACY IN DEFEATING CHRONIC DISEASE.

Examine the medical histories of the chronically ill. See how effective pill popping without healthy behavior has been. As a registered nurse, I frequently work with chronically ill patients, and *I see the pattern played out ever so consistently*. The specific details vary, but the broader pattern is amazingly consistent. (I wish to make it clear here that I speak of chronic diseases of a systemic order and not more superficial health conditions like aches, pains, corns, rashes, congestion, flu and fungus.)

Here is how a chronically ill patient's history typically plays out. Pills appear to work for a season as chemicals contradict the effect of symptoms, but the correction is inevitably short-lived. Over time, the problem and its associated symptoms appear to return—*because they actually never left*. If we do not address the underlying causes of declining health, our health continues to decline, and the symptoms of that declining health will inevitably find expression. So, on these conventional treatments, the same problem will erupt again over time, or it will develop into even deeper problems and impact other bodily systems as well. *This pattern will continue until the underlying behavioral causes of declining health are eliminated and replaced with healthy, self-restoring behaviors.*

This extremely predictable case history pattern can be seen consistently, not sporadically, in the tomes of medical documentation. They provide overwhelming evidence that chemical medicine alone is absolutely futile at preserving physical health. Funny, we don't hear about this utter futility on the television, magazine, and radio ads.

A Typical History Of Chronic Disease Treatment And Progression	
Patient Informed:	Patient given generalized information about proper behavior, diet, exercise, precautions, and restrictions.
Patient Unsupported:	Essentially no lifestyle modification support provided. Essentially no medical fitness centers provided. Essentially no health-promoting guides, no health coaches, no health managers responsible for evoking optimal health in individuals, no health mentors, no emotionally and motivationally supportive consultants, no medical doctors prescribing optimal lifestyle, no prescription of optimal nutrition, no system of patient accountability designed to encourage compliance with progressive health and fitness and nutritional regimens. No group support. No health care team support. No financial, employment, or insurance incentives for compliance with a high standard of health-restoring personal discipline. No praise for patient success and no behavioral accountability contracts to reward positive health maintenance and admonish self-defeating non-compliance. No ongoing monitoring of health-promoting lifestyle success or failure. No appropriate rewards, incentives, and deterrent measures to encourage and monitor for continuing success.
Patient Prescribed:	Pills emphasized early and aggressively. Improving habits lightly recommended, but the doctor *orders*—that is, *prescribes*—medication to be taken.
Patient Trajectory:	90% failure in recovery from disease. A progressively deepening slide down a progressively more slippery slope characterizes the typical case history of the chronically ill.
Patient Outcome:	Ongoing, progressive physiological degeneration and physical de-conditioning, which results in predictably high rates of re-hospitalizations and ever deepening disease states.

The unhealthy people of America need to learn the pleasures of healthy living and also the consistently progressive hellish discomforts of letting your health deteriorate. Instead, they are drawn for refreshment to pools of stagnant water. Yes, stagnant water can sustain the life of those dying of dehydration, however, in the long run, it will poison patients and kill them as surely as severe dehydration. Only clean, pure healthy fluids will sustain long-term health.

The corporate medical industry, however, fails to inform and, more importantly, fails to encourage, mandate, prescribe, instruct, enforce, support, facilitate, and foster these well-proven healing practices. To this degree, they are responsible for the pain and losses whose prevention they knowingly fail to support.

1-28. THE AGENDA OF THE MEDICAL-PHARMACEUTICAL SYSTEM IS FOR YOU TO RECEIVE ONLY THEIR PRODUCTS—AND ONCE YOU'VE CHECKED IN TO RECEIVE, THEY'D PREFER THAT YOU NEVER LEAVE.

Patients usually begin taking medications as consequences of their own actions, making themselves prisoners of their own devices. However, given their 'druthers, most patients would prefer not to be taking massive amounts of medications … but the chapter on when and why to stop taking a great many medications isn't addressed. It's time that it was. A program for departure from medications should be a national agenda, as medications poison, damage, and kill thousands of patients every year.

Seriously now, we are in a state of war. The drug companies, through their authorized representatives, recommend you begin a life of gradual but progressive chemical inebriation. Chemicals are unnatural, unhealthy, toxic substances that damage organs, tissue, and the body's natural immune system. *Medications should be taken as a last resort, and aborted as soon as healthier, less toxic methods of recovery can be implemented.* The proper place for most medications is to perform a short-term "fix" till a long-term solution can be implemented. The problem is that the long-term solutions are not prescribed, because drug lords rule the tribe.

We should also mention all those healthy people who regularly pay elevated healthcare premiums to compensate for the "frequent flyer," that is, those who just can't get enough of being hospitalized. We, the hardworking and healthy, have to pay elevated premiums because the medical system has fallen short of its promises to actually care for its clients. We realize quite well that good advice about being healthier is so much hot air to those who aren't listening or don't have the ears to hear. For these people, admonitions to "live healthier" (without a 12-step support system) is like giving them tea bags and saying "drink up" without any cups of hot water.

We realize that the steep cost of care for the chronically ill falls upon our backs and hits our wallets. We realize that these high costs are largely because the medical system has failed to proactively guide, support, and facilitate the healthier lifestyles that would disarm the causes of ongoing and progressive decay.

If the true intent is to turn lives around, then they should target the people who are struggling with chronic disease. You might call them "chronic disease-aholics" who daily attract chronically deepening unhealthiness to themselves in many ways, without even being aware of it. Or maybe they just aren't motivated enough or capable enough to stop the self-attracting snowball of chronic decline. Whatever the reason, *these people*—the unaware, unmotivated and incapable ones—need much more than merely hearing the message.

And where can the unaware, unmotivated and incapable ones be found? In the beds of our hospitals and in front of TVs in their homes. But through these specific venues, this specific "target" population hears volumes about drugs and only faint whispers about the value of adopting a healthy lifestyle. Why aren't these culprits of mass medical expenditures being persuasively, overwhelmingly encouraged and urgently compelled into programs that promote effective lifestyle reformation?

The inclusion of drugs (which themselves are chemically toxic to the human body) rarely does anything more than alter symptoms of degenerating health. They do not give health; they cannot. Drugs do not impart health. They can lower blood pressure but they cannot improve the underlying cause of the rise in blood pressure. They alter the effects but do not address the cause. Treating effects of declining health does not stop health from declining. It only alters the symptoms. Only restoring a healthy lifestyle pattern and health-infusing behaviors and activities will turn the decline in health into the recovery of health.

Instead, these industries confirm the weak in their current behavior, comfort them with a treatment of their symptoms, and thereby encourage and enable their health-destroying habits. And so the weak get weaker, have more symptoms, undergo additional treatments and additional pills, and thereby yield increasing profits to the strong.

1-29. THIS IS OUR MODERN MEDICAL DILEMMA: PEOPLE DESIRE TO GET WELL AND HAVE THE SOURCE PROBLEMS REMOVED—NOT MERELY HAVE THE SYMPTOMS OF THEIR PROGRESSIVE DECLINES TREATED. THIS IS THE INTENT OF THEIR CONTRACTED AGREEMENT WITH MEDICINE, BUT GETTING WELL IS NOT A PREDICTABLE OUTCOME OF THE CONVENTIONALLY PRESCRIBED TREATMENTS.

Consumers must realize that prescriptively drugged, progressive physical declines are the only logical, predictable outcomes of the great majority of the treatments they are being prescribed. Also, people living wholly out of context with health-fortifying behavior come to the medical system seeking relief from the ailments they have largely brought upon themselves.

Meanwhile, the modern medicine machine—operating largely with high economic goals and without high ethical ideals—treats those symptoms without addressing the underlying causes (i.e., the ailment-attracting lifestyle). While profitable to certain aspects of the medical industry in the short run, this approach is injurious to individuals and to society in the long run.

For instance, with obesity and its myriad of accompanying afflictions quickly becoming the number one preventable cause of death, modern medicine continues to treat symptoms and not sources. They work on diabetes, high blood pressure, and joint pain (and other results of obesity) while making little attempt to identify, grapple with, and modify the underlying causes (which are sourced in human behavior).

When our chronically ill patients continue in the same behaviors or omission of behaviors that led to their current degeneration, and add another 1,000 pills' worth of chemical toxins, they are giving their exquisitely wise biological computers ample data inputs for continuing physical deterioration. But decline cannot last forever. Still, the modern medical model is a whiz at saving those who are about to die from dying. Also, medical recidivism (a tendency to relapse into a previous condition or mode of behavior) is not being adequately addressed. Just as California has severely overcrowded prisons because of prisoner recidivism, we have skyrocketing medical costs because our highest-risk, most costly patients are not getting well, but rather keep reentering the system.

I hate to be so cynical, but I need to point out, it just makes good financial sense for them to do so. If your business is to profit off the treatment of people who are medically unstable, it's certainly not good to let those clients slip from your hands to the clutches of death. No profits can be derived from the grave; it is essential to keep debilitated patients alive because their ongoing treatment is where all the big money is. Letting patients become (and stay) medically unstable is good for business, but letting them die is not.

This model needs people to stay sick and dependent, not get supported and empowered, or die. It is through the portal of patients' prolonged weakness that the medical-pharmaceutical machine's system will get ahead. And so, it will come as no surprise: Modern pharmaceutical medicine's failure to reduce the prevalence of chronic disease in America has been so financially rewarding as to position it consistently in the top three most profitable industries in the world.[23]

1-30. THE PHENOMENAL FINANCIAL SUCCESS OF THE MEDICAL-PHARMACEUTICAL INDUSTRIES' FAILURE TO HEAL PEOPLE AND KEEP THEM WELL HAS CREATED SEVERE ECONOMIC BURDENS ELSEWHERE.

They take the forms of lost work, Medicare costs, disability, unemployment, bankruptcies, and uninsured medical costs. Most of these fall upon the shoulders of the government to pay, which means that the American taxpayers are underwriting the vampire-like systems of the medical-pharmaceutical machine. Remember that for medical/pharmaceutical corporations in America, their equation is "Disease = Profit." While those industries reel in the cash, the American economy (and its taxpayers) experience an ongoing and ever-deepening financial burden.

Chronic disease and obesity are epidemic problems in the United States, and while this is great news for the medical industries that profit off human misery, it is damaging to the strength and vitality of our nation. The healthy are already living out healthy, self-preserving lives, and they should be rewarded for the low cost of medical care they require from the health insurance system.

The real culprit in skyrocketing medical costs for our country is the absence of support for healthy lifestyle transformation for *the one to five percent most chronically ill, who account for 65% of all medical dollars spent in America.*[24] This singular population is responsible for both the incredible medical costs and incredible medical profits that our country simultaneously experiences. If those who are highly disposed to chronic disease—and they can be easily identified—were approached early and supported in adapting their lifestyle and they followed through, they could counteract their strong proclivity to attract disease.

And through this one successful action alone, we would dramatically reduce overall medical costs in America. The top one to five percent most unhealthy are responsible for 65% of every medical dollar spent in America. And the treatment of the chronically ill in general is responsible for 75 cents of every medical dollar spent in America.[25]

Meanwhile, modern medicine's ongoing aversion to teach, instill, and support a transition to healthier lifestyles among the chronically ill robs the American economy of trillions of dollars. Their inordinate gains are largely because the lifestyles that promote chronic disease are winked at.

America can no longer afford to take her medical guidance from an industry that profits from her physical degeneration. Our society's wealth, our health, and our tax dollars are continually being sunk into this cannibalistic money pit.

If you were to poll 10 million chronically ill people, I doubt making the pharmaceutical and American medical corporations filthy rich would be one of their top priorities. Americans desire a system of healthcare that provides relief and long-lasting remedy from illness. Fundamentally, American medical consumers don't give a rip about the profit of *any* industry, health food, fitness, pharmaceutical and/or otherwise; they care about themselves, their parents, their kids. So why are our medical research and medical care systems so dominated by the interests of corporations instead of the interests of the American people?

I contend that large corporations, agencies, and government do not have a right to feed upon the failing health of the weak, especially for the sake of excessive profits. It is detrimental to society as a whole. It damages the American economy. And it promotes weakness and dependency within the American people. Surely we can do better …

Chapter 3.
Problem Two—
How Do We Promote "Chronic Wellness"?

WHAT ARE THE KEY DYNAMICS OF CHRONIC DISEASE, AND HOW DO THEY TIE IN WITH THE MEDICAL-PHARMACEUTICAL MACHINE?

Problem Two mostly focuses on "prescriptive practices" for preventing illness through promoting wellness. This section still embodies a systems-orientation, but there is more of an emphasis on people and processes here than on products or politics as in *Problem One.* Personal practices for amplifying the benefits of health and wellness are detailed in the section titled *Solution Two—Living Beyond the Affliction Zone.*

2-1. MOST CHRONIC ILLNESS IS PREVENTABLE, BUT IT ISN'T BEING PREVENTED.

Choose one—and only one!

a] Healthy people think right, take little to no drugs, and behave right. Unhealthy people do the opposite.

b] Healthy people think about and do healthy things, take little to no drugs, and behave responsibly. Unhealthy people do the opposite.

c] Healthy people think about and do healthy things, take little to no drugs, and behave responsibly with a view to the consequences of their thoughts and actions. Unhealthy people do the opposite.

Here's a movie idea, similar to the documentary *Supersize Me* (which chronicled the physical decline of a person who put himself on a diet made up of *exclusively* fast food for 30 days):

This movie/documentary starts with a very healthy individual (Patient One) and shows him in his healthy habits and healthy lifestyle, and demonstrates his high degree of health and fitness. Then he embarks on a medical treatment plan for congestive heart failure or other major chronic disease (according to his family's genetic propensity for chronic disease), even though he demonstrates no symptoms, because his healthy lifestyle has so reinforced and strengthened him against those health declines. The film follows him as he begins conventional medicine's chemical treatment regimen, and we see the inevitable physical decline that results as a natural consequence.

At the same time, the film chronicles the journey of a middle-aged person (Patient Two) whose behavior over the last 30 years has brought him to his first major diagnosis of chronic disease, and stands on the brink of the usual diagnostic and prescriptive process. But instead of plunging in, he decides to get a second opinion and prefers it, and is instead prescribed an entirely natural regimen of optimal health revitalizing products and practices.

The film shows the chronically well (Patient One)—firmly planted in the life of the healthy and fit—*rattled and removed* from his stronghold of fitness and set "a tumblin' down" a spiraling descent into physical decline. And it is all from simply aligning his life with the teachings and recommendations of modern medicine for the chronically ill.

On the other hand, the chronically ill person (Patient Two), whose gradual descent came about by his own hand (personal lifestyle choices), now takes a serious look at his life and the future typically facing the chronically ill. After deciding against conventional medical advice for the chronically ill (i.e., "swallow your pills and call me when conditions worsen"), he instead takes upon himself a lifestyle designed to restore optimal health. We see his rise out of defeat and decline, and into rebounding health and recovery.

The film concludes by pulling Patient One off all the pharmaceutical agents recommended for a patient with that condition. As the "poor unfortunate" recovers from the American Medical Approach's "cure" (that almost killed him), he resumes his prior lifestyle, that is, an Effective Medical Approach of optimized healthy living. Over time, he is fully restored to his former strength. In conclusion, the two patients meet and discuss their past habits and medical histories and personal experiences with the program.

Now, you might argue that these chemicals were unhealthy for our poor unfortunate *to begin with* because he *didn't possess the underlying condition* for which he was receiving treatment. I would argue that these chemicals are unhealthy for everybody (with or without the condition).

However, they only *kill* patients *very slowly* because these lethal substances are consumed *in such minute doses*. I am *not* arguing for non-treatment; I am arguing for an Effective Medical Approach to replace a toxic and *ineffective* medical approach.

An unhealthy person cannot and will not get healthy by taking lots of drugs, but a healthy person can definitely get unhealthy by taking lots of drugs. If a healthy person (with robust strength and resilience to disease) gets sick from taking lots of chemicals into his/her body (because those chemicals are unnatural and toxic substances), why do we think that an unhealthy person (so much weaker than a healthy person) will get well by taking lots of chemicals into his/her body?

2-2. LONG CONTINUANCE IN UNHEALTHY BEHAVIORS—INCLUDING TAKING MEDICATIONS—PLACES STRESSES UPON THE BODY THAT EVENTUALLY OVERWHELM ONE'S IMMUNE RESERVES. BY PLACING EVEN A SMALL BATTERY OF HEALTHY BEHAVIORS INTO ONE'S LIFE, ONE CAN STAVE OFF SIGNIFICANT DECLINES IN HEALTH FOR YEARS.

What I am saying is a little prevention goes a long way if it's applied consistently. A senior need not be training on a masters competitive swim team five days a week in order to avoid cardiovascular disease; swimming easy laps or taking an aqua aerobics class for 45 minutes, three days a week, will keep him/her relatively healthy for years. Yet drop off the regular fitness program completely and rapid declines in health are highly probable. Such is the law of entropy, especially as we get older.

Regarding healthy lifestyle, we know from statistics that:

- Those who have the healthiest lifestyle are also the healthiest segment of the population.
- Those who have the least healthy lifestyle are the sickest segment of the population, and a hill of pills isn't able to do a thing about it.
- Those who take the least drugs are the healthiest segment of the population.

Please reflect on your own mom, dad, grandparents, friends, brothers, and sisters, and ask yourself the following questions:

- Which ones are enjoying glowing health? What is their lifestyle?
- Which ones are enduring chronic frailty, ailments, and pain? What is their lifestyle?

I cannot speak for you, but it has been my personal experience that the people in my life who attend diligently to a healthy life achieve exactly that, with minimal use of drugs and the highest regard for healthy self-discipline. Those returning to a healthier lifestyle act likewise. However, it has also been my observation that those who take the least responsibility for their health are the least healthy and suffer the most ailments.

2-3. THE COST OF NEGLECTING YOUR HEALTH IS FAR GREATER THAN THE COST OF TAKING RESPONSIBLE CARE OF YOURSELF—AND THE COSTS ARE MORE THAN JUST MONETARY.

People choose unhealthy behavior because (select one or more):

a] It's easy, comfortable, and familiar.

b] We're "predestined by genetics/family"—or so we say.

c] We don't have the support to choose otherwise.

d] Our thinking/worldview/belief system is skewed/erroneous/ignorant.

In a sense, there is simply no avoiding a certain amount of discomfort and struggle in this life. It is sad to observe that many people attempt to avoid remaining healthy because it's, well, inconvenient. It requires effort. It hurts a little. And so they avoid it, extensively, for years, with the frequent result that they end up acquiring a far deeper and far more despairing form of inconvenience, discomfort, exertion, and struggle in the form of chronically degenerating health. It is uplifting, even inspiring, to observe other people who willingly and fortuitously subject themselves to the rigors involved in remaining fit.

It never ceases to amaze me how people will suffer considerable pain associated with the old rut that brought them into chronic illness, but are unwilling to embrace the difficulties and challenges of making lifestyle and behavioral changes that would restore them to health and eliminate the sources of their daily pain. Go figure. Why would anyone choose behaviors that, over a lifetime, destroy the chronic health of their youth and replace it with chronic disease in their latter years? Why choose behaviors whose consequences will result in chronic unhealthiness? People initially choose behaviors that are comfortable, convenient, easy, and afford immediate gratification.

However, if one is not careful, the end result of those choices can be a life that is anything but easy, comfortable, convenient, and gratifying. A simple, straightforward example would be of a patient with cirrhosis of the liver caused by alcoholism. The person obviously did not choose to die by one of the most pathetic and painful ways available to man. Rather, it appears the drinker simply prioritized immediate gratification and escape over deferred gratification and growth. The personal values of self-care and self-discipline were apparently lacking. The emphasis was on short-term (impulse) gratification.

2-4. AN ENORMOUS PROBLEM APPEARS TO BE UNHEALTHY PEOPLES' AVERSION TO HEALTHY ACTIVITIES—THEIR PERSPECTIVE, PRIORITIES, AND ATTITUDE TOWARD HEALTH. HOW DO WE BREAK THROUGH THIS MENTAL MAGNET FOR PHYSICAL DECLINE?

I have a friend in his 40s, who, like millions of Americans, is suffering significant health problems, and I cannot for the life of me convince him to adopt a healthier lifestyle. You might assume from my penchant for preachin' on health that I nag the livin' hell out of him, but I don't. Furthermore, I never have, because I know it's a subject he is completely unreceptive to. I have, on rare occasions, politely recommended adding walks and a diet rich in fruits, vegetables, whole grains, and a couple of nutrient-rich food supplements to his numerous pill bottles and his exclusively sedentary life. But I know by his existing choices of activity, the way he shrugs his shoulders and sighs, and the comments he makes, that his health is a very, very low priority to him. He suffers though, oh yes, chronically, from life-threatening conditions no less. Yet any time I do suggest taking up walking in the hills or joining a health club or drinking carrot juice and eating lots of fruits, salads, and vegetables, it's almost as if he makes the sign of the cross against me.

Why do so many unhealthy people endure considerable and progressively worsening states of disease and suffering without even trying to establish a non-self-diminishing lifestyle? It appears as if they would rather endure physical limitations, daily discomforts, and the press of easy tasks made difficult, rather than the challenge of making the changes in habits and behaviors that would generate inner and outer health and vitality. They consume daily medications that are toxic to the human body, eat a diet that's largely nutrition-less, and daily plod along overcome by fatigue and weakness precisely because they do exactly *nothing* to build strength, reserve, and immunity.

They strain mightily at everyday, basic tasks like standing up, bending over, putting on socks and shoes, walking short distances, or climbing stairs. But the idea of beginning a gentle progressive program of exercise, flexibility, cardio, and strength training that would yield dramatic improvements in physical function, and increased independence and freedom—this makes them wince and cringe. They do not appear to begrudge the act of struggling day in, day out in a battle with weakness, stiffness, shakiness, shortness of breath, chronic pain, and a severely limited existence. No, this is a struggle they are familiar with and therefore comfortable with. But a struggle with regaining a healthy identity and establishing health-promoting activities that would help them thrive and be happy—appears to them to be rather improbable and quite frankly not worth the effort.

"Take care of your body with steadfast fidelity. The soul must see through these eyes alone, and if they are dim, the whole world is clouded."
- Goethe

My heart goes out to these folks. They have unconsciously succumbed to a helpless, self-paralyzing lifestyle and point of view.

To be overrun by chronic disease is not something one consciously chooses, but it is usually a consequence of choices one has made. We frequently choose to be comfortable, and for many that involves retreating from the vibrant, bold, energetic possibilities that surround us. The pursuit of pleasure precludes the demands of growth. *We sacrifice the rewards of initiative for the indulgences of inertia.*

"Those who think they have not time for bodily exercise will sooner or later have to find time for illness."
- Edward Stanley, 19th century Earl of Derby

Taking responsibility is scary and demanding. It necessitates doing what is best by behaving responsibly, morally, intentionally, and healthfully—in a word, intelligently. This is simply too painful and too huge a jump for most people to make from their lifetime assumptions about reality that are familiar, comfortable, self-limiting, insecure, and just plain lazily accepted. This is the heart of good healthcare: to assist patients in the journey towards becoming aware, responsible, and fully human. It is the journey towards behaving in our own best interests, which is in harmony with the universe whose laws underwrite all we see and the breaking of which undermines all we are. It is the journey to not merely exist till we die, but to thrive while alive.

2-5. HOW DO PEOPLE ATTRACT CHRONIC DISEASE TO THEMSELVES—AND WHY?

In the big picture of things, here is how people typically act like magnets for chronic disease:

- *They immerse themselves in debilitating physical/concrete forces,* such as environment, lifestyle, stress, and behaviors. (However, keep in mind that people choose most of these factors themselves; the degree of their influence is mostly within people's direct control.)
- *And they immerse themselves in de-energizing and destabilizing psychological forces,* such as inaccurate self-image, negative attitudes, false identity and other faulty beliefs, fears, emotional wounds, bitterness, inaccurate perceptions of reality, and unhealthy mental preoccupations and desires. (The degree of their influence is fully within people's control.)

Why do people attract chronic disease to themselves? At the deepest level, it's primarily because of their personal paradigm—their mental constructs, attitudes, belief system—and then because of their resulting choices, habits, and priorities. All of these, working together as a system, automatically magnetize to attract chronic disease. This is not fatalism, though. Paradigms can shift and people and their lifestyle systems can be transformed. But the problem is that people become too comfortable with their infected paradigm and their diseased choices. These are far more familiar (and intimately customized to their own likings and preferences) than living connected and in concert with the "health and tension" of reality, nature, and truth.

It becomes far more comfortable to live in a self-created, self-limited version of reality that we have fabricated to our own personal likes, dislikes, opinions, beliefs, and desires than to admit to our smallness and our need for enlightened perceptions. Living in a well-constructed lie becomes more comfortable than facing the unknown of change. Dying slowly from a horrible, self-attracted, personally-embraced disease becomes more comfortable than surrendering to the fullness of our responsibility for living a healthy life. They view life this way because they are mildly depressed, apathetic, wounded, hurt, lacking confidence, misguided, and/or many other possible reasons.

We become what we love. The mere act of opening one's eyes should convey to all that the mystery that surrounds us is wild, wooly, and wondrous. When we concern ourselves only with the small and mundane, we become small and mundane. When we fail to consider the beauty and grandness and mystery around us, we shrink to the size of the petty things we idolize. Instead of looking for the best in life and responding to it by becoming a wiser, deeper, more aware individual, these people ask themselves simpler questions like: What's for dinner? What's on the boob tube? What may I enjoy now, with little effort and pay for mañana?

In the case of the alcoholic, gambler, and drug addict, their chosen *perceptions and priorities* become so contracted that they cannot appreciate the world beyond the shadows of their addiction. None of us are essentially any different, however. Uncontrolled gambling, alcoholism and drug addiction may hold a lower rung on the social ladder, but our socially acceptable addictions like eating junk food, watching TV, and a lack of exercise are only slightly less self-destructive.

Millions are leading lifestyles that aggressively *attract* chronic illness to themselves and maintain it—and they do not even realize it. They simply do not make a connection between their personal behaviors and physiological outcomes. Science has clearly identified a relationship between lifestyle and the presence or absence of chronic disease. Chronic disease, then, is the result of living largely out of congruence with the thoughts, attitudes, behaviors, habits, and lifestyles under which we as humans were ideally designed to live.

2-6. TRANSITION IS POSSIBLE. THE ONLY WAY TO DO A U-TURN ON DECLINING HEALTH IS TO RESTORE AND SUSTAIN HEALTHY LIFESTYLE HABITS, AND THIS CAN HAPPEN DESPITE ANY FAMILY PROFILE OF APPARENT GENETIC PREDISPOSITIONS.

Your body is not punishing you, genetics are not punishing you. God is not neglecting you, *you* are neglecting you and your body. And *you* are experiencing the punishing lifestyle of yourself—and learning the painful lessons of that self-neglect. We are rarely *victims*; we are the directors of our own plays and many are creating a tragedy for themselves.

Those with chronic diseases that have a genetic component are experiencing physiological breakdowns along genetically inherited lines of weakness and culturally adopted behavioral patterns. They reason, "Oh, I am experiencing heart disease like my mother and grandmother before me," when in reality they are living out of harmony with what is best for them. That is, they are failing to express a wholesome connection with their physical gifts, natural talents, and creative abilities. They are out of touch (like their predecessors) with a self-nurturing, self-cultivating and self-understanding way of life that is best for them, and it is destroying them. As a natural flow of cause and effect, their decline logically manifests itself along culturally and genetically inherited lines of weakness.

In the specific case of weight gain, the issues of hormonal, metabolic, and genetic abnormalities are real. But it's not fair to ascribe the problem to these abnormalities until one has engaged in a sensible, well-designed weight loss, exercise, and strengthening program. Until one has done the work that reasonably produces effective weight loss in "normal" populations, for at least a year, one cannot fairly write off weight gain as part and parcel of being born into a family with weight problems.

Indeed, if one is able to tolerate the self-analysis, one may realize his/her family culture never emphasized regular and consistent exercise. It may be a family that gains weight and attracts chronic disease through habits, traditions, and perspectives. These are difficult patterns to break, but they are from inheriting the family's *behavioral* flaws, not *genetically* inherited abnormalities. If your genetics fail to respond to industrious, robust, and consistent behavioral modifications, and remain stubbornly fixed in obesity, physical degeneration, and chronic disease, then you don't need new behaviors, you need new genetics, and until then, drugs to treat the symptoms of your inevitable decline.

But I believe this is extremely rare. I believe 99.9% of the time, people from families with strong histories of obesity and chronic disease will *not* suffer the same fate if they implement this strong change of behaviors. *Frequent recurrence of specific chronic conditions in a family history reveals not only a familial genetic weakness but, more importantly, adverse familial behavioral norms, habits, traditions, patterns and perspectives.* It is the similarity of familial *behavioral norms* rather than the similarity of familial *genetics* that is responsible for the similarity of familial chronic disease patterns. The solution is not in discovering new genetics or new and stronger drugs, but in breaking the illness-attracting familial behavior patterns and replacing them with wellness-attracting behavioral norms.

2-7. WHEN IT COMES TO MOTIVATION FOR LIFESTYLE TRANSFORMATION, THE OLD ADAGE OF "NO PAIN, NO GAIN" IS WORTH PONDERING FOR HOW IT RELATES TO THE GENERAL ROLES OF INTERVENTION AND RESPONSIBILITY.

Change requires motivation, which is why organisms have a nervous system. That's how we detect pain, which signals that a pattern or behavior is injurious and needs to be changed. Unless we sit in a negative consequence and accept it as a logical result of our own causes, it is very difficult to find sufficient motivation to change the deeply ingrained habituated patterns that led to that consequence. When consequences are removed or significantly reduced (which medications do) and personal responsibility is never recognized, it is extremely rare that behavioral change will ever take place.

After reorganizing a self-damaging pattern, accepting its consequences, and desiring authentic change, the next phase is to implement a plan or program of change, that is, lifestyle transition. However, the *next step (as a program)* is not currently available as part of our national health system. Currently, each individual is forced to tread this tenuous journey of lifestyle transition alone. This process is very difficult. It is extremely rare that a person is capable of genuine self-transformation apart from extensive external support.

Unfortunately, the vast majority of medical consumers do not have the motivation to study and become well-informed about their condition and embark upon a path of health recovery. It is so much easier to do as they are told and leave personal responsibility out of the equation. Modern medicine often requires little more than swallowing as directed, and that is very appealing because it's so easy.

To tell obese people to eat right and exercise more is nothing more than passing gas; it feels good to the one passing it, but does very little that is positive for anyone else in the room. Most chronically ill people would rather die a hideous and slow death by dreadful chronic disease than change habitual patterns that are deeply inbred and ingrained. This is human nature and the evidence is overwhelming. The chronically ill rarely change course midstream.

It's been my experience that patients either get a big scare, "get it," make dramatic lifestyle changes, and bounce back, or they don't get it and just continue on, hoping for a change of results to flow out of an unchanged cause. It sounds absurd when you think about it. But that's just it, they *don't* think about it; they've been conditioned and indoctrinated to just keep swallowing the powders of promise that they are sold. Given the options of familiar and easy versus new and difficult, it is human nature to choose the former—but *for* the chronically ill, the familiar and easy path is one of gradual self-destruction.

We need something *stronger* than our propensity for habituation to get people willing and excited about a higher standard of healthier living. I am sure patients agree that taking pills is easier than taking responsibility. But if patients were given the realistic and supported option of getting well as an alternative to getting treated, they would be enthusiastic about it even if it required genuine effort. All a brother and sister needs is a little help along the way. It's time that disease stops serving as a means to wealth. Give health promotion a chance to rectify what a mountain of pills has merely buried.

Health and wellness are the result of intelligent, well-ordered living. We need to rise above becoming the prey of calculating and predatory corporations spewing out ad copy about the heroic works of the powdered marvels (drugs). We need to resist the urge to succumb to the easy, slick, sugar-coated promises of *relief without responsibility*.

2-8. ADDRESSING KEY NEEDS OF PEOPLE WHO STRUGGLE WITH CHRONIC ILLNESS.

I wish now to speak primarily about the needs of those who are chronically ill. Millions of people lead lifestyles that attract chronic illness to themselves and do not even realize it. They simply do not make a connection between personal behavior and physiological outcomes.

We are what we eat, drink, breathe, think, feel, sense, read, do, love, hate, hope, fear, perceive, and believe. Genetic pre-disposition to unhealthy conditions exists, but chronic disease is far more responsive to behavioral choices than it is to genetically inherited predispositions. Chance can take you out in the blink of an eye, but for the vast majority of cases, a person reaps a crop of the seeds he or she has sown.

For out of a man's thoughts
Proceed his actions,
And out of his actions,
Flow his consequences.

I work with patients in the acute care medical setting. I am exposed on a daily basis to the needs and dilemmas of those suffering from years of prioritizing everything *but* their health. I see lives run aground on the rocks of self-neglect. I witness the pains and foibles of lives caught in the jaws of the often-unrecognized laws of cause and effect. There is a proverb that states "Whatever a man sows, this shall he also reap."

On the floors of a thousand acute care hospital units, the seriousness of this law is all too clear. Again, chance can impose itself, but for the most part, the chronically ill *are* as the chronically ill *have done*. There simply is no way to escape reaping what we have sown. Your body responds to and manifests, clear as a mountain lake, every thought and action you conducted within it. This is particularly shocking to observe in those who have indiscriminately neglected their health for many years. Whether we like it or not, we are students of our bodies, each day experiencing a report card of how well we are conducting our health behavior.

2-9. SO, ONCE WE'RE MOTIVATED TO CHANGE, READY TO TAKE RESPONSIBILITY AND START ACTING MORE CONSTRUCTIVELY—THEN WHAT?

Comparison and contrast would be a great tool to consider chronic illness versus chronic wellness, and the transformation process that links the two. Let's apply some scientific research logic to the following scenario:

Visualize two groups of 55 to 70 year-olds. Each group contains 100 people. In one group we have healthy, active seniors: runners, cyclists, swimmers, triathletes, backpackers, hikers, surfers, those who participate in community team sports, etc. In the other group we have 100 chronically ill seniors with a history of frequent re-hospitalizations.

Let's conduct health information surveys from all members of each of these two groups using scientific rigor. In the research phase we gather extensive data about the daily activities, pursuits, employments, diets, behaviors, beliefs, goals, attitudes, past and current medical conditions, medications, surgeries, accidents, physical and emotional traumas and amount of time spent watching TV.

First, we compare the data of each member in a group with data from all members in their own group. From this analysis, we identify any recognizable, consistent patterns of behaviors and outcomes within that group. Then we compare and contrast the patterns of behavior we found in the two groups—remembering that we have before us one group of chronically healthy, active seniors effusing vigor and strength, and the other a group of chronically ill seniors overcome by progressive physical degeneration. And we ask questions like:

- Would we expect the health information collected from the health histories and past and present activity/behavior logs of the members of each particular group to be similar or unpredictable?
- Within each group, would we expect to find similar practices and patterns of behavior?
- Within each group, would we see similar health practices and outcomes?
- Were each member of the two groups to be examined by a doctor, would the physical appearances, shapes, and tones of the bodies (within each group) be similar or different?

- Could we, from the health inventory data compiled before us, derive reliable principles about not only what promotes chronic disease but also what *effectively* prevents it?
- Are the physical bodies of the individuals within these two groups compliant with their personal choices (activities and lifestyle), or is there some cruel twist of fate that deposits health *consequences* piecemeal?

I want you to first think about your own conclusions to those questions and the ones below. Then review my thoughts, found in the next section.

- Do the bodies of seniors with "continuous wellness" and the bodies of seniors with "continuous illness" look the same?
- Do the health histories and behavior/activity logs of the vibrantly well and the corrosively ill read the same over the last 20 years of their lives?
- Are the behaviors of the continuously healthy and the chronically ill identical or very different?

2-10. . . . AND WHAT EXACTLY IS THE BIG PICTURE OF THIS LIFESTYLE TRANSFORMATION PROCESS? WHAT EXACTLY SHOULD WE BE AIMING FOR?

Here are my intuitive opinions from years of personal observation about the scenario defined above, though my desire is to see this scenario conducted as a formal and validated scientific experiment.

First, let me say that in reality, these two "groups" as groups are rarely seen together. The athletic seniors tend to abide in the great outdoors and the fresh air and sunshine or, when kept indoors by the weather, nonetheless in proactive environments of healthy vibrant living. They spend their retirement years in socially engaging activities, productivity, creativity, exercise, and recreation.

The chronically ill, on the other hand, appear to go outdoors as little as possible, even when capable of doing so. They appear to have a strong tendency to remain indoors all of the time, away from the fresh air and sunshine. In addition, they appear to confine themselves to smaller and smaller fields of interest, and smaller and smaller circles of activity and behavior.

The healthy and active seniors are outside engaging in and with their environment as runners, cyclists, swimmers, surfers, cross-country skiers, mountaineers, and hikers. They typically have lean, well-muscled bodies, albeit with a few more wrinkles than in their youth. They have a clean, focused, confident aura about them. They are vibrant because they are fit and energetic, and they are confident because they have retained their capabilities into the golden years and because they are enjoying the ongoing benefits of a life lived well.

The seniors of continuous illness come in many different physical shapes and sizes, but poor circulation is a significant and consistent hallmark. They are often overweight. They are usually of pale complexion, and have lost almost all muscle mass, tone, and strength. Their daily activities are very limited, and even these appear to be very taxing for them. They appear to have lost a lot of their self-confidence. Of course, this is quite understandable, considering the losses they have sustained. They have become intimately acquainted with their own vulnerability through the nagging symptoms of degenerating health and progressive declines into chronic disease.

I would expect that the health histories and behavioral data accumulated from each group would demonstrate a direct link between their behaviors and their health outcomes. I would also expect that the group's pattern would remain significantly consistent within its members. That is, the group whose outcome is one of chronic illness will be directly linkable to histories of non viable disease-attracting behaviors; and the group whose outcome is one of chronic wellness will be directly linkable to histories of viable health-attracting behaviors; and that these two sets of behaviors and their relative outcomes will remain predominantly consistent within each group. The healthy live well and fare well, and the unhealthy live poorly and fare poorly.

For instance, *in the chronically diseased group* I would expect to see:

- More unhealthy habits than in the chronically well group, and (more importantly) a significantly uniform absence of healthy behaviors.
- Their health histories to show a consistent pattern of initial symptoms followed by more serious systemic disorders, all treated by increasing drugs, diagnoses, and surgeries in an ever-descending cascade of physical degeneration.
- Significantly poorer health over a great span of their latter years, while simultaneously consuming a significantly greater volume of medications.

In the chronically well group, I would expect to see the reverse set of patterns:

- Their behaviors in general demonstrate fewer unhealthy habits than in the chronically diseased group, and (more importantly) the active presence of consistent health-promoting, life-giving activities.

- Their health histories show more frequent mobility (joint/muscle) injuries, but a notably consistent absence of deeper systemic disorders.
- Their health histories show diagnoses and treatments for minor problems that heal relatively quickly, far fewer diagnoses of deep-seeded systemic problems, and increased wellness over a greater span of their latter years, while consuming significantly fewer medications.

I would expect that the athletic seniors would not be free from aches and pains and progressive limitations, but these would be of a more external (musculo-skeletal) nature.

I would expect to see that the chronically ill suffered more from symptoms stemming from systemic declines and overall progressive de-conditioning.

I would expect that the long-term behavioral patterns of each of these two groups as a whole will reveal a gold mine of information about how to behave (and how not to behave) in such a way as to enjoy an active and competent retirement.

The law of entropy states that *things left to themselves* tend to go from a state of organization to a state of disorganization. When we apply this law to our bodies, we see that the lack of emphasis upon a healthy lifestyle removes a powerful, natural, self-protecting, resilient barrier to this propensity for things to go toward a state of disorganization. The long-term effect of applying little to no effort toward healthy living has, as its natural consequence, the physiological degeneration of our own body.

The athletic seniors will possess comparatively empty medical files, only an occasional flu, sprain, strain, or other joint disorder. Their personal histories are marked by clean, healthy, active living—travels, rides, races, climbs, adventures on land, sea, and river, as well as community volunteering and other social activities. Though their bodies slow and weaken with the years, they nonetheless remain highly functional adults with an intact capacity to enjoy life's richer pleasures. *They decided to "use it" and have slowed the rate at which they lose it.*

The ever-ill, on the other hand, can recite long litanies of their ever-growing portfolio of medical diagnoses. They can tell you when they received their first regimen of powdered marvels. Later, of course, came more symptoms and with that a greater variety of panacea in pill or bottled form. Later came second, third, and fourth diagnoses and/or complications from previous medications or procedures. Now these people don't have time to exercise with all the pills they have to swallow and doctor's appointments they have to keep. *They have decided to "swallow it" and have increased the rate in which they wallow in it.*

In the two groups' profiles, I see consistency of behaviors and physical outcomes.

Seniors of consistent wellness exhibit:

1] A high volume of healthy behavior and a high volume of healthy consequences.

2] A low volume of unhealthy behaviors and a low volume of unhealthy consequences.

3] Consistently responsible self-care.

4] Determined and intelligent self-maintenance.

5] Aversion to relinquishing self-control.

6] Aversion to becoming dependent upon drugs for symptom control.

Seniors of consistent illness exhibit:

1] A low volume of healthy behaviors and a low volume of healthy consequences.

2] A high volume of unhealthy behaviors and a high volume of unhealthy consequences.

3] Considerable apathy toward self-maintenance and preservation of their health.

4] Aversion to self-discovery and healthy adaptation to negative environmental feedback (symptoms).

5] Aversion to bearing personal responsibility for wellness.

6] Reliance upon chemicals rather than commitment to more responsible living.

The chronically ill choose short-term personal ease over the long-term priority of the health of their body and spirit. Over time, I witness such a disconnection from themselves and their ability to positively influence their own health that they begin to feel helpless. They become passive and dependent upon others to control their own bodies. They become victims and begin depending upon modern medicine to solve the problems that have resulted from their own behaviors. I see a consistent unwillingness to accept responsibility for the condition their body is currently in, or responsibility for resolving their illness through healthier living. They constantly look for some new external solution or some new pill to replace their personal responsibility for behaving in ways that promote wellness.

The chronically well, on the other hand, refuse to relinquish control of their body's health to another, except when truly necessary. They instead pursue an honest and responsible examination and elimination of causes of physical degeneration. They trust that they have within themselves the power to reverse consequences of unhealthy behavior by implementing healthier behavior. They do not believe that the corporations responsible for promoting drug consumption love them as much as they love themselves. They aim to rectify their health problems from the roots upward and not from the symptoms downward. They reason that whatever behavior or lack of behavior has led to their health problem can be unwound, and they can return to health.

2-11. WE ARE WHAT WE DID, AND WE BECOME WHAT WE DO—CORE PRINCIPLES FOR MAKING A LIFESTYLE TRANSITION TO WELLNESS AND PREVENTION.

That's a lot of details and patterns and principles. So how did each group get the way they did? As Forrest Gump's mother said to Forrest in the movie by his name, "Stupid is as stupid does."

I'm not trying to ascribe blame, but to promote breakthrough.

Please hear me: "Stupid *is* as stupid *does*." "Athlete *is* as athlete *does*." "Alcoholic *is* as alcoholic *does*." Alcoholism is the result of the commission of an unhealthy behavior habitually. Chronic disease is the result of the omission of healthy behaviors *omitted habitually*. "Chronically ill *is* as chronically ill *does*."

No pill is going to get you out of this. I'm sorry, but you've been fed one long line of ad copy. Did you stop to read the fine print? You know, the part they read through at a million miles an hour under their breath? Entropy is a universal law; things fall apart naturally unless you make considerable effort to maintain them. A rolling stone gathers no moss, but a stationary stone in moist environments will get green and slick. Flowing water remains fresh, but water blocked up becomes stagnant. Chronic disease will enter into anyone who slows down enough, that is, abstains from health-promoting behavior enough to let it in.

The activities that healthy seniors engage in result in the bodies that healthy seniors enjoy. The activities that the chronically ill engage in result in the bodies they are burdened by. Look at the senior athletes in our group. What have they been doing all these years to end up with slim and powerful bodies in their 50s through 70s (and beyond)? Swimming, hiking, cycling, dancing, running, skiing, climbing, lifting weights, hoisting packs, and clambering up mountains. You don't get these kinds of bodies—or this kind of health—by sitting still and vegetating.

Look at the ugly side now. Look at the seniors of chronic illness in our group. What have they been doing all these years to end up in such a dilapidated, weakened, and pathetic condition in their 50s through 70s? They have prioritized many different things, but as a group, they consistently de-prioritized responsibility for their own fitness. All along, entropy is actively disorganizing every cell of every organism that is not actively exerting effort to stay strong, fit, orderly, and organized. So, *neglecting to actively promote your health is to actively pursue your own disintegration.*

Chronic disease does not "steal from us."
It settles into the sedentary places.
We surrender to it.

The "Habits of Health" were presented earlier in the book but bear repetition here:

The chronically healthy embrace and thus *proactively promote* the daily regeneration of their health through the following activities. The chronically unhealthy neglect and thus *proactively promote* the daily degeneration of their health by avoiding the following activities.

WATERS OF LIFE: BEHAVIORS THAT PROMOTE HEALTH OF BODY, MIND, AND SPIRIT

Entering into: Embracing	Avoiding: Neglecting
Proactively Promotes the *Regeneration* of Health	Proactively Promotes the *Degeneration* of Health

LIFESTYLE HABITS OF THE CHRONICALLY WELL

(As outlined in the previous section, titled "How Does Our 'Healthcare' System Really Work?")

1] Drinking freshly juiced/blended vegetable and fruit juices and smoothies.

2] Engaging in aerobic activity.

3] Engaging in resistance exercise and strength training.

4] Consuming a predominantly alkaline diet with large amounts of fruits, salads, and lightly cooked vegetables.

5] Consuming almost entirely whole foods, i.e. whole grains, nuts, seeds, legumes, vegetables, lean meats, and fish.

6] Supplementing an optimal diet with nutrient-dense (whole food) supplements rich in vitamins/minerals, trace elements, and phytonutrients (i.e., plant-derived compounds with healthful benefits).

7] Practicing yoga, tai chi, dancing/rhythm, Zumba, combination cardio/resistance, stretching and other activities that improve flexibility, coordination, and muscle strength.

8] Practicing periodic fasting and use of heat therapies (Jacuzzi, steam & dry sauna) for detoxification through sweating.

9] Taking extended walks in nature to get lots of fresh air and sunshine.

10] Meditating, journaling, prayer, Sabbath rest, and spiritual discipline.

11] Engaging in outdoor recreation amidst the wind, surf, sun, sea, mountain air, crystal clear pools, trickling brooks, and powerful waves.

12] Engaging in self expression through music and the arts.

13] Remaining socially engaged in the community.

These are the things that the chronically ill *first* give up, then, in that retreat, they are gradually and insidiously overtaken by stagnancy and chronic disease. Just as fresh running water is healthy and useful, but when blocked off, disconnected and isolated, still water over time becomes stagnant; so also as we retreat from and cease to engage in healthy behaviors do we give disease a favorable environment, well suited to taking up residence.

"For my people have committed two evils: they have forsaken me, the fountain of living waters, and hewed them out cisterns, broken cisterns, that can hold no water."

- Jeremiah 2:13, American Standard Version

It's so easy for the chronically ill to say, "I don't walk because I'm exceedingly obese," but I contend that if they take a good hard look at their past they will see that they *first* ceased to live a healthy life, and *then* were overtaken by obesity and chronic disease. It was when they chose to retreat from engaging in healthy activities like low-impact aerobics, swimming, sauna, lifting weights, fasting, heat therapy, hiking in the woods and other forms of outdoor activities that they were then overcome with crippling obesity, and *now* they are caught in a vicious "catch-22."

Way back when, when chronic disease was an option instead of a sentence, they withdrew from the battle. And *then* stagnation settled in, and chronic disease followed.

So they find solace in the TV and recliner. As a rule they find observing life less demanding than fighting for it, so they just float along with the currents. They're awake, or at least their eyes are open, but their life priorities don't include a real effort to regain control of their downwardly spiraling health. I sincerely believe many of them trust and comply with the advice of their medical practitioners. They are never told the dire truth about the consistently poor outcomes of those who comply with modern medical direction. They follow the instructions as to what and when to swallow, but that's where the personal responsibility ends. They swallow what the good doctor tells them to swallow, but beyond that they don't engage in the battle for their own salvation. They may work hard to follow the medical orders that they are being given, but they fail to consider that they are being led along a path of progressive chemical dependency from which *their release is of little concern* to those placing them on the path.

It may appear from the foregoing dialogue that I am jeering at the chronically ill, or that I do not respect them, or that I am angry with them and contending that they are simply getting what they deserve. It is not animosity or disrespect for them but *a compassionate frustration that is driving me.* This book is a pleading ache resulting from a clear apprehension of the complex and difficult challenge before us. Not only do we have the parasitic pharmaceutical and medical corporations to contend with, but we also have the chronically ill who have established a lifetime of familiar habits that oppose their own health. I stand at the crossroads and beckon to the chronically ill, saying "Our health is largely up to us, and we have tremendous power to improve our health if we will simply improve our course."

In the case of chronic disease, with its huge behavioral component, the person's unhealthy behaviors plus lack of healthy behaviors condemn the body to a self-imposed early demise. As previously discussed, I want to reiterate: "Be not deceived; God is not mocked: for whatsoever a man soweth, that shall he also reap" (Galatians 6:7, King James Version). Granted, behavior doesn't explain all medical phenomenon. Chance and genetics are also at play, but behaviorally produced conditions require changing the behavior, not simply adding toxic drugs.

People need to realize (and medical science needs to admit) that our bodies operate much like an exquisitely wise and complex biological computer. A computer cannot override the data fed into it. Remember the law of cause and effect. GIGO: Garbage In, Garbage Out. If you have disease-attracting behavior going in, you will have disease-congruent results coming out. Our extremely wise biological computer manifests all the data inputs we feed it. When you *feed in unhealthy* foods, environments, behaviors, thoughts, emotions, information, stress, relationships, entertainments—and *avoid feeding in healthy* foods, environments, behaviors, thoughts, emotions, information, stress, relationships, and entertainments—you cannot expect to achieve anything but unhealthy results.

So to paraphrase Galatians 6:7-8: "For he who sows to his own flesh (lower nature, sensuality) will from the flesh reap decay and ruin and destruction, but he who sows to the Spirit will from the Spirit reap eternal life (freshness, youth, inner strength and ongoing vitality)."

I believe when we behave in ways that promote our greatest wellbeing, we are behaving as we were designed to behave. I believe health and wellness is a physiological incentive, speaking to us from the cognitive level all the way down to the cellular level, to live the way we were ideally designed to live. And this health and wellness is most effectively achieved through properly ordered, properly guided, and properly prioritized self-interest. Nature rewards behavior that strengthens the species with health and wellness, and discourages behavior that weakens the species with decreasing health and wellness. HIHO: Healthy In, Healthy Out.

At the core of chronic disease is lifestyle compromise, which leads to compromises in cardiovascular and metabolic health and function. As these core systems suffer compromise, they lead to compromise of the body's structural integrity (bones and joints), and/or "building material" (skin, organs, and tissue), depending upon genetically inherited lines of physiological weakness. The entire breakdown process is especially aggravated by unresolved stress.

2-12. IT'S A NATURAL THING THAT ONLY BEHAVIOR MODIFICATION WILL RESTORE HEALTH.

I am more deeply aware and convicted of humans' likeness to plants in their physiological responses to stimuli. A plant will naturally thrive with the ideal balance of soil conditions and mineral balance, nutrition, light, warmth, and moisture. Given a sick plant, a horticulturist will spend most of his or her energy attempting to identify and eliminate environmental imbalances and thus restore the plant to an ideal growing environment, believing that as this happens, the plant's sickly condition will very likely resolve itself. And it works, because contained within the plant's own organic design are self-healing systems that quickly restore the plant if the offending environmental imbalances are removed.

The message of nature is to behave in ways that promote your health and vitality. The message of nature is to listen to what works for you. If whatever you're doing decreases your power to adapt, overcome, and survive, then *revise those behaviors*. Pain and decreasing function become wise guides directing you away from what weakens the system. Health and wellness become wise guides directing you to continue whatever it is that's making you more healthy and well.

Return to what inspires.
Drink in nature's good tidings.

Chronic (slow-developing) problems do not require expensive technology and powerful drugs; they require a healthy diet, healthy exercise, healthy recreations, healthy walks, fresh air, healthy interests, mental and spiritual enrichment, music and the arts, and, last but not least, connection and engagement with others in likeminded healthy pursuits. Health inspires health in upward spiraling circles.

We are not patients suffering personal misfortune; we are students within our bodies, suffering the consequences of noncompliance with the natural laws of vibrant health. Robust health will result from a robust, healthy lifestyle. There is no other way!

2-13. HEALTHY IS AS HEALTHY DOES: LIFESTYLE MANAGEMENT THAT BRINGS ABOUT TRANSFORMATIONAL CHANGE.

Reversal of chronic disease is yielded by absolutely impeccable lifestyle management. By this I do not mean a life upon which many restrictions and limitations are being placed, but a life into which many life-giving activities are being flooded. A large and growing body of scientific evidence demonstrates that participation in healthy behavioral approaches to medicine (lifestyle modifications, exercise and other natural therapies, improvements in diet, and consumption of specific nutritional products) are far superior and much more economical in restoring health and maintaining resilience to disease than modern medicine's method of chemically saturating symptoms.[26]

The *only thing* that can beat the effects of a lower degree of health, i.e. a chronic disease, is a health-restoring lifestyle. *Period*! The only thing to amend a bad effect is the introduction of a better cause. Get on the right track or forever lack. Nature has provided no other way. Chronic disease in particular is highly amenable to modifiable factors over which we possess a considerable degree of control.

Healthy is as healthy does. This is good news because if poor health and chronic disease are self-induced, then they can also be self-erased! In most cases of chronic disease, genetics is a "weak link" in the individual's chain, but it is *unhealthy behavioral choices* that snap the link. Even if you are genetically predisposed to any chronic condition, behavior modification will be your most powerful tool and greatest ally in remaining healthy.

The only solution for a breakdown in health (revealed by a symptom) is rebuilding the health that you have destroyed. We have been mistakenly taught (or intentionally deceived) to view health and disease as different entities that require entirely different fields of investigative study and research. Instead, I suggest we consider viewing them as one continuum of health, ranging from least to most healthy. Utilizing this view simplifies the physiological puzzle. Chronic disease is not a *different* condition from health, but simply a *lower degree* of health. The lower degree of health—chronic disease—is the result of a weaker discipline of healthy living. The only solution to suffering a lower degree of health (a chronic state of disease) is to rebuild the health you have destroyed or allowed to decay.

It then reasonably and sequentially follows that to reverse a lower degree of health, we need to add *improving habits of healthier living*.

Keep reminding yourself: "This is your life, buddy. Don't let it slip away." Stay healthy for the grandkids. Live your later years with dignity and pride. Stay young, fight hard at living healthily, and don't believe the hype that drugs will meet your needs. Healthy living is the ONLY thing that will yield health of mind and body.

Treat your body with respect, give it the optimal nutrition and exercise it needs, and it will serve you well for many years. Abuse it or neglect its needs for long enough, and its inevitable self-imposed degeneration will come back to haunt you tenfold. Modern medicine does little to promote personal responsibility in remaining healthy. You must put responsible effort in, that is, suffer being responsible on the front end so as to avoid suffering debilitating losses on the back end.

A healthy lifestyle that results in disease avoidance can be taught. But it requires a significant investment from both health facilitators and the chronically ill in order to work. Reading a book about healthy principles will not change anything for patients who are deeply entrenched in self-destructive habits. However, consistent participation in a safe, positive, supportive program that is run by gentle, patient, supportive staff—and the support of fellow patients on the same journey—has profound transformative power.

2-14. PEOPLE LOOK FOR ANSWERS IN EXTERNAL SOURCES—PILLS, PRODUCTS, PROCEDURES, ETC.—TO BRING THEM COMFORT IN THEIR SUFFERING. BUT REAL RESTORATION OF HEALTH STARTS FROM INTERNAL SOURCES—MOTIVATION, COMMITMENT, HEALTHIER HABITS AND CONSISTENT FOLLOWING-THROUGH.

You see, the truth is, self-preservation is a personal responsibility. Yes, you can beat or at least greatly minimize a myriad of chronic diseases, even if your family has a genetic propensity for one. But self-preservation requires discipline; it requires pluck and stamina and sincerity. Even though degenerating health is highly preventable, people are prone to take the low road—self-emolliating dependence upon the purveyors of patented powders. It's just human indifference to our own well-being.

So, what is the answer to the question? How could the country be so easily lulled into dependence upon a medical system that cultivates their own defeat? The answer is that people seem to feel self control is apparently far more costly than the consequences of self neglect, as long as they can continually medicate their chosen path instead of working to remain strong, healthy, and complete.

It has been my observation that those who take the least responsibility for their health are the least healthy and also suffer the most ailments. They continuously seek a panacea outside of themselves. They go to doctors the most frequently and return home again and again with an undying hope set yet again upon others for their suggestions, prescriptions, or further testing. And they obediently consume their recommended drugs, the assortment of which grows as new, more complex diagnoses replace older, simpler diagnoses. They appear ever hopeful, thoroughly mesmerized and progressively dependent upon external remedies to their nagging, frustrating, discouraging, ever-present chains of illness that weigh them down. Ever they look externally for relief and ever externally they catch glimmers of hope in new prescriptions (in all the pretty colors they are offered), but never in any of this growing emporium of external treatments is there evidence of a genuine reversal of a downward trend in health.

My heart goes out to the millions of people who have unconsciously heard and unwittingly succumbed to the calculating persuasion of the pharmaceutical corporations and their control over the product lines that medical doctors are allowed to prescribe, endorse or recommend.

The swallowing of toxic drugs is producing a poly-pharmaceutical epidemic in America. In many, many cases it can be well defended that one of the side effects of the medications you are taking is the worsening of the condition for which you are taking it.[27] On a larger scale, we see that the drugs being prescribed for entire patient populations, along with the American medical system's narrow emphasis upon chemical compliance, is effectively grooming and indoctrinating those patient populations into lifestyle and drug-consuming patterns that produce progressive degeneration, disability, and dependency.[28]

I work with people who are chronically ill; I am surrounded by their dilemma. I see their mass exodus out of the comfort of a healthy existence into self-imposed misery—not out of willful rebellion, but out of weakness, apathy, and ignorance. They are spinning their limited "life straw" into pharmaceutical gold, while they themselves are locked up in a castle tower made by their own behavior. You see, the vast majority of medical consumers do not have the motivation to embark upon a journey of health recovery. It is so much easier to "do as told" and leave personal responsibility out of the equation.

2-15. THE PHARMACEUTICAL AND MEDICAL INDUSTRIES PROMOTE UNHEALTHY BEHAVIOR AND DISCOURAGE HEALTHY BEHAVIOR. IN OTHER WORDS, CORPORATE MEDICINE DOESN'T HELP, SO DON'T EXPECT IT TO.

To be sure, pharmaceutical and medical science will continue to find ways to profit off of people's *reluctance* to live healthfully and responsibly. Actually, given the nightmarish consequences of chronic disease, *reluctance* to live healthfully is not a strong enough word. These corporations will continue to profit off of people's *repulsion* to healthy, responsible, self-controlled, self-empowering behavior.

Pharmaceutical corporations have done their best to fund the vast majority of medical research and thus guide its direction, focus, and outcomes. But unfortunately, self-enabling, self-preserving healthy lifestyles (while profitable to the individual in profound ways) do not support the pursuit of profit. Profit requires consumer dependency.

Healthy people (or those returning to healthy lifestyles) tend to avoid the use of drugs as much as possible. The relative lack of medical research being conducted into the effects of health promotion upon chronic disease prevention is simply a matter of economics. The big money is in the formulation of pill solutions rather than the discovery of real solutions.

The medical model system knows its drugs almost always target the symptom and not the originating cause. The chemist may claim the drugs will target the receptors or processes that have been compromised, but if you look deeper, they do not really target the originating causes of physiological compromise. And that is because *the systemic footings of chronic disease are almost always the absence of healthy diet and lifestyle*—and these cannot be formulated and sold in a pill or liquid form.

Do blood pressure pills lower blood pressure? Yes they do. Is high blood pressure bad for your health? Yes it is. Well, there you have it; people with high blood pressure should take blood pressure medicine.

Do insulin injections lower blood sugar? Yes they do. Is a high blood sugar level bad for your health? Yes it is. Well, there you have it; people with high blood sugar levels should take insulin.

Sounds like a slam dunk right? But not so fast! There are other questions *not* being asked because the answers are not so sales worthy.

1] What are the negative side effects of these medicines?

2] Do these chemicals actually improve the health of the physiological systems they affect?

3] What is their long-term effect on my liver and kidney health and function?

4] Can these medications damage my heart and general physical health?

5] What will happen if I take my medications as prescribed but do not exercise and watch my diet closely over time?

6] What will happen if I don't take my medications, but watch my diet very closely, exercise consistently under the close direction and guidance of a health-and-wellness instructor, and consistently immerse myself in evidence-based health rejuvenating recommendations from around the world?

The spin on drugs is they help the patient get well. The reality is that they merely modify the symptoms of the problem(s).

Almost all information patients receive about a medication is designed to sell the patient on its worthiness and thereby promote its consumption. It's all about increasing corporate profits, and not about patient welfare. The medical information being "sold" to the public is not deceptive because it contains outright lies, but because it tells only partial truth.

And we don't even realize we are being *sold* anything. We assume we are entering the halls of scientific medical care and that all therein is objective. We assume we are being objectively assessed, diagnosed, and informed of all of our medical options. We assume we are being instructed in a course of most effective care based upon the best resources and most up to date information. But the system has been infiltrated by financial interests that have strongly influenced the entire modern medical delivery system, from the types of approved medical research and education, to the design of the hospitals, medical clinics, and pharmacies and the choice of products and services which these facilities provide.

In his excellent book, "Overdosed America—The Broken Promise of American Medicine: How The Pharmaceutical Companies Are Corrupting Science, Misleading Doctors, And Threatening Your Health" Dr. John Abramson exposes the commercial takeover of medical knowledge. The drug merchants have one agenda: Profit through the expansion of chemical dependency as far and as wide a possible. The corporate drug merchants who are in charge of the marketing of modern medicine have kept out of the limelight the body's incredible ability to recover from illness, injury and chronic disease when the constant assault of unhealthy thoughts, diet and behaviors are replaced with healthy thoughts, diet and behavior. Remember what's at stake! The average cost of hospitalization in the United States amount to $15,734.00. The profits derived from those who are chronically ill and not getting better are significant.

The 2011 Comparative Price Report found the average cost per hospital stay in the United States was $15,734 followed by $5,004 in Germany and $4,948 in Chile. Total hospital and physician costs for coronary artery bypass averaged $67,583 in the United States compared with $40,954 in Canada — the next highest cost.[29]

Learn about the average cost per stay for the 20 conditions with the highest total inpatient costs in 2009. These include a newborn baby ($2800), septicemia ($18,500), osteoarthritis ($14,800), coronary atherosclerosis ($16,100), acute myocardial infarction (heart attack, $18,200), congestive heart failure ($10,400), pneumonia ($9000), stroke ($13,400), COPD ($7400, physical rehab ($11,800), diabetes with complications ($8700), hip fracture ($14,300), heart valve disorders ($36,700) and more. Average for all diagnoses was $9200. These numbers are estimated costs, NOT prices.[30]

Whether Americans like it or not, their doctors, nurses and therapists are paid by "the system", that has also been referred to as the machine, the corporation, the beast. They simply do not have the right to fully represent the patient; they have an approved line of products, care plans and instructions to impart that have been deemed appropriate by their employer. These and only these are what you will receive from them.

We are led to believe that doctors, nurses, and therapists represent us when we confide to them our physical ailments, pains, symptoms and health concerns. For the most part these professional healthcare providers are well-educated, genuine, caring and qualified; however, what they provide is simply what their employer deems appropriate and profitable to offer. They provide their patients with a plan of care and line of products that is appropriate for the treatment of the complaints, i.e. the symptoms, but they are not paid to offer holistic, comprehensive care. They are largely offering symptom management for conditions whose causes they rarely explore in adequate depth. Hence they are not representing *our interests* in genuine recovery, but the *industry's interests* in sales. Doctors, nurses and therapists are not employed by patients—they treat patients; but they are employed by the industry and they recommend (prescribe) the products that the industry sells. He/She who is paid to pipe, must play the company tune.

When we have an ailment or symptom that is bothering us either intensely enough or long enough, we go to a doctor. The doctor leans upon his/her body of knowledge to give us a definitive diagnosis. We go home with a word or phrase labeling our condition and a treatment plan. If the problem runs deeper we may go home, having been told we have a disease.

They are called diseases, but I propose that it would be more correct to call them "disease indicators." These indicators are signals, symptoms, outward manifestations of more serious problems within the body.

These indicators are the body's effort to get our attention, telling us that it needs supportive help to correct underlying conditions of imbalance which, if left unchecked, will develop into more serious conditions.

When we take medication to make a discomfort go away, we may be trading short-term gain for longer term pain, lower levels of energy, and ill health in the future. Shouldn't we be focusing our attention, not on the *annoyance* of the symptom, but on what the symptom or indicator is trying to tell us.

What have we been doing wrong that is causing the body to complain? The symptom is not the problem; it is our friend.[31]

The medical model can still be effective, but that hinges upon whether it is actually correcting a cause or merely treating an effect. To cut a weed yields a different result than pulling it out by the roots. When medicine pulls at the roots of systemic problems, it acts with integrity and ethical concern for patient welfare. When medicine merely "trims back" at the symptoms of inadequately addressed and removable causes, its motives are suspect. Unfortunately, much of modern medicine falls into this latter category—and it acts as if its "weed management" is really "crop development." This is fundamentally a deception perpetrated upon the naïve for the profit of the cunning. This deception is most polished and insidious in regard to the treatment of chronic conditions, because lifestyle modification is so essential, and the omission of it is both so devastating to the patient and so lucrative to the industry.

When degeneration of a physiological system of the body is defined honestly and forthrightly as a degeneration of a physiological system of the body, then it becomes clear rather than a mystery. The obvious and appropriate course of action is to restore, strengthen, and rectify the system. It makes sense, right—even to the uneducated? But if you redefine degeneration of a physiological system of the body as a *disease,* then the issue becomes a mystery, and its solution cloudy, distant, and difficult to unravel. When you define the *consequences* of degeneration of physiological systems of the body as *consequences* of unhealthy behavior, then the importance of restoring *healthy* behaviors becomes obvious, even to simple minds. But when you define those same consequences as the *symptoms* of *disease,* then it becomes a mystifying quandary, and who can we turn to except the medical experts to resolve this mysterious curve ball that life has thrown at us? Such terms as "disease" and "symptoms" carry a vague and ominous mystique about them, which gives modern medicine the ropes to lasso the public into a chokehold of dependence upon chemical corporations for their physical salvation. It is my intent to bring sight to the blind and to set the captives free.

Modern medicine emphasizes (prescribes) what it sells for profit—not what advances, blesses, benefits, and prospers its patients' medical welfare. Patient compliance with pharmaceutical mandates yields extremely little hope of recovery. Elimination or reversal of chronic disease requires profound lifestyle reformation, and modern medicine offers virtually no effective support. They may offer health education courses at excessive fees, but nothing close to an effective support system for personal health transformation.

2-16. OUR PHYSICAL RECOVERY AND WELLNESS IS INCONSISTENT WITH THE MEDICAL-PHARMACEUTICAL INDUSTRY'S FINANCIAL OBJECTIVES. SO, THE CHRONICALLY ILL MUST LOOK WELL OUTSIDE OF MODERN MEDICINE FOR THE RESOURCES, SUPPORT, GUIDANCE, AND TOOLS THEY NEED TO RECOVER. THE CURRENT MEDICAL MODEL SIMPLY DOES NOT PRODUCE HEALTH.

What's the big deal? The chronically ill will continue to suffer progressive deterioration, and eventually collapse under the weight of their own chronic disease, never again feeling physical freedom or vitality, only progressive decay, disability, and misery. This is all quite lucrative to the pharmaceutical and medical industries, but a horrific loss of joy, pleasure, and independence for the victims.

We—medical capitalists that we are—have placed corporate financial gain above recovery from self-appointed pits. Yes, it is personal behaviors that bring the unenlightened and undisciplined down into pits of chronic disease, but for us medical capitalists to warm ourselves around the fires of their decay is a most hideous legacy that we will someday have to explain. Take obesity as an example. Obesity continues to grow in America today at epidemic proportions not because solutions do not exist or are not known, or even are too costly, but because of the financial interests of the food, drug, and medical industries in harvesting the profit generated by rising rates of obesity. Some of the financial rewards are:

- Obese people eat much more food than thin people, which obviously increases profits to the food industry.
- Obese people suffer far more health problems than thin people—problems which deteriorate into chronically diseased conditions that profit the drug and medical industries.

Conventional Treatment

Let's examine a conventional scenario.

Noncompliance with a health-attracting lifestyle does not happen in a void. It happens within a dynamic environment of active forces. If you are not complying with health-*generating* behavior then you are, because of our dynamic environment, complying with health-*degenerating* behavior. Into this phenomenon, conventional medicine offers chemicals to treat your symptoms of degenerating health. The chemicals themselves are a toxin and, as such, further degenerate your health. So, conventional medicine steps in to provide another health-degenerating substance to treat symptoms resulting from a health-degenerating lifestyle.

If you don't modify the behaviors that produce the symptoms, your health continues to degenerate until another/different symptom manifests. Again, conventional medicine provides another health-degenerating substance to alter this new symptom resulting from your health-degenerating lifestyle. This pattern continues over months and years, except that over time the symptoms become more serious, and the chemical toxins used to modify the symptoms also become stronger, more toxic, and more damaging.

Statistically, patients on this path never step out of the declining health trajectory; they simply survive declining levels of health as their symptoms are treated with a progressively wider assortment of chemical toxins that further damage the patient's health. Eventually the symptoms of the uninterrupted physical degeneration erupt into full-blown chronic disease and require hospitalization, diagnostic testing, surgery, and/

or more drug treatments. Eventually the human immune system and the human physiology are so overwhelmed with the unrelenting health-degenerating habits and the unrelenting toxicity of the chemicals that this process then escalates into critical physiological collapse of entire physical systems, such as the circulatory, respiratory, or digestive system. When such physiological systems are deeply compromised, the cumulative strain of habitually unhealthy behavior, increasing drug toxicities, and overwhelmed bodily systems combine to culminate in multi-system failure and, finally, death.

Old Model:

1] Noncompliance with health-promoting lifestyle = Compliance with health-degenerating lifestyle.

2] Compliance with health-degenerating lifestyle = Degenerating health.

3] Degenerating health = Symptom manifestation of poor health.

4] Symptom manifestation = Trip to doctor and prescription of a symptom modifier.

5] Consumption of symptom modifier = Symptoms modified but degenerating health unmodified .

Repeat steps 3-5 each time with more deeply troubling symptoms and additional toxic drugs, for a final, fatal result.

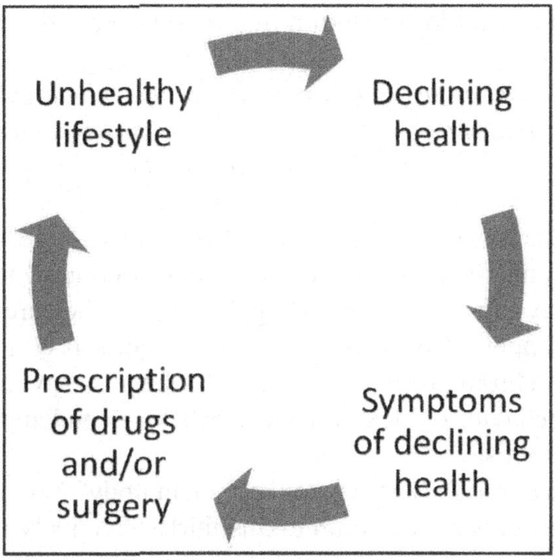

2-17. IN THIS GROWING EMPORIUM OF EXTERNAL TREATMENTS, HAVE YOU EVER SEEN ANY EVIDENCE FOR A GENUINE REVERSAL OF THE DOWNWARD TREND IN A CHRONICALLY ILL PERSON'S HEALTH APART FROM BEHAVIORAL REFORM?

I have seen good results from many types of surgery … but I have also witnessed ongoing drug and surgical treatments that treat the symptoms of decline while leaving patients in the behaviors responsible for their downward spiral of debilitation.

Seldom have I seen a patients' renewing sense of inner strength and physical regeneration. Never have I seen in these patients' lives a real personal transformation and genuine recovery. The personal health history, taking the form of a slow, drawn-out tragedy, continues. Delayed? Maybe. But a genuine improvement in health and reversal of physical decline rarely materializes.

Let's look at the results. Who do you know who has ever gotten better over the long haul, simply by adding drugs to an unhealthy lifestyle? Sure, in the short term the blood pressure goes down, the cholesterol goes down, the blood sugars are closer to normal ranges, or the pains are temporarily decreased—because they start taking one pill for this symptom and one pill for that symptom. Sure enough, individual symptoms change, but … do these patients get better? Do the diseases disappear? Or do they simply continue downhill, like a water course which, when one waterway is blocked, simply builds up until it finds another way downhill?

"Medications largely alter symptoms of a downhill journey of degenerating health, like rearranging the deck chairs on the Titanic."

After patients swallow their next 1,000 pills (largely because they have been adamantly directed to do so), while continuing to behave in the same unhealthy lifestyle patterns (largely because they are *not* adamantly directed and supported to do otherwise), the outcome is virtually inevitable. In the case of chronic disease, which has a huge behavioral component, the person's behavior or lack of healthy behavior condemns the body to a self-directed demise.

Are all medicines *very* toxic to the human body? No, our body's liver and kidneys process a lot of mild toxins fairly effectively for a long time. (However, many, many, many patients suffer kidney damage secondary to years of swallowing the powdered marvels.) These chemicals don't kill you quickly because they are consumed in such minute quantities. However, they do place a stress on the body and, over time, these take a toll on your health. You cannot consume a mild poison in minute doses without being mildly poisoned. The body does its best to eliminate those toxins and mitigate those damages—but the process fatigues the body and depletes the immune system. The damage from one medication is minimal, but this is doubled with two medications, and so on.[32 33]

The question is not whether medication should or should not be taken. But rather, is it treating an initial cause or is it merely treating a symptom of a cause? Medications—such as antibiotics—directly addressing underlying causes are necessary evils. Are antibiotics mildly toxic to the body and do they inflict mild damage to the healthy system? Yes. And antibiotics are also a stressor to the eliminative organs and digestive tract. But what are they treating? They are treating invading bacterial organisms, which are far more damaging to the body than the antibiotics.

Conventional medicine has a forte, and that is, "Fourth down, goal to go!" The system seizes upon patients in acute scenarios, and it assails their problem with aggressive solutions. This is what it does best. Most medications merely treat symptoms and not underlying causes, and that works well for emergent conditions. However, for chronic conditions, that is, long term, slowly developing conditions, it is highly questionable whether the effect of temporary symptom suppression is worth the physiological damage and toxin accumulation that lifelong treatment imposes. Plus, the medication rarely eliminates the real causative agents, which are behavioral in nature and can only be effectively addressed with behavioral modification.

The general information disseminated about chronic disease is usually reliable but entirely inadequate. The full information needs to be openly disclosed. The untold reality is that modern medicine's dependence upon technology and chemicals to treat chronic disease has been a dismal failure. The only thing they seem to have succeeded at is an astronomically profitable increase in the sales and distribution of pharmaceuticals.

2-18. ONLY FULL DISCLOSURE ABOUT CHRONIC DISEASES AND THE PATHETICALLY INEFFECTIVE TRACK RECORD OF CHEMICAL MEDICINE WILL DISPEL THE LIMITED MEDICAL INFORMATION (PROPAGANDA, REALLY) THE PUBLIC HAS BEEN SOLD FOR THE LAST 80 YEARS.

Both telling *and showing* us how utterly inept chemical medicine is at successfully controlling chronic disease would give a clear picture of what devastations await those who simply swallow the little pretties and await their redemption. We, the consuming public, deserve full disclosure not only of specific harmful side effects of these chemicals but of the chemical model's failure in general to generate successful outcomes. The chemical system's failure must be exposed if we are to grasp the gravity of the situation and begin placing our faith and investments into systems that do work—and have consistently demonstrated transformative results.

The full disclosure about chronic disease is that compliance with pharmaceutical protocols result in progressive physical degeneration of the cardiovascular, digestive, eliminative, immune, metabolic, musculoskeletal, neurological, and respiratory systems of the body, and, over time, progressively deeper states of chronic disease. The harsh reality is that the medications you are taking for your chronic disease will not stop that disease; they will barely even slow down its progression. Allopathic medicine is based on a twisted logic by the ingeniously self-serving. A medical system designed to treat the ongoing progressive symptoms of unaddressed underlying causes is truly an abomination. And oh, what a cunning and slippery weasel this system is to get a hold of.

Patients: Deepening Drug Dependency Model
Stagnate → Decondition (repeat)

STAIRWAY TO DISINTEGRATION

Patients approach medical system with symptoms:

Protocol:

Patients arrive with symptoms and are given a diagnosis of a "Disease" (any chronic disease) related to those *Symptoms* → Symptoms are treated (drugs prescribed)

Pattern of Stairway to Disintegration:

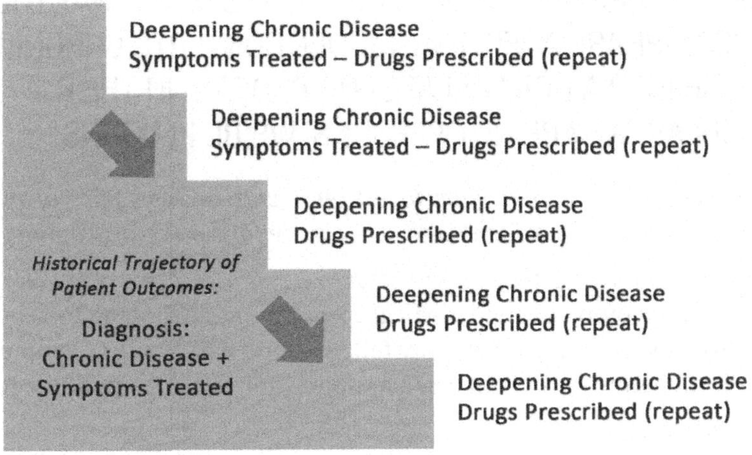

Symptoms are treated, but the underlying cause of disease is not addressed. More symptoms develop due to a negative reaction to prescribed pharmaceuticals, as well as increased problems with underlying cause.

Here's the full disclosure about *high blood pressure/cardiovascular disease*: taking blood pressure medications without engaging in a healthy diet, a customized exercise/recreational program, and stress reduction practices may lower the blood pressure (through chemical means), but it will manifest again later at a more serious level of cardiovascular compromise. The short and skinny is that compliance with high blood pressure management by pharmaceuticals will result in further cardiovascular compromise—for which additional pharmaceutical chemicals and/or other treatments will be prescribed.

Here's the full disclosure about *diabetes*: compliance with blood sugar management by pharmaceuticals, without engaging in a healthy diet, a customized exercise/recreational program, and stress reduction practices may manage the blood sugar levels (through chemical means), but the issue will manifest again later at a more serious level of metabolic compromise. The short and skinny is that compliance with high blood sugar management by pharmaceuticals will result in further metabolic compromise—for which additional pharmaceutical chemicals and/or treatments will be prescribed.

2-19. DID YOU NOTICE, THE LAST PARAGRAPH IS THE SAME AS THE ONE JUST BEFORE IT—EXCEPT THAT THE DISEASE BEING "PLUGGED IN" IS DIFFERENT? THIS IS THE WAY THE MEDICAL-PHARMACEUTICAL MODEL CONVERTS CHRONIC DISEASE INTO A BOILERPLATE FOR PROFITS. IN THEIR FORMULAS, WE ARE NOT PERSONS, WE'RE PLUG-INS.

To see how you and your loved ones can become part of modern medicine's "great American harvest," simply follow the instructions:

Harvest plans for the coming year:

The drug companies and medical corporations are hoping for a bumper crop! Sounds exciting. What, pray tell, are they harvesting? Complete the claim form below to find out. (See footnotes for explanation of the terms.)

Instructions:

Fill in the statement below for each of the medications that you are taking, where the medication *is not directly addressing an underlying cause* of physical decline. Fill in the class, symptom, and system for that medication. Repeat for each medication.

> The * _____ medication that I am taking will temporarily modify my ** ______ but will not support the recovery of my *** _____; it will in fact impose additional stresses upon my already compromised health.
>
> So please fill in your blanks:
>
> 1] _________ Drug class (purpose)*
>
> 2] _________ Symptom class (type of symptom)**
>
> 3] _________ System of the body affected***
>
> EXAMPLE #1
>
> 1] Hypertensive medication (purpose)*
>
> 2] High blood pressure (symptom class)**
>
> 3] Cardiovascular system (bodily system compromised)***
>
> EXAMPLE #2
>
> 1] Blood sugar controlling medication (purpose)*
>
> 2] High blood sugars (symptom class)**
>
> 3] Metabolic system (bodily system being effected)***
>
> * *Drug Class (Purpose): Medications are classified*

by their action, that is, the type of effect they produce in the body. Fill in the main classification of the medicines you are being given.

*** Symptom Class: Modern medicine places great emphasis not upon underlying causes, but upon symptoms, i.e. high blood sugar, high blood pressure, instead of emphasizing health problems at their point of systemic dysfunction, maladaptation, weakness, or toxicity. Enter the primary symptom(s) you are being treated for.*

****System of the Body: Enter the system of the body whose symptoms are being treated: i.e., cardiovascular, digestive, eliminative, immune, metabolic, musculoskeletal, neurological, reproductive, respiratory, etc.*

And that is how you or your loved ones fit in to modern medicine's template for turning chronic disease into a cash cow.

There are a small number of drugs that are very effective at treating physical ailments and disease. For these the benefits outweigh the risks. When evaluating any drug you are considering taking, these are important things to ask:

1] Does this drug/treatment address the underlying cause of my symptoms?

2] Does this drug cater to and thus *enable* an unhealthy lifestyle by simply *diffusing the consequences* (symptoms) of poor lifestyle choices?

I cannot recommend any medications as genuinely safe or effective because every body is different and what is safe and beneficial for one person may produce a life threatening Adverse Drug Reaction (ADR) in another.

> **I am not advocating the use of any drugs—just making the point that there are valid reasons to take *some* medications *sometimes* because they address causes of problems, not just symptoms, and may contribute to the restoration of health and well-being.**

Many more chemicals do very little that is truly helpful to the consumer, and over time, compound health problems rather than resolve them. Use of these chemicals is like placing towels around the base of an overflowing toilet: yes, they soak up the overflowing sewage but they neither address the cause of toilet overflow nor change the downward trajectory of progressive floor damage. That is, they treat the symptoms of decline but do not address its causes or change its trajectory of degeneration.

When people do not live a healthy and balanced life, they become unhealthy and imbalanced. Just one example would be a person who fails to exercise and eat properly who then becomes overweight, and then tires even more easily and then exercises even less, whose muscles become weaker as they bear heavier body weight. All body systems are taxed. The body's metabolic system cannot keep up with a level of food intake that exceeds bodily requirements. The cardiopulmonary system cannot cope with the unnatural demands of obesity. The heart cannot keep up with the task of circulating blood through excessive adipose (fat) tissue. Lungs are overtaxed in attempting to meet excessive oxygen demands and oxygenate excessive adipose tissue; joints are over burdened and bones are overstrained and become inflamed.

This individual will be prescribed bronchodilators for shortness of breath. Insulin for excessive blood sugar levels. Pain killers and anti-inflammatory medication for joint pain and inflammation. As the cardiopulmonary system fails under excessive loads and unnatural demands, the patient's blood pressure will rise, cholesterol will collect, and their heart rhythm will be altered, and blood pressure, cholesterol, and heart rhythm medications will be added to the regimen. The toxic burden of taking many medications puts additional strain upon the kidney and liver, which over time will impair kidney and liver function, for which additional symptoms will be treated with additional medications, creating additional chemical burden upon the body.

All these medications are being taken to address symptoms of an unhealthy lifestyle, and not only will those drugs *not treat* an underlying problem—they will actually create *additional underlying problems* for the body to cope with.

THE GOOD, THE BAD, AND THE UGLY

The purpose and function for which a drug is taken must be weighed in the balance closely if medicines are to serve our purposes as humans rather than for us as humans to be reduced to serving "medicine's" purposes.

- If taking a medicine (a chemical) strengthens, empowers and enables growth and a deeper participation in a full life for the consumer, *then* it is good.
- If taking a medicine (a chemical) does not strengthen, empower and enable growth and a deeper participation in a full life for the consumer, *then* it is bad.
- If taking a medicine (a chemical) caters to and ameliorates

symptoms of an unhealthy lifestyle, thus encouraging that unhealthy lifestyle—promoting complacency and discouraging corrective action, *then* it is ugly.

Ask yourself: Could a significant change in lifestyle eliminate the problem for which I am considering taking this drug? If the answer to that question is "yes," then think twice, no, three times, *very hard,* before taking a medication to do *your work* for you. Many diabetics take insulin simply because they fail to control their weight. Many people take blood pressure and cardiovascular drugs simply because they don't get adequate exercise or eat a lean healthy diet. Many people take many drugs to treat the effects, symptoms, and consequences of a lack of self discipline! The problem is that this approach doesn't work in the long run—it simply masks those symptoms while the underlying problems gain muster, like the build-up of dark angry clouds on the horizon which eventually rain down upon the person in a cloudburst and flash flood of critically poor health.

During my analysis of large numbers of medical case histories over the last 9 years, I have often seen what has become a statistically significant, highly predictable pattern in patient outcome. Patients approach the medical system with a complaint of some symptom that is bothering them. That symptom, however, is merely an indicator of a more fundamental imbalance and compromise of the health of a physiological "system" of the body. Underlying the external manifestation (symptom) lies a more fundamental compromise of the person's cardiovascular, digestive, eliminative, immune, metabolic, musculoskeletal, neurological, reproductive and/or respiratory system(s) within the body.

The symptom simply indicates the underlying more fundamental compromise of the integrity and physiological health of the patient. Within the American Medical Approach, the symptoms of the problem are evaluated, further tests and examinations are performed, and the symptoms are then classified and a diagnosis is given. This is followed by drugs, which treat those symptoms. Lifestyle recommendations *might* be lightly glossed over, but *drugs* are ordered with authority. In reviewing case history after case history over the last many years, I have observed the following pattern so frequently that it is highly predictable:

> **Chemically treated systemic problems that are not met with lifestyle modifications continue in a pattern of unrelenting physiological descent, leading to ever more drug-dependent living.**

Here are four models of medical intervention that patients are currently offered within the American Medical Approach. None are successful at preventing or reversing chronic disease.

Designed To Fail Treatment Model # 1

Health Care Systems manage chronic disease with a drug regimen to be consumed by patients—that is, between predictable hospitalizations for ongoing progressive physiological compromise. This model of treatment would not be acceptable to patients if they were asked—but their input is never sought. This model of treatment is, however, highly profitable to the parasitic medical and pharmaceutical corporations, which make a great profit off the slow and insidious demise of their patients.

Designed To Fail Treatment Model #2

Health Care Systems promote "health education classes" which attract those who are motivated and ready to change their own behavior—at least investigate making a change in their behavior. This "health education" tactic simply retains the health-motivated health care consumer and costs the health care system virtually nothing; but does virtually nothing to reach, "grab hold of" and evoke personal transformation in those caught in a deeply entrenched lifestyle-induced vortex of progressive physical decline, especially in the 1%-5% costing the most money.

Designed To Fail Treatment Model #3

Health Care Systems discharge patients from the hospital with a short list of medical instructions to return to the lifestyle that brought them to the hospital in the first place. "Discharge Orders" in effect informing the chronically ill (who have thus far demonstrated a consistent and predictable pattern of indolence and incompetence in maintaining a healthy state of existence) to "Go home and be better!" "Try harder!" "Pull yourselves up by your bootstraps!" "Be all that you can be!" All these counsels are little more than stinking gas in a cramped elevator to those who have been trapped for years in various "habits of decline."

Designed To Fail Treatment Model #4

Health Care Systems hand out "disease management" information to patients and their families for various chronic diseases: Congestive Heart Failure, Diabetes, Chronic Obstructive Pulmonary Disease, etc. Again, these pamphlets cost the health care system very little to produce and are only the very first step in promoting effective recovery. Patients and their families do not care how much you know until they know how much you care.

UNDER THE CURRENT HEALTH CARE SYSTEM:

The entire focus of reimbursement is around payment for "the treatment of decline" and none of it is aimed at payment for "the prevention of decline."

Until the economic basis for medical reimbursement changes from one of payment for "treating crisis" to one of payment for "preventing crisis," health care systems will not develop successful methods to "prevent the hand that feeds them." To do so would be economic suicide.

Economic incentives aside (and I promise we will return to them), patients deserve to get what they are paying for and what they genuinely need: a fully supported program of disease reversal and health recovery.

2-20. THOSE WHO ARE CHRONICALLY ILL SIMPLY CANNOT PICK THEMSELVES UP BY THE BOOT STRAPS, MAKE THEMSELVES BE GOOD AND EAT RIGHT, AND GET BACK ON TOP OF ALL THE HABITS THAT WOULD RESTORE THEIR HEALTH. IT IS SIMPLY BEYOND THE SCOPE OF THEIR STRENGTH AND VISION.

Chronically ill patients by definition are stuck! They *cannot* lift themselves out of the grip of self-entrenched physical decline. I contend that it is a moral, ethical and financial obligation of the medical system to use clients' dollars in ways that best serve clients' needs. Ask the client, "Do you need to be given the resources, guidance, and support you need to prevent your present condition from worsening? Or do you need a greater selection of pills, products, and medical services to treat the symptoms associated with your continuing decline?"

I propose that if patients were given a choice, the majority would choose first to have the modifiable causes of their declines squarely identified, and then to actively accept considerable 12-step support to make the changes needed to stop their chronic disease in its tracks.

If you were to have patients complete the following survey, what do you think they would select?

1] Do you want to get well, or

2] Do you want to be treated for the progressive symptoms of your ongoing physical decay?

I contend that it is the patient's right to receive the care they deem effective and supportive for lifting them out of the descending spiral of chronic disease in which they are trapped. Again, I contend that patients have invested considerable amounts of their income into their health care, and therefore have a right to have their best interests and preferences considered. They have a right to the forms of medical care scientifically demonstrated to offer the most effective healing and recovery. They deserve access to the forms of treatment that science has confirmed to be the least harmful, least invasive, least expensive, and most effective.

It's time consumers begin demanding what will yield rapid achievement of their objectives. And we need to demand that the large premiums we pay for insurance reflect our needs for health recovery and maintenance, not the profit needs of maintaining the medical-pharmaceutical machine.

Effective methods of chronic disease prevention have been clearly understood for many years. *The medical community can no longer ethically deny these methods, and so the overt omission of them in treatment is equivalent to chronic disease promotion.* But instead, the medical establishment protects, incubates, cultivates, and harvests chronic diseases for their profit-making symptoms by withholding the well-known, scientifically verified methods of their prevention.

> ***So much is already known about what gets people well.[34] We the consumers are paying the medical insurance premiums and federal medical taxes, and we the consumers should be offered medical care that reflects the growing and irrefutable body of evidence that proper nutrition and healthy lifestyles are superior to chemical saturation.***

What incentives do pharmaceutical companies have to stop promoting drugs? What incentives do medical supply companies have to not grow rich profiting off advancing disease and disability? What incentive do medical students have to pursue lower paying primary care positions over higher paying specialties that depend upon advancing states of disease to be treated? What incentive is there for researchers to specialize in the arena of health promotion for which there is little funding?

What incentive is there for the exceedingly wealthy ruling medical paradigm to make changes that will diminish their wealth and decrease their power? Shall they surrender higher profits out of respect for higher principles? They say, "An ounce of true preventive gold is *far less profitable* than a pound of pyrite cure."

"The problems that exist in the world today cannot be solved by the level of thinking that created them."
- Attributed to Albert Einstein

The treatment of the malady rather than the introduction of the cure lies at the heart of the commercialization and corruption of modern medicine.

On the other hand, how about the creation of an entirely new branch of medicine dedicated to optimizing the health of the chronically ill, borderline chronically ill, morbidly obese, and other "at risk" populations? How about the government stimulating this health-promoting economy by subsidizing medical reimbursement and providing a whole host of economic incentives to both healthcare providers and healthcare consumers and especially those most in need of its services?

The government pays hundreds of billions into the treatment of decline—why not have the government pay hundreds of millions into YMCAs and Silver Sneakers and newly budding lifestyle transformation programs dedicated to encouraging and supporting every phase of transition into healthier lifestyles?

What if we invest millions into lifestyle transformation centers such as supercharged YMCAs that offer a multitude of the best evidence-based health-restoring exercises, classes & programs under one roof. What if we create lifestyle transformation centers that implement all the best evidence-based revitalizing lifestyle modifications under one roof, proving to be one mega health-fortifying, self-empowering, self-restoring circuit of health-attracting behavior modalities.

Rationale: If you can't join 'em, beat 'em!

Why fight for change of a system that has no reason to stop committing treason? "Wealth through medical deceit—forever treating *preventable* decline" has worked quite well—so leave it well enough alone. Why should the one taking our country's wealth through the forsaking of her health have any more to say? Shall they give up ill-gotten gain and forsake their present reign? For what? Principles? Because it's the right thing to do? Hell will freeze over before pharmaceuticals and every other form of medical corruption gives it all up for "God and Country."

Why not form a new industry? A new capitalistic endeavor for the aggressive competitive nature of capitalism "to sink its teeth into." A new means of corporate wealth—only this one *with positive outcomes* for society.

> **Instead of government stimulus of Corporate wealth for the progressive chemical treatment of preventable declines in health, we stimulate Corporate wealth for the progressive restoration of the chronically ill's achievable health.**

"Currently, modern chronic diseases, including cardiovascular diseases, Type 2 diabetes, metabolic syndrome, and cancer, are the leading killers in the Westernized society and are increasing rampantly in developing nations. In fact, obesity, diabetes, and hypertension are now even commonplace in children. Clearly, however, there is a solution to this epidemic of metabolic disease that is inundating today's societies worldwide: exercise and diet. Overwhelming evidence from a variety of sources, including epidemiological, prospective cohort, and intervention studies, links most chronic diseases seen in the world today to physical inactivity and inappropriate diet consumption."
- (Christian K. Roberts and R. James Barnard, Effects of exercise and diet on chronic disease.)[35]

For a concise review of the study cited above please refer to the appendices at the back of this book. I would also encourage readers to go online to see the study in its entirety at the websites provided. The study provides extensive research and overwhelming evidence which 1) substantiates claims about the superior effectiveness of exercise and diet in the treatment and prevention of chronic disease, 2) highlights the effects of lifestyle modification for both mitigating disease progression and reversing existing disease, and 3) suggests potential mechanisms for beneficial effects.

Chapter 4.
Solution One—Health is the New Wealth

LET'S REVIEW THE LAST SECTION

Problem One addresses medical system issues in contemporary America: people, processes, products, and politics. This includes a look at such groups and organizations as chronically ill patients, hospitals, treatments, research, political entities, and the current "medical-pharmaceutical machine" in America. It also explores what kinds of key interconnections exist among these players in the processes of illness and wellness, who benefits (or doesn't) and why from the current paradigm/model, and offers some core recommendations for spurring the system to be more ethical and economical. This leads to political and economic proposals for constructive system change, which are detailed in this section, titled *Solution One—Health is the New Wealth.*

I have heard that in ancient China doctors were paid *more money* when the people of their district were well. What could happen in our country if institutions with a "contract with health" were paid more when the people under their charge *stayed well* rather than when they stayed ill?

The only hope I see for our society—apart from individuals rising to the personal responsibility and challenge of lifestyle self-management—is for healthcare reform led by corporate or government entities with a direct *financial* incentive to maintain the well-being of their customers. Such entities—which would make up a new medical system—would exert preventive and wellness influences upon their customers, and especially upon the most chronically ill. That new system would prescribe, convince, and require its patients to co-actively take responsibility for their health. It would provide the facilities and guidance to ease the very difficult transition from unhealthy lifestyle habits into healthy ones until the healthy ones become ingrained. Lastly, it would reward healthcare providers for promoting such compliance.

The federal government needs to stimulate and catalyze the development of a *whole new industry* of disease prevention. I am not talking about promoting yearly pap smears for women and other tests for earlier detection of opportunities to begin profitable drug treatments, but *a new wellness industry committed exclusively to the reduction and even outright elimination of patients' chronic illness.* I'm talking about effectively saving millions, billions, even trillions of dollars through intelligent investment of limited financial resources. We simply don't have the liberty to waste financial resources any longer. The escalating rate of medical claims demands that our resources be employed as strategically as possible.

Ethically, one could argue that improved patient outcomes should be the sole determinant for the course of all medical research and treatment simply because it is the right, noble, correct, and only compassionate course of intention. However, saving government and insurance companies money will prove a far more effective argument. The question ultimately boils down to, "Who is the biggest gun in the West?" Who will have the last word in this drama? Will it be the arm of the medical industry that profits handsomely from heavily-treated-yet-never-resolved illness and disease? Or will it be the arm responsible for paying for every ongoing sickness?

Please note what I am calling for here is not another institution dedicated to "fighting disease," but the creation of an institution or industry that will actually *profit* from restoring health to the chronically ill. This is a *new* medical ideology—an Effective Medical Approach—that honors health acquisition.

MY PROPOSAL WILL ONLY BE PICKED UP BY AN INDUSTRY WHICH PROFITS FROM A *DECREASE* IN CHRONIC DISEASE, NOT AN INCREASE.

Of course, patients have personal and social reasons to adopt this model, (that is, adopt an Effective Medical Approach) because getting and staying healthy is about quality of life. Good health is true wealth. Here is a partial list of organizations with a strong *financial* incentive to see preventive behavioral medicine flourish:

- Large health insurers
- Federal health insurance programs

- Small and large employers
- Health and fitness centers
- Nutritional supplement producers
- Organic food producers and distributors
- Athletic clothing manufacturers and distributors
- Recreational equipment manufacturers and distributors
- Adventure, travel and outdoor sports industries

All of these institutions and industries have a vested interest in promoting the health and wellness of all people. It would be profitable beyond comprehension for Medicare, Medicaid, private insurance organizations, large and small employers, and fitness organizations like the YMCA to band together in discovering paths to wellness for their clients, consumers and patients—especially their most costly, ill, and frequently re-hospitalized patients. Let's break this down a bit and look at some different angles on the impact of this proposal for promoting wellness as the better profit base for the business of healthcare.

It behooves all employers and medical insurers:

- To consult with experts in the *cultivation and management of health and wellness,* which is a totally different industry than that of the *cultivation and management of disease.*
- To pay special attention to supporting the *prevention of chronic diseases,* because those are the financial drains that keep on draining.
- To promote the health of individuals, groups, and eventually entire societies, and to develop a plan that discourages obesity, diabetes, heart disease, cancer, respiratory disease, and degenerative joint conditions.
- To discard the myth of big medicine, which is that the solution to chronic disease challenges lies in diagnostic wizardry and pharmaceutical wonders. The reality is that chronic diseases are lifestyle-induced and lifestyle-reversed.
- To cover costs for the fitness promotion of the "normal" (i.e., healthy) clients and employees.
- To pay special attention to restoring the health of clients/employees/patients who are at risk for a slow but increased rate of progressive degeneration. We must see precisely the prescribed, mandated, facilitated lifestyle transition and health and wellness promotion of this particular group. They are the medical population at the highest risk, and the most costly. So, we must focus on their

restoration to health if we are to enjoy the huge financial dividends of declines in chronic disease, frequent re-hospitalizations, and staggering number of lost work hours each year.

For the sake of our patients and our healthcare system, we need to encourage the development of synergistic relationships among corporations, organizations, agencies, and individuals whose chief profit comes from health and wellness. I hope to see organizations with a vested interest in a new healthcare paradigm band together, develop their own authority and power, and strongly influence medical care in America for an effective wellness approach.

Huge employer groups, large health insurers, large philanthropic foundations, as well as federal, state, and local governments—they all have a vested interest in seeing health and wellness flourish among their employees, patrons, and citizens. These industries must *form powerful consortiums of influence* to demand that:

1] opportunities for fitness, lifestyle modification, and recreation abound.

2] concepts and skills for a wellness lifestyle are taught, trained, and ingrained, specifically for the most at-risk populations - to restore the possibility of health. And among the young to rpomote a healthy lifestyle - steering them in a healthy direction during the formative years.

This is a win-win-win system situation. For instance, the *health product vendor* profits through an expanding business with happier and healthier clients. The *health insurer* profits by spending a little on the front end for prevention, and saving a lot on the back end through averted hospitalizations and health crises. The *patient* profits by having the support, tools, and guidance needed to form new health-restoring habits, thus reaping many more years of empowered and independent living.

Now, it is true that capitalism is the foundation of business in America. It is as central to American business as spinal cords are to the nervous system. What needs to change is the corporate control of medicine. It must be shifted from a sector which profits from disease to one which profits when people are healthy, drug free, and medically independent. Until then, we will continue to see chronic disease rates increase because there will never be an incentive for them to decrease. The crucial question is: Where will the locus of power in medicine be positioned?

When we place a corporate power with a vested financial interest in the successful healthy outcome of the patient in the patient's corner, we preserve the rights, dignity, and choice of the individual against the appetite of the medical-pharmaceutical corporate beast. Ultimately, the only way the consumer's interests can be effectively represented will be when the powers and authorities in control of the medical sector see profit as patients get healthier and suffer loss as patients fare poorly. Only then will there be a truly patient-centered system of intelligent and cost-effective medical care.

Unfortunately, the disease mongers are in charge and have set up the rules of engorgement upon their prey. However, an appeal for ethical and financial integrity in medicine is being raised by patient advocates everywhere.

WHO DECIDED THAT THOSE WHO PROFIT OFF DISEASE SHOULD BE IN CHARGE OF HEALTHCARE ANYWAY? UNTIL THIS INHERENT CONFLICT OF INTEREST IS ELIMINATED AT THE HIGHEST LEVELS OF MEDICAL ADMINISTRATION, PATIENTS WILL CONTINUE TO GET THE SHAFT.

Economically speaking, and for a large portion of the medical industry, the poorest patient outcomes provide the greatest profits at the highest levels. Until the controlling agency of medicine makes its profit from patients becoming well and staying well, patients will continue to suffer as collateral damage in the medical system's pursuit of medical profits.

Now, why should I want to restore health to those who have lost the path? Because I believe it is more blessed to give than to receive. This proposal is, I believe, inherently more ethical but also intentionally more economical. If any industry is to profit, it should be one that imparts health *renewal*, not manages health *declines* for profit. The key to change is uniting industries with a genuine financial interest in seeing the chronically ill actually get well, then empowering them to sustain their healthy status. It will require the consolidated efforts of patient advocacy groups, private and federal insurers, and all other parties interested in seeing the establishment of an ethical and economical medical delivery system.

It is time to place the welfare of the chronically ill, and ultimately everyone, into the hands of corporations who have significant financial incentive to see them get progressively healthier. Only then will we see effective care emerge. Any medical direction not founded on this principle is a shameful, unethical, parasitic conflict of medical interest. In this way, tax- and premium-paying patients become the prey of the current medical-pharmaceutical system, which has become a grim but very wealthy reaper of the proceeds of disease.

Let us remember that the great majority of these patients are (or have been) hardworking American citizens; they have paid their income, social security, and medical care taxes. They have paid their medical insurance premiums faithfully every year. They have upheld their end of this financially binding contract, and they have a legal and moral right to have their medical intentions, focus, and goals addressed directly and effectively.

For their sake, we need to launch an ethical and just medical system. This paradigm shift is desperately needed to replace the ruling authority of parasitic medical pirates whose business depends upon progressive illness. I encourage government and medical insurance leaders to brace up for a war with the pharmaceutical corporations. The outcome of this conflict will define the future of American medicine as either continuing to follow a trend toward parasitic medicine that feeds upon the decay of its host, or toward the genuine prevention and reversal of disease through the promotion of health.

But a radical paradigm shift is rarely accomplished solely by "insiders." It's even more unlikely when the "insiders" have financial incentives to "go with the flow" and few incentives to advocate for reform. So, it is my deepening conviction that the recovery of healthcare systems will only be realized by institutions outside of the conventional medical establishment. In other words, it must be instigated by industries and entities outside of corporately-funded disease-for-profit medical approaches. This includes pharmaceutically-funded medical research, medical schools, medical clinics, and conventional hospitals. These institutions and the corporations which fund them simply have too much revenue to lose if effective and economical medical solutions become commonplace.

> **Only institutions and groups with something to lose from the presence of ongoing and increasing chronic disease will possess the fortitude and presence of mind to push for effective and economical medical treatments.**

We have to believe change is possible, not just necessary. Corporate greed and political lethargy may be as unavoidable as the pull of gravity, but the good news is that many industries and entities profit from the presence of healthy individuals.

Who will stand with me in putting corporations who profit from health and wellness in charge of medicine? Who will help me promote wealth for those industries that promote health for their clients as they support those clients in adopting the healthy lifestyles that produce healthy outcomes?

Let's look closer at what kinds of groups have incentives to see healthcare paradigm change take place, why, and how they could make a difference. I'll focus on what I see as five key clusters of change agents who have clear incentive to see people get healthy and stay well, and some of the dynamics they face:

1] Government agencies.
2] Health/wellness-related industries.
3] Employers.
4] Health insurance organizations.
5] Individuals and families.

1. GOVERNMENT HAS FINANCIAL AND ETHICAL INCENTIVES TO SEE PEOPLE HEALTHY AND WELL.

Surely we the American people want our government to acknowledge the superiority of disease *prevention* over disease *crisis management.* Surely we want our government to enforce ethical medical care, which requires a primary emphasis upon disease prevention. Surely we wish to be *well,* not merely *well-medicated in our decline.* Surely we want our medical systems to meet our acute care needs—but not to secretly groom us toward increasing needs from and dependence upon that system. For all this to happen, we need our government to do certain things that no individuals can enact or enforce. In this section, I will explore points and proposals dealing with our government and:

- The look of an ethical system of medicine.
- Protection for food consumers from the damages of fast food
- The government's purpose in protecting its citizens; the importance of a social conscience, and the refusal to let medical-pharmaceutical machine lobbying control national purposes or policies.
- Universal healthcare and related health/medical policies.
- The pragmatic financial issues of a healthy economy.

AN ETHICAL SYSTEM OF MEDICINE

I recommend the federal and state governments encourage this medical paradigm shift by demanding that *restoring fitness be the primary tool for chronic disease prevention.* They have the authority to create an agency or institution with the power, strength, and mandate to demand that our medical system emphasize two key concerns:

- Early detection of health risk factors.

- Stalwart *prevention* of chronic disease.

The federal government should demand that our medical care providers place a strong emphasis upon health restoration as the first, strongest, and most effective defense against disease progression, and to not merely talk about healthy lifestyle. The federal government should demand that medical care providers *require (prescribe)* health-restoring behavior the same way they *require (prescribe)* drug consumption; that they not only *prescribe* health-restoring behavior, but actually *provide* high-quality, comprehensive, health-restoring programs, and the facilities to carry them out.

This is the only logical, just, and compassionate stance for a government purporting to support its people's physical health. Any government institution or position that keeps medical power in the hands of corporations that profit from growing rates of disease is the enemy of its own people. Diseases will advance un-resisted until a new, powerful player operating out of compassion governs the course of medicine. Until that day, Americans will continue to be harvested for the veins of gold their sickness yields.

Ethical governance of medicine will:

- Enforce medical protocols that reward disease prevention above all else.
- Demand that medical care systems *provide* (not just suggest) a complete array of health-restoring activities for all patients, especially for patients who are high-risk or already chronically ill.
- Condemn the construction of huge hospital complexes that cash in on the diseasing of America.
- Demand that for every billion dollars spent on hospitals, these corporate disease mongers spend $200 million on five-star fitness centers dedicated to promoting health.

Ethical medicine begins with a combination of research, awareness, and action:

1] Compile health/medical research evidence that demonstrates healthy people cost less to insure than chronically ill ones.

2] Research how it benefits society financially to manifest due diligence in bringing people to a healthier state of responsible living.

3] Create a centralized controlling agency that receives medical insurance premiums from patients.

4] Authorize this agency with the autonomy to both designate preventive medical care as a means of capital preservation, and to disburse current funds effectively while also reducing long-term costs through disease reduction.

5] Invest money into the front end of an evolving paradigm of disease prevention in order to save big money on the back end through lowered pharmaceutical and hospitalization costs.

Pharmaceutical and medical lobbyists have gotten in the deep pockets of the federal government to discourage measures for a healthier America for their profit. I propose there is an even bigger profit to be had for the government and large health insurers by making its people healthy and glad. The federal medical insurance programs and large health insurers, to really "make a killin'," need to clot off the flow of all the money "they be spillin'."

PROTECTION FOR FOOD CONSUMERS FROM THE DAMAGES OF FAST FOOD

As part of this paradigm shift toward wellness, we as a society need to create protections for food consumers as well as medical consumers in America, as food relates directly to health. I do not believe we demand salt and fattening agents in our foods. I do not believe we want to eat foods that are unhealthy. I do not see people in Safeway or other grocery conglomerates asking clerks to direct them to the "unhealthy" section. I don't see people at fast food establishments squinting their eyes, looking for the "especially fattening foods" section of the menu. Why? Because almost every processed item (except a very few) qualifies as "especially fattening."

Why does the Food and Drug Administration wink at conglomerate fast food chains with hordes of fattening and artery clogging recipes on the menu, while simultaneously oppressing the interests of health food stores? Why do drug ads proliferate on TV with Federal Trade Commission approval, while simultaneously the FTC actively suppresses information about the value of non-pharmaceutical and preventive forms of therapy?[36] Suffice it to say that we as a society are in a battle to protect ourselves from the very institutions that may (or may not) have been originally set up for our protection, but which now operate entirely co-opted by commercial interests—yet still under the guise of providing protection for "we the people."

Yes, Americans as a whole have been lazy, ignorant, and irresponsible with their health for a long time, but interest has gradually been picking up for diet habits that are healthier. Our society is gradually becoming more aware of the cause and effect relationship between damaging our environment and damaging ourselves. Grocery chains such as Trader Joe's and Whole Foods are becoming household words among discerning consumers.

I believe it is time for a health-promoting business model to begin to permeate mainstream conventional medicine. People are turning to healthier food retailers because they don't want to drown in the salts, refined flours, sugars, and preservatives of mainstream grocery stores. I contend that it's time to give genuine, certified, instructed, supported, supervised and accountable health promotion a chance within our "healthcare" system. And healthy food is a crucial part of health promotion. Many people are ready for the discipline and sacrifices required to lead healthier, happier lives; what they need is benevolent support to replace parasitic exploitation.

PROTECTING ITS CITIZENS, DEMONSTRATING A SOCIAL CONSCIENCE, AND REFUSING TO LET LOBBYISTS CONTROL NATIONAL PURPOSES OR POLICIES

Imagine if the federal government can be pulled away from its well-documented acceptance of payoffs from the medical and pharmaceutical lobbies, which are paid to protect these industries.[37] Imagine a government of integrity committed first and foremost to the benefit of its own people. Imagine if the federal government backed up its Healthy People 2010 and 2020 resolutions by financially rewarding medical corporations that actually decreased the medical expenditures of their patients by promoting their wellness.

But our nation lacks social conscience in government and industry. Things aren't horrible yet, but they could be much better. The government protects corporate interests while the corporations exploit people and the environment—for personal gain in both cases. Their means have gained clout in our cannibalistic—I mean capitalistic—society. Their activities are no longer called by their real name, "bribery." No, they have moved up to the penthouse suite and what they do is now called "lobbying," and "making corporate campaign contributions."

Either government will continue to be the backroom prostitute of corporations by taking greasy palm payoffs to look the other way while corporations exploit, extort, neglect, deceive, and destroy the nation's own people—or it will change drastically in order to defend the interests of the people it has sworn to protect. What would that defense look like? A truly democratic government would:

- Establish socially responsible goals to improve the welfare of all Americans.
- Enforce laws, restrictions and provisions to reform and impugn the unrelenting pathological pursuit of profit.
- Apply its power to punish and reward corporations in such a way as to socially reform corporate criminal behavior.
- Stop taking payoffs from those corporations.
- Increase the cigarette tax, call it the "Smoke and Choke Tax," and use the money to restrain the pernicious influence of the tobacco industry in their wholesale promotion of lung disease and cancer.
- Create a Fast Food Association Tax and call it the "FFAT Tax" and use the money to restrain the pernicious influence of the fast food industries in their wholesale promotion of cardiovascular and metabolic disease.
- Tax unhealthy, preserved, processed, fat-laden, salt-soaked foods (as part of the "FFAT Tax") and use the monies to lower the costs and improve accessibility to healthy foods and products.

It is time for political action and social change. I wish that our government and corporate powers (which may actually exceed governmental powers) were our allies in this battle to restore health to Americans. But such is not the case. It is time for our currently sleeping society to recognize their rights, and to realize the violations that are being perpetrated against our health and well-being for the purpose of corporate gain.

The primary role of effective government should be to protect its citizens from those who would endanger their freedom, health and safety. The application of that role to this arena would be to create an environment that economically rewards industries that promote the improving health of Americans, and to economically discourage the industries responsible for the degeneration of the health of Americans. Financial incentives are a highly effective way for the government to assure corporate compliance with the government's stated objective of decreasing chronic disease in America.

The American government needs to protect its citizens at home from corporations that feed upon their own countrymen to further their private ambitions. American medicine needs to be held responsible for its duty to effectively control, reduce, and/or eliminate their patients' chronic diseases.

Recommended National Patient Safety Goals:

1] Reduction of the incidence of patient re-hospitalization, secondary to (i.e., as a result of) chronic disease exacerbation.

2] Reduction of the incidence of patient harm resulting from poly-pharmacopeia (many medications).

Recommended Healthcare Policy Reforms:

1] Healthcare institutions shall be responsible for their duty to optimize the fitness of the chronically ill patients under their care, and to minimize the number of medications each takes. They shall demonstrate comprehensive efforts toward these outcomes, including the provision of fitness facilities, fitness programs, and 12-step support groups directed specifically at supporting the special needs of their chronically ill patients.

2] Healthcare providers shall demonstrate evidence of the enrollment and participation of their chronically ill patients in physical fitness programs and classes.

3] Healthcare providers shall make all necessary efforts to support the ongoing participation of their chronically ill populations in Lifestyle Transformation Programs and Classes.

4] Healthcare providers shall acknowledge responsibility for their patients' health outcomes and demonstrate evidence that their healthcare recommendations, prescriptions, decisions, and actions are made with the best interests of the patients in mind, and as such are balanced, unbiased, and based on the best medical evidence available and not unduly influenced by "for profit" corporate interests.

5] Healthcare providers shall demonstrate extensive efforts to support healthy lifestyle transformation before prescribing more toxic, harmful, and invasive medications and procedures for the treatment of chronic diseases and conditions. They shall demonstrate the conservative, prudent, and wise use of any toxic substances and invasive procedures, and that, only after more natural, less toxic, less harmful alternatives are fully explored and exercised.

Healthcare providers shall demonstrate that, after a patient has been hospitalized two times for the exacerbation of an underlying chronic condition, that patient will be enrolled in a total immersion lifestyle transformation program of no less than 32 weeks duration. I detail the proposal of such a program in chapter six titled, "Establishing An Effective

Medical Approach".

Measuring Healthcare Performance and Rewarding Wellness Appropriately:

"Never mistake activity for achievement."
- John Wooden

"Our major obligation is not to mistake slogans for solutions."
- Edward R. Murrow

How well are healthcare providers fulfilling their promise to help us thrive? I propose three measurements that will give us the evidence we need about the current status of our healthcare institutions and system. These give us milestones from which to calculate improvement over time in the reduction of chronic illness through active promotion of health and fitness. These three measurements are as follows, with the first two for patients/hospitals/healthcare institutions, and the last one for our national system;

- Chronic Disease Fitness Scorecard
- True Quality of Healthcare Score
- National Healthcare Quality Report Card

Healthcare systems shall be given a *Chronic Disease Fitness Scorecard* rating based on the "degree of fitness improvement" that chronically ill patients under their care demonstrate over a one year period, and that score will become part of that healthcare system's score on a *National Quality of Healthcare Report Card*. The Chronic Disease Fitness Scorecard will be a significantly weighted factor in measuring and defining a healthcare institution's *True Quality of Healthcare Score*.

The focus of these institutional ratings is the improvement of these institutions' reduction and prevention of chronic disease. Once patients are diagnosed with a chronic disease, they will be included in the scoring and evaluation of a healthcare institution's successful reduction and control of those chronic conditions. Once patients have been identified as chronically ill, they will be referred to a Lifestyle Transformation Program, and their health and wellness will continue to be monitored and given a yearly fitness evaluation to determine how well they are doing in the seven key health indictors listed below. The patients' individual scores will be tallied together and contribute significantly to that healthcare provider's True Quality of Healthcare Score. The True Quality of Healthcare Score will be a strong indicator of how well those healthcare providers control, reduce, and eliminate their patients' chronic diseases through that healthcare provider's concrete proactive support of their patients' adoption of healthier lifestyles.

Healthcare providers will not only be required to *minimize harm* in the provision of medically necessary care but to also *actively promote* and consistently monitor their chronically ill patients' health and wellness in seven key areas: Strength, Endurance, Flexibility, Health & Wellness Habits, Diet, Stress Management, Life Engagement.

We do not control chronic diseases so much by their treatment as by the proactive promotion of the lifestyle responsible for their reversal and elimination.

Healthcare providers shall be required by law to submit information annually about each of their chronically ill patients, indicating his/her:

1] Age.

2] BMI (body fat measurement).

3] Number of chronic illness diagnoses.

4] Level of participation in health and fitness activities or exercise programs.

5] Level of sedentary and/or unhealthy activities.

6] Patients' fitness evaluation score.

This information can be utilized to measure three areas: 1] a patient's health trend toward healthier or unhealthier, 2] a healthcare provider's success at promoting healthier lifestyles among its chronically ill patients, and 3] used as a patient's Health Prediction Tool.

This data can be used to generate a *Health Prediction Tool* for each patient. This is based on the patient's *Indicators of Disease* (age, level of obesity, and number of chronic diseases, unhealthy habits, sedentary lifestyle), divided by his/her *Indicators of Healthy Lifestyle* (level of participation in a health club or fitness program, fitness score, diet, associated health behaviors). Or, shown as a formula:

Indicators of Healthy Lifestyle → Indicators of Disease
= Future Health Prediction

This formula measures a healthcare provider's success at supporting, motivating and facilitating a healthy lifestyle for their chronically ill population.

- The formula defines factors (indicators) of health, and factors (indicators) of disease.

- The formula assigns values to the indicators of health and the indicators of disease, which I define as HIP (Health Indicator Points) and DIP (Disease Indicator Points).
- The formula totals the values of the indicators of health (HIP) and the indicators of disease (DIP).
- The formula then takes the total value of health, and divides it by the total value of disease.
- The formula also adds an additional (0.5) point value for every health indicator point earned. (HIP multiplied by 1.5.)

Example: If a patient received 4 points for health indicators and 2 points for disease indicators, then the patient would receive an additional (0.5) point value for each health indicator point earned, but no additional point value would be added to the disease indicator total.

Health Indicator Points = 4 (HIP) x 1.5 = 6 (Health Indicator Points).

6 Health Indicator Points (HIP)
(divided by 2 Disease Indicator Points (DIP)
equals 3

This becomes patient's Health Acquisition Value Estimate (HAVE)

The more the chronically ill are HIP even though they DIP, the higher their score will be and the higher their healthcare provider's score will be for assisting and garnering their patients' success.

The formula assigns greater value (additional points) to a patient's Indicators of Health, and assigns no extra value (points) to a patient's Indicators of Disease, because a healthy lifestyle has the power to overcome disease. Indicators of Health are stronger than Indicators of Disease, so they are positively weighted at HIPx1.5.

It is also true that an unhealthy lifestyle has the ability to overcome health, but even the healthy are eventually overcome by age. For example, a patient may have a fairly serious chronic condition and also be obese—but if they are actively participating in a healthy lifestyle and thus attain fairly strong fitness scores, then their Future Health Prediction Value (score) will reflect positively because their healthy lifestyle will go a long way to negate the effect of other indicators of disease, such as a chronic condition and obesity. The positive effect of a healthy lifestyle upon the chronically ill and obese reflects admirably on the "parentage" and mentoring of their healthcare provider, and actually serves to bolster that healthcare provider's ratings.

It is not the chronically ill members under a healthcare provider's care that bring that provider's scores down; it is the healthcare provider's willful neglect of the underlying causes of their patient's decline that brings that healthcare provider's scores down.

The better the patient's individual scores are, even though they are effectively coping with a chronic disease, the higher their healthcare institution's rating will be, and the government will then provide financial incentives to those institutions whose patients' improving wellness produces (for the provider) high institutional ratings. The financial incentives will be given to those healthcare providers because they are strongly fulfilling their promise to help their chronically ill patients to thrive.

Thus the patient's health and wellness becomes the vested financial interest of the healthcare institution. This is in stark contrast to the way the financial incentives are set up now, which works in such a way that disease is actually *good* for the bottom line *because* medical fees are based on disease.

All scores will be made public and medical institutions who score more highly in their True Quality of Healthcare Score shall attract well-informed consumers (who review the public healthcare ratings) or hear of those ratings through the grapevine. Those providers will also receive government incentives (based on their high scores) which will allow them to keep their fees lower and/or further improve the quality of their care, thus attracting more consumers. Medical institutions with lower scores shall be avoided by well informed consumers (reviewing those ratings) and by those who hear of those ratings through the grapevine, and they shall also receive decreased financial incentives and revenues from the government (which will not allow them to offer lower, more competitive fees, or better services) which will further decrease their consumer appeal and ultimately diminish their market share.

In addition to that, the government will *investigate* those institutions generating lower scores and apply additional scrutiny—even *intense* scrutiny over those healthcare institutions that fail to effectively promote and support their patients' health and well being. Ongoing failure of healthcare providers to effectively support their patients' maintenance of a healthy lifestyle will result in the decrease of that healthcare provider's financial reimbursement for their treatment of the exacerbation (flare ups) of the chronic diseases (that they scored so poorly at reducing). Poorer (publicly viewable) institutional scores and rising institutional costs combined with decreasing public appeal *generated* by the institution's poor performance will result in progressive loss of market share. Thus the consequences of failure to promote the wellness of their chronically ill patients will provide them with strong institutional incentive to genuinely care not only for the lucrative treatment of their patient's decline but for the even more lucrative *preservation* of their health.

All you have to do to get healthcare institutions to start encouraging, supporting, guiding and facilitating their patients' health and wellness is to start decreasing their public "ratings and revenues" for failure to do so. Two economic principles are at work here.

- For healthcare institutions, profit is the driver of decisions. "Where is the money?" is the burning question that most medical "science" questions boil down to. Create laws that attach medical institution's financial reimbursement (Profit Incentive) to genuine and sustainable patient recovery, (that is, *improving* patient outcomes) and those institutions will change the coordinates and course of their migration as quickly as the migration across the American west took place after the profit incentive of gold was discovered at Sutter Mill in California.
- For chronically ill patients: nature repays healthy living with healthy returns! A return to the principles and practices of healthy living can be a downright pleasure once you get the hang of it. Healthy living is actually *addictive* once you get a hold of its substance.

Increasing freedom from disease and infirmity will provide the chronically ill *ongoing incentive!*

If a disease cannot be beaten, healthy living will at the *very least* provide a slowing of the process of decline and a genuine improvement in the quality of life remaining.

CHANGING THE FEE-FOR-SERVICES PAYMENT MODEL

There is an inherent conflict of interest in medicine's fee-for-service reimbursement system: It pays healthcare providers more to keep a patient's chronic illness going by treating its various and sundry symptoms than it does to address and reduce the disease's underlying causes. So, anytime a patient's "exacerbation of disease" generates a medically billable event, the fees-for-disease cash cow starts mooing again! The healthcare industry's only incentive is to provide cheap care in order to receive its agreed-upon fee for providing what? The cheapest quality of *disease* care that it can legally bill for.

If providing cheap disease care results in a patient getting sick again *soon*, the bull snorts "the sooner, the better"—because their new "problem" generates another *billable event* about which the cash cow begins 'amooing agin' and the bull just eyes her with a twinkle and a grin.

> **As long as the fee for treating disease is great and the reward for preventing disease is small there will exist for modern medicine an unspoken contract, covenant and business with disease.**

Until this cycle or paradigm is broken, medicine's incentive, choices, and direction will always be to treat progressive decline, not promote fitness and wellness.

As of 2004, there were more medical/pharmaceutical lobbyists in Washington, DC than any other form of special interest group.[38]

The economy stunk. Corporations slashed jobs. And some firms, once juggernauts of American industry, simply ceased to exist.

But for federal lobbyists, 2009 proved to be a year of riches unlike any other, a Center for Responsive Politics analysis indicates.

At nearly $266.8 million, the pharmaceutical and health products industry's federal lobbying expenditures not only outpaced all other business industries and special interest areas in 2009, but stand as the greatest amount ever spent on lobbying efforts by a single industry for one year.

The pharmaceutical and health products industry was followed last year in overall lobbying expenditures by business associations ($183 million), oil and gas ($168.4 million) and insurance ($164.2 million). In each case, the 2009 totals are greater than that of 2008. Electric utilities, at $144.4 million, placed fifth, although this industry's 2009 lobbying total is slightly off its 2008 pace.[39]

Until the federal and state governments squash the bribery and corruption of our political leaders, and the exorbitant profitability of corporations harvesting human disease, no chronically ill American will be safe from being targeted for the depredations of disease.

UNIVERSAL HEALTHCARE AND RELATED HEALTH/MEDICAL POLICIES

I believe universal health care is an important step toward medical accountability. At least then there will be an advocate in the patient's corner, attempting to implement cost-effective treatment. "The realization that our illogical, mistaken health care system can't go on forever has dawned, and so it will end. The question now is what replaces it."[40] When it comes to that replacement system, there are *at least six positive reasons I have found for establishing universal medical coverage*:

1] Oversight and incentive to administrate best medical practices and achieve most cost-effective medical outcomes.

2] Improved quality assessment and quality control.

3] Medical research and evidence objectively compared and evaluated.

4] Universal implementation of evidence-based best medical practices.

5] Improved pace of implementing advances in medicine and treatment protocols nationwide.

6] Ability to wield the leveraging power of high-volume purchasing.

Big Pharma and medical corporations are strongly against universal health care. Why? In the current system, huge health insurance providers can sidestep their losses by denying coverage to high-risk clients, but under universal coverage, the federal government gives no such option. So, universal coverage opens the possibility that our government might actually give a damn about improving these clients' health, and might actually do something about it. I contend that universal healthcare plus a health-promotion/disease-prevention paradigm provides the greatest hope for significantly reducing medical care costs in America.

This may be an overly optimistic assumption about the American government, that it might actually care, but it is at least a viable starting point. From here we can point out the government's potential to save trillions of dollars by taking control of the health insurance of all Americans. From this position of bulk purchasing power, it can demand that corporate medicine both be forced to focus its foremost attention on lifestyle modification and disease prevention, and that it also be held accountable for what appears to be the intentional grooming of patients with chronic disease for profit.

A national medical policy needs to be established "by the people, for the people" to replace the closed-door policies of corporate leaders looking only to enhance company profits. The current federal goals, guidelines (Healthy People 2010 etc.), and healthcare policies are actually designed to promote wellness and conserve medical spending by improving the efficacy of medical care and its delivery. However, while these goals and guidelines are a positive place to begin, it is a shame and a sham that *the federal government leaves it to private industry to design the means by which to reach those goals.* Disease-profiting companies are not the entities that should be in charge of implementing "health" policies. It behooves the federal government and corporations who profit from health and wellness to create their own forums and think tanks.

Promoting wellness among the most chronically unwell is the most direct path to improving their lives and dramatically reducing our medical expenditures. But for this to be realistically pursued, medicine needs to be governed by a power that would actually profit from those goals being achieved.

The Healthy People 2010 goals must be more than positive affirmations of a brighter tomorrow; they need to include and enforce severe consequences for non-delivery. It is preposterous, ludicrous, and utterly fanciful for the federal government to propose that the pharmaceutical and medical industries, which make billions of dollars off chronic disease, be proactive about decreasing it just because it is the right thing to do. I would like to believe that the American government would pursue these actions because:

1] They actually care about the American people.
2] They actually care about the American people more than their own personal gain.
3] They believe that it is their sworn duty and responsibility to protect the interests of the American people and not compromise those interests by succumbing to the lure of bribes from the medical/pharmaceutical lobbying industry.

1. THE PRAGMATIC FINANCIAL ISSUES OF A HEALTHY ECONOMY

But these ethical reasons may not resonate with our duly elected politicians, and so I turn to the pragmatic subject of money. The American government may not choose to defend the American people from the parasitic pharmaceutical and medical industries because it is the right thing to do. But it may still rise up to protest the costs it incurs as a result of those industries' whoredom.

The truth, though not admitted by industry-financed medical research, is that prevention of disease is responsible for 9/10ths of the battle's success at 1/10th of the battle's cost, while the treatment of the symptoms of chronic disease is responsible for 1/10th of the battle's success but 9/10ths of its cost. The financial treasuries of federal and private health insurers pay this price.

This is, in part, why I encourage the federal government, plus federal and private health insurers, to link together and join forces with wellness industries to sponsor memberships, health coaching, emotional support, and 12-step groups for the one to five percent most chronically ill patients. As a result, insurance funds would be diverted away from pharmaceutical and medical parasites to a new model which focuses upon recovery and elimination of chronic disease.

The American government may not care enough about the American people to defend them from exploitation. But it should look well to its own pocketbook and not allow the national budget and entire American economy to be undermined for the exclusive interests of a small number of pathologically greedy corporations.

The American government needs to recognize that demanding health-restoring protocols for the chronically ill is a wise and effective way to contain skyrocketing medical costs. It is worthy of the substantial effort required to transform the existing disease-for-profit medical paradigm. Under the current paradigm, we have experienced spiraling medical costs, increased consumption of drugs, and increasing use of medical services, and all of these factors impose a growing economic strain upon our society.

2. INDUSTRIES RELATED TO SUSTAINABLE WELLNESS HAVE AN INCENTIVE TO SEE PEOPLE HEALTHY AND WELL.

Health and fitness organizations and health coaches have a valid profit motive: charging a reasonable fee for products and services that meet a reasonable need—health acquisition. Including these organizations and instructors in our medical paradigm shift can do nothing but improve the prognosis of our chronically ill patients. Why? Because these individuals and institutions are only rewarded as their clients become healthier.

Consider with me some of the "systems synergy" to be found when health-promoting corporations contribute to each other's wealth through promoting, supporting, and safeguarding the health of their clients.

1] The first and most obvious relationship is among patients, health and fitness organizations, and the health insurance industry. *Patients* with chronic conditions win because they receive subsidized, supervised, and guided lifestyle modification into a healthier life. The *fitness industry* receives additional clients and recognition for providing a highly effective, low-cost way to prevent or dramatically reduce chronic disease. The *health insurance industry* wins by dramatically reducing the frequency of medical crises and patient hospitalizations among their highest-risk clients, who also prove the most costly and relapse the most often.

2] Another profitable alliance would be among patients, health coaches, and the health insurance industry. *Patients* benefit from the concerned advocate they find in *health coaches*, who also serve as a source of emotional support, guidance, and practical help in moving them toward wellness. And again, *health insurers* benefit from fewer claims because they have proactively prevented problems.

What we need to do is give the highest levels of medical authority and control to corporations that earn reasonable profits from keeping patients healthy, independent, drug-free, and self-empowered.

These corporations already exist, but they have been cleverly excluded from healthcare considerations regarding medical direction, medical protocols, medical research, medical education, and mainstream medical advice. These entities, coaches, and institutions have been relegated to provide "care and direction" for those who already take "good care of" themselves. It is not hard to find the advice and support of entities, coaches, and institutions that care for clients' health and wellbeing; you simply have to look where people who "take really good care of themselves" and enjoy higher levels of health spend their time, expend their energy, and invest their financial resources.

Let's be serious here. If we want to defeat chronic disease, we need to optimize personal fitness. If we want to restore health and fitness to the chronically ill, the chronically ill need to access and rely upon the same sources as the most fit among us regularly access and rely upon.

Let's put on our thinking caps here: who do Americans turn to for medical advice, and who do those people work for and what are their employers selling? I am extremely serious. Why don't we as a nation consider asking recreational equipment manufacturers (like bicycle makers) what their recommendations are for the treatment of high blood pressure, cardiovascular disease, diabetes, and chronic respiratory conditions? Why don't we ask health clubs, fitness centers, and aquatic centers for their advice on the treatment of chronic conditions such as obesity and arthritis? Why don't we ask producers and distributors of athletic shoes and organic foods for their medical prescriptions and treatment recommendations for cardiovascular disease, diabetes, and circulatory, respiratory, and cancerous conditions?

Better yet, why don't we go to the best examples of health and fitness among us and seek their advice and prescriptive recommendations for the treatment of all manner of chronic disease?

Why don't we ask seniors who compete in triathlons or swim

from Alcatraz Island to the San Francisco Aquatic Park about their recommendations for managing hypertension, blood sugar levels, and cholesterol levels? Ask them how they keep their waists trim and their vitality high.

3. EMPLOYERS HAVE AN INCENTIVE TO SEE PEOPLE HEALTHY AND WELL.

Corporations profiting from an increasing prevalence of disease are in direct contradiction to the prosperity, health, wellness and good of man. They are also in contradiction with the intent of a great many insurers and employers who want their medically insured clients and employees to excel in health and wellness.

Let us consider the business and economic implications of medicine's covenant with disease. How many employee work hours are lost and Medicare claims are paid each year because the medicine system cleverly, with premeditation and complete self-awareness, harvests the fruit instead of cutting the roots of chronic disease and developing disability?

Employers need to encourage prevention of behaviorally-caused chronic disease. *It behooves employers to keep its workers working.* Employers should think of it like this:

Happy and healthy
Cultivates for us
Workers for the wealthy.
Giving back to employees
To help them keep healthier
Means they log more hours
To help the wealthy get wealthier.

Health insurance corporations and major employers must hire their own experts who will defend *their* corporate interests—by maintaining a "healthy and well" employee population. If you rely on experts paid in any way by conventional medicine and its profit-driven research, you can expect answers that will defend the interests of modern medicine. And that is, whatever increases distribution of products and services to increasingly sicker populations. This is simply a corporate reality.

4. HEALTH INSURANCE ORGANIZATIONS HAVE AN INCENTIVE TO SEE PEOPLE HEALTHY AND WELL.

There are corporations that profit from health and wellness. Their profit incentive is no different from corporations who have a business with disease; they are not more benevolent or noble. But which corporate objective of profit do you want in charge of overseeing the medical research, course, emphasis, and practices that direct your medical care?

Medical health insurers are potentially a strong ally and advocate for the patient. We must demonstrate to these cost-conscious corporations the superior cost effectiveness of prevention over crisis management and intervention.

The health insurance industry should consider the cost-benefit analysis of proactively preserving and redirecting the wandering health of its prodigal patients.

> **I propose that if you invest in proactive health restoration of the chronically ill, you will actually spend far less in the long run than you are now spending in medical interventions for health crises that were completely avoidable.**

Conventional medicine has a business with *disease.* For advice on achieving health and wellness for customers, health insurance agencies need to go to corporations who have a business with *health.* These corporations profit from increasing rates of health and wellness in society; they have a heavily-vested, for-profit financial interest in seeing clients physically healthy, spiritually wealthy, and nutritionally wise. There can be a great profitable financial agreement between health *insurance* corporations and health *promoting* corporations.

As self-empowered living replaces cowering, confused, self-defeating resignation, people will begin to rebound to progressive recovery. Health insurance corporations will save billions of dollars in averted health care costs. So, their profit incentive to actively invest in the health of at-risk clients is huge. Health insurance corporations need to define their own "prescriptions for health" that are not the same as those prescribed by a medical system whose wealth depends upon Americans' *loss* of health. Presumably health insurance corporations would desire all of their clients to be well. We can assume that when health insurance corporations and employers say they wish us to "live well and prosper," they actually mean it. Meanwhile, the medical and pharmaceutical corporations that constantly tell us how much they wish us to "live well and prosper" would actually lose billions of dollars if that becomes a reality.

5. INDIVIDUALS AND FAMILIES HAVE AN INCENTIVE TO SEE PEOPLE HEALTHY AND WELL.

It is in the best interests of the American people to have vast amounts of money poured into research and facilities that transform the chronically ill into fit, trim, strong, well-balanced, internally cleansed, whole, happy, complete people. They have a personal vested interest in moving from a self-depleting lifestyle to one of self-promotion.

So, if you ask patients what they want from their medical care providers—what they have been paying their monthly premiums, out-of-pockets costs, and Medicare taxes for—what would they say? "I want to swallow pretty colored pills that treat the symptoms of my continuing decline!" Or would they say, "I want to be assessed and advised by wise and caring medical professionals who have access to all products and all healing traditions. I want them to advise, guide, support, and facilitate a healing contract with me in which I actively participate in a mutually agreed-upon plan of care. I want the care plan to be scientifically verified, evidence-based, and contain all of the behavioral, nutritional, and chemical components currently known to expedite as rapid and complete a physical recovery as is possible." Would this not be the stated intent of medical consumers around the world? Surely!

Imagine if every patient were asked at the beginning of every medical visit to answer the following two questions:

1] Have you come to this medical appointment to acquire drugs to treat the ongoing *symptoms* of your continuing decay? Or,

2] Have you come to this medical appointment to regain your health and wellness, and in particular to find effective methods of eliminating or resolving the underlying *causes* of your current symptoms?

You see, our current medical system ingeniously glosses right over that common assumption. It is, of course, obvious that patients go to the doctor's office seeking resolution or elimination of the problems, symptoms, and ailments at their *source* of origin, not merely the *symptoms*. Further, every patient currently *assumes* that source-removal is being provided for them. Instead, you enter the doctor's office, and he/she says, "What's the matter? What's ailing you? Where's the problem located? Where's it hurting?" The doctor then prescribes a medication that treats the specific problem, with little discussion of strengthening the physiological system whose degeneration produced the symptom(s) that brought you there.

The medical system falls far short in providing the healthcare tools for transforming the lives of patients who are deeply entrenched in the cycle of chronic disease. Transformative influence upon the chronically ill involves *more time* and *more support,* but ultimately costs a lot *less money* than is currently spent on frequent emergency care. Preventive guidance and support will save thousands, millions, or billions of dollars, depending on the size of the patient population this new medical paradigm is applied to. A membership to a senior-friendly YMCA program which offers a superior arrangement of ongoing classes in yoga, tai chi, water aerobics, and more, costs a low monthly fee of $65. The challenge lies in changing the system to encourage, promote, and support patients in reversing their condition, rather than medicating and invasively treating their continuing downward spiral.

Health education classes introduce and expose patients to healthy behavior, but they leave those who need it most—the chronically ill—with little more than their doctors' ongoing recommendations to swallow their next 1,000 pills and call back as soon as their condition worsens.

Even though many may choose pain and disabling chronic degeneration over becoming personally responsible individuals, the lifestyle transition programs within which to make that *conscious choice* should be provided, and healthy responsible living should be deeply encouraged. Facilities that bring the opportunity and extensive motivational support needed to commence upon the journey into ideal lifestyle modification should be far more abundant, and fully covered by medical insurance premiums.

People are ready for medical alternatives that will result in healthier and more positive prognoses. I believe great numbers of sufferers from chronic disease would embrace personal responsibility, step up to the plate, and make necessary lifestyle modifications if the facilities, guidance, and support needed were made available to them.

Simply put, *the pleasures of the undisciplined unhealthy lifestyle have been exceeded by the pains of its consequences*. Patients are ready to regain the control they lost when they first set aside personal responsibility and started swallowing, injecting, and absorbing chemical solutions *on command* instead of living out behavioral solutions *by choice.*

The chronically ill are sick and tired of being sick and tired, and the pharmaceutical promises have not delivered on their claims of panacea. These patients are getting progressively worse and feel overwhelmed and trapped in their dilemma, and with good reason. The vast hordes of pill-popping Americans (who do not modify their lifestyles) are going down in slow spiraling ruins. This is all quite profitable to the pharmaceutical and medical industries, but not to the people!

As evolving organisms with a strong instinct for survival, it behooves us to discover what will most rapidly convey strength and fitness to our species. It is in our best interests as individuals, families, and societies to study and comply with principles, standards, and behaviors which will make us strong, fit, resilient, vibrantly alive, and well-protected from physical defeat, disease, and premature death.

This will be a hard-won battle! Those who have a business with disease realize the extreme cost (to them) of the chronically ill being set free from the bonds of their affliction, that is, their chronic disease. I am calling upon brave, mindful activists and socially-conscious organizations to work both independently and interdependently to reach toward the goal of protecting our people, our parents, and our children from being exploited by amoral capitalistic medical parasites.

> **A new model is gravely needed to replace the worn out win-lose-lose model handed down to us from the medical wolves in sheep's clothing. And new attitudes about wellness, illness, and aging are all part of this paradigm shift.**

There is lip service to better living in many areas of healthcare, but most people *cannot,* by themselves, pull themselves out of the habitual pits they have fallen into. Most people in unhealthy lifestyles cannot or at least will not respond to good advice alone. So, there is a great need for health coaches and group support systems to provide personal attention that promotes personal accountability and helps the chronically ill navigate the difficult transition to a healthier lifestyle.

I propose we explore a radically different form of medicine, in which patients both learn the initiating causes of their growing, progressive trajectory of disease and receive the inpatient and outpatient resources necessary to make the *huge leap of lifestyle* necessary to reverse that trajectory. Once they achieve this difficult feat, health coaches, lifestyle transformation programs, and group support systems can continue to provide the ongoing support and resources necessary for them to sustainably remain above the "disease afflicting zone."

Done on a larger scale, health would become the popular norm, and the disease-free lifestyle would become the rage as people in larger and larger numbers turned to its benefits and freedoms. Gradually, the setbacks and disappointments of allowing oneself to fall apart, as is the case in chronic disease, would become a source of embarrassment, while remaining healthy would become a source of personal pride and sought after by increasing numbers of citizens. Gradually, norms would change and older people would be bragging about their health exploits, rather than their most recent hospitalization, drug, or operation. As with any paradigm shift, the changes take at least a generation or two, as the younger generation grows up with the newly prevailing perspective "on their radar" from birth. So, as health becomes the norm, the view of what older life is supposed to be would elevate, and growing old would be viewed as a healthy challenge instead of an unfortunate reality that barely beats its alternative.

To the senior population (and next wave of soon-to-be seniors) I would assert that your health should be very important to you. When you lose your health, you lose your independence and the pleasures of independent use of your significant free time. You lose your power to govern your affairs. You lose self-esteem and confidence, and the freedom and vitality to engage in your community—and, thus, lose your sense of invested participation in your community. You may then begin to perceive yourself as a drain upon society and a burden to others, instead of a positive contributor. To seniors, I say that remaining healthy is *central* to retaining everything else you hold dear. If you love opera, you need to stay in shape. If you love your grandkids, you need to stay in shape. If you love bingo, you need to stay in shape. If you love travel, you need to stay in shape. If you love volunteering, you need to stay in shape. Loss of your fitness means loss of your independence, your interaction with the community, your contact with friends, your ability to travel with ease—in short, the freedom to really be alive.

When I speak of senior fitness I mean *total* fitness, which includes much more than merely being able to walk. I mean the ability to still be passionate, to get excited about tomorrow's contribution. I mean remaining vital, engaged and alive both physically and intellectually. Reading, thinking, reflection, walks, recreation and hobbies, visiting friends, travel, attending shows and enjoying your retirement are all largely dependent upon remaining healthy.

The alternative is to lose so much of your vitality that life begins to look more like, well … more like … waiting. Waiting for what? Well … just waiting! When you seniors have lost your fitness and vitality, you lose your ability to choose until … well … all that's left is the ability to … wait, till … well … to just wait, till whatever is to happen to you next … happens to you. When you lose your health, your quality of life diminishes extremely rapidly.

Since behavior follows thoughts, it could be deduced from the way people behave that at some level, people consider it more difficult to *give up* being a victim than it is to give up their health, vitality, independence, personal dignity, and joy of living.

Principles:

- Lifestyle is the incubator of chronic illness and chronic wellness.
- Medications are impotent when compared to the effect of lifestyle.
- Through a certain lifestyle, the chronically ill create their condition

and no amount of medications taken prevents their course of decline.

- Through a certain lifestyle, the chronically well create their condition, and not taking medication actually contributes to their wellness.

Consider a person who has had a cast on for an extended period of time because of a broken bone or severely injured joint. When that cast is finally removed, he/she initially experiences a considerable amount of weakness, stiffness, and pain in the affected limb because it has been immobilized for so long. But as the person begins to gently and gradually increase the demands and ranges of motion required of the joint, the joint and surrounding tissue adapt and strengthen in response. And, over time, normal strength and function return.

But consider what would happen if people with this condition left the limb in the cast, or, after taking the limb out of the cast, they never again progressively exercised it? Such is the life of the chronically ill. They have adopted a "casted" life, lived it month upon month, into the years, and that life is devoid of health-promoting activity. Their chronically ill state creates a cast upon them by their long-standing and uninterrupted set of non-health-promoting daily habits. Into this reality step medical doctors who diagnose the effects of their casted existence and prescribe pharmaceutical agents. The emphasis, need I say, the *agenda* of modern medicine is to leave people "casted" in the exact behaviors that brought them into their current health crisis, and add to it the consumption of chemicals that have known toxicities, numerous subtle side effects, numerous not-so-subtle side effects, and a few downright dangerous adverse reactions (paralysis, coma, and death). These patients stay in the unhealthy lifestyle that led to the health crisis, but now with additional toxic behaviors i.e. the consumption of toxic chemicals.

A person "casted" into his or her own brand of health-degenerating habits will never return to a healthy, functional state without also returning to health-generating activity … Never. No matter how many drugs you convince them to swallow. It is not the absence of chemicals in one's diet that leads to chronic illness. It is the absence of a healthy lifestyle. It is not the addition of chemicals into one's diet that will restore health; it is the restoration of a healthy lifestyle.

If the chronically ill do what they have always done, they will get what they have always gotten, which is to become progressively more ill. To get something different, they need to behave very differently. To get something different, they need to do something different. To arrive somewhere new, they need to follow a different path. They have neither the enlightenment to see the trench in which they travel, nor the strength and discipline necessary to climb its narrow walls into the light and freedom of healthy living. Without significant lifestyle guidance and strong support to break their addiction to an unhealthy lifestyle, these patients are virtually guaranteed to:

"Continue doing as they've always done
Continue winning as they've often won
Harvesting the rewards of the seeds they've spun
They'll be goin' downhill till their ruin is run."

And to the chronically ill, I would say: "Please do not be offended by this summary of your behavior, but please be real. You have lost your first love of energy and vitality and replaced it with the shards of empty satiations. Remember your first love. Return to the preservation of your energy and vitality, and your energy and vitality will return to preserve you. My counsel and program is designed to remind you of what is real *and* what is *real* wealth. Unless you follow the steps to health, you won't get healthy, so stop looking to the pill-pushers to do your work for you. Healthy is as healthy does."

We need to make it more profitable to get and keep people well.

Until it is profitable to support recovery, capitalist corporations will continue to milk disease. But if a profit incentive is put in place to keep people well, and corporations will be born to reap that harvest. Since disease is currently more profitable than wellness, disease is groomed and harvested. The only way to turn that around is to reward wellness and lessen the profits of treating (harvesting) disease. When it is more rewarding to keep people well than it is to treat their ongoing decay, then ingenuities to promote wellness will emerge. The corporate ingenuities to promote wellness must be well-rewarded, or those bright and capable corporate minds will be drawn to the rewards of treating disease.

Accountants need to consider the cost of non-prevented disease and pay "health corporations" a reasonable profit for preventing it. How long has the great reward gone to the harvesters of disease? It is time to pay the greater honor to the preventers of disease.

Health insurance should increase their profits by actively researching, promoting, and supporting (vis-à-vis generous coverage) disease prevention, i.e. health promotion and health maintenance.

I am proposing that the health insurance industry should make itself wealthier by investing prudently, against conventional medical "wisdom." It should politely demand aggressive support for the lifestyle reformation that alone will redirect the health of the most chronically ill patients.

I believe health insurance organizations have a valid profit motive: saving revenues from the health premiums of their clients. Is this not best achieved by maintaining patient wellness? By reducing the need for hospital stays and emergency room visits? This is an acceptable, ethical insurance incentive to promote wellness. Unacceptable insurance incentives are seen when companies cancel or deny coverage for high-risk clients, and insure only those who seldom need coverage.

Preventive health maintenance programs need to be incentivized by federal and private insurers, since the chronically ill are so steeped in their own quagmire that they are incapable of responsible health maintenance, much less articulate self-advocacy. Many of the chronically ill are so entrenched in the lifestyle and identity of illness that they may be reluctant to try, or feel they have very little to lose; whereas health insurers stand to lose trillions of dollars in avoidable losses. The short and skinny is that conventional medicine has no incentive to see patients well, but, presumably, health insurers *do*.

"It is unreasonable to expect that people will change
their behavior easily when so many forces in the social,
cultural and physical environment conspire
against such change."
- Institute of Medicine

To the health insurers, I say: A generous investment in the health and wellness for your highest-risk clients will bring you far more wealth in the future than your tight-fisted approach has ever netted you in the past. *Beat the disease mongers at their own game.* I am not asking you to give up the pursuit of wealth for benevolent causes. I am asking you to expand your wealth by *investing wisely*. The basic premise here is a considerably better cost-to-reward ratio from spending upfront on health preservation, in comparison to a tight-fisted yet dependent relationship upon the advice, counsel, guidance, and rationales of modern medicine.

"Is there any organization that would spend 35 times more money to deal with the effects of a problem than it would to solve the problem? It makes no sense in the private sector, and, with current concerns about spending rates and budget caps, it should make no sense in government."
- Mike Milken

Currently the patient has two corporate industries fighting over his or her viability as a financially harvestable organism. The medical industry reaps a rich financial harvest from a patient's progressive decline while feigning to be the patient's greatest ally. The health insurance industry is tight-fisted when it comes to covering the cost of expenses that restore and preserve health, but are simultaneously financially obligated to cover a basic level of medical care.

However, there is one patient population that *has the insurance industry by the gullet*, and their behaviorally-induced chronic disease is raining on the health insurer's financial parade, as well as raising the premiums of all the healthier folk. Health insurers appear to hand these sick patients over to the medical feeding frenzy to do with as they deem most profitable, and the medical machine empties the health insurer's pockets. But there is a more profitable way. Health insurers can have their cake and eat more of it, too. The industry can do much to salvage title on the chronically ill and restore them to a much lower medical cost profile.

The health insurance industry can win the game over *who* is to glean the harvest of those patients' financial viability. If they can re-establish the health and wellness of their most costly clients, they will retain them as *partners* in their corporation's acquisition of wealth. As soon as patients deteriorate into the "affliction zone" of *uncontrolled* chronic disease. those patients become partners with the medical industry in the harvest of their own physical declines.

Health insurers—wake up and smell the coffee! If you want to save big cost outlays from the claims of your ungoverned, wayward clients, then you need to educate, encourage, inspire, and support transformative realizations about the bigger highs of healthier addictions. We're all habituating people, that's what we do. We find a groove and dig it deeper. It's just that some people are digging grooves that are good for them, and others are digging grooves that ultimately hurt them, but either way we're all just digging our groove thang.

The chronically ill have largely found their groove thang in ways that don't produce health. It might produce wealth or stealth or girth or mirth, but their groove thang doesn't produce health.

And it's costing health insurers a lot of wealth. I recommend health insurers sit down and think about what your high school principal tried to instill in you: Just say *no* to drugs. You need to stop the merry-go-round, politely take your wayward children—the most chronically ill—by the hand, and place them in the hands of caregivers who prosper when they are well.

For health insurers to be rollin' in the dough, they need to proactively support and promote the health and wellness of their most unstable patient population, *through health maintenance programs that are inexpensive by comparison*. This will medically stabilize them and reduce the *huge costs* normally incurred when they (the health insurers) comply with conventional medical direction, which is to subsidize (pay for) their clients' prescribed medications and ongoing medical appointments and tell them to "hold steady," until further medical crises arise. Insurers who step directly into proactive care of their clients assure patient care and outcomes that are more ethical, more humane, and far more economical.

Conventional medical advice to health insurers is comparable to mechanics telling car owners to "fill her with gas and run her till she makes funny noises and then bring 'er in." My more economical advice to health insurers is to "invest on the front end in oil changes every 3,000 miles and perform regular scheduled maintenance in order to improve performance and reduce costs of care."

The funds invested by health insurers to subsidize health club memberships for the chronically ill create financial incentives for health/fitness organizations like the YMCA. Those payments should encourage them to provide specially-adapted programs that help keep this particular clientele well and out of the hospital. In a fee-based system, healthier clients mean fitness organizations continue to receive fees for "treating" those patients. It's a win-win scenario. It's the health/fitness organization's *profit incentive* to create health-restoring programs and to maintain the health of the "at risk" population. My goal is to take the power and profits from medical parasites, which feed off physical degeneration, and shift them to the market forces that are more closely aligned with the will and intent of people for recovery, and of health insurers for fewer and less expensive claims.

I'd prefer to see health insurers become wealthy because they subsidize keeping their clients well, rather than see pathologically greedy medical-pharmaceutical corporations become wealthy as they wallow in the fees received for the treatment of preventable disease.

I have heard dark tales of health insurers denying coverage for some life-saving medical procedures, which ended up costing the patients *their lives*. If insurers are willing to endure the staining of their public reputation (not to mention their decision's terminal effect upon the patient) and the possibility of ensuing lawsuits all for the goal of reducing their costs—why on earth shouldn't they consider funding entirely independent medical research to investigate what is the most effective and economical approach to eliminating disease, and not simply treating its progression?

The profit incentive of health insurance corporations to actively invest in the health of at-risk clients is huge. Health insurance corporations need to define their own "prescriptions for health," which will by necessity *not* be the same as the dictates prescribed by a medical system whose wealth depends upon *loss* of health.

Health insurance organizations need their own independent medical research experts. It seems that in many respects the health insurance industry's cost analysts are up against a wall in navigating the challenges of:

- How to discern effective from ineffective medical care.
- How to discern economic, cost-effective care from expensive, wasteful ineffective medical care.
- How to choose wisely and therefore preserve their capital by only authorizing cost-effective medical treatments.

Currently, health insurers are dependent upon outside "experts" from the American medical-pharmaceutical machine for information about cost-effective treatment options.

And what do these "experts" approved by the American Medical-Pharmaceutical Machine Approach recommend? Well, the health insurers will certainly *not* be told that an ounce of prevention would go a lot further than a pound of costly cure. Instead, the doctors and research *experts* will recommend to health insurers exactly what their employers (the pharmaceutical and medical industries) pay them to recommend: chemicals, diagnostics, and procedures to alleviate symptoms.

Scientists discover what they are paid to discover; doctors profess and prescribe what they are paid to profess and prescribe. If these experts stray from their employers' party line, they will soon cease to be employees, and will be replaced by other "experts" who will toe that line.

Say a patient is morbidly obese, and his health insurance company is alarmed about the financial risk he poses because they know obesity is fast becoming the #1 preventable cause of death and medical expenses in the U.S. So the health insurer asks the medical industry how best to prevent this from becoming a bigger medical expense. Well, from the type of treatments health insurers are approving payment for, it appears that the medical "experts" recommend that the patient begins a chemical regimen to address his high cholesterol, high blood pressure, elevated blood sugar levels, increased risks of blood clots, pain associated with his excess weight, flare-ups of his cellulites and various ointments for skin eruptions. There you have it: These are the authoritative, "American Medical Approach-approved" prescriptions for dealing with the symptoms of obesity.

But I hope you caught something there. We went from a question of how to prevent the increasing risks and costs associated with obesity, straight into recommendations about how to treat its ongoing symptoms. Treatment of obesity symptoms is not, however, the best solution to the problem of obesity. These treatments are simply the products being sold for profit by the employers of the medical doctors who make recommendations to insurers. These medical "experts" recommend what they're paid to recommend. Furthermore, the patients are being sold this same line of persuasion, and the results of patient's compliance with medical orders is often quite devastating, and also quite expensive for the health insurance companies.

The insurance companies want patients to be well and remain "claim free," right? So they need to hire experts who have a vested interest in keeping people well. The health insurance industry—both government and private health insurers—must fund independent medical research organizations that are completely uncorrupted by the disease-for-profit paradigm. These organizations must discover the most effective ways of stopping the advance of disease and thereby reducing expensive claims. Public and private health insurers need to do their *own* independent thinking and fund their own *independent* medical research, and then pony up and pay for what their independent thought and research has deemed the most health-effecting, cost-reducing strategy.

We need to change the way medical claims are processed and paid.

An ounce of prevention is worth a pound of cure. For instance, why can't a health insurance company pay for a health club membership *if*—and this is an important contractual if—its customer signs a form agreeing to attend regularly and in that way "contracts" to remain well? Why do medical insurance companies refuse to pay preventive health costs while they readily dish out 10 times that much for a critical "health care crisis" resulting from chronic self-neglect?

Before health insurers approve payments for drugs, what if their healthcare policies and protocols required evidence that medical providers have first exhausted health-promoting, disease-preventing, health coaching, fitness facilities, and group support systems? It would radically change the system if payment for drugs and surgeries were a last resort if and when wellness treatments were exhausted, instead of drugs and surgical treatments being virtually the only kinds of payments allowed. What incentive it would be to a shift in the medical paradigm if insurance payments for care must be denied unless dedicated, mandated, facilitated, prescribed, counseled, coached, and financially fostered compliance with healthy lifestyle has been provided repeatedly and refused by patients or was unsuccessful, before payments for drugs and/or surgical treatments are (so handsomely) remunerated!

The chart on the next page captures when the medical insurance industry needs to say, "No!" on paying insurance claims.[41]

Effective Medical Approach—Criteria for Insurance Claim Payments				
Questions/ Criterion	COLUMNS A - D: SCENARIOS AND CONSEQUENCES			
	A	B	C	D
Was patient informed of the Effective Medical Approach?	No	No	Yes	Yes
Was patient provided comprehensive lifestyle transformation support?	No	No	Yes	Yes
Was patient self-empowerment restored?	Failure	Failure	Success	Failure
Patient health outcome.	Repeat Hospitalization	Repeat Hospitalization	Patient compliance & Long term recovery	Repeat hospitalization despite best efforts
Insurance claim payment results.	Accepted (first time)	Denied	Accepted	Accepted
Instructions: Columns A-D are answers to the questions/criterion in column 1.				

1. Please note that the insurance claim payment is not dependent upon patient outcome, but upon provision of comprehensive lifestyle support.
2. When patients receive a course of treatment but lack empowerment

(i.e., comprehensive lifestyle support) to prevent future declines, then the medical system will receive a payment denial or deeply reduced payment. When patients receive both a course of treatment and the resources that empower them to overcome their affliction and adversity, then, even if they are re-hospitalized, the medical system receives full payment.

3. Payments are not based on patient outcome but upon providing best evidence based (preventive) practice. Patients don't always defeat chronic disease, especially in its advanced stages. But what is crucial, and a moral mandate, is provision of the tools, resources, and support essential to their success. In fact, without such provisions, *failure* is almost 100% *guaranteed.*

Insurers, take note: as payers of medical fees, insurance companies should be able to demand that the products and services prescribed to patients are not only profitable to the medical corporation, but actually *effective* for the patient. This may sound absurdly obvious, but I would argue that standard medical care for chronic conditions is frequently *profitable* but infrequently *effective*.

We need to make it less profitable for medical care providers to be apathetic about disease prevention.

This revised system of processing insurance claims would actually give healthcare authority to the insurance company—a company that has a financial vested interest in seeing patients get well and stay well. It also gives them a means by which to demand that patients are not simply treated in ways that bring profit but in ways that also evoke *effective physical recovery*. It's not that insurance corporations should have the authority to deny medical corporations due profit, but they should have the authority to demand that medical corporations provide *effective* (evidence based) medical care as well. The effectiveness of medical care has been deplorably lacking since pharmaceutical and medical corporations became the direct employer of medical doctors, which has meant that medical doctors have become vendors of drug products and medical services *for* the pharmaceutical/medical complex rather than the healthcare representatives and wellness advocates of their patients.

Individual patients do not have the power, expertise, or wherewithal to demand this for themselves. They are simply limited to accepting or rejecting what health care options are offered by their plan. When we place a corporate entity with a strong financial incentive in seeing patient's health improve in the patient's corner, we preserve for a little longer the rights, dignity, and choice of the individual against the beast of corporate appetite.

Why don't we charge medical corporations for the chronic diseases they have knowingly *not prevented* through the *required prescription and provision* of a fully-supported, comprehensive, chronic disease rehabilitation/reversal program? Why don't we demand that Medicare will *only* pay hospital systems for the treatment of chronic conditions *after demonstrating* clear evidence of extensive efforts to refer and enroll the 1%-5% most chronically ill in comprehensive health promotion/ disease reversal programs? If these medical corporations can first prove they have prescribed and performed all that research reveals will assist in disease prevention/reversal, then they can justifiably profit off merely treating the progressive symptoms of chronic disease.

What about applying a similar restraint strategy upon the fast food industry? Obesity is the primary byproduct of fast food consumption. As the fast food industry's wealth grows, so do the waistlines of millions of Americans. The secondary byproduct of fast foods is seedbeds of obesity-induced chronic disease cultivated in the lush, fertile soils of fat-saturated body cells and tissues. Fast food scientists so chemically alter their food products that they become chemically addictive substances, and the thickening of Americans is proof of the success of their grand scheme. An article published in Healthy Life entitled, "Fast Food is as Addictive as Heroin," claims, "Scientists have previously proven links between drug addiction and fast-food addiction, but increasingly there is a growing body of research that is finding out how junk food is hard wiring our brains for cravings."[42] Therefore, shouldn't these fine and upstanding institutions share in the costs to America that result from their successful campaign of promoting food addiction?

"Why is it so hard for obese people to lose weight despite the social stigma and health consequences such as high blood pressure, diabetes, heart disease, arthritis, and even cancer, even though they have an intense desire to lose weight? There are specific biological mechanisms that drive addictive behavior. Nobody chooses to be a heroin addict, cokehead, or drunk. Nobody chooses to be fat, either. The behaviors arise out of primitive neurochemical reward centers in the brain that override normal willpower and overwhelm our ordinary biological signals that control hunger. It is not because they *want* to be fat. It is because certain types of food are addictive. Food made of sugar, fat, and salt can be addictive, especially when combined in secret ways that the food industry will not share or make public. We are biologically wired to crave these foods and eat as much of them as possible. We all know about cravings, but what does the science tell us about food and addiction, and what are the legal and policy implications if a certain food is, in fact, addictive?"[43]

If you would like to explore this topic in greater detail you can easily perform your own research by performing a Google keyword search. Just type into the search engine the following keyword search: Fast Food—Chemically addictive substances.

Isn't it time that we as a nation share the costs of obesity with the industries that are promoting it?

We as a nation finally got fed up with the tobacco companies promoting tobacco addiction and demanded that they give back to America a portion of what they cost her people in their highly successful campaign to promote tobacco-induced chronic diseases. We demanded an accounting of the cigarette manufacturers whose successful addiction of the public (including its youth) to tobacco products resulted in an average cost of 75 billion dollars annually in medical expenses in the United States alone.

Excerpts from WhoCanISue.com website:

1] In a 1,653 page ruling, the judge stated that the tobacco industry had deceived the American public by concealing the addictive nature of nicotine plus had targeted youth in order to get them hooked on cigarettes for life. (Appeals are still pending). . .

2] Non-smokers are [also] exposed to second hand tobacco smoke by being in the same room as a smoker. Victims of secondary smoke exposure are more likely to develop lung cancer, asthma, chronic bronchitis, pneumonia, heart disease, sinus cancer and eye and nose irritation . . .

3] According to the Centers for Disease Control and Prevention (CDC), nearly one in every five deaths in the United States is smoking related, and tobacco use totals more than $75 billion in annual medical costs . . .

4] Various Tobacco Lawsuits. In November 1999, lawsuits against large tobacco by 46 states, four territories and the District of Columbia were all settled for $206 billion, which made this the largest civil settlement in U.S. history.

Known as the Tobacco Master Settlement Agreement (TMSA), this agreement specified that tobacco pay the various states and territories the agreed amount in installments over a 25-year period. The MSA also restricted the tobacco company's ability to win over younger audiences to smoking by marketing cigarettes at large sporting events, on transit systems, billboards or on TV.[44]

Please honk if you believe in the establishment of a tax which would be added to the cost of every "fat inducing, artery clogging" concoction coming off the grill and deep fryer of the "fat food industry." This would be written up as the "Fast Food Association Tax," which we would call it the FFAT Tax.

The tax revenues generated would be dedicated to Lifestyle Transformation Programs and used to treat the effects of declining health through the introduction and support of the behaviors responsible for promoting robust health.

The centers and programs would serve as a model for all people in need of health rejuvenation. The programs' intervention will be a prescribed benefit and will become an insurance-covered intervention for the most chronically ill.

On that thought, why don't we seek damages for every chronically ill patient who has not been aggressively supported in preventative modalities for the last 5-10 years? Why don't we also seek medical insurance reimbursement for every disease whose costs (to the insurer) rose because scientifically proven methods of disease prevention & reversal were never even attempted? How many patients could be brought in on this class action suit? The number of patients thus treated (that is, maltreated) is easily in the millions. What kind of settlement could be expected to repay both the patients for personal losses and the insurers in capital losses? If I were to make an estimate of the ill-gotten gains extorted from our society in the pursuit of profits (at the expense and sacrifice of principles) I would estimate that amount to easily be in the hundreds of trillions of dollars.

America's medical machine and its propaganda mill has cultivated a medically compliant yet highly vulnerable and poorly defended people. Patients are groomed (through medical "orders") to swallow and absorb chemicals through every available orifice; yet those patients' own disease-encouraging and -attracting behaviors are only lightly addressed.

Again, we can see the system— in its use of scientists—applying their education and skills in the work of falsely presenting, that is, "spinning" medical information in such a way as to deceive the public into relaxing implementation of *the only truly evidence-based defense against chronic disease (health promotion)* and instead persuading them to rely on drugs to do their work for them. And we can see the fruit of this system's work in the declining trajectory of public health as people listen to and put faith in this system's chemical propaganda.

If profit is the exclusive bottom line according to corporate culture, then make the fines for violations, damages, abuses, costs to society, and "failures to rescue" so painful as to significantly reduce corporate profits. We need to financially reward socially responsible corporate behavior and fine the hell out of corporate violators. Let corporate profit mongers who violate the earth or any of its people experience such heavy fines as to severely threaten their company's profitability for a long time. Let's consider violations against mankind and the environment to deserve fines and punishment equal to the damage they cause.

Individuals caught for crimes against others or the environment usually experience a considerable penalty for doing wrong. So if a person is caught for such and such a crime and the punishment for that behavior is *sufficiently devastating* so as to be a strong deterrent to that behavior, we as a society consider that to be a successful use of legal deterrence. This same standard should be applied to corporations. After all, *corporations are considered legal "persons," too*. But on the contrary, corporation's penalizations are so pathetic that they actually encourage wide-scale violations of the law. For corporations, getting caught occasionally for their oft-repeated violations is actually more profitable than compliance. Getting caught (and receiving a fine) occasionally is simply factored into the cost of pursuing higher profits. The level of corporate violations taking place is a clear indication that slap-on-the-wrist fines and penalties are ineffective at achieving deterrence of socially deviant behavior. So increase the penalties, make it really hurt and *voila*! We will immediately experience effective deterrence.

So let's say that Pfizer pharmaceutical is guilty of violations to a people or the environment, and they are fined $2.3 billion, and thus their profits for that year are reduced from $48.3 billion to $46 billion. That is so ineffective as to be a huge *incentive* on the corporation's part to continue violating society and the environment. A weak-kneed punishment for corporate violators is tantamount to encouraging them to violate the law. Make corporations hurt in the only area in which they have the ability to experience concern or remorse—their profit margins. So bump the fines up to something they'll respect.[45]

Asking corporations to behave honestly and then laying upon them insignificant fines when they don't is equivalent to pleading with them to *continue* with their abuses. I say, give them something to sweat about if they want to break the law to make more profits. How about making the first fine very painful, the second fine utterly devastating, and the third fine completely wipe them out. Three strikes, you're out. That would not be a profitable outcome for the corporation, and profit is the corporation's only priority, so corporate "persons"—i.e., corporations—would either have to become law abiding members of society or suffer severe consequences.

Irresponsible corporate behavior is entirely modifiable by

implementing laws that truly enforce responsible corporate behavior. This requires a federal government that cares more about protecting people and the environment than about receiving "greased palm" payoffs to look the other way. So, the government needs to step up to the plate and demand corporate accountability. Yes, a corporation's responsibility is to promote profits for the shareholders; this is not being argued. What will no longer be tolerated are violations of any people, animals, or the environment, and all these socially irresponsible acts will be so heavily fined as to obliterate that year's profits.

To the industry which has enjoyed astounding profits as a result of failing to accomplish what they claim to be about—health care—I recommend that they be named after what they actually do: "disease care." However, because patients are paying their hard-earned medical premiums to actually get *well,* the medical industry should be required to turn over a significant amount (say $200 million of every billion they spend on harvesting the ill) to restoring them to optimal wellness.

For instance, medical corporations are paying *billions* to build hospitals to harvest the proceeds of highly preventable diseases. They should be required to spend *millions* on fitness centers to fully facilitate their prisoners' releases. Why should Medicare have to pay the bill for the fruit of fully-blossoming chronic diseases when the medical care system knows full well how to prescribe and facilitate the prevention of those diseases? Profits are what non-prevention of disease progression is all about. It's about the money! What is the cost to society of un-prevented diabetes? The exact same amount as the profits derived by the medical industry for not preventing it.

Chronic disease prevention through comprehensive health promotion should be prescribed. Omission of this "prescription" is very damaging and expensive to society. Corporate profits derived from preventable disease are strangling America by the throat -- bringing it to its knees. The medical-pharmaceutical system is financially responsible for the costs of this broken system. Dramatic lifestyle changes resulting from supporting lifestyle transformation of the 1%-5% most costly and chronically ill patients is this nation's most promising hope for achieving significant reduction of the healthcare costs that are undermining the American economy. Failure to refer the most chronically ill to comprehensive health promotion programs should be a finable offense.

We need to conduct independent research and figure out the legitimate costs of intelligent medical care.

Compared to the ever-expanding, exponentially-increasing cost of medically treating *lifestyle-driven* progressive decline, the upfront costs are nominal for preventing disease through Lifestyle Transformation Programs that are physician-prescribed, community-based, fully-facilitated, insurance-funded, attendance-monitored and 12-step group-supported.

We must conduct financially independent medical research that upholds the highest standards of scientific objectivity and reproducible testability, in order to find the most effective and the most economical treatment protocols available. We must then publish said findings in fully accredited medical review journals, and hold the neglect of these findings as evidence of a *medical conflict of interest*, that is, a demonstration of outright contempt for the medical welfare of the patients those institutions have pledged to serve.

We need medical research not funded or influenced by special interests (i.e., pharmaceutical companies, hospitals, or, for that matter, industries related to organic foods, health foods, and vitamin and mineral supplements). It must be independent of all ulterior motives.

> **The exclusive research objective is finding the most effective treatment protocols and scrutinizing those findings using evidence-based standards of cross-examination.**

Healing protocols would be further refined and updated as ongoing test data becomes available. Evidence should then be presented to government and large health insurance systems of the best patient outcomes, most effective treatment protocols, most economical application of insurance monies for long-term savings, medical effectiveness, and overall viability of the insurance industry and governmental agencies.

The difficulty comes not in the rationale of this construct, but in the corruption of it. The original reason for the American Medical Association was to clearly distinguish and separate scientific medical treatments from the bogus "snake oil" treatments of medical charlatans. It was under this guise (and the political clout it bought) that they oppressed and largely shut down the competition of medical midwives, female physicians, and all natural approaches to treatment. From the advent of the chemical medical model, which sprang out of the occult practices of alchemy, the stated rationale and mission were good, but its motive was the gold.

Things have changed little. The medical-pharmaceutical systems with a vested interest in disease will undoubtedly conduct their own research to disprove the extent of savings gained from boldly preventing disease, just as they resolutely insist on relentlessly drugging the *progressive* symptoms of what is actually *preventable* decline. Research into the cost of disease *prevention* versus the cost of disease *progression* must be conducted by those not influenced in any way by the medi-drug cartels which profit from disease.

Almost all current medical research is funded in one way or another by the pharmaceutical industry. But there is considerable evidence of people who use a diagnosis of chronic disease as a wake-up call to embark upon a lifestyle of impeccable self-care, one that involves redirecting life energy and priorities toward personal development and health restoration activities. These resolute and resourceful few have an extremely convincing track record of overcoming their initial diagnosis, reversing their physiological decline, and regaining health. They regain independent function they had gradually allowed to let slip away. They decrease dependence upon pharmaceutical products, and they decrease dependence upon conventional medical services, both of which depend upon disease to remain financially lucrative.

What is lacking (and I implore this to be rectified out of my desire to see a healthier society and happier people) is research into the effect of profound lifestyle transformation toward healthier and healthier lifestyles, and the effect of this transition process upon chronic disease. My plea is that we defeat disease by employing health. This plan will work, and medical research done with integrity will reflect it. I believe we will find that an absolutely impeccably healthy lifestyle brought to bear upon most chronic disease states will prove the fastest, clearest, most direct path of recovery for all willing to take on the challenge as an individual. Meanwhile, the challenge for us as a society will be to finance medical research whose aim is patient wellbeing and health recovery, instead of merely pharmaceutical treatments for existing symptoms of ongoing and progressive disease.

I request intelligently conducted, evidence-based research into the disease-reversing effects of lifestyles that:

- Promote health.
- Restore vitality.
- Remove toxins.
- Fortify nutrition.
- Release destructive emotions.
- Improve relationships.
- Release captives from addiction.
- Enhance the overall healthiness of behavior and life.

I believe these benefits will be seen when people are placed in a program with absolutely life-enriching health disciplines. We need to observe what happens when people in such a program are encouraged daily into widening circles of healthy participation in vitality-restoring habits and relationships. This is a measure of the accuracy and validity of our independent research on health and wellness.

We need to establish independent industry watchdogs and patient advocacy groups.

We need to initiate a revival of genuine concern for patient welfare. We need to bring compelling draconian forces of much stronger laws and stiffer fines to bear upon the medical/industrial complex to break through:

- Scientific hypocrisy.
- Medical monopolies.
- Anti-trust violations.
- Medical conflicts of interest.
- Corporate greed.

The key is uniting industries with a genuine financial interest in seeing the chronically ill actually get well, and then empowering them. It will require the consolidated efforts of patient advocacy groups, private and public insurers, and all parties interested in seeing the establishment of an ethical and economical medical delivery system.

Here is my appeal. We need to establish a set of moral and ethical dictates that protect society from corporate self-interest, dictates that will be enforced by huge fines for violations. Help me advocate for disease prevention through health promotion for our society. I invite communication about ways to raise public awareness about the plight of the chronically ill and upon the darker forces controlling the direction of medicine in the arenas of: Medical Politics, Health Insurance, Medical Science, and Conventional Medical Treatment.

I encourage you to become proactive, and there are many other ways to become involved in discovering, participating in, or creating vehicles that truly advocate for patients. This could involve websites, informal groups, and/or institutions. We need to:

- Create *patient advocacy groups* with the aim of generating a powerful movement for social and political change—in this case, redirection of medical dollars from pill creation to fitness formation, and from building huge drug infusion centers (hospitals) to building fitness centers and funding Lifestyle Transformation Programs.
- Attract bright-minded social activists who are keen on creating informational *watchdog websites* that slice through the schmooze. There's a need for clear, concise, and well-informed

perspectives on medicine, nutrition, fitness, and healthy lifestyles to counterbalance the stress-inducing, disease-promoting gospel of consumption being propagated from virtually every pharmaceutical advertisement and billboard.

- Create ways to *identify* effective methods for mobilizing social change, *inform* large numbers of people on key social and political issues surrounding this cause, and *mobilize* people for action.
- *Encourage corporate responsibility* in broader issues than merely turning over quarterly profits.

Create watchdog groups and agencies that remain above bribery, do the difficult and time-consuming research necessary to uncover facts, and inform the public about relevant issues affecting wellness. This includes government, corporate and industry trends, social directions, healthcare policy decisions, and laws affecting their health, safety, rights, freedom and quality of life.

If these agencies or organizations were given great credibility and authority in their particular areas of research, they could provide a lighthouse of insight and clarity for the rest of us. They will help us vote and spend from a position of fact-based evidence instead of from a promotional spin. We would have greater power to fight for environmental protection, consumer advocacy, patient advocacy, public education, and public health. We would have greater possibilities for transformation of societal constructs like fast food chains, conglomerate grocery stores, and healthcare services covered by medical insurance.

An informed, united people will get the attention of our self-centered government, expose its protection of corporate exploitation of the earth and its people, and require that government fulfill its commitment to serve and protect its people. The strong voice of a united people will effect positive change in a stubbornly self-centered political environment. Our government, once made responsive to an informed public, will finally rein in the pathologically selfish behavior of corporations that are attempting to increase profits by damaging the environment and oppressing weaker peoples.

"When the people fear their government, there is tyranny; when the government fears the people, there is liberty."
- Thomas Jefferson

What we need is a patient protection and medical consumer advocacy organization. What we need is the heroic return of idealism to medicine.

What we need are organizations such as "Doctors and Medical Consumers for Integrity in Medicine." This organization would identify "improving patient outcomes" as its only driving force. It would look at evidence-based medicine from *all* medical traditions and not limit its investigations to the discoveries of corporation-funded research. It would provide independent evaluation of medical treatments, best practices, and most effective approaches to satisfactory patient outcomes—all from multiple healing traditions—and it would advocate on behalf of the patient's interest in wellness. This organization must be completely independent, entirely unsubsidized in any way by any market, corporate or industry interest, whether it be a medical, pharmaceutical, natural, or holistic product/service provider.

> **However, I would caution against simply depending upon the federal government to solve these problems. We can effect change if we work together. Together, we can raise a powerful voice to shake the walls and create a breach in the fortified defenses of this corporate and political empire. We need to empower advocacy groups, consumer protection groups, and teams committed to finding ways to consolidate the people's power and the people's voice until we can no longer be ignored.**

We need to establish Lifestyle Transformation Programs and their related Lifestyle Transformation Centers.

CONCEPTUAL FRAMEWORK

What does this Lifestyle Transformation Program include? Modified yoga, tai chi, water aerobics and resistance exercises, heat therapy, stretching, drinking organic juices, and group support. The program would build up to four hours a day as tolerated, starting with as little as 15 minutes a day and increasing the duration and intensity of effort over time. Attended three to five days a week, these programs would include activities that are ultra health-restoring, weight-reducing, muscle-toning, nerve-relaxing, systems-detoxifying, endurance-enhancing, socially-activating, and nutritionally-fortifying.

The wellness treatment model and methods I am promoting are highly effective and should be implemented at the onset of all chronic diseases in order to reverse their advances, minimize their impact, and manage what isn't reversible. The program I am pushing for would be a health recovery program for the chronically ill that would be strongly encouraged and incentivized by medical insurance, prescribed by doctors, and subsidized by federal and corporate sources. It doesn't get any clearer than this. Healthy lifestyle recovery programs are one fifth the cost of treating progressive chronic disease.[46]

When added up, the additional costs over 20 years for those not living a healthy lifestyle, compared to those who do live a healthy lifestyle as defined by the CDC guidelines and eat a mainly all-natural diet, are astronomical.[47]

I submit that utilizing existing health clubs (such as the YMCA), and providing funding for group classes designed specifically for the chronically ill, fits just such a strategy. It can make the act of getting well a pleasant and rewarding experience, which offers both the tangible gains of physical breakthroughs and the support of fellow sojourners on the path to recovery. Further, it can offer the great chance of reducing the exorbitant fees associated with unnecessary hospitalizations.

What I am appealing for in medicine is the "Real Thing." I want modern medicine to retard the human propensity for physical degeneration. I want it to shine a light into the underlying causes of disease and prompt people to clean up their act and their diet, and help them shine as humans. I want modern medicine to get real and offer:

1] Doctors who prescribe wellness and demand medical compliance in line with the patient's highest self-interest.

2] Five-star medical fitness centers—top quality, fitness-exploring paradises, with a large portion of the facilities dedicated to the senior and chronically ill populations.

So, if the cause of hospital admissions in a majority of cases is related to neglect of health-promoting behavior, then phase one of hospitalization would be stabilization, but phase two would be immersion in an optimized health and wellness Lifestyle Transformation Program. If sub-optimal lifestyle and health habits produce hospitalization, then introduction, immersion and ongoing support in healthy behavior pose the greatest promise for preventing re-hospitalization.

VISION FOR LIFESTYLE TRANSFORMATION CENTERS

The current hospital/medical system simply treats the outward effects of unhealthy self-determinants, and then releases patients back into them. The hospital/medical model of the future will introduce patients to a new set of self-determinants (healthy behaviors consistent with restoring fitness), and then supports their turning those newly introduced healthy behaviors into life-long habits.

Subtracting the destructive self-determinants that led to hospitalization—*adding* healthy self-determinants that restore fitness while *not adding* pills—results in lasting avoidance of re-hospitalization. The model of the future utilizes this understanding: A healthy lifestyle historically succeeds in sustaining wellness for those who are already well and replaces the destructive lifestyle of those who have been chronically ill.

What is currently missing from the mix is community and medical support *that reaches into* peoples' vortex of health decline *and provides the lift and support* necessary to bring them back into the light of a happy, self-nurturing, self-improving life structure. People need help pulling themselves out of chronic indolence and the spiraling vortex of physical decline. People need a 12-step program to gain support for release from their habitual lifestyles that attract chronic disease. People need a 12-step program, complete with deluxe health spa and sauna, with various forms of detoxification, as well as juice fasting and optimal nutrition. People need activities like pilates, exercise programs, aqua aerobics, Tai chi, dance, yoga, and many other forms of physical and spiritual refinement. Wellness and health promotion centers will work because we can see from those who are immersed in these "healthy intoxications" that they are in vibrant health and literally high on life.

One might ask, "Well, this is wonderful and all, it sounds like paradise for the medically enfeebled, but where will all the money come from to host such an elaborate recovery program?" My response is that the money is already there—and boatloads more! The cost of the current medical system is already far greater than the one proposed here. A YMCA membership that includes all of the above outlined services except nutritional support costs $65 per month. As of 2011, the average cost per stay in the hospital in the United States is $15,734.

New York: A hospital stay costs an average of $236 per day in India, $655 per day in France and an average of $3,949 per day in the US, according to a report — 2011 Comparative Price Report Medical and Hospital Fees by Country—released by the International Federation of Health Plans.[48]

The United States has some of the highest prices for medical products and services in the world, according to a report by the International Federation of Health Plans. The 2011 Comparative Price Report found the average cost per hospital stay in the United States was $15,734, followed by $5,004 in Germany and $4,948 in Chile. These are the average total hospital and physician costs for coronary artery bypass.[49]

The money for my paradise to benefit the medically enfeebled is already in the system—except that the current beneficiary of that money *is* the system.

It is our moral and ethical mandate to actually provide centers for lifestyle rehabilitation. It is no more than empty lip service to tell people who are entrenched in a lifestyle that has given them a chronic disease that they need to "get healthy," but then set them up for failure by not offering the resources and support they desperately need to achieve that goal.

Remedy is difficult when people are addicted to the lifestyle that brings on the chronic disease. *Very difficult.* How many trillions of pills and tons of bills have been choked down without halting the advance of chronic disease that people bring upon themselves? Oh, so profitable to the pharmaceutical/medical complex, but oh, so unethical. It's like selling crash helmets to blind people who are allowed to walk off a cliff, in order to "protect them" from head injuries associated with falling.

When we see doctor-prescribed 12-step supported programs of lifestyle transformation and attendance-monitored participation in comprehensive chronic disease reversal programs, we will be on our way. People typically live in a drug-induced, indeed drug-enabled, unhealthy lifestyle that progressively encapsulates them and finally kills them. Patients that have spun themselves into a sticky web of chronic disease *need to be required to participate* in healthy lifestyle activities until the benefits of their improving health become so enjoyable that they can make the psychological, emotional, and behavioral leap into healthy *self*-maintenance.

These centers of health promotion and chronic disease reversal through lifestyle modification will provide proof that efforts to avert chronic disease, instead of profit from them, are finally taking place. Attendance by patients should be mandated (prescribed and attendance-monitored) until they demonstrate real adaptation and "addiction" to the benefits of vibrant health. Then the prescriptions for healthy living become unnecessary, because people will voluntarily behave healthfully—because it feels so damn good to be healthy!

Peoples' immersion in unhealthy lifestyles is rarely affected by pep talks alone, so lip service from current medical professionals proclaiming the ideal of healthy lifestyles does not constitute proof of genuine interest in reversing chronic disease. Proof comes when community-based chronic disease-reversal programs are part of mainstream society, and doctors prescribe adherence to healthy lifestyles to the chronically ill until its benefits become "addictive" to patients. The critical breakthrough for patients will be when they realize that the benefits of transition to a healthier state outweigh the difficulties of the journey. People who were previously unable to pull themselves away from deeply-ingrained unhealthy habits begin to get excited when they enjoy a renewed sense of energy and freedom from pain and physical limitations. That excitement builds enthusiasm and a vision of self-empowerment that is intoxicating. It gives them the vigor and wherewithal to see it through from the initial medical/health intervention to a sustained personal transformation. Once released from their imprisonment, they will possess tons of motivation to remain autonomous members of a healthier category of Americans—those addicted to joyful, empowered, vital living.

I firmly believe that comprehensive behavioral interventions, which fortify the entire human physiology and strengthens the entire human organism, will prove a most effective treatment in terms of both reduced medical costs and improved patient outcomes. My belief is that, like the plant under the horticulturist's care, when we take humans out of self-imposed, self-damaging lifestyle routines and place them in a healthy environment—limiting their behavior to healthy choices—the amazing self-healing powers of the human immune system will then be able to break forth and rapidly repair the physical damage.

Immersing a patient population in an ideal environment and set of behaviors will result in rapid, effective, and long-lasting physiological recovery—far superior results as compared to conventional treatment outcomes. This holistic approach is superior because it strikes at the core (and not merely at the surface) of the medical and behavioral problem. It also carries significant economic impact and implications.

I believe the implementation of Lifestyle Transformation Programs will dramatically reduce overall medical costs of the one to five percent most chronically ill patients—who currently consume 65% of every medical dollar.

"If we look at the problem systematically, the first fact we can all recognize is where the costs really are. As the exhibit demonstrates, less than 1 percent of Americans actually require care at the [precise] level of the average premium. There is a vast inconsistency in healthcare spending. In fact, 20 percent spend virtually zero percent of total costs, and 70 percent spend only about 10 percent of total costs. Clearly, solving the problem of healthcare cost crisis does not reside among the 70 percent of all insured Americans.

A mere 1 percent of the insured are consuming 30 percent of total costs, and the top 5 percent account for as much as two-thirds of all costs. Herein lies the problem—as well as the massive potential for what we might call a "5 percent solution." That solution lies in identifying the specific chronic and acute conditions that move people into that high-cost 5 percent bracket, and then systematically and consistently bringing to bear strategic, targeted, consistent, high-leverage interventions to keep those people from migrating to the high-cost end of the curve. When people are in crisis, we need to provide best care. But we also need to stop large numbers of people from progressing into that crisis.[50]

Let's look at these statistics for a moment. For every 100 insured people in a room, only 1%, (1 person) spends 30% of the total expense for the entire group and only 5 % (five people) spend 65% of the total expense for the entire group. Clearly, if we could successfully intervene in the lives of those five individuals and bring them and their behavior above the "disease-attracting zone," we could reduce the overall costs of the entire group dramatically. Skyrocketing medical costs in America is not a mysterious and overwhelming problem, it's a "5% problem." The problem requires we apply 100% of our energy into achieving a 5% solution.

I propose that, through a proactive and aggressive investment into the wellness of these most chronically ill patients, we can drastically reduce the frequency of their clinic visits and hospitalizations. That, in turn, will dramatically reduce the economic outflow due to failure to remove the source causes that continually lead to ongoing chronic disease effects. I submit that the upfront cost of running patients through Lifestyle Transformation Programs and Centers will prove economically insignificant when compared to the overall reduction in medical costs that will result from proactively keeping patients well.

The program I have outlined is not a moneymaker for the current pharmaceutical-medical industry. However, it holds huge potential for reducing the prevalence of chronic disease, human misery and the astronomical costs associated with the treatment of advanced chronic disease. The creation of community-based chronic disease reversal programs will lead to disease regression, and capture profits for insurers from the decreasing prevalence of chronic disease.

Hospital systems capture profits from providing interventions that treat chronic disease and its progression. Lifestyle Transformation Centers capture profit from providing interventions that promote health and *decrease,* or reverse, chronic disease.

COMPARING THE TWO PARADIGMS OF MEDICAL REIMBURSEMENT:

Conventional Medical Approach: Fee-for-service = Fees-for-disease	Effective Medical Approach: Fee-for-health promotion = Fees-for-disease reversal
Hospital Systems capture profits from treating chronic disease and its increasing prevalence. (Profit incentive for medical providers)	Lifestyle Transformation Centers capture profits from promoting health and decreasing the prevalence of chronic disease. (Profit incentive for health insurers)

We need to create "personal health assistant" jobs.

In addition to health coaches, we should create a new job category and description for health assistants. These individuals could do much to assist patients in maintaining higher physiological homeostasis (i.e., "wellness") when they would otherwise live with a high rate of medical recidivism. That's a fancy sentence I conjured up to define a person employed to take patients for walks, to the pool, or to an exercise facility, and assist them through a basic exercise routine. So many patients are in need of a little boost in the right direction to turn their entire life picture around. Instead, they hang precariously on the edge of a precipice of physical misfortune and frequently fall off simply because they weren't given a little strategic support to maintain their life balance, personal equilibrium, and physical fitness.

Health assistants could be employed by assisted living communities, home health agencies, and even hospitals. Their one purpose would be to support the basic health and fitness of their patients. It doesn't require a master's degree in physical therapy to walk Mrs. Jones around the complex where she lives, or help her into the pool for an aqua-exercise program, or assist her through some basic exercises. But the consequence of no one providing these simple supports can result in her being hospitalized more than once a year. And just one hospitalization resulting from losing her balance on that tricky tightrope can easily cost $15,000, when all she really needed was a little scheduled exercise, a glass of organic juice before and after her exercise program, and assistance with taking a few high-quality nutritional supplements, and she'd become virtually trouble-free for years.

These new low-cost, personal health assistants, given the *exclusive* task of providing fitness maintenance support to the most costly and highest risk patient populations will greatly strengthen and stabilize the most vulnerable populations and cost very little compared to the *costs averted* in re-hospitalizations.

We need to implement a "Senior Corps"—an army of healthy senior role model volunteers who serve as advocates and evangelists for healthy senior living.

Envision with me a group of robust, vitally alive seniors who refuse to give up, roll over, and let others decide everything for them. Let's call them "The Senior Corps." Organized a little like the Peace Corps or the Marine Corps, this group's sage mission is to instill vitality and preserve meaning for the seniors in our communities. The Senior Corps would be a group of dynamic seniors who have overcome age- and health-related challenges to continue as vibrant, connected, and thriving citizens. Senior Corps members would serve as examples, encouragers, and advocates for the senior community, pushing for improved health facilities and wellness programs for their peers.

They would urge other seniors, through public speaking and mentoring:

- To rise out of broken, health-defeating lifestyles.
- To re-ignite the flames of enthusiasm.
- To embrace lifestyles that preserve youthfulness regardless of age.

They would encourage people to guard against the threats of poly-pharmacopeia—such as drug-induced heart block, auto-toxicity, and/or drug-induced dementia—and to instead promote their health with due diligence. This would be a national organization of seniors assisting seniors to strive toward a drug-free and superior quality of senior life.

We need to implement "health institutes"—schools of health promotion—whose graduates become advocates for chronic disease prevention.

I also propose establishing health institutes for the aging, funded by multimillion-dollar donations or grants. Here, retirees past the age of 65 could enroll as students in a program of health promotion and chronic disease prevention. After two semesters of full-time curriculum in wellness, disease prevention, and lifestyle transition, they would graduate with program diplomas or even accredited degrees in illness prevention. This would certify their work as senior representatives, licensed mentors, and volunteers to reach other seniors and the chronically ill.

These volunteer representatives would serve as models of vitality and healthy senior living. The goal would be to reach out and exhort other seniors to remain as healthy, productive, drug-free, and independent as physically possible by adopting healthy lifestyle principles that are scientifically proven to guard elder citizens from premature aging and physical decline.

The following outline gives an example curriculum for an "Institute Of Health Promotion" or "Institute of Self-Healing and Personal Growth." It would not only teach principles of health maintenance and disease prevention, but also instill a sense of responsibility to teach others.

CORE (REQUIRED) CURRICULUM COURSES:

- Physiological Detoxification
- Organic Hydration
- Optimizing Nutrition
- Fasting for Health and Rejuvenation
- Yoga Lite/Tai Chi Lite
- Cardiovascular Transformation (From Anoxia to the Oxygen-Enriched Lifestyle)
- Core/Musculoskeletal Strengthening (Reversing Osteoporosis and Becoming Strong)
- Modified Triathlon—Safe and User-Friendly for the Physically Challenged:
    - Modified distances
    - Buoyancy vests for the swim portion
    - Three-wheeled (adult) tricycles for the cycling portion for the elderly
    - Walking acceptable for the run portion

Additional Lifestyle Elective Courses:

- Massage and Aroma Therapy
- Gardening Therapy
- Pet Therapy (including grooming and massage for dogs and cats)
- Music Appreciation (such as singing and dancing to the music of the 1930s, '40s and '50s).
- Photography: Appreciation and Practice.
- Art Appreciation and Creativity.

LIFE ENRICHMENT ELECTIVE COURSES:

Focus on self-examination, life reflections, and deepening contribution to society. Sample course emphasizes:

- Aging, spirituality, and scriptural reflections.
- Inspirational compilation of most memorable quotes, stories, and writings.
- Prayer journaling and writing letters to children and grandchildren.
- Discovering the volunteer within.
- Leaving a legacy and making a contribution after age 65.

These institutes need to be developed with a complete budget that accounts for operations, faculty, and curriculum resources. You might say I'm dreaming again, but think more deeply. Compare the typical costs of education with those of hospitalization:

Average Class Costs: Community College (Semester)	
Part-time (1 – 2) classes	$26 to $120 per class
Full-time (3 – 6) classes	$75 to $500 per semester (16 weeks)
Average Class Costs: State Universities (Semester)	
Part-time (1 – 2) classes	$800 per semester (6 units or less)
Full-time (3 – 6) classes	$1,700 per semester (7 units or more)
Average Conventional Hospital Costs (as of 2011):	
One day	$3,949
Four day hospitalization	$15,796 [51]

Obviously, education geared toward prevention is far less costly than treatment of conditions that could have been prevented.

We need to appeal to our national policy makers to implement these new paradigms. What follows is a sort of "executive summary" for the policy side of establishing an Effective Medical Approach for national healthcare.

AN APPEAL TO NATIONAL POLICY MAKERS

Dear Sir or Madam,

I appeal for your support of the Effective Medical Approach. This model for wellness will change the dynamics of our national healthcare system into one that is more economical and ethical.

Please fund and build Lifestyle Transformation Centers that immerse patients in ideal patterns of behavior that, over time, generate vitality and thriving longevity for those who practice them. Educate patients and steep them in the enjoyment that comes from restoring health. Show, encourage, and promote these healthy patterns to patients until the enjoyment of vitality overtakes the pull and impulse toward unhealthy behaviors.

I hope to participate in the creation of Lifestyle Transformation Programs that teach the joy of responsible, healthy living. (By *responsible*, I mean people living in harmony with the pathway that achieves their stated objective of being healthier, i.e., that improves their fitness, renews their vitality, restores their independence, and increases their freedom to enjoy the good things in life.)

When people begin to renew their sense of personal strength, independence, and vitality, they will naturally want to hold onto it. They will shun ever returning to the victimized, dependent, and irresponsible existence they used to call life.

Initially, patients will come into a Lifestyle Transformation Center from self-imposed health-degenerating lifestyles and self-defeating habituated patterns that frequently make them ill and always profoundly weak. As patients surrender old habits and lifestyles, and begin adopting healthier ones, they experience withdrawal and an internal psychological battle begins. This provides the first opportunity to educate them about the growing benefits of renewing health and to impart to them the fortitude to see the process through. This is the time to initiate and support new perspectives and attitudes and a renewed vision of what they are capable of as they begin to adopt a new and healthier way of life. Progressive restoration of vitality, wellness, and an increasing freedom from the weight (and shackles) of physically degenerative symptoms will provide the motivational fuel required for them to continue with the difficult work of physical recovery and lifestyle reformation. The provision of a doctor-supervised, medically-prescribed, health coach-guided, health club-facilitated, 12 step-like group-supported program will continue to be necessary as patients become progressively accustomed to a healthier lifestyle. Over time patients will become progressively stronger and more capable of stabilized independent healthy function.

Through the universal law of cause and effect, a healthy lifestyle produces health and vitality. Continued compliance with health-generating behavior results in ever-deepening physical fortitude, resilience to disease, vitality, and gratitude. With gratitude comes a shifting of attitude, and then a shifting of priorities, and, finally, a gradual habituation of the health-promoting lifestyle.

The Lifestyle Transformation Center staff will work very hard at bringing patients to an awareness of the many ways in which they have fought against their own stated self interests.

Though familiar and very comfortable, unhealthy perspectives, attitudes, and habits usher in chronic disease.

Left to our own devices and the comfort and predictability of familiar ways, the question arises: why would anyone "raise the warm blanket" of familiar habits to let in the cold draft of clearer thinking, wiser choices, and healthier habits *even if* those changes promised to produce a better quality of life?

Well, Lifestyle Transformation Centers are here to help you to "wake up" from the slumber of a comfortable rate of decay, from which point you will *want to* "pull back the covers" and enter into a life of greater vibrancy. This happens by degree—here a little, there a little—until, over time, patients become stable, strong, and capable of the efforts and progressive rewards of responsible and healthy living.

Respectfully yours,

____

The objective of the Effective Medical Approach is to prevent the costs of chronic disease by focusing on promoting health and wellness.

This is accomplished by teaching, facilitating, and supporting the behaviors that consistently produce chronic health in the clients at greatest risk. This involves proactively immersing the highest risk population in an expertly supervised health rehabilitation program. A customized combination of exercises, activities, practices, and classes designed specifically for their needs will go a long way in forming a solid foundation for the restoration of health and reversal of chronic disease.

The emphasis of all these adjuncts is to gradually adjust the disease-attracting mindset. It needs to be transformed from "It's the medical system's responsibility for my healthy outcome" to "It's my personal responsibility for my healthy outcome." By gradual progression, from primary dependency upon doctor visits and drug regimens, to primary dependency upon healthy living coupled with the positively-reinforcing and addictive pleasure of improving health, I believe we can affect permanent change in a patient's mindset and health behaviors. These in turn lead to permanent improvements in a patient's health outcome. The aggregate of changes from all Lifestyle Transformation Program patients who are successfully rehabilitated results in dramatic and permanent reductions in healthcare costs.

Patients need a healthful program that gently strengthens them and increases their endurance—that rebuilds their flexibility, independence, confidence, and self-esteem. I propose that if you provide a program that is enjoyable, refreshing, supportive, interactive, invigorating, vitalizing, and detoxifying, then most patients will grow to love the daily exposure to what makes them well as much or even more than the sweet delicacies of mindless TV, easy reading, salty and fatty foods, non-exertion, non-productivity, and general retreat from healthy and vibrant living.

Most self-help books can be distilled down to a few simple principles:

- Do what you know to do.
- Prioritize goals, carve out opportunity for successful completion of them, and reduce distractions.
- Surround yourself with supportive peers and coaches.
- Identify major obstacles and develop specific strategies for overcoming them.

The Lifestyle Transformation Program goes beyond information and provides the embodiment and practice of those kinds of core principles in a complete health recovery system. The aim is not merely to provide recovery from a particular episode of illness, or intervention for a specific condition. It is a holistic lifestyle program that provides the "missing link"—a favorable environment for sustainable self-healing, self-recovery, and emancipation from the habits that can drown any of us at our own bidding. The chronically ill are particularly numb and disconnected from their own implicit culpability. Oh, that they could say with dawning realization, "I have seen the enemy and it is me."

Envision with me the hospital/institute/center of the future: Lifestyle Transformation Programs with lifestyle transition facilities, health consultants/coaches, and a support network—a positive, patient-centered, health-focused environment for students of their body—not victims of misfortune. They enter this place to become the health they want to experience in the world. They are admitted as "students" (who see themselves as agents of their own health status) and here they are taught, begin to practice, and come to understand that the *cost* of living healthfully is far less than the *consequence* of progressive decline and frequent re-hospitalizations.

The new Effective Medical Approach model of medical intervention works because it addresses causes; it does not cash in on symptoms.

The Effective Medical Approach seeks to:

- Identify health-degenerating behaviors.
- Introduce optimally healthy behaviors.
- Generate incentives and enthusiasm to engage in behaviors that are truly health-regenerating and vitality-restoring.

Please understand that the Lifestyle Transformation Program is not merely establishing a natural way to treat chronic illness versus a chemical method. It is, rather, a school of correction that teaches people how to stop attracting disease through unhealthy habits and attitudes, and to start attracting health. Its goal is also not to merely demonstrate a better way to treat the consequences of poor lifestyle, but rather to break the lifestyle habits that brought about those consequences in the first place.

Please consider that the proposed program is not attempting to heal chronic disease with natural healing modalities versus chemical healing modalities. The emphasis of the program is to implement and habituate such healthy patterns of living as to get people addicted to a physical condition that is in need of *no medical treatment*. That is what *prevention* is about—to create physical systems that no longer require ongoing *intervention*. The goal of the program is to generate a return to such richly renewed vitality that patients need neither natural nor chemical interventions; they are simply healthy.

The Effective Medical Approach is research-based and research-driven.

Numerous studies have already been conducted which demonstrate the superior effects of a "diet and exercise" approach to health over a "chemical and surgical" approach. Those studies are identified elsewhere in this book. I appeal for continued unbiased, impartial, publicly-funded medical research into the effect of comprehensive health and wellness lifestyle programs that treat the whole person.

I advocate for publicly-funded medical research designed to benefit people rather than corporations. I propose using public funds for medical research aimed at optimizing human recovery as an alternative to corporately-funded research aimed at maximizing the profits derived from the ongoing treatment of preventable conditions. I advocate focusing on not-for-profit medical research aimed at measuring the cost/benefit analysis of immersing patients who are "at risk" for imminent decline in practices and programs that offer optimal health-restoring regimens. Some of those studies will analyze and confirm the body's specific recovery mechanisms that are stimulated by adopting a progressively healthier lifestyle. Other studies will, over time, articulate the best or easiest means of supporting, encouraging, and facilitating the difficult journey from a lifestyle that is self-defeating to one that is self-empowering. Other studies will examine how best to maintain health gains and sustain the healthy lifestyle responsible for improved health status. All of these studies are examining various aspects of the natural reality being played out in every human body: "The healthy are as the healthy do."

I am convinced that a lifestyle modification focused on diet, exercise, behavior, and environment will prove the most effective and economical approach to chronic disease management known to man. I appeal for continued medical research to be conducted with complete objectivity by scientists with integrity, over a fair test period, and with a specific test population of frequently re-hospitalized chronically ill patients.

There is already extensive, repeated historical evidence from countless thousands of former seriously chronically ill patients demonstrating the health-altering effects of lifestyle modification. I have no doubt that reliable research will continue to validate those same findings, plus point to the specifics of why and how such behavior modifications work.

> **If this preventive theory that I am presenting gets fair medical investigation and proves to be superior, then naturally we should move this superior medical treatment model into mainstream medical protocols as a best practice in dealing with chronic disease, both for control and prevention.**

I contend that we should have medically prescribed lifestyle management, medical fitness/wellness centers, and medically prescribed fitness lifestyles as the gold standard of effective chronic disease management.

HOW THE TWO COMPETING APPROACHES TO HEALTHCARE COMPARE AND CONTRAST, AND IMPLICATIONS FOR NATIONAL HEALTHCARE POLICY.

The American Medical Approach promotes a culture of dependency upon the fix-it man, whose shop (hospital) repairs victims of disease. There, patients are taught passivity and dependence on others for solutions to what their bodies are "doing to them."

However, the proposed Effective Medical Approach promotes a culture of responsibility through Lifestyle Transformation Programs and Centers—schools of lifestyle correction, where students learn how to take responsibility for their health. They are trained in the tools needed to change and sustain transformational lifestyle outcomes, which promote superior results of self-nurturing, self-sustaining, and independent living.

These two conflicting approaches cannot abide under one roof forever. "And if a house be divided against itself, that house cannot stand." Mark 3:25, King James Version, Bible

Neither can a person nor a political system serve two masters. "No one can serve two masters. Either you will hate the one and love the other, or you will be devoted to the one and despise the other. You cannot serve both God and money."[52] Matthew 6:24, New International Version, Bible

The American Medical Approach and the Effective Medical Approach are utterly different from one another in their assumptions, operating systems, and cultures, and in the lifestyles they promote. One emphasizes powerlessness against illness, the other personal responsibility for wellness. One causes dependence on prescription drugs that mask symptoms while maintaining chronic disease, the other depends upon personal behaviors that self-correct and restore physical systems and sustain health.

The chart on the next page summarizes core differences in these two vastly different approaches to health philosophies, and their implications for policies.

Comparison of Two Approaches to Health		
Issues/ Responses	**American Medical Approach**	**Effective Medical Approach**
Presenting Problem	Non Health-Promoting Lifestyle	Non Health-Promoting Lifestyle
Overall Cause	Lifestyle Induced Self-Determinants for Progressive Decline	Lifestyle Induced Self-Determinants for Progressive Decline
Immediate Medical/ Health Responses	Crisis Intervention: Drugs imposed to counter the symptoms (*effects* upon compromised organs/ systems) resulting from many behavioral and modifiable causes	Crisis Intervention + Root Cause Analysis: Whole person assessment. Assessment includes: diet, hydration, stress, habits, hobbies, priorities, exercise, employment, amount of free time and the ways free time is spent, amount of income and the way money is spent, and beliefs and attitudes about health/fitness/wellness.

Graph continues on the next page...

Comparison of Two Approaches to Health		
Issues/ Responses	American Medical Approach	Effective Medical Approach
Phased Medical/ Health Responses	**Phase 1:** Stabilization of Patient. **Phase 2:** Verbal and written instruction given. Ordering of chemicals to be taken (prescriptions) and behaviors to modify lightly addressed. **Phase 3:** Damage control: Weak efforts to monitor and limit ADRs (Adverse Drug Reactions) These studies estimate that 6.7% of hospitalized patients have a serious adverse drug reaction with a fatality rate of 0.32%.[1]	**Phase 1:** Stabilization of Patient. **Phase 2:** Immersion in optimized behavioral and nutritional regimen. **Phase 3:** Link patient with resources in his/her own community that can support continuing ADRs (Activities of Daily Rejuvenation). "Practices" of health and wellbeing are doctor-prescribed, health coach-administered, insurance-funded, attendance-monitored, 12-step group-supported, and invited daily.
Outcomes for Patient	Patient returns home without any behavioral changes, and so resumes the habits and lifestyle responsible for the underlying health decline.	Introduction and initial immersion into optimal health-restoring behaviors and lifestyle provide patient a small taste of benefits to follow. Continued patient access to facilities, programs, classes, coaching, group support, and scheduled follow-ups support the ongoing, successful adaptation and adoption of a health-restoring lifestyle.

[1]*Centers for Education and Research on Therapeutics*
http://jamanetwork.com/journals/jama/article-abstract/187436

Information from the Centers for Education and Research on Therapeutics makes the following statement in regards to why we should learn about Adverse Drug Reactions (ADR). ADRs are one of the leading causes of morbidity and mortality in health care.

Facts About ADRs (Adverse Drug Reactions):

- Over two million serious ADRs yearly
- Over 100,000 deaths yearly
- ADRs are the fourth leading cause of death. This is more than pulmonary disease, diabetes, AIDS, pneumonia, accidents, and automobile-related deaths.
- Ambulatory patients [those able to walk] ADR rate is unknown.
- On average, a total of 350,000 ADRs are experienced by nursing home patients each year.[53]

Studies estimate that 6.7% of hospitalized patients have a serious adverse drug reaction with a fatality rate of 0.32%.[1] If these estimates are correct, then there are more than 2,216,000 serious ADRs in hospitalized patients, causing over 106,000 deaths annually.[54]

Costs Associated With ADRs:

- $136 billion each year on average.
- Greater than total costs of cardiovascular or diabetic care.
- ADRs cause 1 out of 5 injuries or deaths each year to patients in hospital stays.
- Average length of stay, cost, and mortality for ADR patients are double that for control patients.
- Methodological constraints limit making completely accurate estimates, but these numbers are compelling and should be very alarming.[55]

Principles and Incentives of Effective Medical Care:

- Medical contracts should be awarded to health and wellness organizations that effectively reverse and prevent disease. An ounce of prevention, even handsomely rewarded, still costs far less than the pounds of cure we are currently paying for.
- By building and fortifying health-promoting habits, at-risk patients become competent self-managers of their own wellness. Thus, they become consistently less costly than patients relying on the current system's model of "treatment of decline till more

treatment is necessary."

- Unless financial incentives are created which make "disease prevention through fitness promotion" financially attractive, the medical systems that feed off (profit from) disease will continue without checks and balances. Disease will continue to expand as the continual drip of the continually ill is milked, that is, harvested for conventional medicine's profit.

[1]*Centers for Education and Research on Therapeutics*
http://jamanetwork.com/journals/jama/article-abstract/187436

Chapter 5.
Solution Two—
(Living Beyond the Affliction Zone)

Problem Two mostly focuses on "prescriptive practices" for preventing illness by promoting wellness. It examines human nature's propensity toward sweetness and ease and its subsequent attraction of chronic disease as well as modern medicine's complicit "business with disease." This leads to personal practices for optimizing health and wellness which are detailed in the section titled *Solution Two—Living Beyond the Affliction Zone.*

HOPE PROVIDES A POWERFUL INCENTIVE TO CHANGE OUR BEHAVIOR TOWARD SUSTAINABLE HEALTH AND WELLNESS.

I want to regain my pluck. I refuse to resign my health for other priorities; I am the product of my own doing, and I will love myself back into tighter fitness.

This very day I am taking my mountain bike to the shop to have a broken crank arm replaced. I haven't ridden my mountain bike in well over a year. But something happened yesterday that is changing all of that. You see, yesterday I went with a beloved friend on a fairly long hike out in the beautiful green rolling hills of a nearby park. We were hiking through a lush green canyon beneath a canopy of tall oak and conifer, with lovely ferns growing all around.

Into this peaceful embrace with nature, we were startled by the rapid approach of what sounded like the rushing of many waters. We whirled around to see two mountain bikers who were peeling off a nearby fire road and onto our single track hiking trail. We jumped out of the way while they slowed down sufficiently to respect our sanity. After passing us, they rapidly gained speed and without hesitation went careening down a section of trail so steep we could barely walk down it without sliding out of control—a trail perched on the edge of a steep drop into a rocky creek bed.

Within a few seconds they had disappeared and all was peaceful again. But something had changed for me because of them. They had traversed this steep and narrow trail like Jedi Knights on flying brooms, in just seconds, and this inevitably rekindled in me a memory of my earlier mountain biking days, and the adrenaline rushes on magical brooms of my own. Here I am a day later, with this inspiration, and I have now pulled out my mountain bike and am taking it to the bike shop to get it fixed so that I can continue to get my "fix" off life—off *real* life. Off a wholesome, full, healthy life: off *the type of life* that heals the heart and soul.

If you are reading this and you are not healthy, not leading a life that is truly good for you, what kinds of Jedi memories reside in your heart? What activities from a healthier time and space for you brought a sense of vitality and verve, of love for life? If you could find your way back to those things—by gradual but industrious action, not immediate magical thinking—would you?

I sincerely hope you can open your ears that you may hear, and open your eyes that you may see, and open your heart that you may dream again. Consider discarding what holds you fast and keeps you from entering into healthier disciplines that will yield for you far greater satisfaction. Consider giving up the petty appetites, habits, and indulgences that are holding you fast, stuck in a rut and which prevent you from healthier disciplines that will yield to you far greater pleasures and much deeper joys.

Does it seem impossible? *There is hope—a higher horizon exists beyond the one you now see.* Others have gone before you. There is a path, a way, a set of habits, a lifestyle that following hard after will bring you to a state of greatly-improved health. There are countless examples of people beating chronic disease and completely retarding its negative effects. These individuals have taken personal responsibility to rise to the occasion, do the research, and take the initiative. Then, they applied themselves diligently until they moved themselves to a place of healthier existence.

From the perspective of a health coach, this takes place when a person accepts responsibility for their dilapidated state, and then commits to the discipline of working diligently and intelligently to cleanse, refine, fortify, and strengthen the operation and performance of that physiological system. This can work effectively, whether we're talking about the cardiovascular, digestive, eliminative, immune, metabolic, musculoskeletal, neurological, and/or respiratory system.

Once chronically ill people bring every aspect of their behavior and internal and external environment into harmonious and synergistic compliance with the principles of sound robust health, then—"miraculously"—they drop their former vestments, attachments, and identification with chronic disease.

What is amazing about these examples is the personal resolve and fortitude, the ingenuity and tenacity these people applied to rise above what "modern" medicine had to offer. They actually found a solution that was profitable to themselves, not merely to the procurators of the established medical system. At their first diagnosis and first set of drugs, these rare individuals looked around at the other "chickens in the coop," and, considering their condition and historic outcomes, said, "Hey! It's definitely time to fly *this* chicken coop."

> **But it's a rare bird indeed who can rise to this degree of intelligence, insight, and chutzpah *unassisted.* Most people need help to move toward their hopeful horizon beyond the affliction zone.**

I am making an appeal that we put forth a hearty effort to open blind eyes and set captives free. Most conventionally treated patients end up with very bleak outcomes. It behooves patients who receive a diagnosis to do everything in their power to beat the odds. It behooves them to find out who is not simply *surviving* their diagnosis but who is *overcoming* their diagnosis.

The average car mechanic in town will not advise you to take your car to the best mechanic in town. No, he'll say, "Give me your keys, sign right here, and we'll call you with an estimate." Just as a lot of people don't trust mechanics for a good reason, patients should not assume the medical advice they receive is the best available. There are a lot of medical conditions for which the majority of patients do *not* do very well. And it's not because healthy solutions can't be found, but because healthy solutions are less profitable for the usual advisors and so, therefore, are never advised.

You owe it to yourself to obtain the healthiest physical outcomes you can from any serious conditions in which you find yourself. Some people can and do fully recover from many full-blown, serious medical conditions by using standard advice from the American medical-pharmaceutical machine, but statistically it's rare. You and your family need to search diligently for the wisest advice and most effective treatments if you hope to rise above the dismal outcomes of most patients. I'm just trying to provide a sober picture of the odds you are up against. A majority of patients coming into the medical system and receiving a diagnosis of diabetes, high blood pressure, congestive heart failure, or any one of numerous other chronic conditions fair very poorly by their 5th, 10th and 15th year of treatment.

I don't say this to scare you; I say it to prompt you to rise well above the conventional medical advice to "Take your pills as ordered and call me when conditions worsen." I say this to help you see the importance of rising to the challenge. Your health and wellness are largely in your own hands—they always have been and always will be. The medical staff is there to earn a living that comes from treating those who are ill and providing them with their products and services. As I said, their continuing services are dependent upon your continuing illness. Health and wellness are what "some other vendor" is selling. To get well, you truly do need to go to a *different* kind of vendor.

These other vendors are "Health and Wellness" vendors. Their business deals with your recovery, and they will have a lot more to say about the underlying causes (that is, the lifestyle factors) that lead to physical decline and chronic disease. They will also be far more forthcoming with information about specific modifications of lifestyle and behavior (diet, exercise, massage, stress reduction, and other means and resources) for restoring you back to wellness. They will also be motivated to support your transition from less healthy ways to progressively healthier ways, because they have a business with your recovery—that is, a financially vested interest in your getting well. We don't hear that kind of thing from members of the medical establishment.

The doctors usually don't say, "Yes, Mr. or Mrs. Johnson, you have this condition, and the vast majority of patients receiving this diagnosis and following our advice and prescriptions fair very poorly and end up having their legs amputated; first the toes, then the leg. This usually takes place within 8 to 15 years of diagnosis. That's just the beginning of the hell that is to become your life. Shall I continue, or would you like to put in for a treatment order now?

"This condition has a very high probability of generating progressively deteriorating health and declining quality of life for you. Furthermore, the poor quality of life that goes with this condition is in most cases completely avoidable, if you were to dramatically change the lifestyle that brought you here. The short and skinny of it all is that your future health is largely in your own hands. Many, many conditions are largely reversible through lifestyle changes, but we the medical system do not proactively support, prescribe, or provide the resources to enable those changes, because we make more money off your continuing illness.

"And I must say, most people with your condition *do continue* in the same self-defeating lifestyle that brought them here. As a result, they continue into deeper and deeper levels of pain and disability. This is a personal tragedy and especially sad because it is so readily avoidable. However, we are not keen to support your lifestyle modification because a health-preserving lifestyle would cut too deeply into our profits. And, without a group of committed professionals and health facilities to support you in this difficult transformation, your chances of success are miniscule. But I'm sorry, I've digressed. How many treatment plans leading to a dismal quality of life would you like to order today? You have the right to discontinue your treatment plan and embrace the lifestyle modification necessary to secure a happy wholesome life, but we don't really encourage it. It's easier to just take your pills like a good patient and try to hit the ground running along your chosen course of ever-deepening, self-determined physical demise."

The above dialogue is the haunting reality that so often takes place in the lives of our patients, because the reality of corporate evil is not exposed.

I would advise you to be wise and sober-minded. Live compliant to and consistent with the highest behaviors of health you can attain. Be steadfast and vigilant because, statistically speaking, very few ever escape chronic disease to see health again unless they actively change directions.

Make no mistake: people have to take responsibility for their own health. The captives must choose to leave behind the dungeon of behavioral patterns that promote their own decline. However, we as a transformed medical system could serve mankind by giving them support, guides, and tools—things they cannot succeed without—and thus dramatically assist their rise back up into the light, back into the solid wealth of robust wholeness. The only hope for our patients is to make this transition of lifestyle (which is responsible for chronic health) as palatable as possible, and to support that difficult transition until the healthy patterns are habitual and outweigh the benefits of the behaviors and habits that brought them chronic disrepair.

The effects of being healthy will, over time, permeate your whole being and saturate you with enthusiasm. As the old proverb says, "Hope fulfilled is a tree of life." And as the wealth of health replaces the pill of the ill, rejoicing in regeneration becomes one's rule.

The ill can become well
by their own behavioral hand;
nature faithfully complies
with the obedience of the wise.

But the primary benefits of being healthy can permeate your whole being with renewed vitality and confidence, and your hopes can center more on the exquisiteness of life rather than merely the postponement of death. It holds such benefits as:

- Bending over and putting on your own socks.
- Actually getting off the couch and getting food out of the refrigerator for yourself instead of constantly depending upon others.
- Shopping without requiring major and taxing effort.
- Sensing once again that your strengths and capabilities are expanding instead of retreating.

> **As increasing strength and independence replaces the burdens of chronic disease, your identity percolates with the enthusiasm of overcoming previous limitations. You begin to see yourself as a victor rather than a victim. A string of victories replaces your prior history of progressive disability. Overcoming the walls of your prior prison becomes your daily business. As this grows, you become convinced of and committed to a whole new paradigm of behaviors, values, and pleasures. You are onto a whole new paradigm of right thinking for robust health.**

The old paradigm of identity was one of being a victim. The old paradigm of pleasures came from receiving sympathy and from being *relieved* of responsibility to manage oneself, or to make a contribution, or to bear responsibilities, or to form and follow a path to personal health, or of being expected to be a happy person. Those "pleasures" are replaced by a new paradigm of pleasures that come from embracing personal responsibility, enjoying the rewards of engineering a worthwhile existence, conducting oneself toward a happy state, and choosing to actively participate in the unfolding mystery of the universe.

If you *are not* swimming upstream in a concerted effort to keep your body and soul vibrantly alive, *you are* simply keeping your head above water in a slow but steady downstream current of physical decay. It takes self-discipline and enduring personal resolve to refrain from our natural preference for ease and immediate gratification.

The mountain is high
The valley is low
Where you end up
Depends on ...
Which way you go.

It is so much more comfortable to follow a well-ingrained pattern of coasting into hell rather than climbing a stairway to heaven. However, this thought is too self-implicating to endure for long. So, instead of admitting our aversion to effort and self-improving behavior, we plot a course of pleasant distractions and mindless entertainments that do not satisfy, nourish, or refresh our body, mind, or soul. The road to poor health is paved with pleasurable inventions. We intuitively realize that the path of health restoration will require effort and change, and we would rather continue along well-trod paths of self-degeneration.

Where is one to find the perspective and inspiration to heartily embrace the harder course of the self-restorative behaviors that heal the body and deeply enrich the soul? The principal focus of successful lifestyle transformation programs is imparting the knowledge, understanding, perspective, and inspiration people need to overcome their stubborn resistance to healthy disciplines and behaviors.

"Motivation is when your dreams put on work clothes. Commitment is doing the things you said you'd do, long after the mood you said it in has left you."
- Anonymous

There is no getting around it: Getting well is hard work. Getting chronically ill is often the result of maintaining well-ingrained, but poorly thought-out habits that are so deeply entrenched as to make any other behavior feel foreign and inconvenient. If the behavioral path that you have been trudging daily has led you into miry bogs of physical misfortune, you need to ask yourself the following questions:

1] It is easy to remain on this well-worn, comfortable path of physical decline, but it results in an increasing separation from a healthy life and imposes upon me increasing levels of pain and loss of independence. Is the ease of the path worth it?

2] I am capable of changing my physical outcome from one of declining health to one of improving health, but am I willing to do the serious self-reflection and hard work necessary to regain a healthy and powerful existence?

3] Am I willing to embrace the difficult work of critical and honest self-assessment, and to identify the areas of my life that are inconsistent with healthy physical outcomes?

4] Am I willing to embrace the considerable challenge of holding myself accountable to reducing those self-defeating behaviors of illness, and replacing them with self-disciplined behaviors of health?

We should not expect chemicals to replace a healthy lifestyle. We should *get real* with life and play the real game according to the authentic rules. We are a part of nature, and nature is not a respecter of persons. Healthy outcomes are the result of healthy causes. Nature cannot be fooled. If you want to experience freedom from the pain and foibles of chronic disease, you must meet life authentically and start behaving in a way that will generate health. Healthy stimuli produce healthy effects; unhealthy stimuli produce unhealthy effects.

I have a message for those who have ears that can hear it. This message is from the spirit deep within, and says that we must turn from ways that are not prosperous, and return to the source of self-renewal and healing.

We need to examine ourselves thoroughly and be honest with how our goals, priorities, and behaviors have been in conflict with our own health. We must embrace ourselves with love and respect, but also be mature enough to acknowledge our errors and learn the lessons of better self-care. We must resolve to bring ourselves back to the optimal footing of wise and responsible thoughts and behaviors, which are alone consistent with regaining optimal health.

"To the writing of books there is no end," said King Solomon. Self-help books rarely do more than reinforce a person's pre-existing thoughts, opinions, inclinations, and conclusions. Hence the person who is inclined to healthy aspirations reads books about healthy aspirations, while those not inclined to healthy aspirations read the buttons on their remote, and push dem buttons so they can stay as remote and free as possible of the noisome thoughts and responsibilities of healthy living. The healthy remain adverse to the lifestyle of the chronically unhealthy, lest they suffer a similar outcome. The chronically ill remain adverse to the lifestyle of the chronically healthy, lest they suffer a similar fate of daily exercise, healthy diet and responsible living. Rarely do the twain meet. The healthy remain chronically free of hospital incarceration, dark stuffy rooms, medical clinics, and pharmacies; and the chronically ill remain free of going to health clubs, getting out and walking in the hills and sunshine, and being productive around the house.

The Health-Disease Continuum is not just a battle for our bodies: it's a battle for our heart, mind, and will. What will we do? Where will we turn for help? To which authority will we listen? Upon what system, approach, or products will we rely? And the battle is not only to the weakened, but also to those striving to remain well. How do we thrive despite life stressors and advancing age? How do we find our spark and fan it into flame?

Youth

Youth is not a time of life; it is a state of mind; it is not a matter of rosy cheeks, red lips and supple knees; it is a matter of the will, a quality of the imagination, a vigor of the emotions; it is the freshness of the deep springs of life.

Youth means a temperamental predominance of courage over timidity of the appetite, for adventure over the love of ease. This often exists in a man of sixty more than a boy of twenty. Nobody grows old merely by a number of years. We grow old by deserting our ideals.

Years may wrinkle the skin, but to give up enthusiasm wrinkles the soul. Worry, fear, self-distrust bows the heart and turns the spirit back to dust.

Whether sixty or sixteen, there is in every human being's heart the lure of wonder, the unfailing child-like appetite of what's next, and the joy of the game of living. In the center of your heart and my heart there is a wireless station; so long as it receives messages of beauty, hope, cheer, courage and power from men and from the infinite, so long are you young.

When the aerials are down, and your spirit is covered with snows of cynicism and the ice of pessimism, then you are grown old, even at twenty, but as long as your aerials are up, to catch the waves of optimism, there is hope you may die young at eighty.

- Samuel Ullman, 19th century poet, Alabama, Ullman Museum

What shall we do to remain inspired? What shall sustain us in the face of life's daunting circumstances? Ideally, we would spend our energy in self-healing ways. We would spend our energy loving God, loving self, and loving neighbor. We would spend our energy in ways that promote health of mind, body, and soul.

However, realistically, people who are living out of compliance with the above principles lose the blessings of such behaviors, and instead fall vulnerable to all manner of afflictions. A person immersed in positive thoughts, proper diet, plenty of exercise, healthy self-expression, and meaningful endeavors rarely gets sick in body, mind, or soul. They are living above the affliction zone by loving God, loving self, and loving neighbor. They are living out meaningful and healthy self-expression. These wise people remain relatively affliction-free.

A healthy lifestyle and thought style is the only safe harbor from chronic disease. Any other port will suffer the ravaging storms of being incongruent with reality. Consider this image: Being born is like emerging from beneath the earth's crust and pushing upward into very high elevations where the trade winds blow. Anything in one's life that is incongruent with pure, accurate, healthy living will be given up voluntarily and replaced with solid healthy behavior—or else it will be ripped from one's grip by the universal trade winds affecting reality.

Being born is not a choice, but how you behave is. Our being pushed up into the trade winds is not a choice, but choosing impeccably healthy behavior that can stand up to the ferocious trade winds is a healthy and advisable option. You, of course, have free will and do not have to live congruently with these laws of the universe. But if you choose to live incongruently, you should also be prepared to be torn apart by the fiercely ravaging effects of striving against the winds.

Here's another illustration: Life is like an airstream and our lives are like jets traveling in that airstream. The speed reached by the jets (that is, our lives) is not a choice; what is a choice is the jet's characteristics and flight pattern. Whatever conflicts with an efficient "flow" in the airstream of life will be torn off by the fierce winds of life's speed. You could open up a window and stick out a hand (and many people do—behaviorally speaking), but you should be prepared to have your entire body sucked out the window and to plummet headlong along the chosen course of decline brought about by such choices.

The human body is composed of the elements of the earth. We can thus conclude that the things closest to nature are almost always the healthiest choices for our well-being. Walks in nature are superior to virtual walking in video games. Raw apples are healthier than cellophane-wrapped apple pie snacks saturated with enough preservatives to maintain a two-month shelf life without refrigeration. Cooking a fresh filet from a fish with eyes, fins, and skin is healthier than microwaving prepackaged fish "meat mush" that is first saturated with salts, preservatives, additives, flavorings, colorings, and texture-modifying agents; then it is stamped into a fish burger, then breaded, cooked, frozen, packaged, and shipped. The less we manipulate, process, refine, preserve, substitute, and replace what nature has provided for us, the healthier it is. Our return to nature is restorative;

our aversion to nature is deleterious.

I believe chronic disease does not forcefully invade our lives. It simply comes in and occupies the territory where healthful living, healthful habits, and healthy stress management have been surrendered. Healthy living is our conscious tool to keep chronic disease at bay.

By consciously reengaging in healthy behavioral habits we can, by degrees, regain control of our health outcomes. Whenever I have been less healthy in my life, I would ask myself, *What is going on?* Upon reflection, I usually realized I had allowed my priorities to be shifted to less healthy aspirations. Unhealthiness simply entered into the healthy areas of my life that I had allowed to go to sleep. I'd lost touch with the healthier, freer loves of my youth, and became overly preoccupied with my work, and with family responsibilities. While I fulfilled those responsibilities and received their rewards, I'd also lost the health afforded me by my "first loves." Specifically, I'd neglected my personal responsibilities to my own health, creativity, self-expression, and love for nature and athletic expression. As a result, I lost their rewards, namely my physical health, my deeply centered peace of mind, and my firm footing on the spiritual bedrock of my soul.

When I came back to my senses and began living more consciously attuned to my highest, healthiest priorities, my behavior followed suit. And lo and behold—my health began to improve (gradually, but noticeably) from that day. Nothing unhealthy invaded me. Unhealthiness simply came in and claimed the territory I had let go.

I encourage you to follow me in regaining the first loves of our lives. Remember when you used to love things because they made your soul take flight? Now try to remember what you are drawn to for its own intrinsic value. These are the whispers of wisdom calling to you to pursue your needs for personal enrichment, improved health, and vim and vigor in your life. These relate to your sense of spiritual freedom. Return to a healthy love of self. Return to what gives you life. Pursue deeply meaningful relationships and settled moments of inner satisfaction derived from the activities you find most enriching. Meditate on God however you conceive Him to be and search for the Truth, for it is the Truth that will set you free.

Let me give you an example of the above concept. A man with his priorities straight places significant importance upon his health. He takes good care of himself and by way of example leads his family in similar life-affirming behavior. The man loves his wife and children and spends time with them in ways that nourish, cherish, and honor their significance in his life. This leads to open, warm, life-affirming relationships. It also teaches children to love their parents and follow wholesome ways (along with the usual adolescent mischief and exploration). This leads to family unity and the health of the family—both as a unit and as individuals.

> **There is a legitimate balancing act that is a core part of responsible living: we need to emphasize some things in order to ensure that we get built up. Other things we need to emphasize in order to ensure that we do not get broken down. And other things we need to let go of because they served their purpose in their season but that season has passed.**

All together, these elements and seasons of life create a principle of a "revolving focus" or "circle of focus." Our circle of focus in turn catalyzes a circle of attraction, which draws its objectives to us. When we apply this power of attraction to the movement of our life, we begin to see, over time, repeating patterns or a *spiral* of attraction. Our lives over time are either spiraling upward toward greater health and liberation, or spiraling downward into a vortex of declining health and increasing limitation.

Last weekend I competed in a half ironman triathlon competition. After the event I reflected on my training schedule that led up to the race. The last two weeks involved a reduced training "load" (called tapering) in order to fully recover from the fatigue of consistent training and to "peak"—be at my best—for the event. I was also engaged in fine-tuning my bike, making travel arrangements, preparing my head for the race and all the while reflecting on my recent life experiences and the training and preparation leading up to my present moment, and all this inspired me further. I became even more confident and excited about training for the next race after this race was run. These thoughts permeated my world …

One week later I find myself again reflecting, but this time it's upon my last week of work *after* the race. I find my heart tugged in a completely different direction. I find myself tugged and polarized towards excelling at my work skills and competency. I am impressed with training strategies for improved competency in my work.

These two goals and their associated mindsets tug me in different directions. When my heart aspires toward work/career success, I emphasize one set of goals and behaviors. When my heart aspires toward athletic success, I emphasize an entirely different set of goals and behaviors.

I find myself shifting among a set of revolving priorities. Shifting priorities result in shifting arenas—some of growth and others of atrophy. One blossoms in its season of focus, while others are to some extent shelved and thus atrophy, until I again shift priorities.

My point here is that, underneath all this swirl of shifting priorities, there is what I call the "principle of attraction." Given one focus, I attract its fulfillment to myself. With a change of focus, I attract a different type of fruit.

In this life the only thing we are guaranteed is that we will die.

Almost everything else we experience, especially as adults, is a direct result of what we intentionally focus upon and thus attract to ourselves. It is in this way that we create ourselves every day. A person can, through their focus, attract to themselves the ability and resources necessary to rise like a phoenix out of severe personal tragedies, handicaps, trauma, and socioeconomic limitations—if (and it's a big if) they can clearly identify and hold on to a healthy focus. By the same token, a person who is born with opportunity, wealth, privilege, talent, intelligence, and good fortune can blow it all away very quickly by simply applying this principle of attraction to an unhealthy focus.

We attract what we focus upon, and we reap what we have attracted. If we wish to reap differently from what we have reaped in the past, we must attract differently than we have attracted in the past. We have no choice in whether or not we reap what we attract; that is simply cause and effect. However, we do have tremendous choice over what we choose to focus upon and thus attract unto ourselves.

Look at your current condition, circumstances, and reality: What you behold is a perfect reflection of what you have attracted to yourself. Don't raise the silly objection about external forces beyond personal control—of course there are external forces that are very real. People in the Twin Towers in New York on 9/11/01 did not "attract" that harm unto themselves. I'm not talking about macro-realities truly beyond our ability to control; I'm talking about micro-realities that are very much within our ability to control.

If you find your life is hell, consider changing residence.

Whether we realize it or not, we are largely the product of our own creation, and we inevitably lie in the beds of our own making. If we are not happy with our lot in life, the ability to change it depends largely upon our ability to change our focus. To change our "lot in life," we need to change *a lot* in the "life" of our focus.

When we emphasize things other than our health, we attract things other than our health. These other things may be good things, but they are other things nonetheless; and if we do not circle back around to emphasize our health frequently enough, we will lose its presence in our life.

Most people who become chronically ill have chronically focused on things other than *their health*, and by and by *it* left and what replaced it has come to bite them in the ass. This can be considered an addiction to an imbalanced and unhealthy set of life priorities. Patterns often repeated and well-worn become grooves; grooves are hard to get out of and become habits; habits settle in and become even more deeply conditioned; and deeply conditioned habits *that produce negative consequences* are considered addictions.

I am proposing that the "lifestyle of self-detriment" or "lifestyle of diminishing returns" that the vast majority of the chronically ill are engaging in has many similarities to the lifestyles of other addicts. Thus, chronic disease, that is, "self-determined low grade health" should be added to other commonly accepted forms of addiction. Alcoholics Anonymous, Overeaters Anonymous, Spenders Anonymous, Worriers Anonymous, Hoarders Anonymous, etc. All these addictions share many similarities. All these addicts admit to compulsively engaging in behavior that is unhealthy.

The difference is that these other "addictions" have been socially recognized (and labeled) as *dysfunctional* behaviors, and as a result, those behaviors are considered to be in need of change. But chronic disease is often still viewed by many as, well, simply *unfortunate* and thus deserving of sympathy or pity. That view, however, while comforting, holds those with chronic disease in their identity as a "victim" and actually *enables* their continuing passivity.

I am proposing a paradigm shift in our society's view of (and relationship with) chronic disease. Chronic disease is not so much a matter requiring pity as it is a matter requiring repentance! That is, it is a matter of turning from behavior that is self-damaging.

The positive message is this: We have the power to change; we are not victims of chronic disease any more than alcoholics are victims of liver failure. We are not being overtaken by a noxious creeping poison; we are clinging to a toxic lifestyle. This is a huge paradigm shift in the social consciousness, perspective, and attitude toward chronic disease. I would even say it is comparable to the shift in the American attitude toward smoking. At one time it was considered "cool" to smoke. Now it's considered a publicly obnoxious pollution of the air space of healthier humans.

I'm here to tell you, the scientific evidence indicates that chronic disease is not a given—it's largely a choice. Please stay with me and hear what I have to say on this. To acknowledge a behavioral problem is the first and absolutely essential step to overcoming that problem and being healed. My goal is not to judge or place guilt on the chronically ill, but to empower and prepare them for a behavioral shift that can lead them to a healthier existence and state of mind, and to give them light and hope. It is my desire to reveal a pathway to recovery—a detour off the well-worn path of their continuing decline—and to give them a pathway back up into the light and warmth of the sun.

Nothing in life fits neatly in little boxes, and nothing is black and white. Sometimes chronic conditions absolutely defy the best of healthy lifestyle disciplines. We cannot assume that every person's chronic disease was precipitated by a lifestyle that attracted it. However, this is usually the case. Please do not be offended if you or your loved one is experiencing a chronic disease and you know darn well that they or you have maintained a very healthy lifestyle. You are the exception. My message is not to the righteous, but to those who are unwittingly defeating themselves.

> **And for those who can see and acknowledge that their chronic disease is directly linked to their past behavior—that is, their diet, exercise, thoughts, priorities, interests, habits, environment, relationships, and employment—in short, what they have attracted to themselves; I propose we create a support group called "Disease-aholics Anonymous," just like the support groups available for others who find themselves under the control of unhealthy influences and addictions.**

Why develop an addiction/anonymous group for those with chronic illnesses? Because:

1] We believe that as we remove the impediments to our own prosperity, God's powerful innate healing forces within each of us will restore health and vitality.

2] We need God (however we conceive Him to be) and His strength in order to march forward in a self-healing lifestyle—in patterns that bless rather than hinder us, and live according to a higher, more optimal lifestyle that is self-nourishing, self-enriching, self-loving, and self-healing.

3] We realize we should educate and empower ourselves by engaging in relevant, natural, non-toxic, non-poisoning forms of therapy, while simultaneously pursuing the active and healthy lifestyle that is responsible for restoring oneself to optimal health and resilience.

4] We realize we are individual members of the whole family of man. We are strengthened by gathering with like-minded persons in order to "work out" our character refinement and recovery.

5] We may or may not be able to do anything to change the length of our lives, but we can do a great deal to affect the depth and quality of them.

It is to the quality of our lives
that we commit the quantity of our days

Or, stated personally:

It is to the quality of my life
that I commit the quantity of my days

Regardless of external circumstances over which we have no control, we still have considerable control over the course and direction of our lives. We create and habituate our silos—our circles of routine—our perceived limitations—our horizons. We are capable of becoming bigger than the shells we contain ourselves in. Become "the do" that takes you to a bigger, freer, healthier you.

"I need Thy Sense of Order
The confusion of the details of living
Is sometimes overwhelming. The little things
Keep getting in my way providing ready made
Excuses for failure to do and be
What I know I ought to do and be.
Much time is spent on things that are not very
important
While significant things are put into an
insignificant
place
In my scheme of order. I must unscramble my
affairs
So that my life will become order. O God, I need
thy sense of order."

– From *Deep Is The Hunger*
by Howard Thurman

CREED OF THE DISEASE-AHOLIC

The "Creed of the Disease-aholic" is a phrase I coined based upon my observations of the similarities between the "disease attracting" habits of the alcoholic toward self-destruction through the *commission* of many self-diminishing bad habits and the *omission* of many self-enriching good habits linked to an inordinate "love of alcohol." This closely resembles "disease-attracting" habits of the chronically ill toward self destruction through the *commission* of many self-diminishing bad habits and the *omission* of many self-enriching good habits linked to an inordinate "love of ease."

The acquisition of chronic disease is largely a matter of how you choose to treat your temple. The question is, will you "Destroy—Deplete—Neglect" your temple or will you "Preserve—Enhance—Restore" your temple. The choice is yours but the consequences are not.

Of course these are not new thoughts. Even back in Biblical times, it was understood that the body was the temple of the soul and that those who dishonored the body damaged the soul.

"Do you not know that your body is a temple of the Holy Spirit, who is in you, whom you have received from God? You are not your own; you were bought at a price. Therefore honor God with your body."
- 1 Cor. 6:19-20 New International Version; Bible

My Advice: Take care of what you love!

The Alcoholic	The Disease-Aholic
The "disease-attracting" habits and tendencies of the alcoholic toward self destruction through self abuse and self neglect, that is, the commission of bad habits and the omission of good habits, combined with an inordinate "love of alcohol," which is closely linked to an aversion to good nutrition and healthy exercise.	The "disease-attracting" habits and tendencies of the chronically ill toward self destruction through self abuse and self neglect, that is, the commission of bad habits and the omission of good habits, combined with an inordinate "love of ease," which is closely linked to an aversion to good nutrition and healthy exercise.

We think sympathetically of grandma with her ankles so puffy and the "pure shame" of her contracting Congestive Heart Failure, so much so that we cannot bring ourselves to consider that her condition is the net effect of her actions. Instead we prefer to cast judgment on grandpa because we know why his tummy is so puffy and we can see that his cirrhosis of the liver is the "just desserts" of his excessive drinking. We tell grandma that we love her and that we are wishing her well and we tell grandpa that his bad habits are destroying him and that he'd better "kick the bottle" before *he* kills himself.

The reality is they are *both* experiencing the fruits of their choices. Their poor health outcome is the net effect of their poor health choices. They both need sympathy and they both need a kick in the pants. They are both victims and they are both guilty. Nature is not capricious. She does not say, "health for this one" and "disease for that one." Nature says, "As you have done it unto one of the least of these—cells of your body—so you have done it unto me—and my reward is with me to give unto everyone according to his deeds." That is to say, that nature's code (as it is written in the human genome) is given to reward everyone according to his/her deeds.

Hard work is the *cost* of becoming fit, but alas, hard work is also the *consequence* of becoming chronically ill. For the chronically ill, *merely existing* becomes hard work. The only question remaining is, which form of hard work will you choose?

The Creed Of The Alcoholics Anonymous	The Creed Of The Disease-Aholics Anonymous
STEP 1: We admit we are powerless over (alcoholism) (other people) (a compulsive pattern)—and our lives have become unmanageable.	**STEP 1:** We admit that we are powerless over our habitually unhealthy lifestyle—that our lives and health have become unmanageable.
STEP 2: We come to believe that a Power greater than ourselves can restore us to sanity.	**STEP 2:** We come to believe that a Power greater than ourselves can restore us to a healthier, saner, more intelligent lifestyle.
STEP 3: We make a decision to turn our will and our lives over to the care of God *as we understand Him.*	**STEP 3:** We make a decision to turn our will and our lives over to the care of God *as we understand Him.*
STEP 4: We make a searching and fearless moral inventory of ourselves.	**STEP 4:** We make a searching and fearless moral inventory of the many ways we have neglected and abused our physical and spiritual temple, the body.

STEP 5: We admit to God, to ourselves, and to another human being the exact nature of our wrongs.	**STEP 5:** We admit to God, to ourselves, and to another human being the exact nature of our self-abuse and self neglect.
STEP 6: We become entirely willing to have God remove all these defects of character.	**STEP 6:** We become entirely willing to have God help us remove our patterns of self-abuse, self-neglect, and other defects of character.
STEP 7: We humbly ask God to remove our shortcomings.	**STEP 7:** We humbly ask God to remove our shortcomings.
STEP 8: We make a list of all persons we have harmed, and become willing to make amends to them all.	**STEP 8:** We make a list of all the ways we have harmed or neglected our health and imposed our poor health on others, and become willing to amend these behaviors.
STEP 9: We make direct amends to such people wherever possible, except when to do so would injure them or others.	**STEP 9:** We make direct amends to our neglected health by introducing healthy behaviors (and increasing their intensity) as our strength permits.
STEP 10: We continue to take a personal inventory, and when we are wrong, we promptly admit it.	**STEP 10:** We continue to take a personal inventory, and when we fall away from healthy behaviors, we promptly admit it.
STEP 11: We seek through prayer and meditation to improve our conscious contact with God *as we understand Him*, praying for knowledge of His will for us and the power to carry that out.	**STEP 11:** We seek through prayer and meditation to improve our conscious contact with God *as we understand Him*, praying for knowledge of His will for us, and for the power to carry that out.
STEP 12: Having had a spiritual awakening as a result of these steps, we try to carry this message to others, and to practice these principles in all of our affairs.	**STEP 12:** Having had a spiritual awakening as a result of these steps, we try to carry this message to other disease-aholics, and to practice, indeed habituate, these principles of healthy self-love.

Ease-aholics and sugar-aholics are over time becoming disease-aholics. These "holics" are destroying their health en masse. Behavioral reforms, on the other hand, reverse chronic disease and are America's greatest hope for reversing the growing epidemic of chronic disease in America.

7 PRINCIPLES OF THE 12-STEP PROGRAM

1] We are committed to searching for what works in light of all that we (the chronically ill) have created (around us and within us) that hasn't worked.

2] We see a vision of clear and just recompense for those committed to right living.

3] We resolve to do the work of restoring the health we have allowed to fall into disrepair.

4] We call upon God—"Our Higher Power"—for support. We need help to unwind the constrictive webs we've woven around ourselves.

5] We recommit ourselves to God (however we conceive Him to be)—and align ourselves with a "lifestyle formula" that is the best way for us to live.

6] We acknowledge we cannot (and should not) have to go it alone—we need each other. We need the support of others in this journey of healthy self-discovery.

7] Having realized better ways of coping with and proactively treating chronic disease than the "swallowing of chemicals," we appeal to an Effective Medical Approach. We will advocate for the "practice" of *living above the affliction zone* through dedicated health promotion.

A growing body of scientific evidence indicates the superior health benefits of specific dietary and lifestyle habits. We need to understand what these ideal elements are—healthy nutrition, activities, thoughts, behaviors, relationships and self-discovery—and how to realign ourselves with them. But what is the direction we need to go? When we lose touch with our innate gifts, meaningful passions, and worthwhile dreams, boredom and quiet desperation replace our enthusiasm and joy. This subtle shift away from activities that most deeply bless us is the subtle beginning of our self-imposed path of decline. Losing touch with the activities that give us life—that is, the "True North" of our lives—allows the opposite pole to draw us in its direction.

"If they can get you asking the wrong questions, they don't have to worry about answers."
- Thomas Pynchon

We have been mistakenly taught to view health and disease as different entities, requiring entirely different fields of investigative study and research. I suggest we consider viewing them rather as one continuum of health, ranging from least to most healthy. Utilizing this view simplifies the physiological puzzle. Chronic disease is not a *different* condition from health, but simply a *lower degree* of health. This lower degree of health is often the result of a weaker discipline of healthy living, is accompanied by the physical symptoms of poorer health, and is most effectively reversed by immersion in healthier habits.

The only solution to this lower degree of health is to rebuild the health we have destroyed or allowed to decay. But how do we do that?

We resolve to fight for our health by fighting with ourselves when necessary. We want to be compliant with our own best interests, but we find it difficult because we are predisposed to ease and convenience, comfort and pleasure.

Here's where the rubber meets the road: good intentions aren't good enough. Healthy *beliefs* without compliance to principles of healthy *behavior* leave you no less chronically ill or prematurely dead.

"Obstacles are those frightful things you see when you take your eyes off your goal."
- Henry Ford

A key to defeating chronic disease is to impart the tools and skills of self-empowerment to those whose *loss of those tools and skills* has resulted in their personally supported and accelerated entropy. *It is essential that this profound transitional process be introduced gently, be fortified by group support, and be made enjoyable.* Entropy simply cannot be reversed on a dime.

The law of entropy is that the universe tends toward disorder. The same principle applies in one's personal life. For instance, the home we live in tends toward disorder. To keep a home in order, both within and without, one needs to constantly input additional energies toward organization and reorganization. Otherwise, over time, disorder reigns. The decline into disorder is just as true for our car, our body, and our relationships; without continual input of energy, they all tend toward entropy.

Only by identifying and removing the habitual patterns that attract chronic disease can the self-defeating, self-dissipating, self-destabilizing person turn from their self-determined trajectory into the entropy of disease. They will kick and scream at first as they waver in their loyalties, but gradually they will adapt to the health-attracting lifestyle, and in this way make peace and ally themselves with the causes of health.

The concept is simple: peoples' chosen lifestyle brings them to a state of chronic disease. Imposing drugs and surgery does not change the effect of that lifestyle. Until you change a cause, you *will not* change an effect. *Remember:* you cannot change a cause by modifying its effects—you can only change an effect by modifying its cause.

People need to accept and reflect upon their responsibility for their bodies' present condition, and in that "sober sitting," gradually become motivated to stop planting and watering the causes that lead to such a harvest. Until they can accept responsibility for their actions, acknowledge the harm they do to themselves, and sit in the resulting pain, there is little stimulus for healthy change. The emphasis of this exercise is *not* to impose guilt, but to help people recognize the cause and effect in play. Only as people sit with their effect will they see the dire need for generating a new cause.

I have one point of instruction here: personal responsibility. Much of chronic disease is completely avoidable through intelligent living. Self-discipline and wise selection of lifestyle behaviors can put strong controls on chronic disease. Period. There is tremendous evidence to support this.

What is lacking for most people with chronic illness is a willingness to accept personal responsibility for their own health. Without that, how will they find the motivation and intestinal fortitude to work hard along a well-conceived, intelligent course to bring about desired improvements?

Let me use an example. Obesity is fast becoming the #1 underlying, preventable cause of premature death in America. It is also becoming the number one underlying cause of preventable disease. Out of the basic underlying *cause* of obesity comes a myriad quagmire of other earthly ailments. Ultimately, obesity-related diseases and their symptoms touch *almost every* primary body system: cardiovascular, digestive, eliminative, immune, metabolic, musculoskeletal, neurological, and respiratory systems.

Conventional medicine will step in and treat the symptoms (i.e., our broken parts), but it inevitably fails to address our being as a whole, or the behaviors and environment that precipitated the breakdown in the first place. So, modern medicine examines all the ill effects of the patient's obesity. Then, after the doctors list all the ill effects of obesity (drum roll please ...), the obese patients get their own diagnosis. But the gift doesn't stop there; they also get a list of medications to treat all the effects of their obesity. Now, I want to be respectful here, but we're walking a narrow fence between what is polite and what is expedient. Doctors *should* tell obese clients that they are overweight; and that they have done themselves a great disservice; and that it doesn't help them to blame it all on their genetics; that they need to take draconian measures to "step away from the food bowl," engage in calorie burning low impact aerobics, resistance training and a whole host of other weight reducing, energy restoring, confidence building activities.

But instead we tell them, "you have this, this, and this symptom, and we have this, this and this solution, powder and ointment and for being such a good patient you get to go home with an extra pill pack today. We have a solution for every problem you have or *even think you have* and it's our aim to serve you and your needs well.

"The first order of business in our covenant with disease-- uh, er, well, our provision of excellent medical care—is the treatment of your pain. Pain is the fifth vital sign behind blood pressure, heart rate, temperature, and respiratory rate. First thing to be treated is the pain in your knees from having such weak legs and carrying so much excess weight; then on to hypertension medications resulting from your high-fat, high-salt diet and your high-stress sedentary lifestyle; then on to the medication for your shortness of breath and to begin use of a 'positive airway pressure' device to improve your obesity-induced sleep apnea; then on to the provision of an abdominal binder to treat your obesity-induced hernia; now let's return to the increase in your pain medication for your ruptured lower disc resulting from your obesity-induced vertebral compression; now let's continue on to medication for your peripheral neuropathy resulting from the ruptured disc; and let's discuss increasing your insulin for your continuing problem with high blood sugars; and now on to medications for venous stasis (poor circulation) to the lower extremities; and a topical medication to treat the leg ulcers resulting from your venous stasis; oh, and we almost forgot to change your medication for fluid retention resulting from obesity-induced heart failure because your old 'water pill' (as well as your medication for peripheral neuropathy) have damaged your kidneys. It's a good thing I caught these lab results because they indicate, sure as shootin, that you have drug-induced kidney damage and we need to take you off your current kidney-damaging medications and put you on different kidney-damaging medications to harm your kidney (and liver) in different ways.

"And about your heart medications . . . well, they're damaging your heart . . . the mechanism of damage is complicated, it's called a drug-induced heart block . . . but, you need to take them, uh well other ones, and if those ones don't work we may need to insert a pacemaker, wo-wo-wo, wait a minute ma'am, don't tear up on me, you need to take these medications because your obese state is putting a tremendous strain on your heart. What, why weren't you told? Well, that's water under the bridge. I don't know who you would talk to about that, please now, let me continue . . . When a person becomes obese, the 'extra' body tissue needs to have blood circulated through it in order to bring oxygen to it. The body creates a vast 'extra' network of circulatory pathways running throughout the marbled halls of adipose (fat) tissue. Adipose tissue has an increased number of very small blood vessels, and pumping blood through those very small vessels increases strain on the heart exponentially. Not only does it strain the heart but it also slows down circulation throughout the rest of your body as well. That's why obese people often have a *pasty complexion.* Your heart has been strained by excess body weight, for which medication has been given, but that medication has damaged the heart's rhythm. This medication, along with others being ingested, impose considerable toxic burdens on your kidneys and liver, which are responsible for detoxifying and filtering poisons from your body. As a result, your 'cure' has now strained and impaired your body's natural ability to fight disease and infection.[56]

"But, I've digressed, we haven't even discussed your most recent symptoms, please proceed.

"OK, yes, I see, OK, let me examine your feet, OK, we'll have you take a urine test and have the lab tech perform a blood test. . . OK your results are in, . . If my suspicions are correct, . . . OK, Yep, OK, that confirms it, just as I thought—you have gout! Those symptoms you have been experiencing, you know, the congestion filtering down into your feet are the result of impaired uric acid elimination, probably the result of your impaired kidney function, which is the result of your drug-induced kidney and heart damage. What's that? Please, I don't want you to get upset again, look, please calm down, we have a growing array of products to meet your every need. Would you prefer taking your gout medication three times per day or as a once-a-day timed release?"

Such are the cures offered daily by physicians across the nation for the treatment of hundreds and hundreds of conditions that have but one cause—an unhealthy lifestyle.

In summary, obesity generates symptoms associated with eating more calories than you're expending. Humans are not designed to carry extra fuel around like bears that hibernate for the winter. It is natural (and healthy) for many kinds of bears to get "fat" before winter, because they hibernate for long periods of time and live off their stored energy (fat). Nature is simply operating efficiently—for bears, that is. Winters are hard for bears, so nature has created an effective solution. Nature has it that they eat a lot when the eating is good and they sleep a lot when sleeping is a lot more efficient option. This is natural, efficient, and healthy *for bears*.

Obesity "works" for bears, but not for humans. For human, carrying excessive weight is not necessary; bigger brains give us better options than building bigger bellies. Nature discourages waste, and obesity, for humans, is wasteful. Nature does not encourage fat in humans; nature designed humans to have much smaller tolerances for excessive fat (energy) storage. When those tolerances are exceeded, we experience the natural destructive consequences as symptoms of deteriorating health.

Into this circumstance steps modern medicine, and instead of digging up and pulling out the behavioral roots of obesity, it views obesity as a plethora of pharmacological opportunities. Modern medicine promptly introduces a growing formulary of chemical products to treat the growing array of fat-induced symptoms in almost every bodily system. Again, you cannot change a cause by modifying its effects. You can only change effects by modifying the cause.

Had at any point the medical system *stopped* the obese individual in their disease-inducing lifestyle, and softly pled and gently led the obese into the disease-preventing methods of the chronically healthy, it could have helped that individual avoid destroying himself. At least then the medical system would have a fighting chance at returning the person to a path of healthy living, a chance at saving that person from a life of chronic self-destruction, and a chance at saving society from the growing medical costs of the resulting chronic illness.

The transformational approach I am proposing is precisely the premise behind much of how "The Biggest Loser" TV program works—extended physical assessment, customized exercise programs with trained facilitators/coaches, adequate hydration, optimal nutrition, exploration of background motivations for eating, group support, and training in holistic/systems approaches and in practical everyday skills for how to keep excess weight off through long-term health promotion.

But not one bit of that approach will work—not at all, never, unless its effectiveness is unleashed through the key of obese persons owning their responsibility for past beliefs and behaviors. They commit themselves to doing something about their current perspective and practices *now*, so that they can begin working toward a horizon that is both more healthy and more hopeful.

The point of Disease-aholics Anonymous is to provide or impart a "transformational perspective" that confronts the myths of victimhood and imparts the truth of personal responsibility—so we can leave the graves of our own digging for the glorious liberty of responsible healthy living. The point of the lifestyle transformation programs is to impart the actual tools and resources and guidance required to follow through with breakthroughs in perspective to a new and healthier way of living. The ultimate goal of this comprehensive process of personal transformation is to impart to each client the power and practice of a healthy lifestyle to repel chronic diseases from entering into and taking over our lives.

> **Many studies identified in this book highlight the superior results obtained from diet and exercise—in other words, lifestyle modification approaches to treating chronic disease.**

Back to our example of obesity: the lifestyle of the obese begs disease unto themselves. Initially, these people will find it very difficult to give up their accustomed patterns of self-destruction, and will find it even offensive to follow the very unaccustomed patterns that the chronically healthy utilize. But gradually, as they become accustomed to the evolving restoration of health and begin to enjoy the benefits of renewing vitality, they will grow less attached to their disease-attracting patterns.

Here is where the battle will be won. Here we have a fighting chance to restore health to those who, *if not rudely interrupted* from their pampered love of ease and indulgence, would remain steadfastly obstinate on a path of self-destruction—especially as modern medicine's drugs soften the consequences of their lifestyle and actually *enable* their continued slide down a slippery slope into irretrievable decline.

"To the pampered love of ease there is no resting place."
- Frederick Douglas

By modifying the disease-attracting lifestyle into a health-attracting lifestyle, we will make significant strides in overcoming chronic disease. We are actually overcoming no external force. Chronic disease is not "out there" attempting to defeat every human being. Chronic disease is simply a natural consequence of the effect of poor lifestyle upon poor genetics. Simple as that. We cannot currently change genetics, but we can currently change lifestyle. Why poor genetics has attached itself to the human race is the subject of another book, but we do know that humans have them, and the impact of poor lifestyle upon weak genetics is to allow disease to gain a foothold. If we live healthfully, we assist nature in defending us from disease. If we live unhealthfully, we assist disease—which is also part of nature—in destroying us.

Whatever underlying causes that led to chronic disease, they cannot be stopped by simply adding drugs and surgery. Only the *reversal of causes* will *reverse the effects*. Any other medical approach is fundamentally designed to profit off treating the symptoms of declining health. We need a medical approach that resolutely introduces patients to healthier lifestyles in order to reverse health declines.

Have you ever considered that symptoms are a good thing? They reflect a declining state of health and alert us to a need for change. They warn us that conditions will worsen if we do not identify and abandon the underlying causes. But modern medicine steps in to emolliate and ostensibly eradicate those symptoms, sabotaging their potentially helpful effect. High blood pressure goes away. Rising cholesterol lowers. Blood sugars stabilize. Pains decrease. Nauseas and heartburn cease. Sour moods are lightened. But this masking of symptoms does nothing to address the state of declining health that is responsible for them. The reason modern medicine fails so consistently in overcoming chronic conditions is because it entirely fails to address and transform the behaviors which are responsible.

Healthy people are highly successful at beating disease because of their lifestyle, just as chronically ill people are highly effective at destroying their health—even against the will and instinct of all the cells in their body, which are unanimously struggling not only to survive, but to thrive. Chronically ill people keep getting sicker and sicker and sicker, and nothing modern medicine does corrects that trajectory of self-destruction. It has prolonged the quantity of life but has not corrected the downward spiral of the quality of life for the chronically ill. No amount of drugs or numbers of surgeries will permanently divert the chronically ill from the results of their chosen course. It is only by helping them change their lifestyle by modifying the underlying causes that we can successfully divert the chronically ill from their course and its inevitable effect—a decline into deeper and deeper states of chronic disease.

> **How shall we assist those entrenched in a health-negating lifestyle? By fully supporting their immersion in a health-affirming lifestyle.**

The chronically ill are not inclined toward healthy activities and so must be given considerable support, guidance, and resources in order to gently but firmly direct them toward healthy self-promotion. They simply demonstrate addictive attractions to things that are producing for them more harm than good; they need to be released from the deeply entrenched patterns that trap them in cycles of decline.

This is good news for the future of the Effective Medical Approach. We finally have an intervention that is proven to be successful, and it is observable and measurable in the lives of the chronically healthy. Drugs, as the American Medical Approach has amply demonstrated, have failed miserably because they simply modify the effect without changing the underlying cause. If you doubt this, look at all the evidence. I've compiled many key items in the bibliography regarding the damage and death inflicted on the American people by the American medical system. *Again, I am speaking almost exclusively of modern medicine's treatment of chronic disease, that is, disease with a highly modifiable lifestyle component.* With chronic disease, behavioral changes alone go very, very, very far toward entirely eradicating those diseases' untoward effects.

I say, in order to end chronic disease, instill chronically healthy behavior. One cannot be both chronically ill and chronically healthy at the same time. One cannot behave chronically well and be chronically ill at the same time.

We know how to instill chronic healthiness—just look at all the personal trainers, fitness instructors, and coaches available. The mystery is gone, the curtain is raised. We know how to improve health dramatically. Let's give optimal health a chance to work its miracle at lifting the plague of chronic disease. Let's apply health-restoring interventions in gradually increasing measure as patients' tolerance and strength improve, until they are capable of a few hours of gentle exercise daily. Let's apply these behaviorally-based restorative efforts into the lives of the one to five percent most chronically ill at a Lifestyle Transformation Center, hosted at health and fitness facilities.

Let's share with others our new strength, insight, and convictions as to how to overcome the myths of dependence, victimhood, and powerlessness through entering into the activities that empower, enlighten, and dignify our lives. Let's assist others in realizing this path of renewal. Let's help others divest themselves of the weights that so easily ensnare them in mists of gloom.

I submit that, as these previously grievously ill patients become stabilized, stronger, and more comfortably adapted to exercise (in fact pleasantly habituated and progressively addicted to the healthy lifestyle), they will require less and less supervision and guidance while continuing to improve. Finally, they'll be living above the affliction zone!

Let me conclude this section with a true story that serves as an allegory. This morning I went out on our back patio to eat a late morning breakfast. I was having some left over omelet from the day before. I heated it up and added some ketchup and went out to the back patio to eat it. After I finished the omelet I set the plate down and just enjoyed the peace and quiet of our backyard. But soon my peace was disturbed. A couple of bees, yellow jackets, to be exact, began buzzing me and started getting menacingly closer and closer to me and even threatened to land on my forearm. I resisted the impulse to swat at them because I felt they had no actual "beef" with me or interest in harming me. Then it occurred to me that what they really wanted and what they were after was the greasy scent from my omelet plate. I got up and moved my omelet plate over to where our backyard grill was and came back and sat down again. Almost immediately the bees widened their circle (and stopped their fly-by buzzing of me) in order to pick up on the scent of my omelet plate. Soon they were completely gone. Again, peace had been restored.

Interpretation: Symptoms of disease "buzz around" the behavioral causes that attract them. You can either swat at the symptoms (with drugs) or you can remove the causes that attract them.

Chapter 6.
Establishing an Effective Medical Approach

Establishing an Effective Medical Approach draws together the proposals and practices from this book in the form of concise plans for implementation. This chapter will likely make the most sense once you are comfortable with the core system concepts related through the rest of the book. But those concepts also needed to find some fulfillment in follow-through, which the plans in this chapter provide.

In this section, I contrast the evidence-based Effective Medical Approach as a far superior alternative to the American Medical Approach. The American Medical Approach still dominates our national healthcare system, though it is ineffective in reversing or preventing chronic disease. My overview includes the following sections, which address the theory, practices, programs, resources, and costs of implementing the Effective Medical Approach:

- Part One: The Medical Science Behind the Proposed Approach
- Part Two: Purposes of the Lifestyle Transformation Program
- Part Three: Lifestyle Transformation Center: Facility, Equipment, and Other Wellness Resources
- Part Four: Commitment→Adaptation→Transformation: "Stations of Transformation"
- Part Five: Purposes of This Schedule
- Part Six: The Components of the Program
- Part Seven: Costs of the Program

PART ONE: THE MEDICAL SCIENCE BEHIND THE PROPOSED APPROACH

Before looking at why the Effective Medical Approach is effective, I need to summarize why the current American Medical Approach, with its emphasis on prescription medications, is often ineffective. Just take a look at the documented damaging effects of chemical consumption:

1] *Drugs impair healthy immune function.* The nature of most pharmaceuticals is invasive. Many independent studies have shown that foreign elements are just that—foreign. The body must not only address the illness at hand, but must also address the issue of the pharmaceuticals ingested. This often taxes the immune system and prevents it from doing its job.[57]

2] *Drugs impede natural healing processes.* It is a well-documented fact that the masking effect of symptoms caused by ingesting drugs hampers the body's ability to recognize disease and therefore disable the healthy working of the immune system. For athletes in training, Ibuprofen has been shown to slow or impede the healing process for muscles, tissues, ligaments, and bones.[58]

3] *Drugs impair normal function of healthy organs.* The side effects listed during most of the television ads for drugs have reached comedic proportions. Often the possible negative side effects overshadow any possible benefit. Certain drugs can even adversely affect a man's reproductive system.[59]

4] *Drugs impose a toxic burden on the eliminative organs.* Most pharmaceuticals are hard for the body to process, and often are not fully eliminated.[60]

5] *Drug toxins are not completely eliminated from the body; they are stored in organs and tissue.* Not only does the system have to deal with the side effects of drugs, but often the pharmaceuticals ingested are stored in the fat cells of the body and will trickle into the body for weeks, months and even years afterward. These pharmaceuticals have a toxic effect on a person's overall health.[61]

6] *Accumulated drug toxins damage bodily organs and systems.* The warnings on the pharmaceutical labels are there for good reason. Drugs often do more harm than good. There are always negative side effects, even to a small degree. According to Life Extension Magazine, the total number of deaths caused by conventional medicine is nearly 700,000 per year.[62]

Some medications can perform valuable functions and short-term symptom management. The problems with medications arise when they are relied upon exclusively, with little regard for discontinuing modifiable (behavioral) causes. One such example is the over-medication of the elderly. This is a major problem because their bodies are far less capable of clearing the cumulative toxins of many medications. Even so, to discontinue a medication abruptly can also cause significant health risks. Consult a doctor before decreasing medications. It is important to take a methodical gradual approach while beginning a healthier lifestyle to correct the underlying problems for which a medication is being taken.

If your doctor is focused on writing prescriptions and does not have a plan for wellness care, please seek out a doctor who will support you in simplifying your medications. Try to opt for the absolute minimum (if it is not possible to completely discontinue them). Find a doctor who will wholeheartedly support your efforts to implement a non-toxic lifestyle and dietary modifications as your first and best defense against disease. The effort you put into regaining command of your health will pay healthy dividends.

In contrast to the health drawbacks of most pharmaceuticals, a comprehensive diet-and-exercise approach to health can have a very positive effect on your body's systems. This diet-and-exercise approach has been demonstrated to show:

1] An improved quality of life.

2] Improved body chemistry and metabolic function.

3] Improved immunity and resistance to disease.

4] Reversal or slowing of declines from existing chronic diseases.

5] A slowing down of the aging process.

6] Improved psychological health and sense of wellbeing.

7] Consistent weight control.

8] Increased energy, strength, stamina, and endurance.

9] Increased bone density and muscle mass.

10] Improved agility and coordination.

11] Effective stress reduction.

12] Improved mental clarity.

13] Restoration of balance and unity to a fragmented sense of self.

Of course any health program comes with some risks. It is best to start a healthy lifestyle before your health degrades to a point that makes transition away from medications inordinately difficult. Many studies have been performed that attest to the benefits of exercise.[63]

"Healthy is as healthy does" and *"We each reap what we sow."* The paradigm of healthy behavior that is behind the EMA is summarized in my personal mission and vision statements.

MISSION STATEMENT

To awaken and empower each individual's capacity for self-healing and optimal wellness. To provide others with the guidance, tools, facilities, and resources to fully self-actualize their own optimal wellness.

VISION STATEMENT

- I believe in the power of the individual to greatly influence his/her physical and spiritual condition no matter his/her current state.
- I believe that pursuing wellness gives me life and promoting wellness shall be my life's work.
- I believe the miraculous healing power of health promotion is our single most powerful weapon against the onset and progression of chronic disease.
- I believe in the power of unhealthy individuals to change their behavior, if given a nurturing, supportive environment.
- I believe the most cost-effective method of controlling the costs and progression of chronic disease is the wholesale promotion and support of a healthy lifestyle.
- I believe that inside every chronically ill person is a chronically well person whose life center, life goals, and optimal lifestyle were never realized.
- I believe that when we affirm life, life affirms us, and when we return to what is our life, our life returns to us.
- I believe that to *fail to plan* to be healthy is to *plan to fail* at being healthy.
- I believe we should labor earnestly to enter into the "blessed rest" that good health affords.

I believe the first order of business is to assess one's current situation; the next is to develop a plan, and the third is to follow it through to completion.

But to have both a plan and motivation is still not sufficient in itself; we cannot sustain major lifestyle transformation alone. We all need resources, encouragement, and a strong support system in order to move consistently toward wellness and health. That is where my proposed Lifestyle Transformation Program, and Lifestyle Transformation Centers come into play, especially for the severely health-challenged.

PART TWO: PURPOSES OF THE LIFESTYLE TRANSFORMATION PROGRAMS AND CENTERS

Modern medicine's corporate mission is to expand the distribution and use of its products, which means it must heavily medicate and frequently treat patients who are becoming progressively more medically and chemically dependent. In contrast to this, the system I am proposing is designed to first promote healthy independent living, and then consistently support the maintenance of that healthy independence.

This set of healthy, *vitality-restoring* disciplines reverses decline and generates a rebounding trajectory of recovery. These disciplines are easily introduced to patients within the therapeutic setting—whether it be a live-in rehabilitation center, an outpatient physical therapy center, or a simple health club/fitness center with a commitment to accommodating the special needs of the chronically ill. The Lifestyle Transformation Program immerses patients in a truly healthy environment of nutrition and behaviors that generate recovery. But these external environmental improvements and behavioral corrections will only yield temporary improvements if these health-promoting behaviors *are not maintained voluntarily* outside the therapeutic environment.

In a sense, Lifestyle Transformation Centers compete with hospitals—as health science's best evidence-based, and most economical means of *preventing* disease. At the point where fully-supported health promotion fails and disease finally does prevail, at least the hospitalization and disease care required will be greatly forestalled, and hospitals will be far less frequently visited. Hospitals *treat* full-blown *un-prevented* medical crisies and exacerbations of chronic disease. Lifestyle Transformation Centers give patients the tools and lifestyle guidance to keep themselves balanced and in the best physical condition they can be in *so as to avoid crisis and forestall decline*.[64]

Let's compare and contrast the American Medical Approach and the Effective Medical Approach.

The way of the American Medical Approach is to treat each progressive cascade of decline with more diagnostics, more pills, and more procedures. Through the marbled halls of hundreds of hospitals, thousands of pale and enfeebled patients shuffle between labs, pharmacies, and diagnostic encounters. Nary a word is mentioned of causes or remedy, only of diseases and treatments.

The Effective Medical Approach that I propose is to treat each evidence of health decline (i.e., each health crisis) with an investigation into its causes, and to treat underlying chronic health declines (i.e. exacerbation of chronic disease) with wholesale health promotion.

The physiological principle at work within the American Medical Approach is this: The person's health declines, resulting in hospitalization or an outpatient visit for symptoms, which results in those symptoms being treated, and then the patient is returned to society (repeat).

The American Medical Approach cashes in—"harvests," as it were—the fruits of health declines by treating for profit only the outward symptoms (effects) of a declining standard of health. Then it returns the patient to the normal population.

The Effective Medical Approach recognizes that each health crisis (i.e. eruption of intense symptoms) is merely the external manifestation of an underlying decline in the wellness balance of the patient (i.e., homeostasis; health equilibrium). So, the Effective Medical Approach seeks to identify the flagging (compromised) physiological systems and restore the lacking lifestyle attributes (fitness-nutrition-detoxification-nurture-health coaching and support) to optimal levels. This gives the body and mind the resources they need to restore homeostasis (balance, vitality, resilience) and thus empowers, supports and sustains the patient's ability to thrive.

So, for the sake of profit, the American Medical Approach plays on the same consequences of an underlying decline in health that the Effective Medical Approach recognizes as a body's cry for help. Conversely, the Effective Medical Approach treats it as a systems-wide health crisis and seeks to restore the underlying state of health rather than treat the symptoms for profit. Health is not merely the absence of life-threatening symptoms, but the presence of life-giving wellness.

To use a mathematic illustration: Let's consider health and disease as a continuum from Olympic-caliber fitness at one end (+10) to a multisystem failure and death (-10) at the other end. An extreme health crisis occurs when a patient's score drops below zero, typically into the range of a -1 to -5.

The American Medical Approach uses a yo-yo approach. It seeks to bring patients whose health has dropped below zero (-1 to -5) back up to zero. When another health crisis drops a patient's health below zero again, that generates another billable cycle. So, the American Medical Approach seeks to raise patients from "critical" up to "critically stable" again, and then leaves them to their own devices, until another crisis drops them down into a "critical" status, which generates another billable cycle, and so on. Intensive actions yank the patient back up to zero, but passivity allows the patient to slip down into yet another crisis—which generates another billable cycle, and so on.

The Effective Medical Approach uses a ladder approach. When a patient's general health and fitness declines from relatively strong and stable (+2 to +5) down to below zero (-1 to -5), it recognizes this as a strong indicator of erosion in underlying wellness systems. The Effective Medical Approach seeks to raise patients from crisis/"critical" up to "thriving and well" by restoring patients back to a *strong* underlying health (+3 to +7), and giving skills and resources to sustain it. This prevents dips down into the affliction zone of chronic illness and the astronomical fee structures of crisis intervention.

A fundamental principle of this approach is that you as a patient *are capable* of taking charge of your own life, health, and recovery process. This approach provides a lifestyle philosophy and framework through which *you are empowered* to prevent unnecessary suffering and physical decline, and to create a long, healthy life. It requires patients to engage in *assertive* self-discovery and *responsible* participation in the restoration of their health. It takes into account the entire person—body, mind, and spirit—and recognizes that the most powerful force at play in the attraction of either health or disease is the mind.

How shall we change the course of those whose daily habits destroy them?

Fundamentally, the modern American Medical Approach starts with symptom manifestation and *goes forward:* Given these symptoms, these are the products and services with which we treat it. *"Your loss is our gain. Now let me convey you to the sales floor. We have pretty pills and potions of every color and description."*

An Effective Medical Approach starts with symptom manifestation and *goes backward:* Given this condition, what caused it, and how do we reverse it?

In most basic terms, the Effective Medical Approach attempts to temporarily disengage patients from the environment, people, and behaviors that contribute to their disease, and instead engage them with the environment, people, and behaviors that contribute to their sustainable wellness.

Fundamentally, it involves progressive immersion in both a health-fortifying environment and the performance of health-fortifying behavior. For the chronically ill—bathed in all the things at home that remind and fortify and further entrench them in their disability—just getting them out of the house and planted in an environment that doesn't "look" downward through the "eye of disease and disempowerment" but rather looks upward through an eye searching for "opportunities for breakthrough" is enough to bring them huge gains in healing and health promotion. This program takes a familial-generational approach to lifestyle transformation. It helps people to see how family of origin, relationships, culture, environment, and employment affect our behaviors, priorities, and attitudes about health—and how these directly affect our health or its degeneration.

Program participants are to be flooded from the moment they arrive, to the moment they leave, with the best and most restorative, rejuvenating, immune system-strengthening, physiologically-fortifying, spiritually-uplifting therapies we can assemble. If we plant the chronically ill in the soil of a healthy environment, among people engaged in healthy behavior, it will get under their skin. Once they are infected with the vitality resulting from healthier behavior, they will begin to be transformed by the renewing of their mind and the revitalizing of their body.

I detail the overall plan below. It is my strong belief that once peoples' fitness has risen to the level where they *can begin* a dramatically increased amount of exercise (relative to their baseline), can tolerate a dramatically increased intensity of exercise, and have begun practicing better nutrition and other health restoring behaviors, then they will be well along their way of metamorphosis from feeble to fit. At this point, *they will be hooked!* No longer will they recede from every exertion, because they will find themselves fortified for the battle. They shall go forth with greater confidence because they will be stronger people. The confidence and satisfaction that come from being so much stronger and healthier will further strengthen their resolve to continue with the "healthy habits of responsible living" that have given them their new lease on life. The paltry pleasures and apathetic indulgences that dragged them down will no longer hold the same sticky appeal. At this point, the battle is largely won and participants become their own champions. They have been restored to a healthy, self-actualizing state and the value of this vital discovery will inspire them to guard it diligently.

At this kind of lifestyle management center, people are not merely educated about a healthy lifestyle. Rather, they are ushered into participation in the activities responsible for promoting optimal wellness, guided by trained facilitators. This, then, is where I would like the chronically ill to check in and start their journey back to chronic wellness—a Lifestyle Transformation Center that is *available, medically prescribed, and group supported.* And if people are wise, they will never leave its principles and practices.

Lifestyle Transformation Centers become your therapeutic place to recover your essential seeds of health; seeds that you may have forgotten you had or, worse, had never bothered to sow, even as a child. This becomes the place and opportunity to give yourself much of the self-care, self-nurturing, and self-correcting tough love you have ignored for years. This is an oasis in the desert to provide the "water of health" to those whose health is drying up.

The goal of this program is to assist clients in moving from a passive dependence upon the work of others for their healthy outcome to a proactive dependence upon their own healthy behavior to promote healthy outcomes. By gradually infusing fitness and vitality into the previously powerless and chemically dependent, we provide them with ample evidence of the value of an active lifestyle and their power to maintain it.

"I find that the great thing in this world is not so much where we stand, as in the direction we are moving."
- Oliver Wendell Holmes

PART THREE: LIFESTYLE TRANSFORMATION CENTER—FACILITY, EQUIPMENT, AND OTHER WELLNESS RESOURCES

Visualize with me for a moment!

Thousands of haggard people—both adults and children—shuffling into the foyer of five-star Lifestyle Transformation Centers across America, being led into top-quality, fitness-exploring paradises, with a large portion of the facilities dedicated to the senior and chronically ill population. Such a center would include these components for basic health and wellness:

- Olympic-sized lap swim pool for stronger swimmers
- A comfortably heated exercise/therapy pool for water exercise classes, guided swim instruction with supervision, etc.
- Multiple cardio-equipped rooms, each with high ceilings, great ventilation, headsets at every station for TV screen, with 132 channels plus 10 different continuous streaming music stations:
    - room with 12-16 stationary cycles (for "spin" classes performed to upbeat music)
    - room with 12-16 recumbent bikes
- A room with rowing machines, elliptical trainers and treadmills
- One Jacuzzi—just cool enough to use as a therapy pool with support bars, and large enough for a group physical therapy class
- Another Jacuzzi—large and warm with deluxe hydro-therapy features
- Top-quality Nautilus equipment stations
- Free weights area
- Weight room and low-impact aerobic equipment modified with safety "sit down" features for the needs of the very weak

- Classrooms and instructors for Yoga, Tai Chi, Pilates, and Feldenkrais movement classes
- Large steam rooms
- Large dry sauna
- Spa-style rooms for detoxification and massage
- Deluxe juice bar and nutrition counter, offering:
    - Stimulating tea or energy drink/energy gel packet/ attention-focusing agent to promote focused application to the core challenges of the program
    - Fresh organic juices
    - Nutritional recovery drinks containing the ideal balance of amino acids, minerals, and vitamins for rebuilding muscle and restoring glycogen energy reserves.

Now, the cost of building new centers specifically designed to address the needs of the chronically ill would be far less expensive *in the long run* than the costs of un-prevented spirals of decline that the chronically ill are currently experiencing. However, the chronically ill are a relatively small portion of society, and it is quite costly to build entire fitness centers. So, I currently feel that this population base would not be sufficient to support such large expenditures for them alone. I recommend utilizing existing fitness facilities and expanding them as needed or adding specially adapted equipment and modified classes adapted for the special needs of the chronically ill. The time to build new facilities will be when the Lifestyle Transformation Program exhibits such proven results that the current and expanded facilities become unable to support the demand. The costs of membership at existing health clubs are very reasonable, while the costs of re-hospitalization of the chronically ill are astronomical.

PART FOUR: COMMITMENT → ADAPTATION → TRANSFORMATION

"The only way around is through."
- Robert Frost

Prior to beginning the program, each participant undergoes a comprehensive health assessment and a baseline physical strengths assessment, from which a baseline exercise program will be established. After that, fundamentally, the program involves participation. It's that simple: The chronically ill show up! The chronically ill show up a scheduled number of days per week and follow a program of customized exercise and therapeutic interventions called the Stations of Transformation. Patients simply "show up" and give themselves to their own recovery. The individualized program and individualized attention will gradually lead them to a profoundly healthier state.

Is the program flexible? Of course it is. This is a boilerplate, a guideline that is to be customized for the individual and made to fit within the resources of the facility. But it must also be rigid in certain respects. The goal is personal transformation—which requires work! Thus, there is a certain amount of "tough love" that needs to be applied to encourage compliance with any program—if that program is to have a transformative effect. So, the program may be worked around life, but may not cater to the forces that promote chronic disease.

Imagine a college that didn't require attendance or submission of assignments, or a wrestling team that didn't require practice. Just how effective would these programs be if they were that flexible? Of course flexibility should be available for different populations, practical constraints, or available resources. But what is not flexible is the consistency, depth of commitment, and level of participation that must be maintained. Otherwise, no transformation will take place.

This Lifestyle Transformation Program is not designed to weigh down or frustrate those already weakened. Instead, it is designed to enlighten, empower, and catalyze the release of the chronically ill from personal limitations. That process of transformation may be bumpy at times, and collisions between old and new lifestyles will occur. The deeply entrenched habits and well-ingrained lifestyle patterns (resulting in their profoundly de-conditioned state) will get disrupted and unsettled by the newly imparted healthy habits and lifestyle patterns. To break through a behavioral paradigm of decline takes some work, like pulling teeth. Bad habits don't fall easily; bad habits will attempt to reestablish themselves in the ground from which they have been uprooted. Few major transformations, even healthy transformations, are continuously pleasant, but are rather unpleasant at times. However, afterwards they do yield a very valuable transformative reward to those who are exercised in that manner. If the clients were not chronically ill, they would not be in need of this program.

So, again: *Is the program flexible?* Yes and no! We can be flexible with "the types and ways and the look of the program," but we cannot be flexible with the "will toward decline"—that is, an inclination (or even an addiction) to behaviors, patterns, and attitudes that pull people down. Gentle? Always. Firm? For sure. Supportive? Definitely.

Please note that patients enter the program at different levels of health and ability. Those with better health and a positive attitude can receive comprehensive familiarization with the facility and equipment, and an explanation of how the program works, and they'll be off and running with minimal supervision. Others may require a lot of repetition of information about the facility and the program, repeated demonstration of proper use of equipment, and direct supervision for a longer period of time. As patients become more familiar with the program and more fit, they will require less oversight.

The heart of the Lifestyle Transformation Program is what I am terming "Stations of Transformation." On the next page is the flow of these stations, in sequence.

Stations of Transformation—Done in This Sequence

Warm Up: 45 minutes
Self-guided portion—warming up
1] Healthy hydration
2] Warm up walk
3] Core (lower back/abdominal)
4] Stretching

Main Focus: 45 to 75 minutes

5] Supervised portion—choose one of the following:
a] Group exercise/movement class (dance/rhythm, yoga, tai chi)
b] Guided resistance training class (resistance machines, dumbbells, gravity/body weight bands)
c] Group aerobics/cardio training class (dance/rhythm, recumbent bike, stationary bike, elliptical)
d] Water aerobics (cardio, movement with music, pool walking, swimming class, easy lap swimming)

Note: A combination of all the above (a little of this and a little of that), will achieve balance.

Cool Down: 45 to 60 minutes
Self-guided portion—cooling down
6] Hydration/nutrition
7] Light core/abdominal strengthening exercises

Then:
8] Stretching
9] Hydration/nutrition
10] Heat therapy (dry sauna, Jacuzzi or steam room) and/or
11] Cool Therapy (cool in the pool, or brave a refreshing cool shower to revive and invigorate your nerves).
12] Hydration
13] Now, weekly recap with your group. Embrace your partners in the journey. Support one another. Recount your breakthroughs and review your frustrations. By working as a team, you support and strengthen one another and hold each other accountable as you strive for the prize of a brighter, healthier, stronger tomorrow.

Total: 2 to 2.5 hours. Maintain a slow, very gentle pace—rest as often as needed until endurance and fitness improve.

After a short period, even within the first seven weeks, it is expected that patients will be able to warm up and cool down with only the assistance of their health partner (i.e., a supervisor for their program group). Over time, supervision will become more about re-gearing their heart and mind toward the fitness lifestyle.

Time and effort at each area are increased as progressively tolerated by one's body, with flexibility to be the rule. For instance, expand limits on days clients are feeling strong; aim for easy recovery and therapeutic volume on days they're feeling tired. The effect of dwelling at those stations—or rather, abiding under the influence of those stations—is to purge, purify, cleanse, refine, strengthen, restore, build, fortify, renew, and revive a person's capacity and aptitude for health and wellness. In the end, supervision becomes much less necessary because making healthy choices becomes a habit. Patients have, in effect, regained healthy self-love to replace indifference to their own best interest; they have remedied the ways they have damaged themselves and have heeded and followed the voice of love and reason. This is the transformational content of the program.

PART FIVE: PURPOSES OF THIS SCHEDULE

The sequential progression through the *modules* or *Stations* of Transformation is basically a systematic approach to physical conditioning. Waking up the body, then warming up the body, then limbering up the body, then increasing strength of the body, then increasing the endurance and stamina of the body, then increasing flexibility of the body, then engaging in heat therapy to soothe and relax and cleanse the body—and all along, getting adequate hydration and nutritional support throughout each session. This approach results in systematic achievement, *with easier weeks periodically* to minimize injury and burnout. Great care must be taken to assure that clients are gently challenged but not overly challenged. Over time, the program causes physiologic adaptation and systematic advances in strength, speed, flexibility, and endurance. Over time, if the client is patient and not overly challenged, he or she will begin to experience increased vitality, energy, and enthusiasm. Successful care and direction will yield for clients gradual improvements in their sense of wellbeing as well as feelings of self empowerment.

Is this some kind of "circuit training from hell?" No, the rigors of this program are designed to gently transform your weakness into strength, to reintegrate compromised physiological systems, and to ease you back into better health. This systematic "flaming" is a scientific means of obtaining the health you will be reclaiming. Performing circuits through "the stations" will lead the chronically diseased toward healthful transformations. These stations of transformation are about spurring on your body's obedience towards you. If you treat your body to a smorgasbord of health-producing behaviors, your body will obediently comply with your direction and lead you into renewed heights of health and fitness.

The goal of participating in each of those stations (in a circuit of activities for each day) is to build endurance, strength, balance, and flexibility—but the results over time will also include increased energy, confidence, and vitality. All of these are "prescriptives" for a more abundant life. Again, this program is flexible. The idea is to embrace what your locale provides. Health clubs are not an option for many parts of the nation, but there are opportunities to develop walking clubs or morning "Tai Chi" programs at the local park. Whatever the environment provides for health is to be employed. Nature is ours to enjoy and can mightily assist us in our return to health.

"Everybody needs beauty as well as bread, places to play in and pray in, where nature may heal and give strength to body and soul."
- John Muir

"Climb the mountains and get their good tidings. Nature's peace will flow into you as sunshine flows into trees. The winds will blow their own freshness into you, and the storms their energy, while cares will drop off like autumn leaves."
- John Muir

"I remember a hundred lovely lakes, and recall the fragrant breath of pine and fir and cedar and poplar trees. The trail has strung upon it, as upon a thread of silk, opalescent dawns and saffron sunsets. It has given me blessed release from care and worry and the troubled thinking of our modern day. It has been a return to the primitive and the peaceful. Whenever the pressure of our complex city life thins my blood and benumbs my brain, I seek relief in the trail; and when I hear the coyote wailing to the yellow dawn, my cares fall from me—I am happy."
- Hamlin Garland, McClure's, February 1899

"In wilderness I sense the miracle of life, and behind it our scientific accomplishments fade to trivia."
- Charles A. Lindbergh, Life, December 1967

There is a pleasure in the pathless woods,
There is a rapture on the lonely shore,
There is society, where none intrudes,
By the deep sea, and music in its roar:
I love not man the less, but Nature more.
- George Gordon, Lord Byron,
Childe Harold's Pilgrimage.

Now, how often will the patient cycle through these stations of transformation? Four days a week. You read right: *four days a week* (except for first two introductory phases). Patients will move through the program in the seven phases illustrated on the next page.

Lifestyle Transformation Program Phases / Days of Attendance / Content: Guided or Self-Guided Days		
PHASE	LENGTH	MIX OF ACTIVITIES
Phase One	Three weeks	2 days guided per week (Gentle introductory phase.) ***Note:*** *may start as gentle as coming down to the facility and performing the "Warm Up" and "Cool Down" phases only.*
Phase Two	Four weeks	2 days guided / 1 day self-guided per week. (Laying a solid base.)
Phase Three	Seven weeks	2 days guided / 2 days self-guided/week. (Building a strong foundation.)
Phase Four	Seven weeks	3 days guided* / 1 day self-guided**/week. (Acquiring the fitness lifestyle.)
Phase Five	Seven weeks	2 days guided / 2 days self-guided/week. (Reinforcing healthy lifestyle.)
Phase Six	Three months	1 day guided / 3 days self-guided/week. (Ingraining healthy lifestyle.)
Phase Seven	Six months	1 day guided / 7 days self-guided per 2 weeks. That is, 4 days/week with 1 guided day every 2 weeks. (Sustaining healthy lifestyle.) This final phase is a maintenance program designed to encourage healthy lifestyle success and monitor patients for declines in health and address those needs preventively, instead of treating them expensively.

**Guided = Attendance/participation is supervised & supported by an exercise trainer. Each client follows a customized workout plan. At each "station of transformation," a trainer is available for guidance and instruction on proper technique, safety, pacing, and questions. This is not one trainer with each client at each station; this is one trainer available to several clients simultaneously, to assist as needed.*

*** Self-guided = Clients check in and bring their customized exercise plan with them to follow as a template through the "stations," but they (with the help of their health partner) are on their own.*

Is this template set in stone? No. Does this template illustrate a far more effective paradigm of medical treatment for the chronically ill, capable of saving billions of dollars in crisis care costs *averted* if it is implemented? Yes! Further, patients will ideally not be alone, but they will have a "health partner"—a person, most likely a family member, who supports the patient but who has the opportunity to participate in the program. This serves to gently introduce a culture of exercise into families whose sedentary familial patterns and habits attract to themselves obesity and disease.

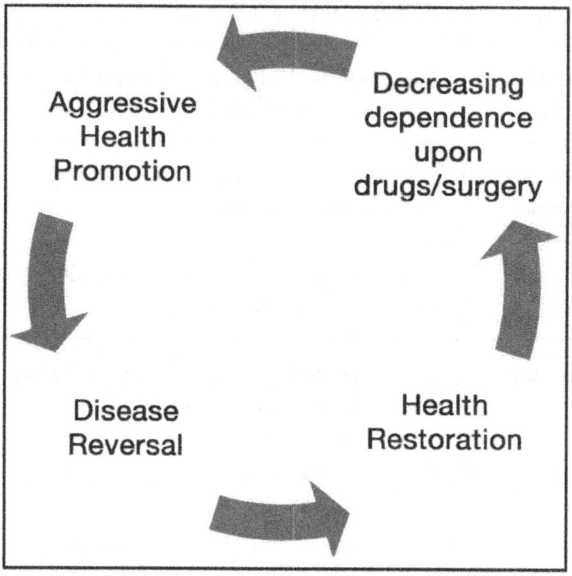

Picture this possible scenario:

A newscaster proclaiming the following news bulletin, "Medicare saved 66 million dollars as a result of refusing to fund a senior wellness program aimed at moving the 5% most chronically ill from their weak and vulnerable state into a healthier and less vulnerable condition. In the next caption the newscaster informs the public in rapid fire bullet points regarding; 1] The alarming rise in Medicare spending associated with the treatment of chronic disease; 2] That two-thirds of all Medicare spending is for the treatment of chronic disease; 3] That Medicare spending is expected to exceed 4.7 trillion dollars by 2020."

The population I am addressing here is very ill; they require a lot of help at home, and are the consuming concern of one or more family members. These family members commit a lot of time and emotional energy to the care of their loved one and often have little respite or support for themselves. The program I advocate allows a family member to partner with their loved one through this program—actually exercising alongside him or her if they so choose. Their first responsibility is to assist their loved one with transition between stations and to monitor their tolerance of the exercises, but they are free to actually "get well" themselves alongside their loved one. This provides two benefits:

- It makes health renewal a family movement instead of an individual phenomenon.
- It provides the direct observation and assistance that the chronically ill often need.

"Don't ask what the world needs. Ask what makes you come alive, and go do it. Because what the world needs is people who have come alive."
- Howard Thurman[65]

Imagine a sink in a hospital room overflowing with water splashing all over the floor, while doctor's and nurses frantically try to clean up the mess, yet no one thinks to turn off the water. That is what the American Medical Pharmaceutical Approach is like.

EXERCISE: HOW MUCH AND HOW OFTEN?

Have you ever pushed yourself one day, but not really realized it till the next day? The idea of this program is to push yourself harder on some days and easier on other days, to stay active but also recover. The program alternates between supervised/facilitator-guided exercise and self-guided days. It also alternates between easier days for "active recovery" and harder days to stretch yourself, push your boundaries, and expand your borders *gently and safely*. In this way, the workouts gradually progress and increase.

For example, in the (introductory) First Phase, Ms. Jones will have two days of guided instruction, and on other days, she may choose to exercise or to rest at home. So on Monday and Thursday, she will gently progress through the stations of transformation (or as far as tolerated)—with a health coach nearby and available to her as much as she needs (more at the beginning of the program, less in the latter weeks of it). On the other days, she will exercise at home or just "rest up," and that will be up to her and performed in her own home at her own pace. In this way she'll not only alternate between guided exertion and self-guided days, but also between harder and easier days.

Please note that the program gradually builds in its physical demands upon the patient as the patient gradually adapts "up to" the physical demands of a healthier lifestyle. Phase One is only two "official" days at the facility with self-direction or just rest on other days. Phase Two is three "official" days at the facility. Phase Three through Phase Seven are 4 days a week at the facility.

Gradually increasing frequency, duration and intensity of exercise *as tolerated* marks the pathway to physical adaptation and ultimately personal transformation. Once this program of physical adaptation and personal transformation is completed, the patients' level of fitness and freedom will be so elevated that they won't want to return to the *easier ways* that entrapped them in the consequences of deconditioning.

Just like an athlete, non-athletes and even the chronically ill can adapt upwardly toward healthier states of being. Listening to one's own body is the key to continuing forward with positive gains and to avoiding undue fatigue, burnout, or injuries from overtraining. The worst thing that could happen would be to push those unaccustomed to a fitness lifestyle too hard and give them a bad taste for what exercise can do to them.

After graduating from the initial program, clients can join the maintenance program. It monitors their participation in classes and continues to provide periodic fitness testing and "check ins" with a health coach in person or by phone. In this way, clients will receive ongoing coaching/encouragement about ways to stay fit, remain motivated, avoid injury, and continue to progress toward optimal health.

Patients: Progressive Empowerment Model (Stairway to Integration)
Fortify → Rebuild (repeat)

Patients approach the system with symptoms:

Symptoms: Patients given diagnosis of: Disease (fill in the blank) related to Critical Loss of Fitness → cause treated (fitness prescribed)

In the following diagram, each step is a threshold of fitness, which - continuing on with the fitness description - consolidates into improved fitness, which then breaks through to the next higher threshold of fitness (repeat). Example: A patient who is weak, inactive, and overweight, begins a fitness program and gains strength → with greater strength, they exercise more instensely and begin losing weight → with a slimmer waistline they find they can exercise more and for longer periods, which increases strength, which increase length of work outs, which intensifies weightloss, which improves appearance, confidence and motivation which increases enthusiasm to watch diet more closely and engage in more recreational activities (outside of the program) → resulting in progressive breakthroughs and consolidations into higher and higher levels of fitness.

Pattern of Stairway to Integration:

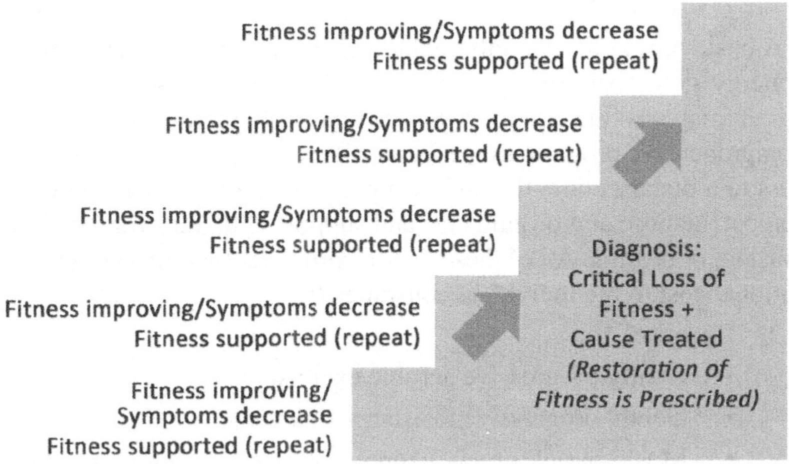

Diagnosis: Critical Loss of Fitness + Cause Treated (Restoration of Fitness is Prescribed)

PART SIX: THE COMPONENTS OF THE PROGRAM

I've listed the equipment and resources of the Lifestyle Transformation Center, and we've looked at overall scheduling aspects of the program. The following lists break out seven clusters of components in the program: dietary ("In with the good …"), exercise, stretching, detoxification ("…out with the bad."), group support, coaching support, and field trips. (Note that some aspects in various clusters would be available only in comprehensive programs.)

1] Dietary

- Ideal phytonutrient-dense liquid nutrition (i.e., bioactive plant-sourced ingredients)
- Raw vegetable juices and healing diet

- Healthy hydration
- Optimal nutrition
- Simple "whole foods"
- Deluxe juice bar and nutrition bar; stimulating tea or energy drink / energy gel packet / attention-focusing agent to promote focused application to the core challenges of the program; fresh organic juices; and nutritional recovery drinks containing an ideal balance of amino acids, minerals, and vitamins for rebuilding muscle and restoring glycogen energy reserves.

A basic program may only include electrolyte replacement drink and an energy gel to sustain energy during the workout. A more complete program may also include fresh squeezed juices and nutritional snack bar. A comprehensive program may include all these elements and also include access to a dietary clinic that offers supervised fasting; chelation therapy; colonic irrigation; and/or guidance and support with diets for detoxifying, cleansing, or healing. All of these "extra" products/services would be at an additional cost to the individual consumer.[66]

2] Exercise[67][68]

- Gently progressive aerobic exercise
- Gently progressive resistance exercises
- Music-based group exercise classes designed to improve flexibility and active range of motion, and to "get the juices flowing." Music-based activities pump life and rhythm back into the soul, and enrich the spirit as well. Types of music/rhythm and movement activities include:
    - Dance/rhythm
    - Tai Chi
    - Yoga
    - Cardio/weight resistance
    - Stationary "spin" cycling class
- Range of motion
- Gentle aerobic conditioning
- Water aerobics. *Water fitness classes are great for bodies that cannot tolerate impact and for those who need to ease back into a healthy lifestyle gently.*
- Resistance exercises

3] Stretching

- Gentle progressive stretching

4] Detoxification

- Sweat "heat therapy"—detoxification. *Dry saunas, Jacuzzis, and steam rooms are great ways to clean out the pores, sweat off bodily impurities, improve the complexion, relax tension, and release stress.*
- Periodic fasting and internal cleansing.
- Guidance and support with a detoxifying, cleansing, and healing diet.[69]

5] Group Support: 12-Steps and "Dream Teams"

- Affirmations, prayers, and focus
- Motivational/transformational coaching
- Building community
- Healing relationships
- Weight-loss accountability support

Accepting personal responsibility for one's present condition is critical to change. After all, if your body's condition is someone else's fault, someone else's doing—genetic predisposition, familial habits, or some other responsible party—then that party still holds the power, and you are simply a (perpetual/permanent) victim. Our ownership is key to success in behavioral reform. This significant shift is more easily embraced when clients are surrounded by others in the same situation. Thus, group support is crucial to lifestyle transformation.

New habit formation is greatly encouraged by the camaraderie of fellow strugglers who are on the path to become "overcomers." The chronically ill may not feel that the healthy have a right to speak of their condition and its remedy. They may feel that those who have not walked in their shoes cannot understand their challenges, and they may discount instruction from such "outsiders" on that basis. But by this same token, they may feel that those who likewise have chronic illness themselves and struggle with its control *have every right* to speak into their mutual struggle and dilemma. Group support and camaraderie is key to doubling the joys and dividing the sorrows associated with new habit formation. Guided (professional- or peer-facilitated) group support is essential to increasing awareness of self-sabotaging tendencies, and to marshaling motivation to "stay the course" with new habit formation.

Group support can make all the difference in the world for those struggling with the challenges, disruptions, upheavals, and discomforts associated with positive change. To know that you're not alone makes the going easier. To hear feedback from those who have gone before gives hope and encouragement to those who have not yet reaped the harvest of positive planting.

For the ill and the aging, survival demands revival. The 12-Step group support program would emphasize emotional support for the journey from "health failure" to "fitness," and put effort into the formation of "Dream Teams" comprised of health-challenged teammates who rally together, striving as one team for mastery over illness and frailty. It's an Olympics, as it were, for the chronically ill. Dream Teams encompass teamwork and camaraderie, accountability and commiseration in their common struggles as they strive individually and corporately for the prize of the high calling of restoring their health. As a team, members share common goals and struggles, and they encourage and support each other. This positive energy generates a cumulative "team power" that is greater than the sum of the teams' individual members. Many hearts make the work light!

On a team, members strive for unity, efficiency, and precision. They spur each other on to be the best they can be. Teams composed of the chronically ill will not merely be striving for a title or trophy, but for a life that is more fully lived and enjoyed. This then is their team's dream. It forms a compelling reason for every Dream Team member to strive for with every ounce of their being. In this team spirit, each member is inspired to new levels and to "take it on" (for the team), and in this way, they rise above themselves to achieve more dramatic health returns.

6] Coach Support

- Individual health coach support
- Telephone health coach support for ongoing "program graduate" support
- Motivational/transformational coaching

7] Instructor Support

At the Center, there will be an instructor available for participants in the program as they go through the Stations of Transformation. The instructor, (and the participant's health partner) will provide the guidance and support needed to ease the participant through the stations that lead to transformation.

Participants, along with their health partners, will choose one of three daily sessions to go through the Stations. Instructors will guide the participants (along with the help of the participants health partner) through either the morning, early afternoon or late afternoon sessions provided at the following times: Morning Session: 9 a.m.-12 p.m.; Early Afternoon Session: 12-3 p.m.; and Late Afternoon Session: 3-6 p.m

8] Field Trips (for comprehensive programs)

- "All work and no play makes Jack a dull boy!" The goal of progressive fitness for the chronically ill is not that they may "exist" longer but that they may arrive at a greater existence.
- Field Trip "Immersions" in nature will expose the chronically ill to nature's extremely powerful healing influence.

Once the chronically ill have been given the basic fitness to get out of the house and up into the hills, an even higher and deeper form of restoration can begin. As personal renewal takes place, the paltry pleasures and apathetic indulgences that used to catch their fancy begin to fade, and they no longer hold the same sticky appeal.

The level of transformation which I believe is possible through the Lifestyle Transformation Program can be more easily illustrated than explained. Every weekend, people flock by the thousands up to Lake Tahoe in the Sierra Mountains of California. They come for many different reasons. Some come up to the lake to remember, some come up to forget. Some come … to hang out in casinos, drink alcohol, engorge themselves on salt-laden fatty foods, and gamble in dark stuffy rooms, where sunlight is blocked out and smoke is trapped in. They come to eschew good nutrition, fresh air, clean water and adequate rest; they come to this dance to forget. But once participants have been through the Lifestyle Transformation Program and have been transformed by the renewing of their mind and body; they will come to this dance to remember . . . they will return to Lake Tahoe to immerse themselves in the lake's cool, pristine waters; walk the pine-scented trails; and imbibe the fresh mountain air. They will then come to Lake Tahoe to experience the sense of beauty it awakes within them, to celebrate life and exult in the glorious healing power of nature. They come to Lake Tahoe to open wide the windows of their soul and to drink in her beauty. They come to this dance to remember.

In a lifestyle transformation *process*:

- The client is introduced to the program and its philosophy of self-empowerment.
- A baseline health and fitness assessment is conducted, involving a detailed health questionnaire and physical fitness assessment.
- The findings are evaluated by a certified health coach/personal trainer.
- A customized workout and nutritional supplement program is established.

What makes this a "Lifestyle Transformation *Program*" is that the content and its sequence are specific, attendance is monitored, group support is provided, and a health coach is assigned to each patient in order to help him/her work through the major challenges associated with personal transformation.

Lifestyle transformation is an individual phenomenon, *but the encouraging environment* within which personal transformation will most likely succeed *can be quantified and prescribed, facilitated, and group supported.* The "prescriptions" patients will have are the guidance, personal support, and resources they need to succeed. They will receive clear direction each day so all they really have to do is comply with the program until the program gets inside them and leads them from frailty into progressive fitness. All they have to do is follow the program.

As an important aside on research, another objective of the program would be to conduct ongoing efficiency studies in chronic disease prevention and reversal, to help establish:

1] The most effective health practices, interventions, and program components for reversing advanced disease states.

2] Development of "best practices" for chronic disease reversal and recovery.

3] Fiscal accountability for the most economical healing and preventive strategies.

4] Development of "Uniform Interventional Approaches, Standards, and Practices" for implementing successful Lifestyle Transformation Programs.

5] Development of specific behavioral modifications (exercises and practices) best suited to recovery from specific conditions (such as congestive heart failure, diabetes, high blood pressure, arthritis, peripheral vascular disease, and gastrointestinal disorders).

PART SEVEN: COSTS OF THE PROGRAM

As you can see, the bulk of each day's session is self-directed. After a thorough introduction to the basic principles of hydration, warm up, and cool down, these portions of each session become self-guided—an extremely economical system for health maintenance. The supervised portion of each session is also economical, because it is held in a group setting, yet remains sensitive to the special needs of the chronically ill population. Eventually, patients transition from medical oversight within the program to self-direction. Initially, the program is prescribed, but eventually it is expected that good results become a persuasive argument to continue with the suffering associated with staying well, in order to avoid the suffering associated with preventable decline.

Since people who are chronically ill constitute a marginalized population, as a *social value*, the program stops the exploitation of the weak cold in its tracks. It is more humanitarian; it restores dignity and power to the citizen and places the emphasis of medicine where it belongs—on imparting health instead of profiting off disease.

The *economic value* of the Lifestyle Transformation Program is that it restores health to the chronically ill at a fraction of the cost of treating their decline.

Before delving into the cost of the program, I want to place the issue of "cost" in its proper place; cost in its relationship to value. The cost of disease *reversal* can only be properly appreciated in its relationship and contrast to the cost of disease *progression.*

The fundamental problem with the modern medical approach is that it costs a great deal, and those costs are *guaranteed to increase* because it only addresses "damage sustained" and does next to nothing to prevent future damage. Whereas the cost of prevention—that is the cost of preventing *a far greater cost in the future*—is really a savings! The following is an excerpt from an article by George Halvorsen; then CEO of Kaiser Permanente, discussing the issue of the rising costs of healthcare and what he believes can and should be done to stem the tide.

> "Buyers are also demanding some answer about why healthcare costs continue to explode: Why is it, they ask, that consumers products such as DVD players, which a few years ago cost $700 per unit, can now sell for as little as $70—with greater functionality—while health care moves in the opposite direction with ever higher costs, fewer benefits, and, sadly, questionable quality?
>
> "Buyers want to know why the cost explosion has not been accompanied by clear and measureable quality improvements or even comparative performance information. The people writing premium checks are asking, what's so different about health care that allows it to defy the cost and quality trends that have reshaped so many other American industries?
>
> "The typical answer for the care system is to throw out the usual cost-increase suspects: an aging population that demands more care: new, expensive technologies that expand the scope of care; new, expensive drugs, many of which provide marginal, if any, improvements in

efficacy; a healthcare worker shortage; consolidation of hospitals and physicians that's giving new price leverage to providers; a national epidemic of obesity that's driving rising rates of costly chronic diseases such as diabetes and heart disease; litigation; etc.

"This is a very good list of usual suspects. Every one of them is genuinely guilty. Each is a cost driver. Each drives up a piece of the cost. Unfortunately, there is no silver bullet that can fix major percentages of healthcare costs by fixing only one of these issues. So the total impact of the cumulative costs is moving employers to a new tipping point—one that has yet to be fully defined...."

The Quality Tipping Point

Reengineering the System

"To answer that question, buyers are beginning to realize that health care needs to do what every other kind of business would do, which is to look systematically at where the dollars are being spent—the total cost of all the processes and tools for getting a healthcare product to market—and to figure out where the cost and quality issues and opportunities lie. Where are the broken or wobbly parts of the core production system that are driving costs and impeding quality improvements, and how can we fix them?

"If we look at the problem systematically, the first fact we can all recognize is where the costs really are. As the exhibit demonstrates, less than 1 percent of Americans actually require care at the [precise] level of the their average premium. There is a vast inconsistency in healthcare spending. In fact, 20 percent spend virtually zero percent of total costs, and 70 percent spend only about 10 percent of total costs. Clearly, solving the problem of healthcare cost crisis does not reside among the 70 percent of all insured Americans.

> "However, if we look at the other end of the cost continuum, opportunities abound. A mere 1 percent of the insured are consuming 30 percent of total costs, and the top 5 percent account for as much as two-thirds of all costs. Herein lies the problem- as well as the massive potential for what we might call a "5 percent solution." That solution lies in identifying the specific chronic and acute conditions that move people into that high-cost 5 percent bracket and then systematically and consistently bringing to bear strategic, targeted, consistent, high-leverage interventions to keep those people from migrating to the high-cost end of the curve. When people are in crisis, we need to provide best care. But we also need to stop large numbers of people from progressing into that crisis.
>
> "We already know what those very expensive conditions are: the leading chronic diseases and certain acute conditions like cancer that account for the lion's share of healthcare spending."[70]

80 percent of Americans typically use less than $1,000 of care in a given year. However, 5 percent of insured Americans account for more than two-thirds of total healthcare dollars—the diabetics, asthmatics, heart patients, patients with kidney failure or cancer, and other chronic disease patients with co-morbidities. If we can bring the strategic, targeted, consistent, high-leverage intensive health-promoting benefits of diet and exercise—in short, successful lifestyle transformation—to the 1%-5% most chronically ill's *vulnerability* (resulting from their disease-attracting behavior patterns), then we can release them from their self-imposed prisons of health decline and save the American economy literally billions of dollars. If we can provide the most vulnerable populations with a gently progressive systematic approach to resolving their symptoms, *at the level of their causation*, then the chronically ill will be well on their way to sustainable recovery. Achieving that one goal alone will reduce healthcare costs in America by billions of dollars.

4 STEP PLAN TO A 5% SOLUTION

1] Embrace and support the vulnerability (need for lifestyle transformation) of the 10% most chronically ill

2] Confront and address their affliction-*attracting* behaviors and hold them accountable to a healthier, happier, higher standard

3] Encourage, support, facilitate, guide, supervise and monitor their recovery from self-imposed prisons of health decline

4] Dramatically reduce the use of the (very expensive and in many cases harm-inducing) hospitalization and medical crisis intervention system

WHAT ARE THE COST VARIABLES OF THIS APPROACH?

Labor is the most significant cost factor in starting a program of this nature for the chronically ill. Other cost factors will vary considerably based on whether a basic or comprehensive program is to be created and so on.

The figures below are for estimates only. Actual costs will vary depending upon local wages, experience, and education of chosen fitness instructors/trainers. These figures offer a starting point for calculating the estimated cost outlay for personnel. I have calculated these labor figures as a starting point for consideration and comparison to the traditional "crisis intervention as healthcare" model.

WHAT ARE THE COSTS OF THE PROGRAM?

Basic Fitness Club Membership Fee:

Many health clubs such as the YMCA, 24 Hour Fitness, Nautilus Fitness Center, and various other sports and fitness clubs already offer exercise classes (albeit not adapted for the chronically ill), and the fee to the individual members is very reasonable . The typical YMCA provides classes such as water aerobics and gentle yoga, aerobics, and dance classes. They already cater to every age and ability; their monthly fees are around $65 /month. 12 mos. x $65 = $780/year for the average member fee.

Lifestyle Transformation Program Fee:

Additional or specialized classes/instruction/consultation/group facilitation for the chronically ill, which would increase the fitness centers' instructor costs, would be covered by the additional Lifestyle Transformation Program Fees. (9 mos. x $300= $2700/program fee)

WHO COVERS THE COSTS?

Medical Care Provider Portion:

Program participants would be "prescribed" to participate in the programs, and therefore should have some or all of their Basic Fitness Club Membership monthly fees covered by their medical insurance premiums. (9 mos. program x $75 = $675 [Healthcare Provider portion])

Medical Insurer/ Payor Portion:

Any additional labor/product costs: (instructors, health coaches, 12 Step facilitators, nutritional supplementation) should be covered by the medical insurer. Insurers should consider the cost/benefit analysis of paying for such a Lifestyle Transformation Program: approximately $2,700/1st year + yearly health maintenance fee thereafter.

Let us remember the costs associated with the interventional crisis / fees-for-disease profit paradigm of the American Medical Approach:

Average Cost of Hospitalization:

Per day: $3,949 per hospitalized day in the US,

Per hospitalization: $15,734 per hospital stay in the US

Many patients with chronic conditions are hospitalized more than 1 time per year for health crises that are largely preventable.

AVERAGE COST PER INPATIENT DAY ACROSS 50 STATES IN 2010[71]

Here are average costs per inpatient day, organized by hospital ownership type, in all 50 states plus the District of Columbia, according to the latest statistics from Kaiser State Health Facts.

Note: Adjusted expenses per inpatient day include expenses incurred for both inpatient and outpatient care. Inpatient days are adjusted higher to reflect an estimate of the volume of outpatient services. It is important to note that these figures are only an estimate of expenses incurred by the hospital to provide a day of inpatient care and are not a substitute for either actual charges or reimbursement for care provided.

Actual (Hospital Incurred) Direct Care Costs Per Day:

United States

State/local government hospitals — $1,625

Non-profit hospitals — $2,025

For-profit hospitals — $1,629

Hospital Fees To The Consumer

Per Day:

A hospital stay costs an average of $236 per day in India, $655 per day in France and an average of $3,949 per day in the US, according to a report—2011 Comparative Price Report Medical and Hospital Fees by Country—released by the International Federation of Health Plans[72]

Per Hospital Stay:

The United States has some of the highest prices for medical products and services in the world, according to a report by the International Federation of Health Plans. The 2011 Comparative Price Report found the average cost per hospital stay in the United States was $15,734 followed by $5,004 in Germany and $4,948 in Chile. Costs reflect an average total for hospital and physician costs for coronary artery bypass.[73]

Actual Hospital Incurred Cost Per Day (Average)	$1,759.00
Hospital Fee To Consumer Per Day (Before Insurance Negotiations)	$3,949.00
Hospital Fee To Consumer Per Hospital Stay (Average)	$15,734.00

Cost/Benefit Analysis: Strategy for Determining Cost/Benefit Value

Let's remember that we have chosen, for this program, a patient population with a known re-hospitalization history. Let's say a patient is eligible for this program if he or she has had at least one hospitalization per year for the last three consecutive years, and at least two hospitalizations/year for two of those years. That would be a minimum of five hospitalizations in the last three years. We then track these patients for the next three years, and assess the cost/benefit analysis.

So we then compare the cost of three years' worth of hospitalizations—a total of five admissions—with the cost of three years' participation in a Lifestyle Transformation program (and any hospitalizations that may happen in those three years).

What Are The Total Costs Of The Program?

Total costs for the Lifestyle Transformation Program for client include a fitness club membership fee ($75/month) + the Lifestyle Transformation Program fee ($300/month) for a total of nine months.

$75.00 x 9 mos. =	$675
$300.00 x 9 mos. =	$2,700
Total Cost:	$3,375

This comes to just under $3,500 for the first year, and much less thereafter. The following years' expenses are projected to be considerably less than the first (intensive) year as the hard-won "practices" become deeply ingrained, permanent health maintenance habits.

Please note that in the arena of medical parlance, "prevention" has a very different meaning from "health promotion." Prevention is merely *early detection* as in the case of problems discovered with pap smears, colonoscopies, and other health screenings. Only a healthier lifestyle can truly prevent disease, but alas, that is not the type of prevention that the American medical system talks about. When the American Medical Pharmaceutical Machine talks about prevention, they are not talking about eating high fiber whole foods or a diet rich in fruits and vegetables, or speaking of maintaining a high volume of physical exercise. What they mean by prevention is having a yearly colonoscopy or breast exam, after a certain age, in order to detect or catch early on the development of a problem such as breast or colon cancer.

DOES PREVENTIVE CARE SAVE MONEY?

> "An intervention is 'cost-saving' if it reduces costs while improving health. Poorly performing interventions can both increase costs and worsen health.
>
> "Careful analysis of the costs and benefits of specific interventions, rather than broad generalizations, is critical. This is important to understanding the impact of cost-saving preventive measures and also preventive measures that deliver substantial health benefits relative to their net

> costs; this analysis could also identify treatments that are cost-saving or highly efficient (i.e., cost-effective)
>
> "In addition to determining which preventive measures and treatments are most efficient, it will be necessary to identify those that are not yet fully deployed and those that could serve a large population and bring about substantial aggregate improvements in health at an acceptable cost. Findings that some cost-saving or highly efficient measures are underused would indicate that current practice is inconsistent with the efficient delivery of health care. Other services might be identified as overused, and such findings would underscore the importance of fashioning policies that provide incentives to shift practice toward more cost-effective delivery of health care. In the face of increasingly constrained resources, there is a realistic way of achieving better health results: conduct careful analysis to identify evidence-based opportunities for more efficient delivery of health care — whether prevention or treatment — and then restructure the system to create incentives that encourage the appropriate delivery of efficient interventions."[74]

Here's the take-away: from the perspective of a health "product" consumer (such as patients and health insurers), the cost of treating "Fitness Lost," i.e. chronic disease, is far greater than the cost of restoring health.

HIGH COST—HIGHLY EFFECTIVE PROGRAM

Pritikin Intensive	$7900.00 - $9900.00
Lifestyle Intervention	2 Week Intensive Live-In Program
www.pritikin.com/	

LOW COST EFFECTIVE PROGRAMS

YMCA	$50.00 - $75.00/month
Silver Sneakers www.silversneakers.com	Silver Sneakers is paid for at the corporate level by Medical Insurers directly to Silver Sneakers. Silver Sneakers is a benefit; which provides members with a free health club membership as a benefit under their healthcare plan.

CORPORATE WELLNESS PROGRAMS

1] Health Project website: thehealthproject.com. *Information presented in the report on notable employee wellness programs was obtained primarily from this website.*

2] Table 2–National Health Expenditure Amounts and Average Percent Change by Type of Expenditure: Selected Calendar Years 1980-2012. CMS website/OACT projections (cms.hhs.gov/statistics/nhe/projections-2002/t2.asp).

3] CDC website: www.cdc.gov/nccdphp

Corporate costs varied based on program components, classrooms, and facilities required, employees in the program, etc. Bottom Line: Reviews on ROI (return on investment) concluded the following cost to benefit ratios: Savings ranged from $1.49 to $4.91 in benefits (corporate cost reduction) per dollar spent on the program, with a median of $3.14 (decrease in corporate costs related to medical expenses, lost work hours, etc).

Now, let's compare the above Lifestyle Transformation Program costs to the conventional, American Medical-endorsed and -enforced approach. Extremely significant to this proposed program is the assessment of return on investment. We can measure past medical expenses for a chronically ill individual, and, from them, project with some certainty what future expenses *would be* in a conventional medical treatment model.

CALCULATING COSTS OF HEALTH PROMOTION COMPARED TO

TREATING PREVENTABLE DISEASE PROGRESSION

We can also measure the *cost of administering* this new prevention-focused model, the *cost for a patient to participate*, and his/her *medical expenses following completion of this program.* Cost can be calculated by subtracting the cost of providing the Effective Medical Approach from the cost of treating un-prevented declines. (The cost of treating un-prevented declines can be *projected* by measuring the client's *actual* hospitalization costs for the three years prior to entry into the program.)

A comparison of one patient's medical expenses before and after entering this new program, as well as future projected costs, will be of vital importance to determining just how financially advantageous the new model is to patients, the government, and insurers. From there, we can determine the aggregate benefit to the insurance and business worlds, and indeed, to society as a whole.

Does it seem ridiculously *unaffordable* to bring the chronically ill and those at risk for steep declines in health out of their comfortable, well-entrenched, disease-incubating ruts—and place them into a program and environment designed to elicit a strongly therapeutic healing response? Let's remember that the average cost of one hospital admission is more than $10,000. Might preventing decline by promoting fitness for the chronically ill help them become more disease-resistant and thus cost society far less? Fitness has a way of gently challenging its citizens to rise up to its tougher demands, but then rewards them with health and vigor and vistas that the unfit never realize.

Expenditures in the United States on health care surpassed $2.3 trillion in 2008, more than three times the $714 billion spent in 1990, and over eight times the $253 billion spent in 1980. Slowing this growth has become a major U.S. government policy priority. Employers and consumers alike are struggling to keep up.

The nature of health care in the U.S. has changed dramatically over the past century, with longer life spans and more attention to prolonging life—even poor quality of life. Chronic illness is up, and this has placed a tremendous burden on society regarding costs associated with the health care system. There is an ever-increasing need for treatment of ongoing illnesses. Never before has there been such an emphasis placed, or need for, long-term care services. It is estimated that health care costs for chronic disease treatment account for over 75% of national health expenditures.

Many employers are providing financial incentives to workers for engaging in the wellness needed to stem the rise of chronic conditions, by encouraging employees to exercise, quit smoking, and choose better diet options.[75]

SUMMARY

Expenditures in the United States on health care surpassed $2.3 trillion in 2008. It is estimated that health care costs for chronic disease treatment account for over 75% of national health expenditures. 75% of 2.3 trillion = 1.7 trillion dollars being spent annually on the treatment of chronic disease.

In regards to the cost/benefit analysis of the patients chosen for this example, the entry criterion for participation was for them to have been hospitalized at least 1 time per year for the last 3 years and at least 2 times per year for 1 of the last 3 years. If we estimate the avg. cost of each hospitalization at $15,000.00 (x 4 hospitalizations), then we have a cost of $60,000.00 for their last 3 years of conventional care. As noted previously, the total cost of the Lifestyle Transformation Program is less than $5,000.00 for 3 years. The only figure remaining unknown is the cost of hospitalizations for the 3 years following entry in the program.

Cost of Hospitalization = $15,000.00 x 4 Hospitalizations = $60,000.00

4 Hospitalization = $60,000.00 x .75 (*Projected* Cost Reduction) = $45,000.00 savings over 3 years

I do not claim that all chronic disease is rooted in behavior. I do claim that an impeccable diet and active lifestyle diminishes the impact of every other contributor to chronic disease. A healthy lifestyle can often reverse chronic disease, but what it cannot fully reverse it can still greatly mitigate; that is, greatly decrease the damage being experienced.

Much of chronic disease is the outright consequence of poor diet and sedentary behavior. And that is my current focus. To use a metaphor, the chronically ill are much like people whose "Health Reserve" is comparable to living paycheck to paycheck. They are getting by - but just barely. Any drop in health status or health "income" and they find themselves out on the street and homeless, which is to say, they find themselves back in the hospital.

The whole purpose of living above the Afflication Zone is to gain some Health Equity and Health Reserve comparable to financial reserve to fall back on when hard times hit, that is, "hits to your health" happen. By supporting the chronically ill population's acquisition of Health Wealth, they thus acquire the physical reserve that they will need to fall back on when hard health times hit.

This all translates into fewer hospitalizations, which translate into the savings of billions of dollars for the nation and the marked diminishment of human suffering for the American people. I strongly assert that hospitalizations of the chronically ill could be reduced by 75% with the implementation of the Effective Medical Approach.

75% *Projected* Cost Reduction = $45,000.00 Savings (minus) $5,000.00 (Approximate Cumulative Cost of Lifestyle Fitness Program for 3 years)

$45,000.00 - $5,000.00 = $40,000.00 Savings (per patient) every 3 years

Projected Savings Over 3 Years:

1 patient	$40,000.00 (thousand)
10 patients	$400,000.00
100 patients	$4,000,000.00 (million)
1,000 patients	$40,000,000.00
10,000 patients	$400,000,000.00
100,000 patients	$4,000,000,000.00 (billion)
1,000,000 patients	$40,000,000,000.00
10,000,000 patients	$400,000,000,000.00

Projected Savings Over 1 year:

[Formula] 3 yr. savings (x .33) = 1 yr. savings

1 patient	$13,300.00 (thousand)
10 patients	$133,000.00
100 patients	$1,330,000.00 (million)
1000 patients	$13,300,000.00
10,000 patients	$133,000,000.00
100,000 patients	$1,300,000,000.00 (billion)
1,000,000 patients	$13,300,000,000.00
10,000,000 patients	$133,000,000,000.00

These projected savings are based upon a projected 75% reduction in hospitalizations.

These projections reflect the savings *after including the cost* of a Lifestyle Transformation Program.

These figures only consider the estimated reduction in cost of hospitalizations. They also do not consider the savings that would result from reduced medication intake, nor do they reflect the reduction in adverse drug reactions, which currently cost $183 billion each year.

Note: These projections only reflect an approximation of the savings achieved among the 5% most chronically ill. Granted, this particular population spends a lion's share of all medical dollars spent (and is why the paradigm shift begins with them). However, these projected savings only reflect the tip of the iceberg as this health movement catches on and *intelligence replaces indolence* among the general population.

The prescription, incentives, and support of a "fitness lifestyle" are by far the most effective solution to the problem of chronic disease among all people the whole world over.

- It is scientifically well-established that chronic disease is largely *a lifestyle-induced condition.*
- It is scientifically well-established *that chronic disease responds* quickly and effectively to the introduction of healthier lifestyle interventions.
- It is therefore reasonable to assume that the massive cost resulting from the unattended progression of chronic disease (resulting from America's opportunistic *treatment-focused* medical paradigm) will be hugely reduced as a result of the institution of an *Effective Medical Approach* replacing the *American Medical Approach.*

I believe that it is reasonable to assume that the total yearly debt resulting from chronic disease in America could be reduced by 50% *if the interventions for chronic disease were to reflect what the best scientific evidence demonstrates.* The best evidence-based, *patient-centered* approach to chronic disease management starts, continues, and ends with strategic, targeted, highly effective lifestyle interventions that result in bringing the chronically ill "down off the ledge" of precipitous health declines, and into the fold of well-managed, low-cost, and healthy self-maintenance. The costs of treating the chronically ill's un-corrected *lifestyle-induced* trajectory of decline is well over 1.5 trillion dollars a year, and I believe it is reasonable to project that this cost could be reduced by 50%, or from 1.5 trillion dollars per year down to 750 billion dollars per year.

In conclusion, let me emphasize that *the money is already in the system* for these far superior, far more effective, considerably more economical interventions. In fact, within the system I am outlining, far less money will be spent on the chronically ill, not more. That is because the cost of the less-effective "treatment model" that is endorsed and enforced by the American Medical Approach for treating the symptoms of preventable declines is far greater than the Effective Medical Approach, which depends upon eliminating/reducing the effects by transforming the underlying behavioral causes.

"We are what we repeatedly do. Excellence,
then, is not an act, but a habit."
- Aristotle

The nation that does not spend a sufficient amount of its resources promoting the health of its people will inevitably spend a far greater percentage of its resources treating the chronic diseases of its people.

"An ounce of prevention is worth a pound of cure."

Improving patient education programs will greatly help in reducing rates of hospitalization and re-hospitalization. However, I believe that the most effective use of limited financial resources will be the promotion of aggressive, targeted comprehensive lifestyle transformation programs committed to supporting the 5% - 10% most chronically ill in adopting a lifestyle pattern that optimizes their health and wellness at every age.

SUMMARY:

Train the mind and the body will follow…

Human personality and behavior respond well to nurturing and positive reinforcement.

To effectively reduce the medical costs of our nation, it will require more effort and energy be applied to training up our patients in the ways of healthy self-maintenance.

The effects of legislative efforts to mandate more effective patient education programs and rapid follow up of patients in the home health setting has led to significant reductions in the costs associated with frequent re-hospitalizations.

But what is still needed is federal funding to support the 5% - 10% most costly patients adoption of a health promoting lifestyle. Once patients begin to participate in healthier habits and reap the benefits of an improving sense of well-being, they will become increasingly convinced of those habits enduring value and strive to maintain their newly acquired habits and lifestyle in order to continue to enjoy improving health. Both wisdom and health are their own greatest reward and once partaken of they are not easily forsaken.

But I want to be clear, the most effective reductions in medical costs for our nation will come from targeted (population specific) lifestyle transformation programs designed to meet the specific needs, challenges and barriers of the 5% - 10% most costly, most chronically ill patient population, that is, meeting the health maintenance needs of those patients that are our nation's highest "utilizers" of medical services. By simply supporting their highest level of health & fitness we avoid the astronomical costs associated with treating their ever deepening cascades of health decline.

For more evidence that demonstrates that "A Healthy Lifestyle

Decreases Hospital Utilization and Medical Costs" please see the appendix dedicated to that topic at the end of the book.

Prelude to Chapter 7.
Re-Orientation—
Getting The Most From The Rest of This Book

When I wrote this book, I held two audiences in mind: those affected by chronic disease (either their own or of someone they love), and those with the responsibility of treating the chronically ill, either on the front lines of direct patient care or in healthcare management, policy and reform. Every healthcare professional has a responsibility to be his/her patients' advocate. If they are not committed to that, first and foremost, then they are in the wrong business. Each of these audiences has a personal responsibility. The first has a responsibility to overcome chronic disease by living in a way that is *consistent* with their recovery. Their only other alternative is to live in a way that is *inconsistent* with their recovery, which is to encourage their own decline. The second has a responsibility to provide treatment that is consistent with the "goal of payment" which, I contend, is for patients *to get well* and not simply to have the symptoms of their progressive decline treated and/or medicated.

The first group consists of people who are chronically ill, as well as their family and their friends. They've been told that their salvation lies in prescription drugs and surgical procedures, and there are strong reasons to believe that this is not so—that these products of the American medical-pharmaceutical machine actually prolong the underlying illness by treating symptoms instead of addressing causes. Members of this group need hope that health and wellness are actually possible, and they also need a specific "framework of help" to make what is a possibility into their personal experience.

The second group consists of all healthcare professionals, doctors, nurses, and therapists, as well as healthcare managers, administrators, healthcare policymakers, and healthcare reformers—men and women involved with legislative groups and non-profit leadership, and with granting foundations and advocacy agencies. Members of this group need to examine their mission, and if it is to improve the health of their patients, they need to lead their patients, practice, and the industry in the direction that will most effectively fulfill that mission. That is, they have a moral mandate to promote the type of healthcare that the best evidence supports.

Both of these groups need to grasp that our healthcare crisis is largely the result of an unwillingness to do the "real work". Real solutions require time and hard work, whereas consumers, corporations, and social systems seem fixated on short-term gratification. Perhaps that is why we are so caught up with providing (or accepting) "solutions" that only treat the effects instead of examining and rooting out the causes. It takes a great deal more time and dogged determination to dig beneath the surface and unearth the real problems, and to discover where the real solutions lie. Throughout this book, I examine threads of connection, some for better and many for worse, between the people, processes, products, and politics of medicine.

PLEASE BE ADVISED . . .

The following are reviews and analyses (interspersed with my own personal commentary) on numerous books, studies, reports and papers. I have reviewed thousands of pages of material over a 10 year period on the subject matter for this book. In this section of the book, I have attempted to provide a review and summary of some of the most articulate voices on the state of our nation's health.

I have reviewed the subject in two broad categories:

Part 1) The Dilemma: Cause, Consequence and Outcomes

Part 2) The Solution: Cause, Consequence and Outcomes

To further elaborate, this section is broken up into two parts.

In Part One, *The Dilemma –Problems with the American Medical System,* I discuss what I believe to be the foundation, or underlying *cause,* of the most complex problem with the American Medical System, which bears a naturally resulting *consequence,* which has matured into full blown *outcomes.*

In Part Two, *The Solution to the American Medical System Approach,* I discuss what I believe to be the foundation, or the underlying *cause,* of the simplest and most effective solution to the problem with the American Medical System, which bears a naturally resulting *consequence,* which has matured into full blown *outcomes.*[76]

Now a word about classifications:

We use classifications to help us understand things, *but life itself* is far too complex, dynamic, fluid, and messy to stuff into neat little boxes.

With that in mind, I have attempted to shed light on America's growing epidemic of chronic disease and what we can do about it.

Chapter 7.
Influences of the American Medical System on Adulthood and Aging,
Part 1: The Dilemma

WHAT CAUSED THE PROBLEM WITH THE AMERICAN MEDICAL SYSTEM

The following is a brief review and commentary of salient chapters of a most excellent book exposing the influences of the American medical system on adulthood and aging in America. For anyone with an interest in this subject, I heartily recommend reading *"Overdosed America: The Broken Promise of American Medicine - How The Pharmaceutical Companies Are Corrupting Science, Misleading Doctors, And Threatening Your Health*, by Dr. John Abramson as the most articulate voice on the subject.

"Of all the forms of inequality, injustice in healthcare is the most shocking and inhumane."
- Martin Luther King Jr.

What happens when the quest for corporate profit guides medical research? What happens when the welfare of mankind is less profitable than the progression of disease? What happens when corporations whose profits depend upon disease are placed in charge of a nation's medical care system?

The following is an outline of the material to follow, as well as an outline of what I believe to be the American Medical System's *worst problems,* along with recommended *best solutions.*

Problems

- We were doing so well! *What happened?*
- Expensive
- Ineffective
- Changing source of funding for medical research
- Changing purpose for which medical knowledge is acquired
- Modern medicine needs advancing disease for its livelihood
- Normal cost drivers are not a real problem—perverse incentives are

Recommended Solutions

- Correcting perverse economic incentives
- Separating real science from commercial distortions
- Applying the right interventions at the right time
- Creating economic stimuli to improve health outcomes

"Everyone knows that high cholesterol is the greatest risk for coronary heart disease, right?... The National Cholesterol Education Program has been remarkably successful in achieving its goal of raising awareness and understanding about high blood cholesterol as a risk factor for coronary heart disease (CHD) and the benefits of lowering cholesterol levels as a means of preventing CHD." So successful, in fact, that about twice as many people discuss cholesterol with their doctors during physical exams (67 percent) as are counseled about the importance of routine exercise (34 percent) as are advised (of smokers) to quit smoking (37 percent). Even the most obvious counseling, advising obese people to lose weight, occurs at only 42 percent of obese people's yearly checkups."

- Dr. John Abramson[77]

America's Changing Health Status In The 70'S—80'S—90'S

"The good news is that the death rate from coronary heart disease has dropped quite dramatically since its peak in 1968." Several factors are responsible for that. Way back in 1964, just a few months after JFK was assassinated, the first Surgeon General issued the first report on the dangers of smoking, and since then, the percentage of adult smokers in the U.S. began to decline; from 42 percent in 1965 to 25 percent in 1990. Continuing along the same track, in the early 70s, the American public became more conscious of the importance of maintaining a healthier lifestyle to ward off the risks of heart disease. As a result, America's per capita consumption of beef, eggs and whole milk began to decline and people started exercising more. The death rate from heart disease went down by half between 1970 and 1990.[78]

American Medicine's Changing Source Of Research Funding

During the 1960s through the 70s, most medical research was funded by the federal government through the National Institutes of Health. But in the late 70s, the federal government gradually withdrew funding for medical research. Into this gap stepped commercial funding by the drug and medical device industry, until, by the mid 90s, the great majority of medical research was commercially funded.

A Medical Revolution Is Launched!

In the wake of industry-financed research, the industry began to make many breakthroughs in drug and medical device technology in the mid 80s, with the creation of a clot-busting medication and the first generation of cholesterol-lowering medications. Angioplasty surgery and wire stent placement procedures were developed, and all these advances in drug therapy and breakthroughs in medical procedures were marketed to Americans as holding great promise for improving the health of all Americans.

WE WERE DOING SO WELL! WHAT HAPPENED?

What effect did all of these breakthroughs and advances in technology have on the death rate from coronary heart disease? "Instead of a dramatic improvement, the rate of decline in the death rate actually slowed during the 1990s (from an average decline of 3.1 percent per year between 1970 and 1990 to 2.8 percent per year between 1990 and 2000)."

Why didn't the death rate decline at an even faster rate after all these great breakthroughs in prevention and treatment? It appears that announced advances in medicines diverted our attention away from the healthy lifestyle changes that had been working so well over the previous two decades.

The declining number of Americans who smoked leveled off in 1990 through 2002. "The percentage of obese Americans nearly doubled between 1990 and 2002 (11.6 percent versus 22.1 percent)." The number of Americans with type 2 diabetes increased proportionately—largely the result of growing rates of obesity. They call this twin phenomenon diabesity. But, I've digressed, the great progress made in lowering high blood pressure in the 1970s and 80s stalled in the 1990s, again probably secondary to growing rates of obesity, diabetes, and increasingly sedentary lifestyles.

"The problem is that all the current medical recommendations, public education campaigns, drug advertisements, and news of breakthroughs in the prevention of heart disease give the benefits of a healthy lifestyle just enough lip service to preempt criticism that these issues are being ignored. The end result is that doctors and patients are being distracted from what the research really shows: physical fitness, smoking cessation, and a healthy diet trump nearly every medical intervention as the best way to keep coronary heart disease at bay." [79]

Timeline of Modern Medicine - Correlation between drug promotion and decline in fitness promotion.

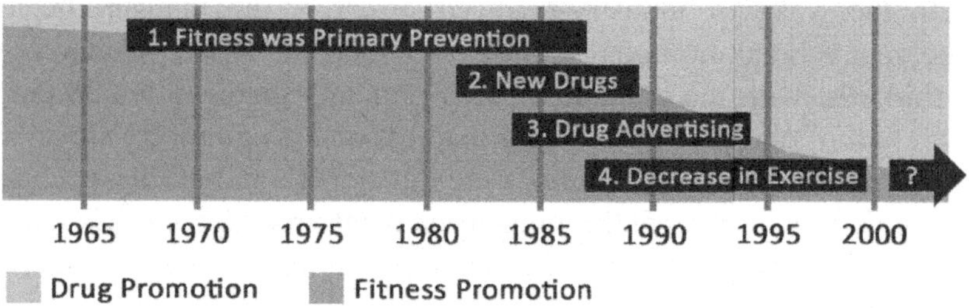

1] At the time of the *greatest advances* in medicine's measurable reduction of the prevalence of heart disease (between 1967 – 1987), lifestyle modification was the primary and *virtually only* intervention available.

2] However, in the mid 1980s modern medicine began unveiling its technological revolution: introducing its medical advances and breakthroughs. In the latter half of the 1980s, modern medicine began to showcase its advances in the "prevention" and treatment of heart disease.

3] The public's interest in and commitment to lifestyle changes in the 1970s and 1980s began to wane in the late 1980s and early 1990s in response to pharmaceutical and medical device marketing through multiple media formats... PhaRMA and its medical advertisers succeeded in pulling the public's attention off the value of exercise and fixating it upon the marvels of its drugs and medical devices.

4] We can see a strong, *negative correlation* between modern medicine's increasing promotion of drugs, devices, and medical procedures in comparison to the public's relaxing of its commitment to exercise. Following modern medicine's revolution in "preventive care" in the latter half of the 1980s and through the 1990s, we see a statistically significant decrease in exercise as well as a statistically significant increase in obesity and chronic disease.

Medicine Stokes 'Em	Medicine Soaks 'Em
• False and misleading medical propaganda. • Pharmaceutical advertising dressed up as medical research. • Pharmaceutically funded *public education*—cholesterol lowering campaigns.	• Over inflated drug costs • World's most costly healthcare • *"Excess health care expenditures* in the United States in 2004 will amount to about $530 billion (based on estimated total health care expenditures of 1.8 trillion)."

Unfortunately, our genes were not as impressed by medicine's educational campaign as we were. Evidently our genes don't read cholesterol tables. For example, in 1999 the Journal of American Medical Association (JAMA) published results of a study of data collected on 25,000 executive and professional men. The study performed comprehensive physical exams that measured diet, cholesterol, and fitness levels of these men, and ten years later correlated that data to the deaths that had occurred from all-cause and cardiovascular disease in order to determine what factors contributed most. What they determined was that "being among the 20 percent least physically fit (as determined by the results of a treadmill test) is a far greater health risk than an elevated total cholesterol level (above 240 mg/dL)." It turns out that, among men with normal weight, low fitness increases their risk of death by 60%, and for overweight men, low fitness increases their risk of death by 70%.[80]

Your morbidity and mortality risk is far more responsive to your lifestyle choices than to what drugs your doctor prescribes to you. However on another note, what has significantly increased morbidity and mortality rates in America is modern medicine's turning of people's attention away from the things that really do work, such as exercise and proper diet, and instead directed their attention to pharmaceuticals. That influence has deeply undermined the health of Americans. The purpose of this discussion of the pitfalls and shortcomings of medicine is not to have you reject modern medicine, but to squarely grasp its limitations.

Let's remember that two thirds of modern medical care are performing their function well. The function for which modern medicine works best and the domain in which it excels is the aggressive treatment of acute health crisis. This is its forte. However, chronic diseases develop very slowly, . . . over a long period of time, and are *far more responsive* to lifestyle interventions. Modern medicine is completely inept and ill-equipped to provide the lifestyle management interventions that the chronically ill so desperately need. But modern medicine's refusal to refer the chronically ill to resources far better equipped to meet their needs (for lifestyle reform) implicates their hand and role in promoting the largely preventable declines in the health of the chronically ill.

Funding Changes Hands

Prior to 1970, most medical research was funded by the federal government through the National Institutes of Health. The purposes of federally-sponsored medical research was the prevention of disease and, where present, it's reduction and cost containment. In the 1970s, medical researchers were said to be thumbing "their academic noses at industrial money" as reported in the Journal of Science in 1982, according to Natural Pedia.

However, in the late 70s and through into the 80s government-funded medical research continued to decline, until in 1990 almost two-thirds of requests for research funding were denied by NIH. As universities and researchers were forced to look for other sources of funding, attitudes toward industrial money changed. As federal funding of medical research became tighter and tighter, the drug companies were more than willing to step in and lend a guiding hand.

As drug and biotech industries assumed an ever-larger role in funding clinical trials (reaching 80 percent by 2002), they increasingly exercised the power of their purse. Drug and biotech industries began controlling research design, data analysis, and even writing up the conclusions and submitting complete articles to prestigious medical journals. In 1999, Dr. Drummond Rennie, deputy editor of the Journal of the American Medical Association, characterized the response of academic institutions to this changing climate: "They are seduced by industry funding, and frightened that if they don't go along with these gag orders, the money will go to less rigorous institutions. It's a race to the ethical bottom."[81]

Changing The Purpose For Which Medical Knowledge Is Used

It is well known that medical research has become big business, risking and making billions of dollars. Scientific discovery based on rigorous research, on the other hand, is, well, unpredictable. There is far too much money at stake to leave the conclusions of medical research to the uncertainties of science. Because of this, the role of the pharmaceutical, drug, and medical-device companies has changed so that the most important product they produce is scientific evidence, not things they make. It is this scientific evidence that drives profits.

Rigorous and well-performed scientific studies are an obstacle to bringing products to market: it is for this reason that the age-old standards of "good science" are being radically undermined—to bend it to the will of its corporate suitors.

If we are to begin to solve the crisis of American medicine, we first need to stop pretending that the current organization of the production and dissemination of medical knowledge is serving the public's interest. The ideal of "well ordered science" (a phrase coined by philosopher Philip Kitcher in his book *Science Truth, and Democracy*) is often replaced in commercially sponsored medical research by the ideal of profit-maximizing science.

This is the mother of all sleights of hand: the transformation of medical science from a public good, whose purpose is to improve health, into a commodity whose primary function is to maximize financial returns.

"The drug companies' funding '*buys them the right* to set the research agenda. The result of commercial sponsorship is that medical knowledge grows in the direction that maximizes corporate profits, in much the same way that plants grow toward sunlight. The questions that do get answered, and thus *become our medical knowledge*, are often not the ones that will contribute most to improving our health."[82]

Over time, the esteemed body of medical knowledge simply becomes a product catalog for its pharmaceutical manufacturers and serves as its prescribing physician's desk reference.

Modern medicine is effective for many acute conditions, but it is not a "Holy Grail," especially for chronic diseases. In fact, as I discuss later, modern medicine is responsible for a great deal of harm. The dazzling lights of advertising and medical "breakthroughs," displace our common wisdom. We get caught up in the plea to "talk to your doctor about it."

The problem, however, goes a lot deeper than simply exploiting doctors and the public's susceptibility to aggressive advertising. By systematically saturating doctors and the public's information sources with new drugs, medical breakthroughs, cholesterol and blood pressure guidelines, and doctor recommendations from a commercially distorted perspective, the medical device and pharmaceutical manufacturing industries are deceiving the American people and leading them deeper and deeper into dependency upon drugs, as well as damaging their health. Most Americans are convinced that the answer to every health problem is in a brand-name pill or over-priced medical procedure.

That is not merely exuberant advertising—it demonstrates fraudulent intent. To advertise is part of business; but to deceive and misrepresent is fraudulent. This crime is costing Americans billions of dollars, and worse, it is eroding the health of countless millions and lowering the quality of their lives. Exposing the distortions of commercially driven medicine is an essential part of restoring integrity to medicine. However, it is still important to remember that "about two-thirds of our medical care is beneficial and even lifesaving."[83]

What IS working in modern medicine → *acute crisis intervention*

"The biomedical model works exquisitely for some problems, from emergency surgery and successful organ transplantation to the cure of strep throats and life-threatening infections. The problem is not the biomedical model itself; but like any good tool, it must be used in the right circumstances. The problem is the illusion that the biomedical approach is the only valid approach to all of our health problems."[84]

What is NOT working in modern medicine → *Falsely inflating the value and effectiveness of medication, leading the public to place their trust and reliance in medications for the treatment of lifestyle-induced chronic conditions.*

Solution: Mandatory referral of the 1% - 5% most chronically ill (by hospital systems) to lifestyle transformation programs. A vast tome of good science indicates the superiority of lifestyle transformation over drugs / invasive procedures for the treatment of chronic conditions.

"Hundreds of billions of dollars are being flushed away because care isn't related closely to need."
– Dr. Donald Berwick[85]

This pattern will not change until economic incentives are closely related to patients' needs for recovery. If you want *to understand* which way medicine has been intentionally going, *follow the money*—down its "fees-for-disease" trail. If you want *to direct* which way medicine will be going, *lead with the money* and blaze a new trail by rewarding better outcomes with higher "fees-for-recoveries."

As discussed earlier, it is estimated that 500 billion per year could be saved by limiting medical care to real medical needs. I estimate that those savings could be increased by another 300 billion per year by providing comprehensive lifestyle interventions to the 1% - 5% most-chronically ill who account for 65 cents of every dollar spent on medicine in America. Stabilizing their condition can dramatically reduce their need for medical care and the costs related to that care.

It will be very difficult to reign in the excesses of commercialized medicine because they are in it for the money, and deceit and sleight-of-hand are the only dealings these predators understand. There will be no end to their distortion of medical studies and their production of medical "evidence" to guide prescriptive practice. Chasing down these devils in the labyrinths of their own tunnels will continually leave us burned. However, there is another way. These disease-mongering predators focus their trade mainly on the most vulnerable of our population. This has always been the way of predators—to isolate and tear apart the vulnerable members of any given group.

If the designated guardian of the American masses, that is, the Federal Government, rises to its designated appointment, it can strengthen the feeble knees and hands that hang down and thus restore the health of this vulnerable and self-marginalizing population and lift them up out of the murky waters of preventable disease, saving our nation hundreds of billions of dollars every year. All that is needed is for the government to create economic incentives that reward health promotion and disease reversal, while at the same time progressively diminish the rewards (reimbursement) for the treatment of the progression of preventable health declines.

Consider these comparisons:

- Toyota was made profitable by producing safe, reliable, efficient cars.
- Airlines were made profitable by providing safe, reliable, efficient air travel.
- American medicine is made profitable through costly, redundant treatment of progressively sicker patients.

Modern medicine made profitable by advancing disease.

"Is there any organization that would spend 35 times more money to deal with the effects of a problem than it would to solve the problem? It makes no sense in the private sector, and, with current concerns about spending rates and budget caps, it should make no sense in government." - Michael Milken

Bloomberg ranked countries based on the efficiency of their health-care systems. Among advanced economies, the U.S. spends the most on health care on a relative cost basis with the worst outcome, say Bloomberg analysts.

Methodology: Each country was ranked on three criteria: life expectancy (weighted 60%), relative per capita cost of health care (30%); and absolute per capita cost of health care (10%). Countries were scored on each criterion and the scores were weighted and summed to obtain their efficiency scores. Relative cost is health cost per capita as a percentage of GDP per capita. Absolute cost is total health expenditure, which covers preventive and curative health services, family planning, nutrition activities and emergency aid. Included were countries with populations of at least five million, GDP per capita of at least $5,000 and life expectancy of at least 70 years.

Country Comparisons For Quality Of Life (Partial List)					
RANK	COUNTRY	EFFICIENCY SCORE	LIFE EXPECTANCY	HEALTH-CARE COST AS A PERCENT OF GDP PER CAPITA	HEALTH-CARE COST PER CAPITA
1	Hong Kong	92.6	83.4	3.8%	$1,409
3	Japan	74.1	82.6	8.5%	$3,958
9	Switzer-land	63.1	82.7	11.5%	$9,121
28	Cuba	46.8	79.1	11.3%	$606
46	United States	30.8	78.6	17.2%	$8,608

The information above is taken from the *U.S. Health-Care System Ranks as One of the Least-Efficient* (September 28, 2016).[86]

In terms of quality (efficiency), the U.S. ranks a lowly 46th out of the 48 countries measured; but in terms of healthcare cost as a percent of GDP (per person cost) we are in first place. No one even comes close to America's combination of poor quality and high cost.

Expensive!

"Despite the poor performance of the American health care system, our health care costs are simply staggering…Even taking into account our higher per person gross domestic product, the United States spends 42 percent more on healthcare per person than would be expected, given spending on healthcare in other OECD nations."[87]

"Whether we say we could spend 30 percent less on healthcare or we say we are spending 42 percent extra, the bottom line is that excess health care expenditures in the United States in 2004 will amount to about $530 billion (based on estimated total health care expenditures of 1.8 trillion)."[88]

Ineffective!

Dr. Barbara Starfield, University Distinguished Professor at Johns

Hopkins School of Public Health, compared the health of 13 industrialized nations. She determined that "the U.S. population does not have anywhere near the best health in the world." She compared these 13 nations and found that the health of Americans was close to the worst on most measures, and overall ranked second to last. Surprisingly, American's rates of red meat consumption, smoking and drinking ranked in the better half for these measures. Dr. Starfield's studies are confirmed by an extensive comparison of the health of the citizens of industrialized countries done by the Organisation for Economic Co-Operation and Development (OECD). Their report again ranked the United States poorly, with 18 industrialized nations having greater life expectancy. One of the best indicators of a country's health was developed by the World Health Organization (WHO) and measures the number of years that a child born now can expect to live in good health (i.e., total life expectancy minus years of illness adjusted for quality of life), and is called "healthy life expectancy".

As of 2004, Americans' *"healthy life expectancy"* is ranked 22 out of 23 industrialized countries, better only than the Czech Republic. Children born in Japan can expect to live 75.3 healthy years, children in the other 22 industrialized nations can expect to live 71.8 healthy years, and children living in the United States can expect to live 69.3 healthy years.

Finally, "performance on the level of health" measures the efficiency with which health care systems improve their citizens' overall health. *On this measure, the United States' ranking drops to a lowly 72 in the world.*[89]

American medicine's corporate cunning is hunting down its own people. The drug and medical device industries have become too powerful for their own country's health. It is the duty of our government to protect the American people from the pathological greed of corporate monopolies and to break up those monopolies when they threaten the safety and economic stability of the nation.

Enough is enough. It is time for a just accounting. The intentional deceiving and harming of the American people must be stopped. How can these conflicts of interest be tolerated? Is there no virtue, no dignity, no power to overthrow those by whom we are being overthrown?

Theodore Roosevelt said, "It is no limitation upon property rights or freedom of contract to require that when men receive from government the privilege of doing business under corporate form . . . they shall do so upon absolutely truthful representations. . . .Great corporations exist only because they are created and safeguarded by our institutions; and it is therefore our right and duty to see that they work in harmony with these institutions."

The U.S. healthcare system clearly stands alone among the nations of the world. No other nation provides such poor quality of care at such a high cost. We must be careful though, in the terms we use to describe this phenomenon. Whether this phenomenon is a success or failure depends entirely upon the economic incentives driving the system. The failure of the U.S. health system to serve America's medical needs *effectively* can be seen in American's poor health status (as compared to other OECD countries) combined with our low quality of medical care (according to a Rand Corporation study measuring standardized health system metrics)[90] and our health system's singularly high cost. However, these results are not failures but predictable outcomes, given the economic incentives driving American healthcare. These are not failures, but successes. The American medical machine has done very well, enjoying astronomical profits, as Americans' health have fallen further behind other nations, and our healthcare spending has stretched lengths ahead of every other nation. Health care spending in the United States has increased almost sixfold, and the percentage of our GDP devoted to healthcare has risen from 8.8 to 17.2 between 1980 and 2012.

The fee-for-service reimbursement model creates incentives for medical systems to rack up charges. "Doctors and hospitals are paid more for doing more, largely without regard for evidence of improved health outcomes (examples can be found in the rapid increase in the number of MRI machines, excess capacity for neonatology and invasive cardiac procedures that lead to excess use, and the approximately 12,000 deaths that occur each year as a result of unnecessary surgery). Health care providers that deliver high quality, efficient care are financially penalized for not delivering a higher volume of more intensive services, beneficial or not (referred to as the 'perverse incentive')."[91]

Normal Healthcare "Cost Drivers"

- Chronic disease, obesity and co-morbidities, lifestyle factors and personal health choices
- Fee-for-service reimbursement
- Unnecessary tests and treatments
- Prescription drugs
- Advances in medical technology
- Lack of transparency about cost and quality, compounded by limited data with which to inform consumer choice
- Structure and supply of the health professionals
- Fragmentation in care delivery
- Administrative burden on providers, payers and patients
- The health care legal and regulatory environment

The biggest cost driver in this list is chronic disease. 65 cents of every dollar spent on medicine in America is spent on the 1% - 5% most chronically ill. The key to achieving the greatest healthcare savings is to identify the most significant cost drivers and handle them. We already know that the greatest cost driver in healthcare is advancing chronic disease, and we also know from countless diet and exercise studies exactly what can be done to bring them under much better control. Chronic diseases are most effectively managed through comprehensive health promotion. We don't need to manage chronic diseases so much as reverse them through the immersion of the chronically ill in exceedingly healthy lifestyles.

The following quote is from Dr. John Abramson. But first, a word of praise: Dr. John Abramson, in his book "Overdosed America," has provided a poignant and compelling exposé of the forces affecting American Medical care. I have quoted him often because there simply is no clearer voice on the subject. He has raised the curtain on medical corruption and invites us to take our place beside him in protecting our health and the health of our loved ones against predatory medical practices. Dr. John Abramson knows, but more importantly, he cares.

> "How could the market have allowed the medical industries to thrive while serving Americans' health needs so poorly and inefficiently? The problem is not with the market itself, but with the inadequate information and flawed incentives that currently shape our health care market. Drug companies earn higher profits when more people use expensive drugs, not when more people achieve better health.
>
> "Of course, the medical industry would do everything in its enormous power to prevent having to relinquish its control over medical knowledge. But what purpose is served by the current situation, in which the public's interest in effective and efficient health care is subjugated to the commercial goals of the medical industry?"[92]

The medical industry will not willingly let go of the chronically ill, whom they have worked so hard to indoctrinate into a lifestyle of drug dependency, and release them to be served by organizations committed to the promotion of their health and self-empowerment.

Dr. John Abramson continues:

> "In September 2001 an unprecedented alarm was sounded. The editors of 12 of the world's most influential medical journals, including the Journal of the American Medical Association, the New England Journal of

> Medicine, The Lancet, and the Annals of Internal Medicine, issued an extraordinary joint statement in their publications. In words that should have shaken the medical profession to its core, the statement told of "draconian" terms being imposed on medical researchers by corporate sponsors. And it warned that the 'precious objectivity' of the clinical studies that were being published in their journals was being threatened by the transformation of clinical research into a commercial activity."[93]

> **When an alarm is sounded, it is not time to stand around and consult, it is time to move!**

These industries have proven themselves unworthy of trust. It is time to turn responsibility for the chronically ill over to the care of organizations with a vested interest in seeing their patients prosper. It needs to become a standard of healthcare policy that the 1% - 5% or maybe even 1% - 10% most chronically ill be referred to community-based, health-promoting, disease-reversing rehabilitation programs.

> **Best Practices should be: The most effective, least expensive, least dangerous approaches to restoring health.**

Who Decides What The "Best Practices" Are Anyway?

Currently it would have to be answered that the "foxes," that is, the industries that make the most money off disease, currently still rule the roost. Take for example the prescription of defibrillators for patients with weakened hearts. The following example illustrates the cozy relationship between industry and medicine. Many medical prescriptions are based on commercially distorted information and imposed upon (that is, prescribed) to unsuspecting patients in the name of "science."

According to an article in the New York Times, the combined cost of a defibrillator and its surgical placement in patients with weakened hearts is between $30,000 and $40,000. [94] Defibrillator placement for 1000 patients is between $30 million and $40 million. According to company data, the cost of each month of extended life is over $100,000—or more than $1 million per year of life saved. According to a study in the New England Journal of Medicine (NEJM), the patients randomly assigned to receive a defibrillator had a 31 percent less risk of dying over the next 20 months than the patients in the control group. The article concluded that, "prophylactic implantation of a defibrillator [in patients with hearts weakened by heart attacks] improves survival and should be considered as a recommended therapy." [95] The question begging to be answered is not actually about the cost of saving lives, but for whom are the benefits of those costs intended?

For instance, the NEJM article failed to mention that there is good evidence that there are other far less expensive and far more effective ways to prevent many more deaths among these high risk patients. Only 3 years before the NEJM study, a group of Italian researchers examined the effect of exercise training on a similar group of patients with weakened hearts. The study randomized patients to either an exercise intervention group or a conventional treatment group. The exercise group received exercise training three times per week for the first 8 weeks and then 2 times per week for the following year while the conventional treatment group received no exercise training. The results published in Circulation (the journal of the American Heart Association) were dramatic: "The risk of death was reduced by 63 percent in the exercise group (more than twice the benefit of the defibrillator group); the risk of hospitalization for congestive heart failure went down by 71 percent (instead of up by 33 percent in the patients who received implanted defibrillators); and both exercise capacity and quality of life improved significantly in the exercise group and remained improved for the 40 months of the study ($p < .001$ for both)."[96]

The superiority of lifestyle intervention to chemical and mechanical interventions are not considered a part of the "evidence" upon which prescriptive "scientific" decisions are being made. This evidence is excluded from being a part of "real medicine."

"How could the free market have allowed the medical industries to thrive while serving Americans' health needs so poorly and inefficiently?" The problem is not with the market per se, but with the inadequate and commercially distorted information being fed to doctors and the public, and the flawed incentives that currently shape our healthcare economy. The problem is with the allowance of deceptive marketing to masquerade as scientific evidence, and the flawed economic incentives that encourage prioritization of medical profits over improved patient health.

Drug and medical device companies earn higher profits when more people use expensive drugs and devices, and not when more people achieve better health. This is the failure of healthcare legislators and fiscal policy makers to incentivize the health of the American people.

"The cost of the oversupply of medical services to our nation's pocketbook is staggering. Fisher and his colleagues estimate that 30 to 33 percent of Medicare expenditures could be saved nationally without compromising the quality of medical care." [97]

WHAT CAN BE DONE TO RESOLVE THESE PROBLEMS?

1] Government intervention to protect public's interests.
2] Separating real science from commercial distortions.
3] Correcting perverse economic incentives.
4] Applying the right interventions at the right time.
5] Creating economic stimulus to improve health outcomes.

The federal government must restore its role as a protector of the people.

"And, finally, the government cannot simply stand by as a paid-off sugar daddy to the medical (and especially the drug) industry. Well-functioning markets require active government oversight to make sure that the public's interests are being served."[98]

Let us remember what the purpose of the healthcare system is and acknowledge that it is the responsibility of the federal government to make sure that it is carried out. As stated by the 1998 President's Advisory Commission on Consumer Protection and Quality in Health Care Industry, "The purpose of the health care system is to reduce the burden of illness, injury, and disability, and to improve the health status and function of the people of the United States." [99]

Government oversight is needed in order to reign in the pathological quest for profit that unregulated capitalism produces. "Americans need to realize that our economy has thrived not in spite of government, but in many ways because of government."[100]

Without a whole host of government rules, capitalism could not exist. Even regulations and social programs help sustain a market economy by fixing many of [capitalism's] serious social and economic problems.

Markets, like governments, are very much social constructs. The market is a set of behaviors that is structured by rules, and many of the most important rules have been developed and enforced by government. Without these rules, our prized free-market economy would be a stunted and feeble version of what we see today.

"The Inherent Problems Of A Market Economy[100]

"The failures of markets are many, serious, widespread, and ongoing. This is not to suggest that capitalism is "bad" or to deny the many economic advantages and achievements of markets. It is simply to acknowledge that when left on their own, market economies will inevitably produce a whole host of economic and social problems. Let's consider a list of some of the basic built-in problems, limitations, and failures of capitalist market economies.

"Economic Bubbles[100]

"Resource Depletion. Like individual businesses, capitalist economic systems must grow or die. But as the worldwide economy grows, depletion of non-renewable resources necessarily increases dramatically. For example, the United States, with five percent of the world's population, currently consumes twenty-six percent of the world's energy—most of it in non-renewable forms. If the rest of the developing world were to rise to our levels of energy use, non-renewable energy resources would quickly be used up. A worldwide capitalist economy engaged in unlimited growth is fundamentally incompatible with a world where many vital resources are limited.

"Corporate Fraud and Theft. Without the government playing watchdog, there is a constant and strong temptation for companies to cheat their investors and their customers. The Bernie Madoff ponzi scheme that defrauded investors of $50 billion is simply the latest example of this problem. This happens so often, it cannot be considered an aberration. In just the last decade, many large businesses, including Enron and WorldCom, have used deceptive accounting procedures to give the illusion of profitability, defrauding investors out of billions of dollars. Insurance brokers have rigged prices to steal hundreds of millions from their customers. Investment companies have routinely told customers to buy stock in companies they have underwritten, knowing full well that these are poor investments. Several prominent mutual fund companies have been convicted of allowing illegal "late trading" by a few favored customers that lowered the profits of other customers. Drug companies have paid hundreds of millions in government fines for bribing doctors to prescribe their medicines. Corporations also routinely cheat the public by using questionable, unethical, and sometimes illegal strategies to avoid paying taxes, thus forcing citizens to pay more to fund public services.

"Neglect of Public Goods. Another classic example of market failure. A public good is something that is hard or impossible to produce for private profit—primarily because once it is produced, you can't limit who enjoys or consumes that good. The classic example is a light-house, because you can't prevent any ships from using it. More important examples are national defense, law enforcement, and clean air. Such goods are inevitably under-produced or neglected in a market economy and we must produce them collectively through government.

"Neglect of Social and Public Investments. Typically, businesses will

not invest in large public projects that are necessary for the long-term health of our economy or society. A typical example is infrastructure facilities like roads, bridges, harbors, airports, etc. Such projects are usually too risky and provide too little profit for most businesses or investors to want to take them on. Education, sanitation, and public transportation are other examples of important social investments that would be neglected if left to the market. [100]

"*Hidden Information.* For markets to work effectively in the interest of the public, consumers must have the information they need about products in order to make an intelligent choice about what meets their needs. But businesses often have an interest in not fully disclosing all relevant information. So government must step in and force companies to reveal that crucial information, such as what is in their food products, how safe their cars are, how efficient their air conditioners are, or what side effects their drugs have.

"*Inability to Plan.* Markets cannot plan. Capitalism is basically an anarchical economic process. Economic development is a function of the activities of separate and uncoordinated businesses and customers—all largely oriented toward the short-term. While this arrangement produces great economic efficiencies, it has the disadvantage of disallowing any coordinated planning to make our lives better. Only government can provide rational, long-term plans for the development of society.

"*Boom and Bust Cycles.* As history has shown, *laissez-faire* capitalism is subject to regular cycles of boom and bust, where economies heat up too rapidly and then cool down into a period of deep stagnation. Only government is in a position to revive the economy through the use of monetary and fiscal policies.

"*Lack of Markets.* Not everything we need for a good society can be provided by markets and business—especially things such as justice, fairness, equality, or basic rights and freedoms. Only government can properly supply things like justice and freedom to all Americans.

"*Monopoly.* Competition in capitalism does not foster more competition—it eventually creates monopoly. Unrelenting competition eventually drives many companies out of business or forces them to merge, thus allowing fewer companies to take over increasingly larger shares of a market. Unchecked, this process leads to monopolies and oligopolies. This inevitably produces price-fixing, low-quality products, and other abuses of overly concentrated economic power. The only cure? Government anti-trust laws and other "regulation for competition" policies.

"*Ignoring Needs.* Markets and business do not respond to our *needs*, they respond to *demand*, as expressed in money. Thus, social needs are sometimes neglected. What concerns producers is not what social needs or functions are fulfilled by their products, but how much people will pay for them. Henry Ford put it best when he said that he was in the business of making money, not making cars or providing transportation. So while there is a pressing need for low-cost, affordable housing in America, what are being produced are huge Mansions and luxury condominiums—because these are more profitable. And while we may desperately need universal health care in this country, it will not be provided by the market alone. It can only be mandated by government policy.

"Devaluing the Future. As a rule, businesses are only oriented to the short-term. The accounting practices of firms utilize "discount rates" that require them to consider money, goods, and resources in the future to be worth less than those in the present. So it is better to develop resources like oil and old-growth forest now, rather than leaving them for later. The result: values like long-term environmental sustainability and the welfare of future generations tend to be neglected in corporate calculations.

"Poverty and Economic Inequality. On their own, market economies tend to produce high levels of poverty and economic inequality. In the last twenty years, the distribution of income and wealth has become more unequal in the United States, and we far surpass other Western democracies in our poverty rate. Also, the top 10% of wealthy Americans now own 70% of the wealth of the country. Studies have shown that Western countries which spend more on social programs and do the most to promote worker interests are the ones who have the fewest poor and the lowest economic inequality.[7]

"Lack of Opportunity and Economic Mobility. The economic inequality characteristic of market economies also undermines equal opportunity. The poor face many obstacles to financial success, while the well-off enjoy the advantages of superior education, social connections, and family wealth.[8] Only government programs such as Head Start, high quality public schools, federal student aid, and low cost public colleges can begin to level the economic playing field and help to equalize life chances for all Americans.

"Taken together, all of these failures and problems totally undermine any notion of the "perfect" and "self-regulating" nature of the market. Virtually all of these problems are *built in* to a capitalist, free-market system. They are *systemic* problems—products of the normal operation and the inherent attributes of this kind of economic system. This means that they occur irrespective of who is running our businesses. They are not the product of greedy owners or evil corporate CEOs; they are a product of the systemic priorities that all companies must adhere to if they are to stay in business and prosper. It is the internal logic of capitalism that forces firms to pay low wages, ignore the environment, devalue the future, and hide information from consumers."[100]

Being systemic also means that these problems cannot be cured from within the economic system itself. These problems can only be addressed from the outside by coordinated collective efforts—the efforts of people acting through their governments.

Pernicious Conflicts Of Interest Need To Be Exposed And Disbanded . . .

As Dr. John Abramson says: "The FDA and NIH should be independent of, instead of seamlessly interwoven with, the drug and medical device industries. Drug company lobbying can no longer be allowed to stand in the way of legislation that clearly serves the health interests of the American people." [101]

Calling All Leaders . . .

Dr. Abramson continues: "Courageous leadership is urgently needed to redirect American health care—not unlike the leadership provided by President Teddy Roosevelt a century ago when the enormously concentrated power of the railroad, steel, and oil "combines" similarly threatened the public's interests. Government needs to be re-empowered, and a good place to start might be public hearings that investigate the commercial distortion of our medical knowledge." [102]

A Word About Quality In Healthcare.

Modern healthcare is a dangerous "theatre of engagement" for patients. This was brought to light by the The Institute of Medicine (IOM) report To Err Is Human: Building a Safer Health System.[103] A major contribution from that report was the introduction of the importance of patient safety into the standard for measuring quality in healthcare. (I will come back to the subject of patient safety shortly.) Another important element in measuring the quality of healthcare is the extent to which patients are actively engaged in their own health outcomes.

While there are many perspectives of quality, the healthcare industry must look to a more comprehensive and integrated vision to improve the health and healthcare of all Americans. While many conflicts of interest exist in the present healthcare system, it is imperative to get beyond these conflicts and create a better vision for the future. The system must look to what is best for the individual patient in order to define quality.[104]

The research of Dr. Barbara Starfield and her colleagues at Johns Hopkins, as well as the research of Dr. Elliott Fisher and his colleagues at Dartmouth, shows that—despite our faith in the latest high-tech medical care—the areas of the country that have higher concentrations of specialist physicians have both higher health care costs and worse health care outcomes; the areas that have more primary care physicians have lower health care costs and better health outcomes.

How important is safety when you go to the hospital?

In a study published in the JAMA in 2002, Berwick et al. [105] asks the question, "What practices will most improve safety?" The Institute of Medicine (IOM) produced a report called *To Err Is Human: Building a Safer Health System*[106], which estimated the deaths from hospital error to be between 44,000 and 98,000 people per year. This figure does not include numerous other causes of death from medication usage and hospitalization.

An article written by Barbara Starfield, MD, MPH of the Johns Hopkins School of Hygiene and Public Health in the Journal of American Medicine on July 26th, 2000[107] shows that medical errors may be the third leading cause of death in the United States. "The healthcare system may also contribute to poor health through its adverse effects. For example, estimates in the US of the combined effects of errors and adverse effects that occur because of iatrogenic damage include:

12,000 deaths/year from unnecessary surgery

7,000 deaths/year from medication errors in hospitals

20,000 deaths/year from other errors in hospitals

80,000 deaths/year from nosocomial infections in hospitals

106,000 deaths/year from nonerror, adverse effects of medications

Total 225,000 deaths per year from iatrogenic causes."[108]

Since the medical system's drugs and procedures are harming so many, and efforts over the last 5 years to reduce that damage has yielded very little improvement in patient safety, wouldn't a better approach be to prevent those health crises from developing in the first place?

Would it not be wiser to provide comprehensive health promotion programs to the 1% - 5% most chronically ill, and thus cultivate healthier, less afflicted, less medicated patients? This would keep them out of harm's way, that is, keep them from being hospitalized and medicated, and bring about the quickest and most effective improvements in patient safety.

"More than five years ago, the Institute of Medicine (IOM) issued its path breaking report, *To Err Is Human,* and fundamentally changed the debate about health care quality in the United States."[109]

"The report recently has been characterized as the most influential health care publication in the past two decades." [110, 111]

"Traditionally, research into quality of care has focused on three areas: variation, patient-centered care, and compliance with guidelines. The IOM report added the domain of *safety* to quality research." [111]

"The product coming out of that report was the concept of "preventable injury," whose burden became the cornerstone of the IOM report." [111]

"Yet at this point, there is a sense of disappointment about the results of the patient-safety movement. There have been few breakthrough interventions. There is little evidence that the health care system is safer today than it was five years ago and certainly nothing to suggest that deaths from error have been cut in half, as the IOM called for in its report. Leading advocates have not found evidence of the transformation of the health care system, or even of individual hospitals, that was thought necessary to make the health care system as safe as other industries. Hence, the answer to the question being asked five years later — how many deaths have been prevented? — is disappointing." [111]

"Patient safety sparked a level of public interest that the rest of the quality-improvement field in health care had failed to excite." [111]

I would like to weigh in on the patient safety issue because it is so important to every citizen entrusting their care to the medical system. People's lives, health, happiness, and future employability are all deeply impacted by the dangers of the medical environment.

Could it be that improving patient safety needs to be pursued from a different angle, since the route we have been following has yielded no breakthroughs? I propose that, in the arena of treating disease and preventing iatrogenic harm, we must identify the heaviest users of the system (the 1% - 5% most chronically ill) and develop mandatory healthcare policies around their care. Those policies would require comprehensive health promotional efforts be taken to keep patients well and out of harm's way. That approach would require mandatory referral of all high risks (high repeat patients) to community-based comprehensive health promotion/ disease rehabilitation programs. The 1% - 5% most chronically ill are the most sick, most medicated, most often re-hospitalized group of patients suffering the greatest percent of iatrogenic harm (patient endangerment), and by improving their health, we can most rapidly, most effectively, and most economically pull them out of acute care's "hazard zone" even before entry, and preserve them from becoming its casualties.

The costs in terms of human suffering are not the only things to be considered. Not only are lives being damaged and destroyed, but billions of dollars are also being wasted as patients re-enter the system as a result of being damaged by being in the system. Prevention, that is, keeping them out of harm's way, truly is worth a pound of cure.

Applying The Right Interventions At The Right Times

John Abramson: "Policy makers and payers should focus their attention on healthcare systems (groups of doctors, hospitals, and other medical services)—especially to figure out how to reward them for providing the right care in the right amount, for achieving high levels of patient satisfaction, and, most important, for improving the health of the people they serve." [112]

We need two independent bodies to oversee effective healthcare delivery:

Board/Body #1:

Securing the accuracy / integrity of medical knowledge, devoid of commercial distortion *that possesses the power to* approve which medical services/interventions/drugs are scientifically well-supported, and more importantly, which ones will be reimbursed. The independent body would be responsible for deciding what *best restores health* rather than what *best promotes commercial interests.* Currently, the questions that do get answered, and thus become our medical knowledge, are often not the ones that will contribute most to improving our health.

Board/Body #2:

Identifying the best in community-based health promotion/disease reversal strategies *and possessing the power to* approve reimbursement for these programs, and requiring referral (of all appropriate patients) from hospital systems into these programs.

About The Independent Bodies . . .

"Such a body must have the independence and expertise of the Institute of Medicine (part of the National Academies of Science), which would be well suited to accept responsibility for evaluating the scientific evidence."
- John Abramson

Lessons from the past show that this public body would require maximum insulation from political and commercial influence, along the lines of the model of the Federal Reserve Board— employing long and staggered terms, no financial ties to industry, and secure funding from Congress. The health of the American people and almost $2 trillion in annual expenditures are at stake here. To fail to fund such rigorous oversight is to knowingly sanction the largest white collar criminal operation in the United States. This industry has become too powerful to be self-corrected by the market. Strong government intervention is required if the public's interests are to be preserved.[113]

John Abramson says: "This new independent board would have a threefold mission. First, it would ensure that medical research was designed, conducted, analyzed, and disseminated with the primary purpose of improving health and in accordance with accepted scientific standards. Second, it would provide oversight in developing clinical guidelines for the prevention, diagnosis, and treatment of specific medical problems and overall health through independent analysis of all the available scientific evidence. Third, it would identify, fund, and oversee research when important scientific evidence was lacking. For example, the absence of evidence from randomized controlled trials precludes informed recommendations about whether routine bone mineral density testing for postmenopausal women has any clinical benefit, or whether drug therapy, lifestyle modification, or both will best prevent hip fractures in women with osteoporosis." [114]

The United Kingdom developed an agency to perform this function in 1999: the National Institute for Clinical Excellence (NICE). Its role is defined as providing "patients, health professionals and the public with authoritative, robust, and reliable guidance on current 'best practice.'" It does this with a budget of less than $30 million per year.

By contrast, Donald Berwick, author of the Institute of Medicines report, "Crossing the Quality Chasm" states that "Hundreds of billions of dollars are being flushed away because care isn't related closely to need." [115]

Three Fundamental Changes

Three fundamental changes are necessary to redirect American medicine toward what most agree is its rightful mission: to best improve the health of all Americans most efficiently.

1] Accurate and transparent information from research studies and the establishment of an overarching federal board (and completely insulated from financial bribery by private interests) in order to evaluate incoming research and use their expertise to find truly cost-effective, evidence-based, outcomes-oriented "best medical practices".

2] Government-stimulated return or rebalancing of physicians into primary medicine. Drawn by the promise of higher income,

PhRMA and big business entice most graduating physicians into specialties—because those specialties increase usage of more expensive procedures and chemical products. Primary physicians, on the other hand, encourage earlier prevention of conditions before more expensive (cost-driving) specialists are required. Also, PhRMA-stimulated enticements to physicians to serve their higher profits must be curtailed, replaced with the creation of more incentives for physicians to serve the patients' needs for recovery instead of the drug distributor's need to increase distribution: incentives for primary care physicians to identify patients at risk for disease progression, and refer those patients to chronic disease rehabilitation/reversal programs instead of merely prescribing medications for the treatment of their ongoing progressive decline.

3] Policy makers and payers must focus on figuring out ways to: A] reward health promotion, disease prevention and disease reversal, and B] limit medical services to the right care (best practices) in the right amount (pay-for-performance). The goal: to more quickly identify patients whose conditions are declining precipitously, and to quickly restore their underlying health and bring them back to the higher health and lower cost end of the payment spectrum.

Separating Real Science From Commercial Distortions

"The public has the right to know that the recommendations that guide their medical care are not nearly as 'evidence based' as they claim to be; that many of the references cited to support key recommendations do not provide that support; that the directions of the estimations and extrapolations presented in the guidelines tend to justify the use of more statin drugs; and that these guidelines are driving up sales of cholesterol-lowering statin drugs while diverting doctors' and the public's attention away from far more effective and far less expensive ways to prevent heart disease." [116] Given that the outcomes of these distortions of truth do not simply sway sales of products but contribute to the destruction of the health of humans—should they not be held accountable for the human cost of their success?

"Commercial interests are so successful in appearing to represent the public's interest that doctors, health policy experts, and the public are unable to discern the commercial distortions of the medical knowledge upon which they rely. 'Quality of care' is now defined largely in ways that best serve the financial interests of drug and other medical industries rather than the health needs of the American people." [117] The distortion of medical information for financial gain has a name—it's called fraud.

"The production and implementation of medical knowledge in the United States is by now so riddled with conflict of interest at virtually every level and every stage that nothing less than a new independent national public body is needed to protect the public's interest in medical science." [118] Let us remember that the interest in conflict is nothing less than the public's health.

"In this context, the most urgent challenge facing American medicine is not how to guarantee adequate access, but first to determine 'access to what.' Nor is it even how to ensure quality of care, because this presumes that the available scientific evidence is adequate to make that determination. The most important health care issue(s) in the United States today are: 1] whether our current method of creating medical knowledge realizes the full potential of medical science to improve our health, and 2] whether this knowledge is then best applied to clinical practice and communicated effectively to the public. By these standards, American medicine is clearly failing to fulfill its promise." [119]

To resolve the issues above, we need to address and resolve the following limitations to medical progress: 1] the very narrow, exclusionary, non holistic biomedical perspective and paradigm, and 2] the commercial interests funding (driving) most medical research which exclude from their paradigm of inquiry/discovery any products that are non-patentable, or that carry low financial margins.

1] Thomas Kuhn coined the term "paradigm" to describe the unspoken professional values, beliefs, and techniques shared by a community of scientists or professionals. The shared paradigm then defines the range of problems that are legitimate to investigate, the range of legitimate solutions, [120] and the criteria that justify the belief that the findings are true.[121]

Michael Polyani developed the idea further: "When we accept a certain set of presuppositions and use them as our interpretative framework, we may be said to dwell in them as we do in our own body... As they are themselves our ultimate framework, they are essentially inarticulable." [122]

2] Kuhn's most important contribution was to show that what appears from the outside to be the unrestricted pursuit of scientific discovery is really the result of scientific inquiry within a tightly restricted field. Facts that don't fit the current paradigm, like the greater reduction of the risk of heart disease by changing one's lifestyle than by statin therapy, are discounted and ignored: "not real medicine," and "not what real doctors do."

In what has become a classic paper published in *Science* in 1977, "The Need for a New Medical Model: A Challenge for Biomedicine," Dr.

George Engel wrote: "The historical fact we have to face is that in modern Western society biomedicine has provided the basis for the scientific study of disease, it has also become our own culturally specific perspective about disease, that is, our folk model." "Folk model" takes some of the shine off the great progress that has been made in biomedicine, but it is the only way to describe the intensity of our commitment to providing and receiving so much suboptimal medical care. [123]

Commentary:

Taken on an individual basis, when any one of us fail to critically examine the nearly unconscious assumptions we hold to be true, we run the risk of making plans and decisions based on these assumptions and taking actions that produce results and consequences that we didn't expect or desire. Viewed on the basis of a medical culture, when medical doctors fail to critically examine the accuracy and validity of the scientific theories, constructs, and foundational assumptions underlying their prescriptive practice, they run the risk of prescribing chemicals that ultimately do more harm than good. When doctors fail to examine not only the patient's condition (i.e. symptoms) and the (sympton-reducing) purpose for which medicines are prescribed, but the long-term negative effects of those medications, they run the risk of diverting patients away from their best possible health outcomes to unsatisfactory outcomes and actually cause more long-term harm than short-term good, that is immediate symptom reduction.

The great challenge of this discussion is that it calls into question the foundation upon which western medical decisions are based. If the integrity of the medical knowledge upon which western medical decisions are based is in question, then the entire system is in question. There is mounting scientific evidence that western medicine's biomedical model falls far short of offering valid solutions to the needs of the chronically ill. The biomedical model was designed to address acute care problems and medical crisis, and these needs are well met by the model.

However, the growing epidemic of chronic disease cannot be effectively addressed without a broader scientific approach that seriously weighs and addresses the underlying causes of declining health.

To the extent that modern medicine refuses to aggressively address the underlying causes of chronic disease, it slips away from being a science, and into a silky smooth, craftily devised sales pitch built upon a foundation of deceit. The difficult challenge facing ethical doctors attempting to live out the highest principles of medical integrity is changing the direction of their medical practice to reflect best evidence, when the powerful current of medical misinformation is flowing so swiftly.

To raise a flag of contention with the existing medical system is to rock the boat and risk becoming an outsider. To question the foundation upon which the system's medical knowledge is based opens up a Pandora's Box and a potential wave of professional derision.

Medical care is at a crossroads in America. The scientific evidence regarding the proper course of treatment for the chronically ill no longer confirms the conventional course of treatment currently being recommended. Regarding chronic disease, doctors must decide whether they will continue to follow the conventional recommendations of their practice, or follow the best evidence and recommend what the science of chronic disease rehabilitation suggests.

WHAT ARE AMERICAN MEDICINE'S PERVERSE ECONOMIC INCENTIVES?

Incentives for increased volume. Providers have a financial incentive to increase the number of services they produce in order to increase their incomes (as long as the payment amount exceeds the cost of producing additional services).

Incentives to deliver more costly services. Providers have a financial incentive to deliver more costly services instead of less costly services.

Little or no incentive for achieving positive results, or for care coordination. Because all providers bear no financial risk for either poor outcomes or higher costs, they have no financial incentive to deliver the most effective care or coordinate care for complex patients among multiple providers.

Little or no incentive to deliver preventive services or other services with low financial margins. Providers have little incentive to provide services that represent low financial margins — including preventive care and behavioral health care. [124]

"Ultimately, the issue is not the quality of our medical science, but the *political context* in which American medicine unfolds. The overwhelming power that the drug and other medical industries now wield over American politics, science, and health care has created an imbalance between corporate goals and public interest that is no longer self-correcting. In fact, it has become resistant to correction. If democracy is to be more than a ritual dance choreographed by powerful corporations in this postindustrial 'information age,' government must actively protect the integrity of the information on which we rely to guide our personal and political choices." [125]

Can somebody just throw me a bone? Can *anybody* throw me a bone?

No, I don't want you to give me a bone, I want you to open up your browser windows. I want you to open up your browser window and go to the following You Tube video. It's only 5 minutes long. I want you to find the following video:

"I'm as mad as hell and I'm not
going to take this anymore!"
(Network - 1976)

I hope I am not alone! I hope you will join with me in taking a stand against medical injustice. The current system is so immersed in convolutions and distortions of truth that it cannot see the forest for the trees. The current system is entirely set up, from top to bottom, to promote the advance of chronic disease. The current system, from its research to its payment structure, focuses upon treatment of decline, which depends upon the presence of decline. There is no reward for promoting health—only for treating advancing illness.

What incentives do pharmaceutical companies have to stop promoting drugs? What incentives do medical supply companies have to not grow rich off advancing disease and disability? What incentives do medical systems have to stop profiting off the treatment of decline? What incentives do medical students have to pursue lower paying primary care positions (aimed at prevention) over higher paying specialties that depend upon advancing states of disease being treated? What incentive is there for researchers to specialize in the arena of health promotion, for which there is little funding?

What incentive is there for the exceedingly wealthy and ruling medical paradigm currently in power to make changes that will diminish their wealth and decrease their power? Shall they step down simply because they are unqualified to rule—because it's the right thing to do?

Convincing the disease-for-profit medical machine to give up all their profit for the principles of the matter will be slow.

We need healthcare policy to link financial incentives—for both individuals and corporations—to improving health outcomes

Let's think outside the box for a moment . . .

How about the creation of an entirely new health promotion industry that targets the as-of-yet unreached "at risk" and obese and borderline chronically ill as well as the fully blown "in risk" and morbidly obese and chronically ill? How about having the government stimulate this health promotion economy / industry by reimbursing the companies providing the lifestyle interventions and the patients needing its services? How about the government paying into a comprehensive chronic disease rehabilitation and reversal industry that is paid (rewarded) for converting the "at risk" and very ill into the healthy and well?

The government pays hundreds of billions in the treatment of decline—why not have the government pay hundreds of millions to YMCAs and Lifestyle Transformation Centers dedicated to encouraging and supporting every phase of transition into healthier lifestyles?

How about we invest hundreds of millions into Lifestyle Transformation Centers, such as supercharged YMCAs that offer a multitude of the best evidence-based and health-restoring modalities under one roof? How about we create Lifestyle Transformation Centers that implement all the best evidence-based and revitalizing lifestyle modifications under one roof, providing one mega health-fortifying, self empowering, self restoring circuit of health-attracting behavioral modalities? The power of optimized health-attracting behaviors and disciplines accessible under one roof has profound capacity to restore, renew, and revitalize the chronically ill and bring them back into a state of chronic health and wellness. The difference between the chronically ill and the chronically well is their behavior—that is, their diet, exercise, activities, priorities, perspectives, and attitudes.

RATIONALE: IF YOU CAN'T JOIN EM'... BEAT EM'!

Why fight for change in a system that has no reason to stop committing treason? "Wealth through medical deceit—forever treating preventable decline" has worked quite well—so leave it well enough alone. Why should the one taking our country's wealth through the forsaking of her health have any more to say! Shall they give up ill-gotten gain and forsake their present reign? For what? Principles! Because it's the right thing to do! Hell will freeze over before pharmaceuticals and every form of medical greed give it all up for "God and Country." We need to expose the darkness, but more importantly, we need to bring in the light.

Form a new industry: A new capitalistic endeavor to lift the chronically ill out of their trouble and pain. Form an industry that profits as they *promote* their patients' gain. Create a new means of corporate wealth—*for profound contributions to society's health.*

> **Instead of Corporate Profits for treating preventable decline in health, We create economic stimulus that promotes Profits for Promoting Achievable Health.**

A Call To Medical Activism

"In retrospect, all revolutions seem inevitable. Beforehand, all revolutions seem impossible."
- Michael McFaul, National Security Council, Obama Administration

As citizens of the United States, it is our responsibility to demand that our government restore the balance between public health and corporate profits, so that the drug, medical device, and other medical industries can only achieve their goals by effectively and efficiently maximizing America's health. Needless to say, these industries, as well as many doctors (whose high priced specialty services would not be needed in such high volume in a more efficient healthcare system) will do everything possible to prevent reform, as they have so successfully done in the past.

"Change is possible if we have the desire and commitment to make it happen."
- Gandhi

Ultimately, the issue is not the quality of our medical science, but the *political context* in which American medicine unfolds. The overwhelming power that the drug and other medical industries now wield over American politics, science, and healthcare has created an imbalance between corporate goals and public interest that is no longer self-correcting. In fact, it has become resistant to correction. If democracy is to be more than a ritual dance choreographed by powerful corporations in this postindustrial "information age," then government must actively protect the integrity of the information that we rely on to guide our personal and political choices.

"Unless someone like you cares a whole awful lot, nothing is going to get better. It's not."
- Theodore Giesel (Dr. Seuss)
Writer, author, poet and cartoonist

"The imperative is to define what is right and do it."
- Barbara Jordan, Congress member
and civil rights leader

"Every great dream begins with a dreamer. Always remember, you have within you the strength, the

patience, and the passion to reach for the stars and to change the world."

- Harriet Tubman, Abolitionist & humanitarian

Ultimate Ends

Our Government needs to be reawakened from its drunken stupor and inspired anew to defend integrity, justice and compassion. America is still a proud people, and we need our government to defend its people from all who would oppress her—from within as well as from without. Government needs to re-empowered, and a good place to begin would be with its independent investigation of the commercial distortion of our medical knowledge.

Postulates

Several things must be accomplished if we are to create a healthcare system that is safe, effective, economical, evidence-based, outcomes-oriented, patient-centered, value-driven, comprehensive, and inclusive.

a] Starting at the highest levels of government, there must be exposure of political and medical corruption. We need to identify and expose conflicts of medical interest and separate commercially biased "science" from real evidence-based science. We need to identify financial ties between institutions, such as the National Institute of Health (NIH) and private industry, because they are being trusted to defend the people's interests while they are, in fact, being paid off handsomely to do and teach that which is most profitable to the medical industry.

b] "He who pays the piper, gets to call the tune." We cannot expect pharmaceutically financed research to produce much more than powders for profit. Some actually do provide a value; but most are merely slight variations on old formulas for the purpose of generating new patents that allow companies a higher profit margin.

c] We also need to remove medical lobbyists' power to influence politicians in their healthcare policy decisions. Again,

While the devil pays the piper,
The nation must dance his tune.

It is unconscionable for politicians and governmental institutions to even entertain, let alone listen, at these betrayers' bargaining table.

d] We need to establish an entirely separated, completely independent, financially insulated medical research institute, and to conduct entirely open and unbiased investigations into both the causes and most effective treatments for disease.

e] We need to then put in place public healthcare policy which demands the implementation of, not the most lucrative forms of medical treatment as it is currently, but the most effective and economical best medical practices. All hospitals and healthcare systems must then be held accountable to that ethical, humane, economical, effective methodology of care.

f] Health Promotion through Wealth Promotion:

Corporately speaking, we need to establish an entirely separate branch of medical care dedicated to the health promotion of its patients. This medical entity would be positively compensated as their patients' chronic diseases diminish and their health, wellbeing, and independence increase. This entity would have financial incentive—positive reward for positive results, and non-payment for non-performance—outcomes-based payment incentives. *Privately speaking*, no medication can produce what successful behavioral modification can produce. We must create ways to financially reward individual behavioral reform leading to physical recovery and financially discourage non-health-promoting behaviors which foster continuing deterioration.

Conclusions

We have a serious challenge ahead of us: to pioneer a transition from our current disease-for-profit "sick care" system into a humane, ethical, and *evidence-based* "health care" system.

Acknowledgement:

In this previous section, I have drawn heavily upon *Overdosed America* for its incredible contribution to the discussion before us. I heartily recommend reading Dr. Abramson's *Overdosed America—The Broken Promise Of American Medicine: How The Pharmaceutical Companies Are Corrupting Science, Misleading Doctors, And Threatening Your Health.*

Dr. Abramson has also performed talks and interviews, which are available online, along with more information on his work.

THE CONSEQUENCES OF THE PROBLEMS WITH THE AMERICAN

MEDICAL SYSTEM

What happens to a nation when integrity does not guide its medical research? What happens to a nation's health when the health of that nation takes a lower priority than the profits of the medical corporations guiding its care? What is the record of our nation's health and what does that "state of health" reveal about the wisdom of turning over our nation's medical direction to the control of corporations, whose fees and profit structure depend upon the treatment of disease?

Following is a personal review and commentary on a major report published by the Department of Health and Human Services (DHHS), entitled *Prevention Makes Common "Cents"*

Health Of The Nation[126]

Our nation is in a war with chronic disease. This is a war that we are clearly losing. The two primary reasons we are losing this war are:

1] We are using very expensive weapons.

2] Science has clearly demonstrated that the weapons that we are using *do not work.*

Point #1:

The fact that so many Americans are without medical insurance is simply another "casualty" of the performance of the American medical system. As of 2013, the United States is the only industrialized nation in the world that does not provide some form of universal health insurance for every citizen.

Point #2:

Everyone gets medical treatment whether they have medical insurance or not. The insured receive better care for sure *and* the costs are covered by their insurance, but everyone does get medical care through the American medical system.

The epidemic of chronic disease in America and the escalating costs associated with the treatment of chronic disease are indications of modern medicine's failure to address the problem of chronic disease effectively. Whether it's truly a failure-to-succeed or intentional success-through-failure is open for discussion.

The following studies use the terms "healthcare expenditures" and "healthcare costs". But that is only one side of the economic coin. That which is a source of *cost* to the nation is a source of *revenue* to the medical industry.

The following data examines the State of the Nation: Chronic Disease in America. I am using this information to create a "report on a report" on the performance of the American Medical System, because the data examines the performance of American medicine in its treatment of chronic disease in America.

Prevention Makes Common "Cents"

In 2003 the U.S. Department of Health and Human Services performed a major study and produced an Executive Summary on the costs of chronic disease and the importance of implementing stronger preventive measures. I inquired as to whether they had performed any more recent studies on the subject, but they have not, and their data is still heavily quoted and considered very reliable. The purpose of my review is to examine costs and trends in healthcare spending and to consider possible ways to reduce those costs.

Expenditures for healthcare in the United States continue to rise at a higher and faster rate than other sectors of the market.

The entire following section is taken from "Prevention Makes Common "Cents"", U.S. Department of Health and Human Services, September 2003.

"Health care spending is growing faster than the gross domestic product (GDP), and is projected to account for 17.7 percent of the GDP by 2012, up from 14.1 percent in 2001."

"Reasons for this are many but a few of them are the rapid advancement taking place in medical technology. A large volume of retiring baby boomers leaving the medical workforce and a rapidly growing elderly population as baby boomers begin entering into the retirement years. Chronic diseases are also more prevalent as people age and that will also pose an increasing burden upon the nation's limited medical resources. Far and away the most significant factor affecting increasing medical care expenditures is the growing epidemic of chronic disease."

Healthcare expenditures were estimated to reach 1.66 trillion in 2003. Much of that cost (approximately 75%) is associated with the care and treatment of chronic diseases and conditions such as diabetes, obesity, cardiovascular disease, arthritis, asthma and Alzheimers disease.

Approximately 129 million U.S. adults were obese in 2000, and that number is steadily rising. Costs are estimated to be between $69 billion and $117 billion per year for the treatment of obesity-related problems. The percentage of adults with diabetes is increasing rapidly, and is closely associated with the increasing proportion of obese adults in the U.S. In 2000, diabetes cost the U.S. economy approximately $132 billion, affecting 6.2% of the population and 117 million people. Childhood obesity is growing at such an alarming rate that they have stopped calling Type 2 Diabetes "adult onset diabetes." In 2003, the same study estimated that 1.1 million Americans would have a heart attack, and approximately 45% of those heart attacks would be fatal and those fatal heart attacks would be experienced by people who do not even know they have a heart problem. The study goes on to conclude that cardiovascular disease, including stroke, cost this nation more than $300 billion dollars each year.

"A much smaller amount is spent on preventing these conditions. There is accumulating evidence that much of the morbidity and mortality associated with these chronic diseases may be preventable."

"Individual behaviors and lifestyle choices greatly influence the development and progression of these chronic conditions. "Unhealthy behaviors, such as a poor diet, lack of physical activity, and tobacco use are risk factors for many chronic conditions and diseases. A high calorie diet and sedentary lifestyle commonly result in excessive weight gain. Overweight and obesity are risk factors for a large number of chronic diseases, most significantly, type 2 diabetes, congestive heart failure, stroke, and hypertension."

"A great deal can be done to encourage people to adopt healthier lifestyles and that is the arena that provides the single most effective means of reducing healthcare spending in the United States. Most costs associated with healthcare spending are somewhat fixed and expanding but by changing the way people live "Americans could change their personal health status and the health landscape of the nation dramatically."

"Increasingly, there is clear evidence that the major chronic conditions that account for so much of the morbidity and mortality in the U.S., and the enormous direct and indirect costs associated with them, in large part are preventable—and that to a considerable degree they stem from, and are exacerbated by, individual behaviors."

In particular, obesity, overweight, lack of physical activity, poor diet, and smoking greatly increase the risk of developing the most serious chronic disorders. Most of the dollars spent on healthcare in the United States, however, are for the direct care of medical conditions, while only a very small portion are being targeted by preventing those conditions.

Continued Statistics And Quotes From: Prevention Makes Common "Cents"

Disease: Obesity[127]

Cost:

One study investigating obesity and its cost to the nation estimated the cost to be 102 billion in 1999 for the direct care costs alone.[128] The following is a list of the conditions and costs closely associated with obesity:

- Arthritis $6.7 - 7.4 billion
- Heart disease $25.5 - $30.6 billion
- Type 2 diabetes $18.4 - $20.5 billion
- Hypertension $8.3 - $9.6 billion
- Stroke $6.1 - $8.1 billion

Risk Factors:

The condition of obesity is almost always preceded by a long period of physical inactivity and poor diet. Choosing to spend leisure time by being sedentary contributes greatly to being obese. Many medications contribute to weight gain as well. Obesity is not genetically inherited. That said, genetics does influence familial tendencies for weight gain. Some families and cultures are more prone to obesity than others; however, familial and cultural attitudes toward exercise and choices in leisure time activities are also strong behavioral contributors to the risk of obesity.

1] *"Weight gain is a direct function of an imbalance between the amount of calories consumed and the amount of calories expended by an individual."*

2] The availability of sugary, fattening, pre-packaged foods, eye-popping big portion restaurant meals, and sweet syrup sodas beckon to us to breach on the beach of life and waddle along its shore.

3] *"Individuals who would be more active often find it difficult to do so because of demands, and other constraints associated with their work, family, and community."*

4] Overcoming lethargy and adopting an active

lifestyle is a difficult task. Deeply engrained patterns are hard to break. But being obese makes everyday activities difficult. The only question is what type of difficulty will you choose.

Prevalence:

Over 129 million U.S. adults are considered either overweight or obese. The prevalence of obesity is increasing in all age groups, and the age group with the lowest proportion of obese ranges from ages 18 through 29 years. "However, this same age group has shown the largest percentage increase in obesity of all age groups, rising from 7.1 percent in 1991 to 14 percent in 2001—a 97 percent increase."

"Contributing to the overall trends, annual hospital costs for obesity-related disorders in children ages 6 to 17 years increased from $35 million to $127 million between 1979 and 2000."

Effects:

Obesity and overweight significantly affect the health and life expectancy of the US population. Obesity significantly blunts the quality of life. "Researchers have suggested that in terms of the physical quality of life, the effect of obesity can be the equivalent of aging as much as 30 years." [129]

"Overweight and obesity also can reduce mobility and physical endurance, can lead to psychological disorders, and can result in social, academic, and job discrimination." Obesity contributes significantly to days lost from work and work related disability. [130]

Obesity is the precursor to many progressively disabling health conditions, without which those conditions would never take root. Obesity is the rich fertile soil in which the seeds of many other chronic diseases are germinated. An estimated 47 million U.S adults have a condition called "metabolic syndrome" which begins with insulin resistance and is characterized by the presence of obesity, abdominal fat, high blood sugar and triglycerides, high cholesterol, and high blood pressure.

Obesity and overweight contribute heavily to the risk for:

Type 2 diabetes, metabolic syndrome, high blood pressure, high cholesterol levels, coronary heart disease, congestive heart failure, angina pectoris, stroke, asthma, osteoarthritis, musculoskeletal disorders, gallbladder disease, sleep apnea and respiratory problems, gout, bladder control problems, poor female reproductive health, and cancers of the: uterus, breast, prostate, kidney, liver, pancreas, esophagus, colon, and rectum.

Disease: Diabetes

Cost:

In 2002, diabetes cost the U.S. economy approximately $132 billion, affecting 17 million people, causing an average of 8 days per year of lost work, and accounting for 14 million disability days. This includes $91.8 billion in direct medical expenditures for diabetic care, complications and secondary medical conditions, and $39.8 billion in indirect medical expenditures for lost workdays, restricted activity days, mortality and permanent disability due to diabetes.

American Diabetes Association: Economic costs of diabetes in the U.S. in 2002. Diabetes Care 26(3):917-932, 2003

Risk Factors:

Most research suggests that obesity, overweight, and a lack of physical activity contribute to insulin resistance and are associated with an increased risk for diabetes.

The risk factors for diabetes are both genetic and environmental. We cannot change our genetic profile (family history of diabetes, race/ethnicity, age/genetic interactions), but we can control our environment—that is, our level of physical activity and the quality of our diet. Diabetes is largely a matter of choice. If you already have diabetes you can still choose whether you will control and reverse your diabetes or if you will be controlled by and promote your diabetes.

Diabetes: The choice is yours

Genetics and Habits: Family genetics and family habits.

Genetics run in families, but so do familial behavioral

patterns.

You cannot change your familial genetics, but you can choose a healthier lifestyle than your family. Diabetes runs in families because behavior patterns run in families. The familial pattern of diabetes can stop with you if you deliberately choose to renounce unhealthy family habits and adopt the habits of healthy athletic families.

Risk factors contributing to diabetes: (that are outside our control)

- family history of diabetes
- race/ethnicity ("African Americans, Hispanic/Latino Americans, American Indians and some Asian Pacific Islanders are at particularly high risk for Type 2 diabetes." - *National Diabetes Fact Sheet*)

Risk factors contributing to diabetes: (that are within our control):

- physical inactivity
- poor diet
- obesity
- impaired glucose tolerance

Prevalence:

In 2000, it was estimated that 17 million people (6.2 percent of the population) had diabetes. Of this number, 7.8 million were men and 9.1 million were women.

"The CDC has estimated that one in three persons born in the U.S. in 2000 have a life-time risk of developing diabetes, unless significant changes occur in patterns of eating and exercising, and that 39 million people in the U.S. could have diabetes by 2050." - *National Diabetes Fact Sheet*

Effects:

1] Untreated or poorly treated diabetes can result in death or significant disability, including heart disease and stroke, kidney failure, blindness, and lower limb amputations. More than 60 percent of non-traumatic lower-limb amputations occur among diabetics. - *National Diabetes Fact Sheet*

2] Other complications of diabetes include: high blood pressure, nervous system damage, macular degeneration, dental disease, complications of pregnancy, acute life-threatening events caused by biochemical imbalances and susceptibility to other illnesses.[132]

Disease: Heart Disease

Cost:

The National Heart, Lung, and Blood Institute (NHLBI/AHA) performed the first comprehensive economic analysis of cardiovascular disease (CVD) based on the 2000 Census data. *"The NHLBI/AHA studies of CVD evaluated both direct costs (physician services, hospital and nursing home services, medications, home healthcare, and other durables) and indirect costs of lost productivity resulting from morbidity and mortality (days of work lost due to absence from work or premature death)."*[133]

For the year 2003, the NHLBI/AHA calculated the direct costs of CVD to be $209.3 billion and the indirect costs to be $142.5 billion.

Risk Factors:

The key risk factors for CVD are physical inactivity, poor diet, tobacco use, high blood pressure, and high cholesterol levels. Physical inactivity is a strong predictor of CVD because exercise improves endothelial function, keeping arteries more pliable and less prone to vascular inflammation and clogging. Physical inactivity allows the lining of arteries and vessels to collect deposits and get thicker, which decreases their inner diameter and constricts blood flow through them. Exercise increases the heart rate and the powerful flow of blood through those arteries and vessels, thus stretching them open, increasing their elasticity, and clearing out deposits before those deposits thicken the arteries or reach critical mass. Smoking is very damaging to the arteries and blood vessels, and results in significant hardening of the arteries and blood vessels, which impairs the transportation of oxygen to every cell of the body. The hardening and narrowing of the arteries is responsible for the pale cyanotic complexion of smokers and heart patients. Their arteries and blood vessels (transport passageways) have been hardened, and they block the transport of oxygen to every cell of the body. Their bodies' tissues are being starved of vital oxygen and are slowly suffocating.

Prevalence:

"Heart disease and stroke are the first and third leading causes of death in the United States, respectively, in both men and women." [134]

"CVD accounts for 40 percent of the mortality in the United States, killing about 950,000 Americans annually.[135] Taken as a whole, CVD is the cause of more deaths than the next five causes of death combined."[136, 137]

"This year, an estimated 1.1 million Americans will have a new or recurrent coronary attack and more than 45 percent of the people experiencing these attacks will die of them." [138]

"About 61 million Americans (almost one-fourth of the general population) live with some form of CVD, including coronary heart disease, stroke, high blood pressure, congestive heart failure, congenital heart defects, and other diseases of the circulatory system." [139]

Effects:

"Cardiovascular disease (CVD) is predominantly caused by atherosclerosis—a hardening of the arteries—due to a thickening of the lining of the arteries. Atherosclerosis results in inadequate blood flow to particular tissues in the body, causing poor function, damage, or death of those tissues. In heart disease and stroke, the principal components of CVD, atherosclerosis affects the arteries of the heart and brain, respectively." [140]

Heart disease (including stroke) frequently results in considerable loss of work, and serious long-term disabilities. Heart disease and stroke can also be very difficult for other family members.

Strokes are especially difficult for the family. Responsibilities for the care and rehabilitation of the patient, combined with the responsibility to maintain the rest of life's commitments, can be very overwhelming to spouses. Heart disease is truly a family affair—a serious life-changer for all those closest to the afflicted. A stroke can truly test the strength of a marriage and the love and loyalty of the entire family.

Disease: Asthma

Cost:

The ALA study of asthma costs in 2001 evaluated both direct health care costs of asthma and indirect costs of lost productivity (school days lost, work days lost, and lifetime earnings lost due to mortality) and calculated these costs to be $9.4 billion and $4.6 billion, respectively.

Risk Factors:

While there is no consensus as to why asthma prevalence has increased, scientists studying the phenomenon have postulated that obesity and lack of physical exercise, along with dietary changes and increased exposure to indoor allergens, are among the reasons for the increase.[141]

Prevalence:

Approximately 22.2 - 23.2 million adults and 9.1 million children (a total of approximately 32.3 million Americans) have had or currently have asthma. Asthma is the 6th-ranking chronic condition among the general American population and the leading serious chronic illness of children in the U.S.

Effects:

Asthma produces inflammation and bronchospasm of the airways, which restricts airflow into and out of the lungs. Asthma sufferers periodically experience attacks of wheezing, shortness of breath, chest tightness, and coughing. [142]

End of Source:
Prevention Makes Common "Cents"

The underlying causes of chronic disease are well known and its costs astronomical, yet very little is being spent to prevent that which is costing so much to treat. This is not an accident, and if we are to lower medical costs in America, we must start with making the economics of "disease progression" less profitable and the economics of "disease reversal" more profitable. The nation's medical industry and the nation's public health will—sure as shootin'—follow the money! The state of the nation's disease will follow the emphasis of the nation's medical focus. The nation's medical focus will follow the path of greatest profit. Those that control the nation's medical economics and define its medical reimbursement system are in control of what will be emphasized by its medical care recipients and its medical care providers.

"Improved public health translates directly into greater national productivity, which underpins all economic growth."
- Mike Milken

WHAT ARE THE RESULTS OF THE PROBLEMS WITH THE AMERICAN MEDICAL SYSTEM

What happens when integrity does not guide medical research? What happens when best evidence is ignored and suppressed in favor of much more profitable distortions of evidence? What happens when medical authorities we trust place profits above principles?

The following is a review, analysis and commentary on numerous scientific health studies, with recommendations for further reading.

Slow Death: Death By Medicine

I have spent hundreds of hours researching thousands of pages on the internet and in print. Below are some resources I believe are important to further understand the issues of the modern pharmaceutical machine. I am calling these resources Slow Death 1, 2 and 3. Consider this a "best of" resources synopsis.

Slow Death 1

Review of *DEATH BY MEDICINE,* By Gary Null, Ph.D., PhD; Carolyn Dean MD, ND; Martin Feldman, MD; Debora Rasio, MD; and Dorothy Smith, PhD

This is a must read. Gary Null, the principle author, highlights just how much damage to our health the ingestion of modern medications can cause. Medicines taken incorrectly can have dire consequences, but even when administered as prescribed, medicines are causing death, disease, and a poor quality of life. Why is this not being heralded from the hilltops?

From overmedicating our seniors to prescribing drugs to counteract the damaging effects of other drugs, modern medicine is reputably the leading cause of death in the United States; causing even more deaths than all the casualties from every war, from the Civil War to present day, we as a nation have fought.

Dr. Null asserts that efforts to restrain the medical-technology industry are opposed by policymakers. Most policymakers are more concerned with the negative impacts on the medical-technology industries than they are about the negative impact on the consumer. Disease is viewed as an "economic stimulus," and the creation of medicine as big business. He further asserts the appearance of carte blanche approval of what he calls the "disease industries" in regards to the development of medical gizmo's claiming to examine, diagnose, and treat, when in fact they contribute to the *progression* of *preventable* disease and disability.

Through an examination of a large body of scientific studies, this publication asserts that chronic disease is largely preventable, and existing disease progression can be mitigated (slowed down) and even reversed when *specifically targeted lifestyle interventions* are prescribed and fully supported.

I guarantee that you will be astounded and informed by the information in this book.

Slow Death 2

Below are some websites that will help you to understand the severity of the problems that modern medicines create.

The website, www.breathing.com, contains information about the extensive negative impact of the consumption of drugs, and the unsustainable nature of the pharmaceutical approach to disease management. Below are some quotes found on this site. [143]

"If they can get you asking the wrong questions, they don't have to worry about answers." Thomas Pynchon

"The whole concept of drug induced disease is much better known now than it was 10 or 15 years ago." "Though some drugs save lives, unfortunately, many drugs create unwanted side-effects . . . illnesses, toxicity and death." Paul Seligman, Director of the FDA's Pharmacoepidemiology and Statistical Services, *USA Today* March 2005.

"Millions of Americans swallow pills that are supposed to make them feel better — physically or mentally — but covertly wreak havoc with their body and brain. Many older folks are dismissed as senile, when in fact their drugs are causing their memory lapses and confusion." *Dr. Julian Whitacker, MD*

One of the articles, entitled "Prescription Drugs Anyone?" by Raymond Francis, FAQ Medical Advisory Panel member, has valuable information regarding the nature of drugs and their misuses. He highlights the suffering created by the use of drugs in modern medicine. He states, "Prescription drugs are one of America's leading causes of disease and death. The problem with prescription drugs is very simple…they do nothing to cure disease. All they do is suppress the symptoms of disease by disrupting normal cellular functions. Abnormal cell function is the very definition of disease, and since prescription drugs *cause* our cells to malfunction, then…"

Mike White, the author of "DRUGS, DRUGS, DRUGS," from the June 2001 *Wall Street Journal*, writes: "In 1999, the Center for Disease Control and Prevention reported more than 600,000 hospital admissions and 700,000 emergency-room visits resulting from medications that were correctly administered but nonetheless produced side effects—from intestinal bleeding to seizures to even death." Mr. White goes on to outline the effects of such drugs like Rezulin, Lotronex, Propulsid, Redux, Pondimin, Durct, Seldane, Hismanal, and Posicor.

Another article that is worth a look was written by Heidi Stevenson, a former shill for Big Pharma. She interviews Dr. Erick Turner, a psychiatry professor at the Oregon State Health and Sciences University, who "tells the truth about drug testing" (April 29, 2008).

Dr Turner is quoted as having said, "Pharmaceutical corporations are so pervasive that, as described by the *Washington Post* in 2002, in the days leading up to the American Psychiatric Association's meeting in Philadelphia [2002], pharmaceutical companies mailed attendees hundreds of free phone cards, as well as invitations to museums, jazz concerts and fancy dinners... And in several dozen symposiums during the week-long meeting, companies paid the APA about $50,000 per session to control which scientists and papers were presented and to help shape the presentations."

Heidi Stevenson notes, "Is it any wonder that doctors have become so utterly disconnected from their responsibility to protect their patients from harmful drugs? It's no wonder they seem unable or unwilling to look at drug company reports critically. It's no wonder that they have become little more than drug pushers, forever pressing the latest pills on their patients, without considering the risks and the obvious suppression of information about the products they prescribe. It's no wonder that when, finally, after a few years of prescribing a particular poison, they're informed that it's been recalled, they immediately jump on the bandwagon of yet another highly-promoted, research-suppressed so-called "wonder" drug. And then, they repeat the pattern yet again."

"The pharmaceutical industry has so controlled the medical industry—and with the doctors' full cooperation—that even the doctor who blew the whistle seems to have no idea how to procede without prescribing the very medications that he knows are ineffective in most cases." [144]

Author segue: *permission to speak, sir!*

As the author, I feel the urge to address the last opinion. I feel that the above mentioned doctor may *have an idea* about how to proceed without prescribing medications he knows are ineffective in most cases, however, he may *have no idea* about how to *make a living* without prescribing the medications he knows are ineffective in most cases. The problem is that the doctor is not employed *to deliver benefits to the patients* so much as he is employed *to prescribe drugs from his employer*. The problem is one of economic incentives.

Medicine is not the answer; except in the sense that Hippocrates meant when he said, "Let thy food be thy medicine and thy medicine be thy food." The rising tide of chronic disease cannot be held back by the levy being raised by modern medicine. Local, state and federal governments are imbued with tremendous powers of influence, and with power comes responsibility to do what's best for their constituents. In terms of public health, effective control of chronic disease will only be possible in societies that encourage disease reversal through economic incentives:

1] Economic incentives placed on medical institutions to reward disease reversal more highly than its progression.

2] Economic incentives that encourage individuals to remain trim, fit and healthy.

3] Economic incentives rewarding those with advanced chronic disease to take significant proactive steps to optimize their health.

4] Economic incentives given to community-based chronic disease rehabilitation programs, to provide comprehensive health-restoring programs for the chronically ill to keep them well.

5] Public funding of projects focused upon improving access and increasing opportunities for citizens to engage in healthy recreational activities.

Whether We Like It Or Not, We Are Students Of Our Body.

In order to rebuild your health, you must stop doing what makes you ill. One's health usually breaks down secondary to an extended period of stress, physical inactivity and poor diet (and drugs are the unhealthiest foods known to man). If you have a symptom that could be corrected by healthier behavior, why would you add yet another unhealthy behavior (consuming toxins) to your already "sickness-producing" unhealthy state? Better to suffer with your body's symptom, that is, your *body's indicator* of a need for change. Behavioral changes are always difficult, but what better stimulus to embrace a difficult *but necessary* change than the experience of *the discomfort* of remaining the same.

The emergence of a symptom is your body's attempt to inform you of a need for a change of behavior, i.e. to identify and remove the cause of the symptom. To mask or silence a symptom through the use of drugs is to cut short our body's *difficult conversation with us* about our behaviors that aren't working. This serves to solidify, strengthen, and engrain the behaviors that are undermining our health and causing symptom generation. To block the body's "feedback mechanism" with symptom-altering drugs is to promote the ignoring of the body's feedback (discussion with us) about behaviors and environmental conditions that are self-damaging. This encourages its underlying cause.

Change is always difficult. It contains two major challenges: *Initiation* and *Action*

Initiation: The more deeply the behavior is engrained, the more difficult it is *to initiate the expulsion* of the unhealthy behaviors for the institution of healthier behaviors.

Action: The more deeply a behavior is engrained, the more difficult it is *to take action to expel* the unhealthy behavior and to instill the healthier behavior.

The discomfort and systemic alarm produced by symptoms is nature's prompt to investigate the symptoms' causes and change our course of action for the better. When we nullify the symptom with symptom-altering drugs, we ignore its warning.

Drugs lull us deeper and deeper into harm's way. Symptom-modifying drugs anesthetize the *initiating impetus* to change, and reduce the *immediate need* to change.

Don't turn off your body's alarm—it's trying to save you! Nature is sounding the alarm—danger—damage, break down, injury in progress—pay attention, take note—identify *the cause*—cease and desist—eliminate or avoid *the cause.* Change your behavior or environment from that of self-harm and self-extinction to self-healing and self-preservation.

Initiating a change in behavior is quite challenging. However, done gently and intelligently—working with your body's need to be *loved and cared for* rather than *neglected, ignored and abused*—is truly one of the greatest gifts you can give yourself.

Take action: Treat yourself to tough love. Emancipate yourself from the dungeons and chains of self-inflicted poor health. Don't reach for a drug; reach for the things that restore health. Reach out for what restores your brokenness of mind and body. Reach out for the source(s) of your salvation and work out that salvation with fear and trembling.

STEPS TO TAKE TOWARDS BETTER HEALTH

Health Impact News (at healthimpactnews.com) provides an outline of effective tools in the treatment of chronic disease. These tools are what I would call "real medicine." [145]

Resource:

http://healthimpactnews.com/2011/prescription-drugs-now-kill-more-people-than-illegal-drugs/

Of course, medications do a lot more than merely reduce your impetus to initiate healthy change and reduce your need to implement healthy change; they actually do much to destroy your health. Let me be clear here: I am speaking about medications designed to treat chronic conditions. Medications taken for short durations to treat specific correctable conditions are often useful; these are medication's rightful place, but continuous use of medications to treat lifestyle issues generate continuous low levels of oxidative stress for the body, which generates reactive oxygen species, which exceeds the bodies oxidative/antioxidative balance and contributes to the progression of many diseases. Drugs designed to be taken for a lifetime (such as medications to alter blood pressure, blood sugar, and cholesterol levels) may, over your lifetime, inflict far more harm, damage, and the initiation of additional diseases than real curative value. That said, if you simply stop taking these medications because of their damaging effects but do not adopt the positive lifestyle changes needed to correct these problems at the level of their root cause, you will also lead yourself into further declines. There is no way to avoid your work. It is only by doing the work, building your house upon stable bedrock, that you can expect to withstand the floods of life. It's a good bit of work, but a great bit of good that comes out of that work.

The most efficient way to stop iatrogenic injury and death (injury and death due to medical treatment) is to *stay out of harm's way!*

Stay Healthy! Prevent Health Decline → Prevent Hospitalization → Prevent Injury & Death By Medicine

Take responsibility for your health so that you can stay well naturally, without the use of drugs or even frequent conventional medical care. If you adhere to a healthy lifestyle, you most likely will never need medications in the first place. This includes:

Proper Food Choices

Look to focus your diet on whole, unprocessed foods (vegetables, meats, raw dairy, nuts, and so forth) that come from healthy, sustainable, local sources, such as a small organic farm not far from your home. Know which foods to avoid. Topping the list is fructose. Sugar and fructose can act as a toxin and as such, drive multiple disease processes in your body. This includes insulin resistance, which is a major cause of accelerated aging.

Comprehensive Exercise Program

Even if you're eating the healthiest diet in the world, you must exercise in order to reach high levels of health. Exercise effectively, including core strengthening, strength training, stretching, and high-intensity activities (such as *Peak Fitness*) that boost human growth hormone (HGH) production.

Stress Reduction and Positive Thinking

Do not avoid addressing the emotional component of your health. Your emotional state plays a role in nearly every physical disease — from heart disease and depression, to arthritis and cancer. Developing effective coping mechanisms promotes longevity. Stress has a direct impact on inflammation, which in turn underlies many chronic diseases. Meditation, prayer, and social support can all work well to fend off illness.

Proper Sun Exposure to Optimize Vitamin D

Get out in the sun daily to receive your vitamin D naturally. There is existing evidence suggesting that oral vitamin D may not provide optimum benefits (although it's still better than no Vitamin D intake at all) .

Take High Quality Animal-Based Omega-3 Fats

This is an important factor in helping people live longer.

Avoid as Many Chemicals, Toxins, and Pollutants as Possible

Included are prescription medications, OTC medications, and toxic household chemicals, cleaners, soaps, hygiene products, air fresheners, bug sprays, lawn pesticides, and insecticides.

PRESCRIPTION DRUGS AND THE SIDE EFFECTS IN THE ELDERLY

This resource is found at:

www.naturalnews.com/036482_prescription_drugs_side_effects_elderly.html

The elderly often have a variety of health challenges. Often, the elderly consume a mixed cocktail of medications. Taking a variety of prescribed medications in order to treat several health conditions can result in side effects that can make problems worse. These harmful side effects are not always readily apparent when first taking a medication. The longer a drug is ingested, the greater the risk of experiencing side effects. These may continue even after the drug is no longer taken. The website Natural News is valuable to further explore both the damaging effects of drugs and the available natural approaches.

The author, Adams, refers to himself as the "Health Ranger." He recommends these additional resources:

- www.bbc.co.uk/news/health-13880553
- www.netwellness.uc.edu/healthtopics/aging/faq16.cfm
- www.tbyil.com/Elderly_Dangerous_Drugs.htm

Researchers have found that commonly used drugs prescribed to those who are 65 or older lead to increased incidences of death and mental health decline (especially when the drugs were prescribed in combination), compared to those who did not receive drugs.

These findings, published in the August 2011 *Journal of the American Geriatrics Society*, suggest that certain types of drugs negatively affect the brain and increase the risk of decline and death.

Elderly people take approximately three times the amount of medications that younger people do. Although the elderly are prescribed a wide array of drugs, the most common are heart medications, statins, benzodiazepines, and antidepressants. Drugs that treat the cardiovascular system can result in nausea, vomiting, weight loss, anorexia, and bleeding problems. Statins' *side effects* include muscle weakness and pain (the most serious that can be life threatening), headaches, nausea, vomiting, constipation, diarrhea, skin rash, and general weakness.

Benzodiazepines can result in sedation, confusion, and falls. The side effects of antidepressants include sedation, confusion, falls, low blood pressure, and urinary retention. Antidepressants also thin the blood. They decrease blood clotting capacity, which increases the risk for stomach and uterine bleeding. Take over-the-counter NSAIDs at the same time and the risk doubles.

Other commonly prescribed drugs also have a host of potentially harmful side effects. Examples include:

* Antipsychotic medications that are used to treat "mental disorders" can result in confusion, sedation, low blood pressure, falls, urinary retention, Parkinsonism (involuntary shaking and twitching), and tardive dyskinesia (repetitive body movements).

- Antihistamines used to treat allergies can result in confusion, sedation, low blood pressure, falls, sleep disturbance, and urinary retention.

- Drugs that relieve nausea can lead to confusion, sedation, low blood pressure, falls, urinary retention, Parkinsonism, and tardive dyskinesia.
- Pain medication can result in constipation, confusion, & sedation. Even over-the-counter medications can result in serious liver and gastrointestinal side effects.
- Drugs to treat Parkinson's disease can result in confusion, dizziness, low blood pressure, and an increase in cardiovascular toxicity.
- Drugs to relieve muscle spasms can result in dry mouth, constipation, urinary retention, and delirium.
- Urinary incontinence drugs can result in dry mouth, constipation, urinary retention, delirium, and confusion.

All of these side effects relate to individual drugs. Imagine how these side effects can be compounded by taking several prescription drugs at a time.

Sources:

- www.bbc.co.uk/news/health-13880553
- www.netwellness.uc.edu/healthtopics/aging/faq16.cfm
- www.tbyil.com/Elderly_Dangerous_Drugs.htm

The author, Luella May, is a natural health advocate helping people to heal naturally, and the author of "The 8 Invisible Stains of Our Souls." She partners with Tony Isaacs, who authors books and articles about natural health, including "Cancer's Natural Enemy" and "Collected Remedies."

Another article worth reading is "Doctors Are The Third Leading Cause of Death in the US, Killing 225,000 People Every Year," published in the Journal of the American Medical Association (JAMA), which documents the tragedy of the traditional medical paradigm. The author is Dr. Barbara Starfield of the Johns Hopkins School of Hygiene and Public Health. She describes how the US healthcare system may contribute to poor health. You can find it at: http://articles.mercola.com/sites/articles/archive/2000/07/30/doctors-death-part-one.aspx

Slow Death 3

I like the term "Dose Dependent Disease"—the question is "How badly do you want to promote your chronic disease?" Results are individual, largely dependent upon your commitment to prescription drug consumption.

Please check the box that best describes your commitment to drug induced disease progression.

Chronic Disease:

[ ] I want it!
[ ] I want it bad!
[ ] I want it really bad!

Remember that results vary, but an enduring commitment to a sedentary life, eating a poor diet and consuming an increasing volume of prescription drugs will aid in the promotion of your chronic disease.

In the following section, I review more specifically the mechanisms by which drugs cause death, disease, and disability.

A Word Of Warning

The following material is drawn from scientific studies, journals and articles. The material is written in scientific terms and assumes a strong grasp of anatomy, physiology, chemistry and pharmacology. I have chosen to include this material as a resource for further investigation and as evidence to support my claims and appeal. I have read through volumes of material and included only the most relevant, concise, and well-written material—however, that only partially eases the difficulty of interpreting the scientific writing style.

Drug Metabolism And Mechanisms Of Drug-Induced Liver Damage

The liver plays a central role in transforming and clearing chemicals, but is also susceptible to the toxicity of these agents. Chemicals that cause liver injury are called hepatotoxins. More than 900 drugs have been implicated in causing liver injury. Drug-induced liver injury is responsible for 50% of acute liver failures.

The human body identifies almost all drugs as foreign substances and subjects them to various chemical processes to make them suitable for elimination. The liver is the principal "metabolic clearing house" for endogenous chemicals (such as cholesterol, steroid hormones, fatty acids, proteins) and exogenous substances (such as drugs, alcohol).

Drug metabolism is usually divided into two phases:

Phase 1 is a reaction that helps prepare a drug for phase 2. Many compounds, however, can be metabolized by phase 2 directly. Phase 1 involves oxidation, reduction, hydrolysis, hydration, and other rare chemical reactions. Water solubility of the drug is often increased and generates metabolites, which are chemically active and potentially toxic.

Most of the phase 2 reactions take place in cytosol and involve conjugation with endogenous compounds via transferase enzymes. Most chemically active and potentially toxic Phase 1 products are rendered inert and suitable for elimination by Phase 2 processes.

The most important family of metabolizing enzymes in the liver are cytochrome P-450. Cytochrome P-450 is the terminal oxidase component of an electron transport chain. It consists of a closely related family of 50 isoforms, of which six metabolize 90% of the drug.

Due to late discovery of hepatotoxicity, drugs continue to be taken off the market. Due to its unique metabolism and close relationship with the gastrointestinal tract, the liver is susceptible to injury from drugs and other substances. Most of the blood, about 75%, comes to the liver directly from gastrointestinal organs and the spleen by way of the portal veins. The drugs arrive in a nearly undiluted form.

Several mechanisms are responsible for either inducing hepatic injury or worsening the damage process. Many chemicals damage mitochondria, intracellular organelles that produce energy. Its dysfunction releases excessive amounts of oxidants which, in turn, injure hepatic cells. Activation of some enzymes in the cytochrome P-450 system also lead to oxidative stress. An accumulation of bile acid inside the liver results when the hepatocyte and bile ducts are injured. Non-parenchymal cells such as Kupffer cells, fat storing stellate cells, and leukocytes (i.e. neutrophil and monocyte) also have a role in the mechanism, and promote liver damage.

Pathways and Mechanisms by which drugs damage the liver:

Drugs are ingested and metabolized to blood → Liver plays a central role in transforming and clearing chemicals, and is susceptible to the toxicity from these agents→ Chemical toxicity damages mitochondria →Energy production declines, and excessive amounts of oxidants are released →Activation of P-450 enzymes (such as CYP2E1) further increase oxidative stress →Hepatocyte and bile duct cell damage lead to bile acid accumulation inside the liver →This further increases oxidative stress and liver damage →Cellular disruption of Non-parenchymal cells such as Kupffer cells, fat storing stellate cells, and leukocytes also take place.

If you want to go deeper, check out "Current Concepts of Mechanisms in Drug-Induced Hepatotoxicity" by authors Stefan Russmann, Gerd A. Kullak-Ublick, and Ignazio Grattagliano.

You can find it at: www.ncbi.nlm.nih.gov/pmc/articles/PMC2765083

Drug-induced liver injury (DILI) has become a leading cause of severe liver disease in Western countries, and therefore poses a major clinical and regulatory challenge. Whereas previously, drug-specific pathways leading to initial injury of liver cells were the main focus of mechanistic research and classifications, current concepts see these as initial upstream events, and appreciate those subsequent common downstream pathways and their attenuation by drugs and other environmental factors. (Genetic factors also have a profound impact on the risk of an individual patient to develop overt liver disease.) This paper deals with:

1] Initial Mechanisms of Toxicity: Direct Cell Stress, Direct Mitochondrial Impairment, and Specific Immune Reactions

2] Direct and Death Receptor-Mediated Pathways Leading to Mitochondrial Permeability Transition

3] Apoptosis and Necrosis

Other Targeted Resources

There are also some very specific articles you can research that deal with specific kinds of health risks due to the ingestion of pharmaceuticals.

The first one I have cited is entitled, "Drug-Induced Nephrotoxicity," written by Cynthia Naughton, PharmD, BCPS, North Dakota State University College of Pharmacy, Nursing, and Allied Sciences in Fargo, North Dakota. It was published in September of 2008 in the American Family Physician. (www.aafp.org/afp/2008/0915/p743.html)

Drugs are a common source of acute kidney injury. Compared to 30 years ago, the average patient today is older, has more comorbidities, and is exposed to more diagnostic and therapeutic procedures with the potential to harm kidney function. Drugs shown to cause nephrotoxicity exert their toxic effects by one or more common pathogenic mechanisms. Drug-induced nephrotoxicity tends to be more common among certain patients and in specific clinical situations. Therefore, successful prevention requires knowledge of pathogenic mechanisms of renal injury, as well as patient-related risk factors, drug-related risk factors, and preemptive measures, all coupled with vigilance and early intervention. Some patient-related risk factors for drug-induced nephrotoxicity are an age older than 60 years, underlying renal insufficiency (e.g., glomerular filtration rate of less than 60 mL per minute per 1.73 m^2), volume depletion, diabetes, heart failure, and sepsis. General preventive measures include using alternative non-nephrotoxic drugs whenever possible, correcting risk factors (if possible), assessing baseline renal function before initiation of therapy (followed by adjusting the dosage), monitoring renal function and vital signs during therapy, and avoiding nephrotoxic drug combinations.

The second one I have cited is entitled, "Drug-induced Atrial Fibrillation," written by Cornelis S. Van der Hooft, MD; Jan Heeringa, MD; Gerard Van Herpen, MD, PhD; Jan A. Kors, PhD; J. Herre Kingma,

MD, PhD; Bruno H. Ch. Stricker, MB, PhD., published in 2004 in the Journal of the American College of Cardiology. (http://content.onlinejacc.org/article.aspx?articleid=1136126)

Atrial fibrillation (AF) is the most commonly sustained rhythm disorder observed in clinical practice, and is predominantly associated with cardiovascular disorders such as coronary heart disease and hypertension. However, several classes of drugs may induce AF in patients without apparent heart disease, or may precipitate the onset of AF in patients with preexisting heart disease. Successively, we discuss the potential role in the onset of AF played by cardiovascular drugs, respiratory system drugs, cytostatics, central nervous system drugs, genitourinary system drugs, and some miscellaneous agents.

The third one I have cited is entitled, "Drug-Induced Hyperglycemia." It is authored by Beatriz Luna, PharmD, BCPS; Mark N. Feinglos, MD, CM, and was published in 2001 in the Journal of the American Medical Association.

It is well recognized that certain classes of drugs can cause clinically significant elevations in glucose concentrations. Historically, the agents implicated have included β-blockers, thiazide diuretics, corticosteroids, niacin, pentamidine, and others. Of recent interest are the increasing numbers of reported cases of new-onset diabetes mellitus (DM) in patients receiving treatment with protease inhibitors (PIs) or atypical antipsychotic agents. In most cases, the mechanisms by which hyperglycemia occurs are not fully understood, although several possible theories have been proposed for each drug class.

Elevated blood glucose concentrations can have significant consequences, especially in high-risk populations. Granulocyte activity may be impaired in the setting of hyperglycemia, compromising the normal immunological response and the host's capacity to resist infection. Hyperglycemia also directly inhibits the development of granulation tissue, impairing the wound healing process. Some evidence suggests that hyperglycemia, even in the non-diabetic range, can adversely affect the development of macrovascular complications. A recent meta-analysis reported that the rate of cardiovascular events (including heart attacks, CAD, atherosclerosis, high blood pressure, and stroke) increased continuously with glucose levels that were higher than 75 mg/dL in nondiabetic subjects.

The fourth one I have cited is entitled, "Autoimmune Disease: Mechanisms," written by Deliza Fairweather of Johns Hopkins University's Blomberg School of Public health in Baltimore, Maryland, USA.

Factors contributing to the development of autoimmune diseases are primarily environmental. Diet, drugs, and toxins are important contributors in determining whether an individual will develop autoimmune disease. Environmental agents are able to amplify autoimmunity in genetically susceptible individuals and can break tolerance in genetically resistant individuals, thereby increasing the risk of developing autoimmune disease.

Genes (30%)

+

Environment: behavior, diet, medications and toxins (70%)

=

Autoimmune Disease

For some time, toxins like heavy metals or drugs intended for therapy have been associated with disease syndromes that resemble autoimmune diseases. For example, drugs like procainimide and hydralazone can induce autoantibodies and lupus-like disorders in patients. Due to the chronic nature of most autoimmune diseases, autoantibodies appear long before clinical symptoms, providing a good predictive marker for the potential to develop disease. In fact, the risk of developing an auto-immune disease rises from about 10% when one autoantibody is present to around 60-80% if three autoantibodies are present for a particular autoimmune disease. Autoantibodies can induce damage to the body by binding to self-tissues, activating the complement cascade and inducing lysis and/or removal of cells by phagocytic immune cells.

The fifth one I have cited is entitled, "Drugs That Cause Parkinson," by Dr. Joseph Jankovic. This article was modified by Dr. Abe Lieberman for readability. You can find the article at: (http://thegoodlylawfulsociety.org/drugs-cause-parkinson/)

There are three classes of drugs that are likely to produce Parkinsonism:

1] Dopamine receptor blocking agents, including the phenothiazines (such as Compazine, Stelazine, and Thorazine), butyrophenones (such as Haldol), and metoclopramide (Reglan).

2] Dopamine-depleting agents, including reserpine (rarely used) and tetrabenazine (used to control dyskinesia)

3] Drugs that act by various known and unknown mechanisms, including the atypical antipsychotic drugs such as Resperidal, Orap, and Zyprexa.

In one series of 95 new cases of Parkinson's Disease, evaluated in a department of geriatric medicine, 58 were drug-caused. The most common offending drug was Compazine: an anti-nausea, anti-vomiting drug. In our experience, Reglan is one of the most common causes of drug-induced

Parkinsonism.

The sixth one I have cited is entitled, "Drugs and Bone Disease," by Alison Pack, M.D. This is located at http://www.ncbi.nlm.nih.gov/pmc/articles/PMC321183/

A growing body of literature indicates an association between antiepileptic drugs (AEDs) and bone disease, including histologic, radiographic, and biochemical evidence. The AEDs most commonly reported to cause decreased bone mineral density and disorders of bone metabolism are inducers of the cytochrome P450 enzyme system (phenobarbital, phenytoin, carbamazepine, primidone). Polytherapy (many-drug therapies) has been shown to be associated with a higher risk of bone metabolism abnormalities than is monotherapy (single-drug therapy). Polypharmacy (many-drugs) also has been identified as a risk factor for low bone mass in adult patients. Several theories have been proposed to explain the link between anti-epiletic drugs and bone disease. Hepatic induction of the cytochrome P450 enzyme system, which leads to increased catabolism of vitamin D, is the principal mechanism reported. Other possible mechanisms include a direct effect on bone cells, including impaired absorption of calcium and inhibition of response to PTH, hyperparathyroidism, and calcitonin deficiency.

The seventh article has to do with a subject I found groundbreaking, titled "Exercise and Gene Expression: Physiological Regulation of the Human Genome Through Physical Activity," authored by Frank Booth, Manu Chakravarthy and Espen Spangenburg. It was published in 2002 on the PublMed.gov website. (http://www.ncbi.nlm.nih.gov/pubmed/12205177) The following is the abstract of this article:

> "The current human genome was moulded and refined through generations of time. We propose that the basic framework for physiologic gene regulation was selected during an era of obligatory physical activity, as the survival of our Late Palaeolithic (50,000-10,000 BC) ancestors depended on hunting and gathering. A sedentary lifestyle in such an environment probably meant elimination of that individual organism. The phenotype of the present day *Homo sapiens* genome is much different from that of our ancient ancestors, primarily as a consequence of expressing evolutionarily programmed Late Palaeolithic genes in an environment that is predominantly sedentary.
>
> "In this sense, our current genome is maladapted, resulting in abnormal gene expression, which in turn frequently manifests itself as clinically overt disease. We speculate that some of these genes still play a role

> in survival by causing premature death from chronic diseases produced by physical inactivity. We also contend that current scientific evidence supports the notion that disruptions in cellular homeostasis are diminished in magnitude in physically active individuals compared with sedentary individuals, due to the natural selection of gene expression that supports the physically active lifestyle displayed by our ancestors. We speculate that genes evolved with the expectation of requiring a certain threshold of physical activity for normal physiologic gene expression, and thus habitual exercise in sedentary cultures restores perturbed homeostatic mechanisms towards the normal physiological range of the Palaeolithic *Homo sapiens*. This hypothesis allows us to ask the question of whether normal physiological values change as a result of becoming sedentary. In summary: in sedentary cultures, daily physical activity normalizes gene expression towards patterns established to maintain the survival in the Late Palaeolithic era."

The last scholarly treatise I have cited is entitled, "Effects Of Exercise and Diet on Chronic Disease." This final resource, by Christian K. Roberts and R. James Barnard, was published in the Journal of Applied Physiology in 2005. Locate the article at: http://jap.physiology.org/content/98/1/3. The following is the abstract of this article:

> "Currently, modern chronic diseases (including cardiovascular diseases, Type 2 diabetes, metabolic syndrome, and cancer) are the leading killers in Westernized society, and are increasing rampantly in developing nations. In fact, obesity, diabetes, and hypertension are now even commonplace in children. Clearly, however, there is a solution to this epidemic of metabolic disease that's inundating today's societies worldwide: exercise and diet. Overwhelming evidence from a variety of sources (including epidemiological, prospective cohort, and intervention studies) link most chronic diseases seen in the world today to physical inactivity and inappropriate diet consumption. This review discusses the effects of exercise and diet in the prevention of chronic disease, and highlights the effects of lifestyle modification for both mitigating disease progression and reversing existing disease. It also suggests potential mechanisms for beneficial effects."

Summary

Overwhelming evidence links most chronic diseases seen in the world today to physical inactivity and inappropriate diet consumption. Poor diet and a lack of exercise attract chronic disease. Chronic disease is a choice. The good news is that restoring your health is also a choice.

> **Body Logic: He who has ears, let him hear what his body is saying.**

Chronic disease is usually the body's accurate reflection of unhealthy behavior.

(Chronic physical inactivity + inappropriate diet) lead to chronic disease.

Medical practice has both an ethical and financial responsibility to the patients under their care to provide interventions that are patient-centered and consistent with the best evidence of the best means of achieving disease reversal.

Chronic disease is largely a consequence of unhealthy choices. Shall we treat the effect or grapple with the causes?

> **As we wage the war on chronic disease, we must keep in mind that we are the enemy. Physical activity and appropriate diet are effective weapons in the war on chronic disease, but we the people covet ease, the easy chair, the remote to push, a pill to pop, instant gratification, and fattening fare; and medicine (as a corporate institution) makes more money off a disease's progression than by providing transformative care.**

Chapter 8.
Influences of the American Medical System on Adulthood and Aging,
Part 2: The Solution

A FOUNDATION FOR THE SOLUTION TO THE AMERICAN MEDICAL SYSTEM CRISIS

What happens when integrity guides medical research? What happens when the welfare of mankind takes precedence over the profits of corporations? What have we discovered as a result of attempting to find the origins and root causes of human health problems, instead of exploiting those problems for personal and corporate profit?

The following is a review, analysis and commentary on numerous scientific health studies, including"Exercise and Gene Expression: Physiological Regulation of the Human Genome Through Physical Activity," authored by Frank Booth, Manu Chakravarthy and Espen Spangenburg. [146]

Exercise And Gene Expression

There are genetic "codes" underwriting human hardwiring. We cannot escape our genetic programming; we can only align ourselves with it, or be swept downstream by it. The technological advances of modern society have made survival and finding food much easier; we are, however, still genetically programmed for intense and prolonged exertion, and when our behavior strays from our genetic programming, we actually trigger or prompt abnormal gene expression. Chronic disease appears to be the result of genetic aberrations that are initiated secondary to a state of "exercise deficiency.

The authors continue, making the following assertions:

In this sense, our current genome is maladapted, resulting in abnormal gene expression, which in turn frequently manifests itself as clinically overt disease.

Mounting evidence from a variety of sources indicate that a sedentary lifestyle and poor diet actually prompt (catalyze) abnormal gene expression. We speculate that some of these genes still play a role in survival by causing premature death from chronic diseases—produced by physical inactivity. However, the same powerful genetic forces that prompt accelerated decay (self extinction) can also act like an "On←→Off" toggle switch, to be harnessed to reverse chronic disease and prolong the quality and length of our lives.

We also contend that current scientific evidence supports the notion that disruptions in cellular homeostasis are diminished in magnitude in physically active individuals compared with sedentary individuals, due to the natural selection of gene expression that supports the physically active lifestyle displayed by our ancestors. The only effective, that is, *genetically approved,* prescription for the treatment of chronic disease appears to be *physical activity and appropriate diet.*

In summary, in sedentary cultures, daily physical activity normalizes gene expression towards patterns established to maintain the survival in the Late Palaeolithic era.

More Commentary On The Interaction Between Genes And Environments

Physical activity is one example of an environmental pressure (demand) that shaped the human genotype and phenotype. The differences in caloric expenditure are not trivial, and hence cannot be ignored. Cordain *et al.* (1998) found that recently studied hunter-gatherers had 72 $kJ\ kg^{-1}\ day^{-1}$ more physical activity than the typical US adult. An exercise deficiency of 72 $kJ\ kg^{-1}\ day^{-1}$ is the work equivalent of a 70 kg (150 lbs.) human walking 19–33 more kilometers per day (12-21 more miles per day).

The human genome was organized during a time when survival depended upon large expenditures of physical energy. To survive, a human needed to expend a great deal of energy hunting, gathering, and sheltering and protecting their clan. That is what humans are hard-wired to excel at. That order, or rule of survival, has been written (integrated) into our genetic code. To do otherwise (in that era) meant we would rapidly disintegrate. To fall short of the high demands of survival meant one did not survive. Survival demanded high levels of exertion and endurance for over 40,000 years in the Paleolithic Age (50 BC – 10 BC) and those *expected energy expenditures* were genetically "hard-wired" (coded) into the human genome.

> **Genetic, Behavioral and Environment Interaction: The human genome (human genetic expression) is influenced by behavioral choices and our environment to prompt survival or extinction.**

Humans were designed to interact with their environment in specifically "coded" ways. When the code of our survival is followed then code-*supported* behavior prompts improved survival. When the code of our survival is not followed then code-*unsupported* behavior prompts self extinction.

Second Law Of Thermodynamics

Any system which is free of external influences becomes more disordered with time. This, along with entropy, suggests that any system will naturally move from order to disorder. If this is true, how do biological systems maintain such a complex degree of order?

Effort is usually required to produce order out of disorder. Energy must be put into a system in order to create and maintain orderly states. This is referred to as "times arrow." If two snapshots are taken of a given system, and one demonstrates more disorder, it is considered to be the later image. Things in nature, over time, tend towards decay, that is, progressive disorganization. It is only through the continual input of additional energy (work) that order is created and then maintained.

Commentary

The medical implications of the principle of "time's arrow" are as follows:

Any physiological system into which energy is not being input to bring improved order and organization will necessarily actualize a trajectory of progressive decline. This principle points to an unalterable course of decline for any system into which additional energy for organization is not being applied. In other words, for any patient who is prescribed medications without being prescribed the facilitation of "the work of physiological reorganization" (fitness training), they are in effect being recommended (prescribed) a course of progressive decline. The prescription of any course of medication without a prescription of a "regimen of physical fitness," that is, a prescription of the work required to stimulate physical reorganization, is necessarily recommending a course of physiological decline for their patients. Unless the work effort to reorganize the disordered system is added to the system, further disorder is the only trajectory and outcome that "times arrow" can predict and produce. The prescription of the work of physiological reorganization is absolutely and inalterably essential for there to be any hope of *improving* health. Without the input of the energy needed to reorganize the systems in decline—that is, the institution and implementation of a regimen of fitness—progressive decline is an unalterable certainty.

- Quick, effective (adaptive) interactions with the environment prompt survival.
- Slow, ineffective (maladaptive) interactions with the environment prompt extinction.
- Activity/exertion promotes adaptive genetic super-compensation, and promotes survival.
- Inactivity/indolence/laze promotes maladaptive genetic aberration, and promotes extinction.

Genetic Impulse Toward:

Stagnation:

Exhibiting Indolence/Laze (Promotes) → Bodily Systems to Stagnate →Accelerating Entropy

Regeneration:

(Healthy/Active) Behavior → According to: Laws of Genetics → Promotes Regeneration → Survival

Degeneration:

(Unhealthy/Inactive) Behavior → According to: Laws of Genetics → Promotes Degeneration → Extinction

It has been demonstrated that brain glycogen supercompensation follows exhaustive exercise. Exercise training elicits an increase in the basal level of muscular glycogen. This happens when glycogen recovers to above its basal level (supercompensation), after it decreases with acute exercise.

There is evidence that exhaustive exercise induces glycogen supercompensation not only in the skeletal muscles, but also in the brain. Furthermore, information provided by the Laboratory of Exercise Biochemistry and Neuroendocrinology at the Institute for Health and Sports Sciences at the University of Tsukuba observed exercise training-induced increases in basal glycogen levels in the cortex and hippocampus, which are involved in motor control and cognitive function. What this suggests is that, like skeletal muscles, the brain adapts metabolically, probably to meet the increased energy demands of exercise training. [147]

"Physical fitness is not only one of the most important keys to a healthy body, it is the basis of dynamic and creative intellectual activity."
- John F Kennedy

Supercompensation is a four-step process:

Step 1 is the application of a training "load" and the body's reaction to this training load, which is fatigue. Because of the load, there is a predictable drop-off in performance.

Step 2 is the recovery phase. This includes either a light training session, recovery session, or rest. The recovery period helps the energy stores, and an individual's performance will return to their baseline (state of homeostasis)—the point of the application of the original training stress.

Step 3 is the supercompensation phase. This is the adaptive rebound above the baseline; it is described as a rebound response because the body is essentially rebounding from the low point of greatest fatigue. This supercompensation effect is not only a physiological response but also a psychological and technical response.

Step 4 in the process is the loss of the supercompensation effect. This decline is a natural result of the application of a new training stress, which should occur at the peak of supercompensation. If no training stress is applied, there will be decline. This is referred to as the detraining phenomenon. [148]

Behavior:

Exercise Abundance → Supercompensation → Transformation & Renewal

Behavior:

Exercise Deficiency → Entropy → Stagnation & Decline

A Little Insight Into Our Distant Past

The period during which the human genome was constructed required hunter-gatherers to walk long distances. (For instance, present-day Aboriginals in Australia walk 12 to 21 miles per day.) They were also required to engage in short periods of intense exertion while hunting or fighting for survival.

The human genome was genetically coded to encourage and prompt the success of this type of behavior. Modern society, on the other hand, requires none of these physiological demands, and indeed encourages and promotes a sedentary lifestyle.

How does a hunter-gatherer's physical exertion compare with a sedentary person's physical exertion?

I draw from the quote at the beginning of this section:

An exercise deficiency of 72 kJ kg^{-1} day^{-1} is the work equivalent of a 70 kg human walking 19–33 more kilometers per day (12-21 more miles per day).

Translation:

The genetic code was written into our DNA so as to favor the survival of the most fit. The period during which the human genome was written required that humans walk 12 – 21 miles more per day than modern man. The very low physical demands of modern sedentary societies as compared to the very high physical demands of the Late Paleolithic Period are equivalent to an exercise deficiency of walking 12 – 21 miles less per day than our predecessors. It is believed that a certain threshold of exertion was expected of humans for the maintenance of normal homeostasis and survival, and that when levels of exertion fall below a certain threshold expected for survival, a whole host of alterations in gene expression are triggered/prompted/initiated as a result of those exercise deficiencies.

What are the physical effects of living an exercise-deficient lifestyle. Phenotypic expressions and changes associated with exercise deficiency are:

- Decreased size and strength of skeletal muscle
- Lower capacity of skeletal muscle to oxidize carbohydrates and fats
- Higher insulin resistance
- Greater homeostatic disruption of cellular metabolism in skeletal muscle at a given absolute work load
- Lesser vasodilator capacity in perfusion vessels to the heart
- Smaller maximal cardiac outputs and stroke volumes
- Sarcopenia: the degenerative loss of skeletal muscle mass quality,

and strength, and a component of the frailty syndrome

Apparently, a lack of understanding by the general scientific, medical, judicial and legislative communities of the magnitude of the "altered gene expression by exercise deficiency" has led to their underestimation (or non-consideration) of the significance of the functions of exercise-induced gene expressions.

If the exercise-deficient phenotype did not contribute to overt clinical disorders, exercise-induced changes in gene expression would only be physiological phenomena (Booth *et al.* 2002). [149] However, *alterations in gene expression by exercise deficiency* contribute to morbidity (chronic diseases) and mortality (premature death). This highlights the importance of using the evolutionary pressures (which have shaped human physiological responses*) in order to reverse* the chronic diseases that exercise deficiency induces. [150]

Morbidity Refers To The State Of Being Diseased. Mortality Refers To Death And Dying

Exercise deficiency → Alterations in gene expression → chronic disease and premature death

The reason that drugs do not work well for the chronically ill is because the most significant interactions are taking place as our genes interact with our behavior and environment. That is a healthy and proactive behavioral adaptation to one's environment, which has been genetically coded to prompt (favor) survival.

Genes←→ABC (Interactions/Relationships)

a] Genes ←→Environment & Diet

b] Genes ←→Behaviors & Habits

c] Genes ←→Thoughts & Stress

Lifestyle Induced Exercise Deficiency prompts self-extinction via chronic disease

Maladaptive behavior, that is, behavior that is inconsistent with optimizing our survival, actually prompts self-extinction. We are genetically coded to interact with our environment in ways that optimize our survival. When we do not behave (interact with our environment) in ways that optimize our survival, we actually stimulate/prompt genetic programming for self-extinction. That is, we prompt our own self-extinction.

The reason that drugs do not work well in chronic diseases, that is, in lifestyle-induced *exercise deficient* conditions, is because the human genome was developed during an era that required humans to expend great amounts of energy gathering food and fighting/struggling for their survival. Survival depended upon exertion and required a tremendous amount of strength, speed, and endurance. Those that did not have or exhibit strength, speed, and endurance did not contribute to the survival of the species. From the evolutionary/genetic perspective, inadequate exercise causes alterations in gene expression, which promote chronic diseases, which accelerate self-extinction.

What do we find when we apply this theory to what we see in society? Does the theory stand up to what we observe in modern society today? Our societies no longer need to expend considerable energy hunting and gathering food and fighting for survival. However, in today's societies, those individuals who expend considerable energy (in exercise) and select the best sources of nutrition will thrive while those who are sedentary and eat foods which do not optimize their chances of survival will succumb much more readily to chronic diseases.

Our genes have not changed
We are still operating with . . .
Stone age genes amidst
Space age conveniences!

Modern society's abundance and ease allows us to be sedentary, and provides a wide variety of healthy and unhealthy food. Modern society's conveniences have contributed greatly to modern societies' chronic diseases.

Let's Recap:

The present human genome was molded and refined through generations of time. It is proposed that the basic framework for physiologic gene regulation was selected during an era of obligatory physical activity, as the survival of our Late Palaeolithic (50,000-10,000 BC) ancestors depended upon walking 12-21 miles per day while hunting and gathering.

It is speculated that genes evolved with the expectation of requiring a certain threshold of physical activity for normal physiologic gene expression, and thus habitual exercise in sedentary cultures restores perturbed homeostatic mechanisms towards the normal physiological range of the Palaeolithic *Homo sapiens*.

In summary: within sedentary cultures, daily physical activity normalizes gene expression towards patterns that were established to maintain survival in the Late Palaeolithic era. [151]

In the past, our survival depended upon being extremely active and eating the best food available, and when we follow that rule today, we thrive—and when we ignore the behaviors *genetically coded for our survival*, we prompt the cellular cascade of our own self extinction. Any time we use drugs to treat the symptoms that poor diet and exercise deficiencies have created, we avoid real and lasting solutions, and accelerate the failure of our health.

We cannot beat our genetic code. At our best we can become aligned with the way we're designed and then, suddenly, powerful genetic forces will energize our recovery.

We have but two paths we can go by:

Exercise Sufficiency → Normalized Gene Expression → Health and Homeostasis

Exercise Deficiency → Alterations in Gene Expression → Disease and Disregulation

Exercise is what our genetic code requires for our bodies' normal physiological operation. We each have to decide whether we are going to "live by the code" or "die by the code." But what about drugs? They are effective in a crisis, but their value is not sustainable with chronic conditions. Growing evidence indicates drugs actually contribute to the progression of the very conditions and diseases they claim to treat.

Exercise Abundantly → Genetic Affirmation → Catalyzing Survival

Exercise Deficiency → Genetic Negation → Catalyzing Extinction

Some Terms Defined

Health: Health is not merely the absence of disease but the presence of soundness and vigor. Synonyms: vitality, strength, fitness, stamina.

Homeostasis: The tendency of a physiological system to maintain internal stability, owed to the coordinated response of its parts to any situation or stimulus that would tend to disturb its normal condition or function. In regards to *psychology*: a state of psychological equilibrium obtained when tension or a drive has been reduced or eliminated.

Disease: A disordered and incorrectly functioning organ, system, structure, or part of the body, resulting from genetic or developmental errors, poisons, nutritional deficiency or imbalance, toxicity, illness, infection, or unfavorable environmental factors.

Dysregulation: The impairment of a physiological regulatory mechanism (such as that governing metabolism, immune response, or organ function).

Living by the genetic code: we must either "live by the code" or "die by the code".

This kind of thinking is not foreign to us historically. We can see passages in literature and history that reflect the same issues:

> *"See, I set before you today life and prosperity, death and destruction. For I command you today to love the LORD your God, to walk in obedience to him, and to keep his commands, decrees and laws; then you will live and increase, and the LORD your God will bless you in the land you are entering to possess. But if your heart turns away and you are not obedient, and if you are drawn away to bow down to other gods and worship them, I declare to you this day that you will certainly be destroyed. You will not live long in the land you are crossing the Jordan to enter and possess."*
>
> - The Bible KJV, Deuteronomy 30:15-17 (1500 BC)

THE CONSEQUENCES OF IMPLEMENTING THE SOLUTION TO THE AMERICAN MEDICAL SYSTEM CRISIS

What happens to a nation when its medical research is guided by integrity? What happens to patients when their health takes a higher priority than the profits of the medical corporations guiding their care? What happens to patients when they are guided by what the best evidence indicates are the surest ways to overcome chronic disease?

Following is a personal review and commentary on a major report published by the *Journal of Applied Physiology* by Christian K. Roberts and R. James Barnard, entitled: *Effects of Exercise and Diet on Chronic Disease.*

The Effects Of Exercise And Diet On Chronic Disease

Currently, modern chronic diseases, (including cardiovascular disease, hypertension, Type 2 diabetes, metabolic syndrome, and cancer) are leading killers in Westernized society. However, overwhelming evidence from a variety of sources link most chronic diseases in the world to physical inactivity and inappropriate diet. The purpose of this summary regarding the effects of diet and exercise on chronic disease is to highlight both the effects and the suspected mechanisms by which diet and exercise provide the most effective remedy for chronic diseases.

Poor diet and a lack of exercise attract chronic disease. Chronic disease is a consequence of daily choices. The good news is that restoring your health is also a consequence of daily choices!

He who has eyes, let him see what his body is saying.

Chronic disease is the body's genetically programmed response to habitually maintained patterns of unhealthy behavior. If you want to see how much and how often you exercise and eat right, just look in the mirror!

He who has ears, let him hear what his body is saying.

If we have eyes and ears and we look and listen, we can observe the results of our genes' interaction with the environment we create.

We create our environment through our behavior (our thoughts and actions).

Consistent physical activity and appropriate diet cause health and wellness.

Consistent physical inactivity and inappropriate diet cause chronic disease.

The human genome or genetic code (written between 50,000 – 10,000 BC) defines what is healthy/unhealthy (adaptive/maladaptive) behavior for humans.

The genetically designated *maladaptive behaviors* of physical inactivity and inappropriate diet frequently result in the genetically programmed *maladaptive effect* of chronic disease.

Medical practice has both an ethical and financial responsibility (to the patients under their medical care) to provide interventions that are patient-centered and consistent with what reliable evidence indicates is the best means of achieving disease reversal.

Chronic disease is a consequence of unhealthy choices. Shall we treat the effect, or grapple with the causes?

The only logical solution to a behavioral problem is a change of behavior. Any other course is like a "shifting of the chairs on the deck of the Titanic."

Chronic Diseases Are Epidemic In Modern Western Society

Chronic diseases develop slowly over a lifetime and their prevalence is epidemic in modern western societies. Their causes are physical inactivity and poor diet and lifestyle choices and there are no effective remedies except lifestyle modification. Chronic diseases are an enormous burden to society by *decreasing* human independence and productivity while *increasing* medical costs and human suffering. Physical activity and diet appear to be the only effective weapons in "the war on chronic disease." [152]

Gene-Environment Interaction

Humans living today inherited a genome that was programmed for daily physical activity and a high fiber diet. Nature has so deemed us that there are ultimately two paths we can go by. Defiance or compliance. If we comply with the lifestyle we were programmed for—we thrive—if we do not, we dive. Simple yes? [152]

So, when we subject our genes to that which our genes determine "begets health" → we get healthier; and when we subject our genes to that which our genes determine "begets illness" → we get unhealthier.

Our genes simply respond to the input we provide them. If you want to know how well you are doing at achieving the health your genes are programmed to achieve then take off your clothes and simply look at yourself in the mirror. The genetic record of all you have done to create your present condition is there before you. Behold your results and, going forward, carefully choose the behaviors that mold you.

Our genes are hardwired to prompt the survival of the fittest.

Survival depends upon successful adaptation:

- Adaptive Behavior prompts an Adaptive Effect → promoting Survival (cellular regeneration)
- Maladaptive Behavior prompts a Maladaptive Effect → promoting Extinction (cellular negation)

In each of the cases above, we see: *Cause* → *Effect* → *Outcome*

"Be not deceived; God is not mocked: for whatsoever a man soweth, that shall he also reap."
- Galatians 6:7 Bible (King James Version)

Lifestyle Modification Can Mitigate Disease Progression And Reverse Existing Disease

There is an overwhelming body of studies indicating that when one hour of daily exercise is combined with "a natural food diet, high in fiber-containing fruits, vegetables, and whole grains, and naturally low in fat, containing abundant amounts of vitamins, minerals, and phytochemicals, the vast majority of chronic disease may be prevented." [151A]

If medical practitioners of every pedigree are not actively and aggressively promoting the importance of increased physical activity and a healthier diet to their patients, they are by their silence actively enabling the disease-attracting behaviors of physical inactivity and poor diet that brought the patient into the medical facility to begin with.

Being an example is not the only factor involved in influencing others, but it is by far the most effective. If you and I know what constitutes healthier behavior and we do not embrace those disciplines, we miss the mark. We thus become co-conspirators in the overthrow of our own health.

Coronary Artery Disease

Physical inactivity and poor diet contribute vitally to the progression of atherosclerosis and the consequent development of coronary artery disease. [152]

Studies indicate that inactivity may be as predictive of CAD risk as conventional risk factors; whereas exercise training has been shown to improve endothelial function. "Combined exercise and diet interventions have been demonstrated to mitigate atherosclerosis progression and may in fact induce plaque regression and/or improve myocardial flow reserve." [152]

"These benefits are, at least in part, due to reductions in plasma lipids, lipid oxidation, and inflammation." [152]

Despite estimates that death rates from cardiovascular diseases declined 17% from 1990 to 2000 (secondary to improvements in disease diagnostics, surgical procedures, and drug therapy), the actual number of deaths increased 2.5% during this period. Scientific research and technology certainly has been "improving diagnostics, surgical procedures and drug therapy" and yet the death rates have increased! [151A]

Let me raise an allegorical question:

Could it be that modern medicine's approach to CAD is comparable to a blind and inept horticulturist who treats a tree for its myriad diseases with the most advanced diagnostics, tree surgery procedures, and chemical therapy without providing for the tree's most immediate needs for the proper volume of moisture, sunshine, minerals, trace elements, fertilizers, and soil enhancements required for its survival? Could it be that modern medicine's answers fail to address the most pertinent questions? The interventions discussed in this section appear to be quite successful in not only controlling but reversing CAD. Why haven't these interventional successes been implemented as mainstream medical practices?

If we analyze the economic (institutional reimbursement) incentives for various options in treatment, do we find greater rewards being given to "primary prevention and disease reversal," or for treatment of progressive decline?

How are trends in treatment protocol's best practices going to be compelled to reflect the best evidence, if not driven by an economic reward system that rewards the most effective approaches more than less effective approaches? Industry will always follow the profits. Do the current economic incentives reflect modern medicine's current course of treatment, or do radical changes in reimbursement policy need to be enacted in order to drive industry to revise its treatment modality to reflect best evidence?

It is obviously financially rewarding for industry to emphasize the treatment of ongoing disease progression, but does it make moral and ethical sense for an economic reimbursement system to reward the treatment of conditions that may otherwise be prevented?

In the article "Conclusion And Future Directions," by Christian K. Roberts and R. James Barnard some arguments against the feasibility of successfully implementing (securing patient compliance) with dietary and behavioral modification are raised; however, the studies cited evidently demonstrated successful navigation of those challenges.

Long-term patient compliance with a "disease preventive lifestyle" is key to successful disease prevention. Are studies being conducted to compare the effectiveness of different motivational strategies and approaches, where staff members support patient compliance with the demanding challenges of lifestyle modification? What are the costs associated with funding the most effective means of motivating patient compliance with disease prevention and reversal, in comparison to the costs of the current chemical/surgical approaches of managing the symptoms of the patients' ongoing lifestyle-induced *progression* of cardiovascular disease?

Money is a great motivator.

What economic incentives are being implemented to drive industry and citizens toward healthier outcomes? Are fat foods being taxed and healthier foods being subsidized? Are industries that encourage inactivity, sedentary lifestyles, and poor behavioral choices being charged for the diseases and collateral damage that follow in the wake of their success?

Are city planners being required to provide adequate space, resources, and facilities for citizens to engage in healthy extracurricular activities? Are medical care providers and the medical care systems receiving financial incentives to provide their patients with free health club memberships, and are the pharmaceutical corporations being fined for promoting, recommending, and prescribing drugs that are documented to cause organ damage and induce chronic diseases?

Hypertension

Hypertension (systolic blood pressure >140 mmHg and/or diastolic

>90 mmHg) is a hallmark risk factor for CAD, stroke, congestive heart failure, and end-stage renal disease. Presently, it has been estimated that hypertension affects as many as 56 million adults in the United States. Several cohort and epidemiologic studies document that both physical activity and diet have blood pressure-lowering effects.

Effects of diet and exercise on blood pressure:

- Mitigation of oxidative stress
- Improvement of endothelial function
- Improved vascular function
- Improved contractility of the heart muscle
- Augmentation of NO (Nitric Oxide) availability
- Improvement of insulin sensitivity
- Lowering of resting blood sugar levels [152]

The effort required to overcome inertia and change behavior, especially in the presence of strongly engrained personal habits and strongly established familial patterns, is great. Overwhelming evidence supports the effectiveness of behavioral change, but very little support is available to the average citizen who is not chosen for special studies and/or who cannot afford intensive lifestyle modification programs on their own (as they are currently packaged). Nor are there many programs available, even for those who could afford them. How is societal shift to be encouraged when so many forces conspire against effective change and so few comprehensive lifestyle modification programs are available?

Hypertension is the most common cardiovascular disease in the United States and is a hallmark risk factor for CAD and stroke. Both physical activity and diet have been shown to affect the development of hypertension, and can lower blood pressure even in those without clinically defined hypertension.

Diabetes

Normally, over 75% of blood glucose is cleared into skeletal muscle by insulin, and insulin resistance in muscle is the primary defect leading to diabetes.

Diabetes prevalence has increased dramatically over the past two decades, contributed to by changes in activity levels (exercise training, television viewing, computers/internet, etc.) and diet.

The current body of scientific evidence indicates that comprehensive lifestyle approaches are most effective. Combined interventions have documented reversal of existing diabetes, even in those on insulin therapy, albeit less than those with oral hypoglycemic therapy.

Finnish and Diabetes Prevention trials unequivocally document that the progression of elevated fasting glucose levels and glucose intolerance into diabetes is mitigated by exercise and diet, primarily due to improvements in insulin sensitivity, and that said diet and exercise is superior to drug therapy.

Metabolic Syndrome

Kaplan called Metabolic Syndrome the "deadly quartet." Metabolic syndrome is the aggregation or accumulation of coronary artery disease risk factors, including insulin resistance, hypertension, high triglycerides, and visceral obesity. DeFonzo and Ferrannint suggest that insulin resistance is the underlying factor, and that once it is established, those with a genetic predisposition easily develop the other aspects. However, they strongly emphasized that diet, physical exercise, and body weight all strongly influence insulin resistance, and suggest that the final phenotypic gene expression was heavily influenced by environmental and behavioral factors. [152]

If the goal of medical care is the health of the patient (instead of the profit of the system), then the first and foremost goal of every patient encounter should be the establishment of 1] informed consent, and 2] patient accountability leading to behavioral contracts, which include the comprehensive and integrative protective benefits of a proper diet and regular exercise.

The metabolic syndrome, although only more recently defined and investigated, exhibits a prevalence at nearly 25% of the US adult population, and epitomizes the integrative nature of modern chronic disease, given its endocrine, metabolic, and cardiovascular underpinnings.

Cancer

An abundance of evidence suggests that lifestyle factors, including exposure to chemical carcinogens (mainly from smoking), physical inactivity, and diet play major roles in the development of many common cancers.

According to Ames, the standard human diet contains many mutagens and carcinogens that promote the generation of Reactive Oxygen Species (ROS). Drugs are known to be significant generators of ROS. When ROS rises above our bodies' tolerable threshold, ROS appears to begin increasing its reactive "initiation" of cancer and other chronic conditions. [153]

Colon Cancer

According to Friedenreich and Orenstein, the extensive studies on the risk factors associated with colon cancer give us the most definitive evidence on the association between physical exercise and cancer. Of 51 studies on colon/colorectal cancer, 43 studies showed a dramatic reduction of risk in the most physically active men and women by 40-50%. Of the 29 studies that examined a possible dose-dependant response to exercise, 25 studies documented that increasing levels of activity were associated with decreasing risks. [154]

In Burkitt's examination of British subjects living in Uganda, he noted a high incidence of colon cancer, while he rarely saw this among the native Africans. He began studying differences between these two cultures and discovered that the Africans consumed large amounts of fiber in a largely unprocessed diet and suggested that fiber appeared to play an important role in colorectal cancer, and that, by the removal of fiber and refining of the carbohydrates, the highly refined and processed British (Western) diet:

1] Reduced stool bulk and increased gastrointestinal transit time as well as adversely affected intestinal flora.[155]

2] Increased glycemic load and raised insulin levels which may affect colonic epithelial cell growth. [156]

3] *Decreases* stool bulk and *increases* stool transit time, which *increases* total stool bile acids—*especially* the secondary bile acids deoxcholic and lithocholic acids, which are thought to be the most carcinogenic bile acids. [156]

In Burkitt's original work, not only did the African natives have a very low incidence of colorectal cancer in concordance with a high fiber intake, but they also consumed a low-fat diet and were physically active, suggesting that comprehensive lifestyle modification is required to reduce cancer risk.[157] Several types of cancer are influenced by behavioral choices, and cancers of the prostate, breast, and colon are significantly influenced by exercise and diet. Dietary factors that affect cancer progression include: fiber, fat (amount and type), and meat consumption (especially red meat intake). Exercise is strongly correlated with reducing the risk of developing several types of cancer.

Conclusion And Future Directions

"The evidence is overwhelming that physical activity and diet can reduce the risk of developing numerous chronic diseases, including CAD, hypertension, diabetes, metabolic syndrome, and several forms of cancer, and in many cases, in fact, reverse existing disease."
- from Effects of Exercise and Diet on Chronic Disease
By Christian K. Roberts and R. James Barnard

Physical activity and diet have also been shown to ameliorate several other chronic diseases, such as osteoporosis, arthritis, and sarcopenia, as well as stroke, congestive heart failure, erectile dysfunction, chronic renal failure, and Alzheimer's disease.

Several studies demonstrate that physical activity helps to deter chronic disease, especially hypertension and metabolic syndrome, but few studies have examined the combined effect of exercise and diet. As a result, further studies on the effects of exercise and diet on chronic disease (using a comprehensive set of lifestyle interventions) are recommended.

Evidence suggests that the following dietary changes contribute to the reduction of chronic disease risk:

1] Elimination of refined carbohydrates, fatty foods, fast foods, and sugar-containing beverages.

2] Consumption of a whole food diet rich in fruits, vegetables, whole grains, and legumes, and high in fiber and nutrient density.

Two things are urgently needed:

1] A concerted (mutually contrived and united) effort to increase the primary prevention of chronic disease through the promotion of health and translation of research data on the superior value of exercise and diet (as compared to any other forms of treatment) for the information of the general public.

2] Legislation that translates best evidence into prescriptive practice, as opposed to parasitic treatment that "plays for opportunity," which can be entirely prevented.

It is commonly argued that it is difficult to change the lifestyle of the obese and sedentary, steeped as they are in the traditions of indulgence and lethargy; however, such pessimism may not be entirely justified. Evidence abounds of participants of rigorous exercise and diet studies rising to meet the challenges placed before them. When presented with the hard evidence, most people choose to rise to meet reasonable challenges rather than succumb to avoidable cascades of progressive decline. It's all in how the opportunity and challenge are presented. And when the historically dismal outcomes of patients following "usual care" are contrasted against the outcomes of those who are made aware and given the tools to rise above disease and despair, it becomes starkly clear just how great the stakes are, and the importance of choosing wisely.

"Chronic disease not only impacts life expectancy but also may significantly blunt the quality of life [during those] years." [158]

Additionally, questions have been raised as to the practicality of rigorous recommendations. An example of this would be the Institute of Medicine's recommendation for physical activity of 60 min/day. This has been questioned on the basis of feasibility. However, it is known that 30 min / 3 x per week can provide many important benefits. This may be inadequate for maximal health benefits, but it is plenty to stave off premature declines in chronic disease. The goal here is to preserve and secure a higher quality of life—to prevent *preventable* declines, and that can be achieved with far less demand than adherence to the highest standards required to optimize fitness.

The same argument can be raised about dietary recommendations: Rigorous adherence to the highest dietary standards will, of course, yield the greatest benefits, but even moderate changes in diet can yield significant health benefits. This is written as a general guideline: individual protein/carbohydrate requirements vary based on activity levels. Fundamentally, foods are either "nutrient-dense" or "energy dense" in nature.

Nutrient-dense foods are foods rich in minerals, vitamins, trace elements, phyto-nutrients, amino acids, and/or complete proteins. Examples include: vegetables, fruits*, nuts, seeds, legumes, yogurt, cottage cheese, fish, poultry, red meat.

Energy-dense foods are rich in "energy"—that is, easily available calories. Examples: fruit*, whole grains (complex carbohydrates), dried fruit*, honey, enriched/refined flour (refined carbohydrates), sugar.

**Fruit & Dried Fruit are both nutrient-dense and energy-rich, providing an excellent source of vitamins, minerals, electrolytes, trace elements, and simple, quickly digestible (rapid-release energy) foods.*

***Combo foods: Fats (nut & seed butters, avocados, cream, oils, butter, and fatty meats) are energy-rich but slowly digested (slow-release energy) foods. Fats are good for sustained energy requirements.*

Proteins are nutrient-dense and needed for normal muscle function and rebuilding muscles after exertion/muscle breakdown.

Consuming a nutrient-dense/energy-lean diet is healthiest for most people, except when engaging in high-exertion activities that require lots of easily available energy from food. Those engaging in a high volume of muscular activities need to emphasize more protein-rich foods. Those engaging in a high volume of aerobic activities need to emphasize more complex carbohydrate (energy-dense) foods.

Weight gain is a result of the following simple mathematic formula: Energy/caloric intake exceeds energy/caloric requirements

By frequently emphasizing nutrient-dense/calorie-lean except when energy demands are high, humans discipline their body to utilize blood sugar wisely, which stabilizes their metabolism and minimizes fat storage.

Refined carbohydrates and refined sugars are high in calories, and are energy-rich and nutrient-lean foods.

They provide a quick boost, but blood sugar drops rapidly again after calories are burned.

Fruit is a nutrient-dense, natural, unrefined energy source.

Vegetables are predominantly nutrient-dense and energy-lean foods.

Lean Proteins are nutrient-dense and energy-lean foods.

A Word About Fat:

Plant fats are healthy in moderation. Nuts, seeds, and avocados, for example, are nutrient-dense foods that provide sustained and slowly released energy. Greater moderation in consuming animal fats is recommended. Foods high in hydrogenated and trans fats are the least healthy.

Basically, the more natural, less processed, and less cooked your food is, the better your health will be.

What To Avoid:

Processed Foods. Avoid the following (or consume them minimally): refined carbohydrates, fast foods, fatty foods, sugary foods and drinks, salty foods, processed foods, hydrogenated foods, and heavily preserved foods, and greatly reduce consumption of red meat and limit dairy intake to low-fat cultured dairy products.

What To Encourage:

Natural Foods. Emphasize a largely plant-based diet consisting primarily of unprocessed whole foods with a high concentration of fruits and vegetables, whole grains, legumes, nuts, seeds, fish, and eggs, with moderate intake of lean meats, poultry, and low-fat cultured dairy products. Encourage consumption of raw fruit and vegetable juices. I love my ultra powerful Blendtec blender, which I use to make nutritious fruit and vegetable smoothies. These machines (Blendtec and Vitamix blenders) are popular and powerful machines and can turn any fruit and vegetable combination into delicious, healthy, nutrient-dense smoothies in seconds (and clean up is a breeze).

While these dietary recommendations will confer the greatest benefits, for the less motivated, simply reducing consumption of fatty processed foods, eating more fruits and vegetables and whole grain products instead of refined flour products, and cutting out sugary drinks will go a long way in reducing "high glycemic load," and confer many health benefits.

The pursuit of health is a dose-dependent relationship with yourself rather than an all-or-nothing proposition.

How is wellness to be encouraged?

"Treat people as if they were what they ought to be and
you help them to become what they
are capable of being."
- Johann Wolfgang von Goethe

If a medical professional or health advisor acts a certain way toward a client, and operates under certain assumptions and expectations, then that "environment" and those assumptions and expectations affect the attitude, behavioral responses and ultimately the health outcomes of those clients. When a person believes a client has the capability of becoming more than they currently are, and they gently push their client to succeed, the recipient often lives up to those expectations and higher standards. By giving clients "another set of eyes" through which to see themselves (and all that they are capable of becoming), they are given the vision and power to become more than they previously were. This is in stark contrast to the modern medical approach that often fosters dependence. Medical doctors do not ask what you want from this visit, but rather, what's wrong with you today. Medical doctors' recommendations seldom lead patients toward becoming the healthiest people that they can become, but rather instruct them to "take this and call back if conditions get worse."

In contrast, a patient-centered approach would not only instruct but provide clearly laid out guidelines and the support needed to reach those goals and recognize that any steps clients take toward positive behavioral reform are steps toward a healthier long-term outcome.

Physical Activity and Nutrient-Dense, High-Fiber, Low-Fat Diet causes:

Increased Insulin Sensitivity →
Decreased Circulating Insulin Levels→ Decreased Obesity
Decreased Inflammation → Decreased Adhesion/ Chemotaxis
Decreased Oxidative Stress → Increased Endothelial Function
Improved Lipid Profile → Decreased Blood Clotting

Physical Activity and Proper Diet Prompt P.A.R. (Physiological Adaptational Response), resulting in:

P.A.R.→ Decreased Diabetes, Coronary Artery Disease, Hypertension → Decreased Heart Attacks, Strokes

And the opposite is also true! Physical Inactivity and Poor Diet Causes:

Decreased Insulin Sensitivity → Increased Circulating Insulin Levels → Increased Obesity
Increased Inflammation → Increased Adhesion/ Chemotaxis
Increased Oxidative Stress → Decreased Endothelial Function
Worsening Lipid Profile → Increased Blood Clotting

Physical Inactivity and Poor Diet Prompts P.M.R. (Physiological Maladaptative Response), resulting in:

P.M.R. → Increased Diabetes, Hypertension, CAD → Increased Heart Attacks, Strokes [159]

MEDICATION SIDE EFFECTS

The biomedical paradigm treats symptoms of disease with drugs that produce more symptoms, but the pharmaceutical manufacturers have distorted our understanding of those symptoms by calling them "side effects." A list of common medication side effects is to follow, but these are actually commonly expected symptoms resulting from taking these medications. The problem gets deeper. Just as symptoms are the result of deeper systemic problems classified as diseases, so also are the symptoms that result from taking medications the result of the deeper systemic problems created by taking medications. The symptoms produced by taking medications are the physiological effects of the diseases being induced by taking those medications. Medications are taken for symptoms such as high blood pressure, high cholesterol, and high blood sugar, which are symptoms of deeper systemic problems classified as diseases, such as cardiovascular disease and diabetes. But the medications themselves produce other symptoms (which have been reclassified as "side effects" by the drug industry) which are in reality external manifestations of deeper physiological dis-harmony or dis-ease being produced by taking the medication. The question becomes: which is worse? Enduring the symptoms of the underlying physiological compromise, or adding the physiological compromise of taking a medication. Now, many times the side effects (symptoms) of taking medications (and the underlying diseases those drugs are promoting) are worth the beneficial effect for which the medication is being taken. For example taking antibiotics are very hard on the digestive and eliminative systems of the body, however, the beneficial effect of killing invading bacterial organisms is worth the damage incurred from taking the medication. However, antibiotics in particular are very constructive medications, in that they eliminate underlying causes (invading bacterial organisms). However, many prescriptions and over-the-counter medications do not eliminate anything—they simply mask the symptoms of underlying physiological compromises while producing other side effects (symptoms of the physiological compromises that the drugs produce), for which there are other medications to be prescribed.

My point is that medications *do not* simply produce side effects (the public *has been and is* willing to accept this); but, on the contrary, medications are producing symptoms, that is, symptoms of the underlying diseases that they are promoting. This is simply a different explanation of the side effects of medications and precisely why the symptoms of taking medications have been reclassified as "side effects." It's one thing for the public to tolerate the undesired side effect of a medication for the positive correction of another problem. It's quite another thing for the public to absorb a self-poisoning, health-destroying, disease-inducing chemical to treat a different symptom of a previous health problem. People would be more reluctant to take medications if they were informed that the medications they are taking for one set of symptoms are producing yet more symptoms of other diseases that they are contracting through taking those medications.

An example of this diseasing of the public by the pharmaceutical industry is its mass cholesterol education campaign to promote the use of statins. Statin drugs—hyperlipidemics, that is, cholesterol-lowering medications, are being promoted by the pharmaceutical companies for the condition of high cholesterol, which (we again, are being told by the pharmaceutical/medical industry) is a primary risk factor for cardiovascular disease. However, what the pharmaceutical industry's pro-drug public education campaign fails to tell us is the overwhelming body of evidence that indicates exercise is much more effective at reducing the risks of cardiovascular disease than taking statins, and that statins actually increase the risk of diabetes, cardiovascular disease, and cancer among a large portion of the population. But I digress.

So the self-serving medical sales model conveniently defines a primary risk factor for cardiovascular disease as patients having such and such a cholesterol level, and then they conveniently provide us with the chemical solution to the "cardiovascular health risk" that they have conjured up. Thus the ad script goes: to reduce your risk of cardiovascular disease, please see your doctor and begin taking Lipitor. However, the real science reveals a different perspective on the effects of taking statins. I highly recommend reading: *Lipitor: Thief of Memory, Statin Drugs and the Misguided War on Cholesterol Paperback*, published on January 28, 2004, by Dr. Duane Graveline. This is a must read for anyone who is even remotely interested in how our sickness care (billed as healthcare) system works. Dr. Graveline, obviously a very conscientious doctor like many, was suddenly faced with a number of dilemmas when he experienced transient global amnesia (memory loss) induced by Lipitor (one of the statin cholesterol-lowering drugs). Interestingly the manufacturer even proclaims that there is no connection with its use to prevent heart disease or heart attacks, yet the use of this useless drug continues through slick marketing. This short and eminently readable work discusses, among other issues, what Transient Global Amnesia (TGA) is, how the statin drugs work, the myth of the Cholesterol/Modified Low Fat Diet, etc. Of special interest is the role of cholesterol, particularly in the brain. It is shown how statins can traverse the blood brain barrier and interfere with the normal functioning of the brain. This is most important in those who have a dramatic reduction in cholesterol levels when using statins. "Abrupt, major decreases of serum cholesterol from statin drug therapy should be taken more as a warning than as an indication of success, for cognitive side effects seemed more likely to occur in these cases." (Lipitor, Thief of Memory: Statin Drugs and the Misguided War on Cholestoral" by Duane Graveline)

Other significant side effects of statin drugs are liver/kidney damage, muscle pain/injury, Coenzyme 10 (CQ10) depletion (which is essential for heart health), and contribution to deficiencies of heart-essential B Vitamins and other nutrients as well.

Statins have a great number of downsides to their use. A recent study examined the effect of statins on post-menopausal women. The study determined that post-menopausal women taking statins experience a 48% increase in their risk of developing diabetes. Diabetes is closely related to an increased risk of developing cardiovascular disease. [160]

So let me get this straight. The pharmaceutical advertisers and cleverly devised cholesterol education campaign (medical propaganda) informs us that post-menopausal women should take statins to lower their cholesterol in order to decrease their risk of heart disease; however, the medical propaganda fails to mention that an adverse effect of taking these blood-lipid altering drugs is the dramatic increase in these women's risk of diabetes, which is closely linked to an increased risk of heart disease.

Statins—Friend Or Foe?

What you decide depends on who you choose to believe. Your doctor and the FDA will more than likely side with the drug industry's educational campaign, which is designed to coerce all adults whose cholesterol level reaches an arbitrarily established level of 200 into taking a statin medication for the rest of their lives. This is a favored gateway drug by which the drug industry seeks to draw all people unto themselves.

Here are a few bits of information to weigh in on your decision:

Memory disruption is a known side effect of statins. In Febuary 2012, the FDA came out with the following warnings:

- Cognitive (brain-related) impairment such as memory loss, forgetfulness, and confusion have been reported by some statin users.
- People being treated with statins may have an increased risk of raised blood sugar levels and the development of Type 2 diabetes.
- Some medications interact with lovastatin (also known as Mevacor) and can increase the risk of muscle damage. [161]

Amy G. Egan, M.D., M.P.H., deputy director for safety at the FDA's Division of Metabolism and Endocrinology Products (DMEP) assures us that, "The value of statins in preventing heart disease has been clearly established, their benefit is indisputable, but they need to be taken with care and knowledge of their side effects." Others who have experienced those side effects are not so sure.

What industry determined the level at which you need to start lowering your cholesterol? That's interesting—it's the same industry that sells the medication to lower your cholesterol. "But Grandmother, what a convenient business model you have!" said Little Red Riding Hood. "The better to eat you with," replied the wolf.

High cholesterol is positively correlated with longevity in people over 85 years old, and has been shown to be associated with better memory function and reduced dementia. In a remarkable recent study, it was found that Alzheimer's patients have only 1/6 of the concentration of free fatty acids in the cerebrospinal fluid compared to individuals without Alzheimer's. In parallel, it is becoming very clear that cholesterol is pervasive in the brain and that it plays a critical role, both in nerve transport in the synapse and in maintaining the health of the myelin sheath coating the nerve fibers. An extremely high-fat (ketogenic) diet has been found to improve cognitive ability in Alzheimer's patients. These and other observations described below lead me to conclude that both a low-fat diet and statin drug treatment increase susceptibility to Alzheimer's. [162]

Old people with high cholesterol live the longest.

"This statement seems so incredible that it takes a long time to fully understand its importance. Yet the fact that people with high cholesterol live the longest emerges clearly from many scientific papers." [163 164]
- Uffe Ravnskov

When we separate the scientific evidence from pharmaceutical sales, we are left with very little to recommend taking statins. When we add to that an examination of cholesterol levels and their relation to mortality among the elderly, the picture becomes even clearer. The healthiest, smartest, longest-living elders have higher cholesterol levels on average than their peers. Another way to say this is that those taking statins are becoming less healthy, slower-witted, more ill, and dying younger with more diseases than their statin-free counterparts. Given that this is a 20 billion dollar per year industry, there is a lot riding on the pharmaceutical industry's perpetuation of its cholesterol misinformation campaign.

A growing body of clinical research now indicates that the cholesterol-lowering class of drugs known as statins are associated with over 300 adverse health effects - research boldly flying in the face of national health policy, medical insurance premium guidelines, statin drug manufacturer advertising claims, and the general sentiment of the public, with approximately 1 in every 4 adult Americans over 45 currently using these drugs to "prevent heart disease."

The Cholesterol Myth

For well over 40 years, statin drugs have successfully concretized a century-old myth about the primary cause of heart disease: namely, that cholesterol "causes" plaque build up in the arteries, ultimately leading to obstruction of blood flow, and subsequent morbidity and mortality.

Indeed, the medical establishment and drug companies have been singing the praises of this "cholesterol myth," to the tune of 25 billion dollars in statin drug sales annually.

While it is true that oxidized low-density lipoprotein is found within the atheromatous plaque that is found in damaged arteries, it is less likely a cause than an *effect* of heart disease. The underlying damage to the lining of the artery, which could be related to infections, chemicals, stress, and/or nutrition, *comes before* the immune response that results in plaque buildup there. Blaming LDL cholesterol for causing heart disease is like blaming the scab for the injury that caused it to form, or like blaming the band-aid for the scab it is covering—this is, after all, the inborn and fatal flaw of allopathic medicine, which focuses only on symptoms of disease, which it then fool-heartedly attempts to suppress by any chemical means necessary.

Death By Statins?

No one can deny that statins do exactly what they are designed to do: suppress cholesterol production and reduce measurable blood serum levels. The question is, rather, at what price do they accomplish this feat, and for what ultimate purpose?

With the National Cholesterol Education Program Guidelines, having been designed by "experts" on the payroll of statin drug manufacturers, requiring ultra-low levels to obtain a strictly theoretical and numerical definition of "health," statin drugs are guaranteed to receive first-line treatment status in the goal of prevention and treatment of heart disease through lipid suppression.

What is at question here is whether the unintended, adverse effects of this chemical class of drugs are less, the same, or worse than the purported "cardiovascular" benefits they provide?

Fundamentally, statin drugs damage the muscles and nerves in the body -- so much so that a dose as low as 5 mg a day (albeit in rare cases) can kill a human. There are well over 100 studies demonstrating the myotoxic or muscle-harming effects of these drugs, and over 80 demonstrating the effects of nerve damage, as well. When you consider that a vast portion of our body is comprised of muscles and coordinating nerve systems, this drug has the potential to cause damage to the entire body, and undoubtedly does so universally, differing only in the matter of degree—the damage occurring acutely in those at the tip of the iceberg, asymptomatically in the majority of others at the base. [165]

Statins and Efficient Brain Function [166]

Yeon-Kyun Shin, a biophysics professor in the department of biochemistry, biophysics and molecular biology, says the results of his study show that drugs that inhibit the liver from making cholesterol may also keep the brain from making cholesterol, which is vital to efficient brain function.

"If you deprive cholesterol from the brain, then you directly affect the machinery that triggers the release of neurotransmitters," said Shin. "Neurotransmitters affect the data-processing and memory functions. In other words -- how smart you are and how well you remember things."

"If you try to lower the cholesterol by taking medicine that is attacking the machinery of cholesterol synthesis in the liver, that medicine goes to the brain too. And then it reduces the synthesis of cholesterol, which is necessary in the brain," said Shin.

In his experiments, Shin tested the activity of the neurotransmitter-release machinery from brain cells without cholesterol present, and measured how well the machinery functioned. He then included cholesterol in the system and again measured the protein function. Cholesterol increased protein function by five times.

"Our study shows there is a direct link between cholesterol and the neurotransmitter release," said Shin. "And we know exactly the molecular mechanics of what happens in the cells. Cholesterol changes the shape of the protein to stimulate thinking and memory." Reducing the cholesterol in the brain may reduce your memory and cognitive skills as well. [166]

Relationship Between Statins & Brain Disease

"Our understanding of how cholesterol is critical for brain health has brought me and many others in my field to believe that statins—the blockbuster drugs prescribed to millions of Americans to lower cholesterol—may cause or exacerbate brain disorders and disease." [167]

In addition to the fact that cholesterol does not cause heart disease and we need not use statins to artificially reduce cholesterol for that reason, there is another problem. Statins have serious side-effects in many people: Memory lapses, muscle pain and muscle weakness (due to statin-initiated depletion of coenzyme Q10), neuropathy, polyneuropathy (weakness, tingling, and pain in the hands and feet, as well as walking difficulties), weakening of the sex drive, heart failure (the heart is a muscle and it cannot work when deprived of coenzyme Q10), dizziness, cognitive impairment, cancer, suppression of the immune system, pancreatic rot, and depression, sometimes of suicidal potency. Statins are powerful drugs.

Dr. Duane Graveline, a former NASA astronaut and flight surgeon, was put on a statin drug called Lipitor in 1999 for moderately elevated cholesterol. Just six weeks later his wife found him wandering around the house unable to recognize her or his surroundings. His memory lapse lasted a few hours. Duane Graveline was in excellent health. The lapse lasted only a few hours but there was simply nothing to cause it .... except one possibility. He suspected Lipitor was the culprit and since it was the only medication he was on, he discontinued its use. His mental health returned. Two years later his doctor insisted he continue taking Lipitor. He returned to using Lipitor and within a short time experienced another memory lapse episode that lasted more than 12 hours. Convinced that Lipitor was causing his episodes, he discontinued its use. [168]

So, what is the "party line" that we are being sold by the pharmaceutical industry through their front line sales reps? The message is gradually coming into focus the older we get: aging is a medical condition that needs to be medicated for the rest of your life.

Dr. Malcolm Kendrick has written a book called *The Great Cholesterol Con*, in which he discusses the pharmaceutical and American Heart Association agenda to put every living American on cholesterol medication by the age of 63. The article he references is called "New ACC/AHA Prevention Guidelines Address Blood Cholesterol, Obesity, Healthy Living and Risk Assessment," located at the American College of Cardiology Website, ACC.org. For further information, you may search the article title in the website search engine.

YOU NEED A STATIN—NOW WHAT WAS THE QUESTION? [169]

By Dr. Malcolm Kendrick

As many of you are aware the American College of Cardiology (ACC) and the American Heart Association (AHA) came out with new guidelines on cardiovascular disease prevention a few days ago. As part of this, they produce a risk calculator. Using this calculator, if your risk of heart attack or stroke is greater and 7.5% over the next 10 years, you should take a statin – for the rest of your life.

I downloaded this calculator, and I have been playing around with it. I think I would tend to agree with the headline in the NY times 18th November 2013:

Risk Calculator For Cholesterol Appears Flawed

To be frank, you can fiddle around with the figures on this calculator for hours. I think my OCD is getting worse. (Maybe I should take a statin to cure my OCD). One of the questions to which I wanted to find an answer was at what age would a perfectly healthy man (with 'optimal' risk factors) have to take a statin for the rest of his life?

So, I fed in the figures, and use the 'optimal' figures for cholesterol and blood pressure on the risk calculator

The Perfectly Healthy Man

- Male
- Age 63
- Race: WH (white)
- Total cholesterol 170mg/dl [This is 4.4mmol/l in Europe i.e. very low]
- HDL cholesterol 50md/dl [This is 1.3mmol/l in Europe]
- Systolic blood pressure 110mmHg
- Non-smoker
- No treatment for high blood pressure
- Non diabetic

CV risk over the next 10 years = 7.5%

So, there you are. You can do absolutely everything 'right,' be as healthy as healthy can be—according to the AHA and ACC. Yet, by the age of 63 you need to take a statin—for the rest of your life.

The next question to which I wanted to find the answer was at what age does a 'normal', very healthy man have to start using a statin? In the UK, the average total cholesterol for men is 5.0mmol/l. [this is 193mg/dl in the US]. The average blood pressure in the UK systolic is 129mmHg. (To be frank, I think the average cholesterol level for men is higher than this, but the World Health Organization (WHO) says not).

Feed these figures in, and you would need to start taking a statin, for the rest of your life by the age of 58. Which means that very healthy men, with no real risk factors for cardiovascular disease—at all—have to start statins at 58.

What of women? Well, they get another seven years of statin free life. A super healthy woman, with optimal risk factors, reaches the dreaded 7.5% risk at age 70. An 'average' healthy women, with average BP and cholesterol levels, would have to start a statin at age 63.

In summary, using this risk calculator, extremely healthy men will be starting statins at fifty eight, and very healthy women at sixty three. This, then, marks the age at which life becomes a statin-deficient state. You can be as healthy as healthy can be. You can do everything right, have no risk factors at all for cardiovascular disease, and yet you still need to take medication to reduce the risk of cardiovascular disease.

Sorry, what was the question again? [169]

"Once they have you asking the wrong questions. They don't have to worry about the answers."
- Thomas Pynchon, Gravity's Rainbow

Before suspending your judgement and conforming your reason and will to the will and intent of the pharmaceutical and medical industry to indoctrinate and drug every living human, please educate yourself about the valuable role and importance of cholesterol, Co Q Enzyme 10, and Vitamin D in the maintenance of the health of your brain and body. Before you commit your body to the consumption of drugs that interfere with the normal functions and processes of the body—do your homework. Also remember that the healthiest and longest-lived people on Earth do not have particularly low cholesterol and are definitely not taking statin drugs.

I make the following two recommendations:

1] Review the following websites:

- www.newmediaexplorer.org/chris/2003/11/07/bad_news_about_statin_drugs
- www.newmediaexplorer.org/chris/2005/06/28/statin_drugs_side_effects

- www.thincs.org/WAPF2003
- www.health-heart.org/

2] Consider reading the following books:

- Lipitor Thief of Memory – November 1, 2006
- The Statin Damage Crisis – July 1, 2012
- The Truth About Statins: Risks and Alternatives to Cholesterol-Lowering Drugs—April 24, 2012
- The Great Cholesterol Myth: Why Lowering Your Cholesterol Won't Prevent Heart Disease-and the Statin-Free Plan That Will – November 1, 2012

What Is Co Q Enzyme 10 - Coenzyme Q10 (Coq10)? [171]

CoQ10 is a vital participant in the chain of metabolic chemical reactions that generate energy within cells. It is found in every cell of the body (the name ubiquinone stems from its ubiquity), but is present in higher concentrations in organs with higher energy requirements, such as the kidneys, liver, and heart. Many medical studies demonstrate supplemental CoQ10's beneficial effects, most of which stem from its vital role in oxygen utilization and energy production, particularly in heart muscle cells.

Why is it necessary?

Coenzyme Q10 is beneficial for heart health in many ways. It assists in maintaining the normal oxidative state of LDL cholesterol, helps assure circulatory health, and supports optimal functioning of the heart muscle. CoQ10 may also help support the health of vessel walls.

What are the signs of a deficiency?

Since this enzyme is found in high concentration in heart muscle cells, deficiency has been associated with cardiovascular problems—including angina, arrhythmia, heart failure, and high blood pressure. Problems with blood sugar regulation, gingival (gum) health, and stomach ulcers have also been associated with CoQ10 deficiency. Those who are taking statins to lower cholesterol are at particular risk for deficiency, because not only do statins reduce cholesterol levels, but they also block CoQ10 synthesis in the body. Low CoQ10 levels in patients on statins can contribute to the common side effects of statin therapy, such as aching joints and muscles as well as fatigue.

How much, and what kind, does an adult need?

Dr. Andrew Weil suggests at least 90 to 120 mg of supplemental

CoQ10 for any adult taking statin medications and for those with a family history of heart problems, or for those who are at increased risk for cardiovascular disease. This dosage is also appropriate for otherwise healthy men and women as a preventive measure, and to help maintain a healthy cardiovascular system. CoQ10 is fat-soluble, so take the supplement with a meal containing fat. Seek out the soft-gel ubiquinol form when taking CoQ10 as a standalone supplement, as this has greater antioxidant efficiency than the ubiquinone form.

How do you get enough from foods?

Although the body is capable of synthesizing CoQ10, Dr. Weil believes that adding foods high in CoQ10 to the diet and taking a daily supplement is advisable for the at-risk populations. Foods such as fish and meats, as well as oils from soybean, sesame, and rapeseed (canola) are good dietary sources.

Are there any risks associated with too much?

There is limited research on the toxicity of CoQ10, but preliminary evidence indicates that supplemental doses of up to 1,200 mg a day may be beneficial for those with certain health conditions (especially Parkinson's Disease), and has no known side-effects.

Are there any other special considerations?

1] More research is needed, but CoQ10 seems to improve muscular dystrophy patients' exercise capacity, heart function, and overall quality of life.

2] There are preliminary indications that CoQ10 may slow the progression of dementia in Alzheimer's patients.

"We are now in a position to witness the unfolding of the greatest medical tragedy of all time - never before in history has the medical establishment knowingly created a life-threatening nutrient deficiency in millions of otherwise healthy people."
- Peter H. Langsjoen, MD

The following excerpts are drawn from the work of Owen R. Fonorow PhD. From his book *CoQ10 and Statins: the Vitamin C Connection*, Dr. Fonorow has given to us a far more natural and effective treatment plan for the prevention and treatment of cardiovascular disease.

Ubiquinone (CoQ10) is a popular heart medication

that until 2001 was only available by prescription in Japan. The public is hardly aware that an increasingly popular class of cardiovascular drugs called statins (HMG-CoA reductase inhibitors) interferes with the body's synthesis of CoQ10. Top-selling statin drugs such as Lipitor® and Zocor® earn their makers in excess of $20 billion per year. These drugs lower the endogenous production of cholesterol and are often touted as "life-saving" by cardiologists and the media.

Are statin drugs really good for us, or are cardiologists mistaken? How can drugs that lower the body's production of CoQ10 benefit heart patients? Are the health benefits attributed to CoQ10 supplementation hype, or are the thinking and the science used by statin drug marketers fundamentally wrong? [172]

CoQ10 BASICS

Coenzyme Q10 is a vitamin-like, fat-soluble antioxidant found everywhere in the body. The highest concentrations have been measured in vital organs such as the heart and pancreas. At age 20, an individual's heart has a higher CoQ10 level than other major organs. At age 80, this is no longer true, with CoQ10 levels in the heart cut by more than half. More than 35 controlled clinical trials in Japan, Europe, and the U.S. have proven that CoQ10 therapy is highly effective in treatment of congestive heart failure, angina and ischemic heart disease, and myocardial infarction. It is now believed that CoQ10 is the key nutrient for generating 95% of the total energy required by the human body.

A healthy, youthful human body can make its own CoQ10. Endogenous production or biosynthesis of CoQ10 has 17 steps, requiring at least seven vitamins (vitamin B2 (riboflavin), vitamin B3 (niacinamide), vitamin B6, folic acid, vitamin B12, vitamin C, and pantothenic acid) and several trace elements.

The pharmaceutical giant Merck has known for more than 15 years that statin drugs interfere with CoQ10 biosynthesis, leading to low serum levels, which cause muscles to atrophy. The following claim from one of two 1990 Merck patents (4,933,165) suggests adding CoQ10 to statin drugs to overcome statin-induced myopathy. [172]

> CoQ10 supplementation has been found beneficial in the prevention and rehabilitation of ALS, heart disease, diabetes, neurodegenerative diseases, mitochondrial diseases, immune disorders, kidney failure, high blood pressure and its value in the treatment of other health conditions such as cancer.[173] Statin drugs interfere with cellular production CoQ10 enzyme.[173] Statin drugs interfere with the synthesis of Vitamin D from cholesterol.[175]

Are statin drugs really good for us, or are cardiologists mistaken? How can drugs that lower the body's production of CoQ10 benefit heart patients? Are the health benefits attributed to CoQ10 supplementation hype, or are the thinking and the science used by statin drug marketers fundamentally wrong?

Vitamin D3: 5,000 IU Daily

Evidence supporting Vitamin D's influence on key biological functions vital to one's health and well-being keeps coming in. Vitamin D contributes to cardiovascular health, immune support, bone and joint health, and much more. These discoveries about D3 are especially notable considering that we are living in a time of widespread Vitamin D insufficiency.[176]

"Humans make thousands of units of Vitamin D within minutes of whole body exposure to sunlight. From what we know of nature, it is unlikely such a system evolved by chance." Dr. John Cannell, Executive Director, Vitamin D Council.[177, 178]

"The chutzpah of pharmaceutical science and medical practice in presuming to control the body's processes, without any consideration for adverse effects that can readily be predicted—such as known disorders related to inadequate Vitamin D and CoQ10 —needs to come to an end."

- Heidi Stevenson

Inadequate Vitamin D causes muscle pain. The purpose of statin drugs is to lower cholesterol. Is there a connection between the muscle pain that results from statins and inadequate Vitamin D?

There can, in fact, be little doubt. The connection is obvious if you know one fact: Cholesterol is required to make Vitamin D. Therefore, anyone taking statins can be expected to have a deficiency in it.

On the next page, let's take a look at the primary conditions associated with inadequate Vitamin D and the adverse effects of statin drugs:

Inadequate Vitamin D	Statins
Myopathy (muscle pain)	Myopathy (muscle pain)
Osteomalacia (bone softness)	Osteomalacia (bone softness)
Peripheral neuropathy	Peripheral neuropathy
Diabetes	Diabetes
	Appears to increase some cancers[179a]

It isn't hard to see that there's a connection between serious conditions known to be caused by both inadequate Vitamin D and statins. It shouldn't be surprising, though. The purpose behind statins is to lower cholesterol. Unfortunately, medical researchers and doctors tend to wear blinders. They focus only on a single item known to be associated with a condition. They believe that cholesterol causes heart disease — but not because it's ever been proven true. They have a theory, and they have decided that their theory must be correct, in spite of a lack of evidence to support it.

The theory says that cholesterol causes heart disease by getting stuck and collecting on the linings of blood vessels to form hard plaques. This limits blood flow, thus increasing blood pressure, which is believed to be another cause of heart disease. Eventually, bits of the plaques break off and travel to an artery in the heart, causing the blood supply in a heart artery to be cut off, resulting in a heart attack. (It's also believed to be the reason for many strokes, with the only difference being that the plaque travels to the brain and blocks an artery there.)

Statins function by inhibiting the enzyme HMG-CoA reductase inhibitor. This enzyme is critical for the manufacture of cholesterol in the liver. Cholesterol, in spite of modern medicine treating it like a criminal, is a critical substance required for a wide range of body functions. One of them is the manufacturing of Vitamin D. It should, therefore, come as no surprise that some of the conditions associated with statins are the same as those associated with inadequate Vitamin D.

Modern medicine and its bought-and-paid-for science have yet again made the fundamental error of assuming that something associated with a disease is caused by it. To have adequate Vitamin D, we must have adequate cholesterol. Medical science presumes to be the arbiter of how much cholesterol is too much, never considering that the body manufactures more for a reason, with the exception of genetic hypercholesterolemia, which is a birth defect.

Presuming that there is an excess of cholesterol and then giving a drug to force its level down is playing with fire. Willingly wearing blinders, medical science and doctors focus on one narrow marker, so the whole story is missed, even when much of the information is already available. By preventing the production of cholesterol, Vitamin D production is also prevented. By the way, the enzyme needed for the production of cholesterol is also required to produce CoQ10 (another critical substance), which may be part of the reason that statins are associated with diabetes.

Does it make sense to supplement with Vitamin D and CoQ10 when taking statins, as is being asked in some medical circles? Perhaps, but wouldn't it be better to ask medical science to search for the real causes of diseases and stop trying to suppress symptoms, which invariably end up causing at least as much (if not more) harm than the diseases they're trying to prevent?

Vitamin D [179]

Vitamin D is finally getting the attention it has always deserved.

Vitamin D promotes healthy bones, largely by promoting the absorption of calcium. "If you have a vitamin D deficiency, particularly in your older years, it can lead to osteoporosis or osteomalacia [bone softening]," says Lona Sandon, RD, assistant professor of clinical nutrition at the University of Texas Southwestern in Dallas.

But there is recent and mounting evidence that links low levels of the vitamin to an increased risk of type 1 diabetes,[180] muscle and bone pain, and (perhaps more serious) cancers of the breast, colon, prostate, ovaries, esophagus, and lymphatic system.

If you want to lower your blood pressure, vitamin D may be just what the doctor ordered. If you're trying to reduce your risk of diabetes, or lower your chances of heart attacks,[181] rheumatoid arthritis, [182] or multiple sclerosis, [183] then vitamin D should be at the front of the line in your daily supplement regimen.

"Activated vitamin D is one of the most potent inhibitors of cancer cell growth," says Michael F. Holick, PhD, MD, who heads the Vitamin D, Skin, and Bone Research Laboratory at *Boston University School of Medicine*. "It also stimulates your pancreas to make insulin. It regulates your immune system."

Just consider these recent studies:

At Boston University, after people with high blood pressure were exposed to UVA and UVB rays for three months, their vitamin D levels increased by more than 100% -- and more impressively, their high blood pressure normalized. "We've followed them now for nine months, and their hypertension continues to be in remission," says Holick, professor of medicine, physiology and biophysics at Boston University. Here's a theory about how vitamin D reduces blood pressure: it decreases the production of a hormone called renin, which is believed to play a role in hypertension.

In a study published in the *Journal of the American Medical Association* in December 2003, of more than 3,000 veterans (ages 50 to 75) at 13 Veterans Affairs medical centers, those who consumed more than 645 IU of vitamin D a day along with more than 4 grams per day of cereal fiber had a 40% reduction in their risk of developing precancerous colon polyps.

In a report in the *Journal of the American Geriatrics Society* in February 2004, researchers at the University of Basel in Switzerland showed that elderly women who took a vitamin D supplement plus calcium for three months reduced their risk of falling by 49%, compared with consuming calcium alone. Those women who had fallen repeatedly in the past seemed to gain the most benefit from vitamin D.

A study in the Jan. 13, 2004 issue of *Neurology* indicated that women who get doses of vitamin D that are typically found in daily multivitamin supplements—of at least 400 international units—are 40% less likely to develop multiple sclerosis compared with those not taking over-the-counter supplements. [184]

Warnings about the use of statins:

In addition to statins' interference with the body's synthesis of CoQ10 enzyme and Vitamin D, there are numerous other negatives associated with taking statins as well. [184]

The FDA has increased and expanded its warnings about the side effects of using statin medications:

- Cognitive (brain-related) impairment (such as memory loss, forgetfulness and confusion) has been reported by some statin users.
- Some medications interact with lovastatin (brand names include Mevacor) and can increase the risk of muscle damage.
- People being treated with statins may have an increased risk of raised blood sugar levels and for the development of Type 2 diabetes. [184a]

Regarding the risks the public is exposed to with the consumption of statin medications; one recent study published in the Archives of Internal Medicine in January 2012 demonstrated a 48 percent increase in the risk of diabetes among women taking statin medications.[184b]

There is also an interesting correlation between the American medical system's history of increasing prescription of statin medications and our nation's increasing incidence of new cases of diabetes. In spite of overwhelming evidence linking diabetes to obesity and a sedentary lifestyle (so much so that the growing epidemic of diabetes is being called diabesity), the American medical system still continues to prescribe medications that actually *increase the risk* of diabetes instead of prescribing exercise and highly effective yet inexpensive weight loss programs like Weight Watchers. Who or what is the American medical system really working for?

The following data is from the Diabetes Report Card 2012: National and State Profile of Diabetes and Its Complications: Incidence of Diagnosed Diabetes

The figure on the next page shows diabetes incidence in the United States, which is the number of new cases diagnosed each year. The number of new cases of diabetes changed little from 1980 through 1990, but began increasing in 1992. From 1990 through 2010, the annual number of new cases of diagnosed diabetes almost tripled. The rise in the incidence of type 2 diabetes cases is associated with increases in obesity, decreases in leisure-time physical activity, and the aging of the U.S. population. [184c]

Influence of modern medicine on Adulthood and Aging.

More Meditation On Medication

When people have a symptom of a systemic (lifestyle-induced) chronic condition, and they take action to correct the underlying health-deficient behavior—whether it be a lack of exercise, poor diet, high stress, or overeating—they take control of their health and stop the problem at its root.

When people have a symptom of a systemic (lifestyle-induced) chronic condition, and they take medication to correct the symptoms of underlying health-deficient behaviors, those symptoms are modified, but the cause (their unhealthy lifestyle) continues to degrade their health, erupting in other symptoms of degenerating health or in symptoms resulting from the medications being taken. These new symptoms are then treated with other additional medications, which produce other symptoms, for which other medications are taken, and so on.

It is obvious that the more diseases one has, the more drugs one takes; however, I propose that it actually works the other way around—the more medications one takes, the more diseases one gets!

The following is just a short list of a few of the most common medication classes and the symptoms they produce—that is, their side effects.

Medication Class	Reason For Taking Medication	Common Side Effects (Symptoms) *** FOR THESE SYMPTOMS CONTACT DOCTOR IMMEDIATELY
NSAIDS (Non-Steroidal Anti-Inflammatory Drug)	Relieves pain and inflammation	Bloating, gas, diarrhea, dizziness, drowsiness, headache, heartburn, lightheadedness, decreased urination, unusual bleeding, black tarry stools***
Steroids	Relieves pain and inflammation	Increased appetite, weight gain, fluid retention, nervousness, insomnia, increased blood sugar levels, bloody or tarry stools***
Antidepressant (Trycyclic)	Nerve pain, insomnia (rarely used for depression)	Bloating, constipation, dry mouth, fatigue, muscle weakness, nausea
Antidepressant (Serotonin Inhibitor)	Treatment for depression / emotional conditions	Sweating, decreased appetite, insomnia, tremors, muscle weakness, drowsiness, heartburn

Medication Class	Reason For Taking Medication	Common Side Effects (Symptoms) *** FOR THESE SYMPTOMS CONTACT DOCTOR IMMEDIATELY
Antihyper-lipidemics / Statins: Cholesterol-lowering agents	Lowers cholesterol and tryglyceride levels	Muscle pain, muscle weakness and tendon damage, muscular atrophy, impaired mobility and coordination, inhibits coenzyme Q10 production*, reduced energy production, fatigue, diarrhea, difficulty urinating, headache, dizziness, stomach pain, impaired cognitive function *Coenzyme Q10 deficiency is linked to heart failure, hypertension and Parkinson Disease
Anticoagulant	Blood thinner: decreases the blood's ability to clot	Bruising, abdominal pain, bleeding gums, nose bleeds,*** black tarry stools,*** bloody urine,*** vomiting blood***
Antihypertensive: calcium channel blocker	Lowers blood pressure	Constipation, leg swelling, drowsiness
Antihypertensive: Ace inhibitor	Lowers blood pressure	Changes in kidney function, elevated potassium electrolyte levels, dry cough
Antihypertensive: Alpha blocker	Lowers blood pressure	Light-headedness, dizziness

Medication Class	Reason For Taking Medication	Common Side Effects (Symptoms) *** FOR THESE SYMPTOMS CONTACT DOCTOR IMMEDIATELY
Diuretic (water pill)	Reduces fluid retention by increasing urination	Dry mouth, dizziness, increased thirst, irregular heartbeat, leg cramps, light-headedness, low blood pressure
Laxatives	Stimulates bowel activity	Gas, diarrhea, abdominal cramping, nausea
Anti diarrhea	Slows intestinal function; absorbs fluid from stools to create formed stools	Abdominal cramping, urinary retention, drowsiness, dry mouth, blurred vision, rapid heart rate***
Anti diabetic (insulin)	Lowers blood sugar levels	Hypoglycemia: blurred vision, anxiety, fatigue, irritability, shakiness, rapid heartbeat, sweating Hyperglycemia: extreme thirst, frequent urination, blurred vision, drowsiness, dry skin
Anti diabetic (oral)	Lowers blood sugar levels	Constipation, diarrhea, nausea, drowsiness, headache, shakiness, decreased appetite, sweating, fatigue, anxiety, rapid heart rate

Information for the above table was derived from references from various sources.

Drug-Induced Diseases

It is well documented that drugs cause numerous forms of physiological damage:

Drugs → Liver Damage → Kidney Damage → Heart/ Vascular Damage → Adrenal Insufficiency → Digestive Interference → Disruption of Metabolic Process → Destabilizing Normal Blood Sugar Levels → Disruption of Cellular Energy Production → Increased Oxidative Stress → Immune Suppression → Slower Healing → Increased Autointoxication (Self Poisoning)→ Tendon Weakening and Damage → Inflammation → Joint Stiffness → Disruption of Cellular Respiratory Processes → Increased Weight Gain

It is a well documented fact that many drugs cause "Drug-Induced Diseases," and it should be understood that many drugs currently being prescribed and/or marketed as OTC drugs contribute to the progression of the very diseases they claim to treat.

THE OUTCOMES—APPLYING THE SOLUTION TO THE AMERICAN MEDICAL SYSTEM CRISIS

What happens when best evidence defines best practice? The following chapter is divided into two sections:

Section 1: Scientific Health Studies. What the best scientific evidence indicates are the most effective means of controlling and reversing chronic disease.

Section 2: Corporate Wellness Programs. Improving health and generating a significant return on investment.[186]

Section 1 is a review and commentary on a great many diet and exercise studies contained in the major report by Christian Roberts and R. James Barnard entitled "Effects of exercise and diet on chronic disease."

Section 2 is a review and commentary on a number of corporate wellness programs and their reported benefits and return-on-investment (ROI) for their respective organizations.

Section 1: Review, Analysis, And Commentary On Numerous Scientific Health Studies

Primary Source: *The Effect of Exercise and Diet on Chronic Disease,* by Christian K. Roberts , R. James Barnard

Human Genes, Lifestyle And Environment

Evidence of Gene-Environment Interaction can be seen among the Pima and Tarahumara Native Americans. Both groups have the same genetic background, but one tribe lives on a westernized diet and has adopted a westernized, sedentary lifestyle while the other group continues to consume a traditional Indian diet of natural foods and engage in a very physically active lifestyle. Among the westernized Pima living on a reservation in Arizona, the incidence of diabetes is among the highest known (at 50%), whereas the Tarahumara living in Mexico have a very low incidence of diabetes at 10%.

Genetics And Diet

Native Americans eating a natural, unprocessed diet consistent with their predecessors' natural diet (during which time the human genome was being constructed) experience a genetic predisposition for adaptation and survival. Those whose diet is inconsistent with the natural unprocessed diet eaten during which time the genetic code was written (programmed) experience the equal and opposite side of that genetic equation (genetic impulse)—the maladaptive extinction of those who eat a diet inconsistent with the diet coded for their survival. This is confirmed by the fact that when the Tarahumara of Mexico do consume a Western diet, rapid hyperlipidemia and increasing rates of cardiovascular disease rapidly ensue. [187]

The same genotype subjected to different environments (diet and lifestyle) generate results accordingly. Those Indians whose lifestyle is in alignment with the human genome for adaptation and survival of the highly active thrive, while those Indians whose lifestyle is *out of alignment* with the human genome for the adaptation and survival of the highly active are experiencing the equal and opposite side of the same genetic equation: that is, the maladaptive extinction of the highly inactive (sedentary).

Lifestyle Modification Can Mitigate Disease Progression And Reverse Existing Disease

National Cholesterol Education Program (NCEP) Step 1 Diet

Many diets have been studied, including the *National Cholesterol Education Program (NCEP) Step 1 Diet* and high-fat, low carbohydrate diets, for which the benefits appeared to be modest. Other studies upon different types of diets have highlighted "the value of diets consisting primarily of whole grains (rich in fiber, antioxidants, minerals, and phytochemicals), fruits, vegetables, and omega-3-containing fish, with limited intake of saturated fats, trans-fatty acids, cholesterol, and refined carbohydrates," which fall in line with the American Heart Association's newer dietary guidelines.

The Pritikin Comprehensive Lifestyle Intervention Program

Most effective by far have been the studies which evaluate the effect of *comprehensive lifestyle modification programs.* Such programs have proven most effective in winning the war against chronic disease. "The scientific evidence supporting the value of daily exercise and a diet focusing on the consumption of whole grains, fruits, and vegetables for the prevention and treatment of the major diseases seen in the industrialized countries today is overwhelming." Christian K. Roberts and R. James Barnard, *Effects of exercise and diet on chronic disease*

There is overwhelming evidence from numerous studies of *comprehensive lifestyle intervention programs* that "when daily physical activity of one hour is performed in combination with a natural food diet, high in fiber-containing fruits, vegetables, and whole grains, and naturally low in fat, containing abundant amounts of vitamins, minerals, and phytochemicals, the vast majority of chronic disease may be prevented." [187a]

It is now well documented that the combined effect of specialized programs of physical activity and diet mitigate the progression of chronic disease and reverse existing disease. From the success of these studies, we can now scientifically confirm what are the most effective means of controlling and reversing chronic diseases. Additional studies are needed to better understand the cause and effect relationship or mechanisms by which proper diet and exercise modulate gene expression and reverse chronic disease. Ongoing studies will also be needed to refine the best means of migrating large numbers of the chronically ill into programs of health restoration in order to prevent their decay into the far more expensive and far less effective chemical management of lifestyle aberrations. Most importantly, economic stimulus must be put in place to require medical systems to prescribe (and facilitate) what the best evidence dictates and not merely "treat the decline" of that which is entirely preventable.

Coronary Artery Disease Trials And Studies

Women's Health Study

The Women's Health Study showed an inverse relationship between dietary fiber intake and coronary artery disease. This was probably due to participants' increased consumption of fruits and vegetables, which has also been confirmed by other studies to reduce the risk of coronary artery disease. Other factors associated with slowing and/or reversing CAD are reduced consumption of proteins, and the substitution of red meat with poultry and fish.

The Adult Treatment Panel III Summary

The Adult Treatment Panel III concluded "physical inactivity" is a major risk for coronary artery disease. Total physical activity, vigorous activity, and cardio-respiratory fitness are all inversely related to coronary artery disease, with the relative risk of inactive individuals being about twice that of active persons for developing coronary artery disease.

Women's Health Initiative Observational Study and Nurses' Health Study

The combined results of these two studies showed that 30-40% of CAD could be prevented simply by walking more than 2.5 h/wk as compared to less than that amount of physical activity.

Harvard Alumni Study and The Health Professionals Follow-up Study

Several studies, including the *Harvard Alumni Study* and *the Health Professionals Follow-up Study,* revealed that CAD risk inversely related to calories expended. CAD risk was threefold greater for unfit individuals as compared to fit ones. There was an inverse relation between maximal oxygen consumption (Vo2 max) and death from CAD. Also, high fitness was associated with slower progression of carotid artherosclerosis. Men who trained with weights 30 min/wk or more had 25% reduction in CAD risk, compared with those who did not.

Oslo-Diet Heart Study

Men consuming a diet lower in saturated fat and cholesterol as compared to a control group reduced their Total-C* by 17.6%, compared to 3.7% in the control group, and after 11 years experienced significantly fewer CAD-related deaths.

Understanding Lipid Panels:

- *Total-C:* total cholesterol, and is a sum of the HDL, LDL and VLDL (very low density lipoprotein). Total cholesterol = HDL + LDL + VLDL
- *LDL:* "bad" cholesterol. LDL should be less than 130 mg/dL, ideally less than 100 mg/dL.

- *VLDL:* "bad" cholesterol. VLDL should be less than 40 mg/dL.
- *HDL:* "good" cholesterol. HDL should be greater than 40 mg/dL, ideally greater than 60 mg/dL
- *Triglycerides:* should be less than 200 mg/dL, ideally less than 150 mg/dL

Total-C does not consider triglycerides. Triglycerides are a type of fat in the blood, not a type of cholesterol. However, triglycerides are frequently used to estimate VLDL ("bad") cholesterol. Here's the calculation: triglycerides divided by 5 equals VLDL cholesterol.

Here is a great link that discusses all of the numbers and how they relate to one another: <http://www.healthcentral.com/cholesterol/c/42538/39391/cholesterol>

Stanford Coronary Risk Intervention Project

In the *Stanford Coronary Risk Intervention Project,* 300 patients with angiographically-confirmed coronary artherosclerosis were randomly assigned to a usual care group and a comprehensive risk reduction group, involving a reduction of fat and cholesterol consumption, an increase in daily activities like walking and household chores, and a specific endurance exercise training program. The groups were later tested on several measures of fitness and CAD risk with the following results: the intensive risk reduction group showed 22% reduction in both of the "bad" LDL/ApoB cholesterols and 12% increase in the "good" HDL_C cholesterol, 20% reduction in triglycerides, 4% reduction in body weight, 20% improvement in exercise capacity and a 47% reduced rate of narrowing of diseased coronary artery segments (with some showing regression) as compared to the usual care group.

Lifestyle Heart Trial as compared to the NCEP Step I Diet (National Cholesterol Education Program)

In the *Lifestyle Heart Trial,* 48 patients were randomized to either a *usual care* group instructed to follow the *NCEP Step 1* cardiac diet or to an experimental group instructed and supported in maintaining intensive dietary and lifestyle changes. The usual care group was instructed to follow the NCEP Step 1 dietary guidelines while the experimental group was placed on a more rigorous whole food and vegetarian diet with only 10% energy from fat, plus aerobic exercise, stress management training, smoking cessation, and group support. After one year of follow-up, the experimental group demonstrated fewer and less intense episodes of angina and measureable quantitative improvements under examination by coronary angiography. After a 5-year follow-up, "the experimental group exhibited a relative reduction in diameter stenosis of 7.9% compared with a 27.7% progression in the control group. The risk ratio for a cardiac event in the control group compared with the experimental group was 2.47." [187a]

The usual care control group followed the recommended dietary recommendations alone, and experienced only modest improvement over no recommendations at all. In fact, after 5 years of follow up, they had a 2.47 times greater likelihood of having a cardiac event than did the experimental group. This is a clear indication as to the importance of implementing comprehensive lifestyle modifications in the treatment of cardiovascular patients. The usual care model has been shown to be 2.47 times less effective then a comprehensive lifestyle modification program.[188] Subsequently, NCEP came out with a more rigid dietary guideline called the NCEP Step 2 Diet, which is far more effective.

NCEP Step 2 Diet (National Cholesterol Education Program)

The National Cholesterol Education Program (NCEP) Step 2 diet focuses upon restricting fat intake and monitoring fat intake very closely: (30% of calories or less as total fat, less than 7% saturated fat, and less than 200 mg of cholesterol per day). The NCEP Step 2 diet was tested and found effective in significantly reducing total and LDL cholesterol levels, without changing the total cholesterol/HDL cholesterol ratio for men and women who had normal-to-high cholesterol levels.[189]

For more information, read *Efficacy of a National Cholesterol Education Program Step 2 Diet in Normolipidemic and Hypercholesterolemic Middle-Aged and Elderly Men and Women.*[190]

Pritikin Combined Physical Activity and Diet Intervention

Comprehensive lifestyle modification programs reduce the risks of CAD by using several mechanisms simultaneously. Several prospective studies suggest that chronic inflammation of coronary vessels is a more significant risk factor for CAD than elevated cholesterol, and that measuring CRP levels serves as a better predictor of CAD. Elevated C-reactive protein (CRP), which is a marker or indicator of vascular inflammation is a more sensitive predictor of myocardial infarction, stroke, peripheral arterial disease, and sudden cardiac death than Total-C (cholesterol levels) alone.

Dietary Component:

There is considerable evidence supporting the importance of eating a diet containing a lot of fruits and vegetables in order to reduce vascular inflammation. "The addition of vegetables to the diet has been shown to reverse the increase in sICAM-1 and sVCAM-1* induced by high-fat meal consumption.[191] Consumption of an array of phytonutrients may be optimal, as the effect of individual supplements on inflammatory markers is not consistent." [192]

*sICAM-1 (soluble intercellular adhesion molecule 1), sVCAM-1 (soluble vascular adhesion molecule 1) are adhesion molecules. The attachment of monocytes and lymphocytes to endothelial cells, *which initiates atherosclerosis*, arises under the influence of adhesion molecules.

Exercise Component:

Glycemic load is also associated with increased CRP levels. Many epidemiological studies indicate that regular physical activity reduces glycemic load and ameliorates chronic inflammatory processes.

Comprehensive Studies:

The most convincing evidence comes from studies combining the use of exercise and diet to control chronic disease. "Wegge demonstrated that the *Pritikin Combined Physical Activity and Diet Intervention* decreased CRP by 45%, serum amyloid A by 37%, and soluble ICAM-1 in postmenopausal women on hormone replacement therapy with risk factors for CAD." [193]

Studies on the effects of exercise conducted with participants in the Pritikin lifestyle intervention demonstrated that cardiac "event-free survival rate was superior with one year of exercise training as compared with percutaneous coronary angioplasty, and that this occurred at a [substantially] lower financial cost secondary to reduced rehospitalization and repeat revascularizations." [193]

The following is a list of some of the known and/or suspected mechanisms by which exercise and diet reduce the risks of Coronary Artery Disease (CAD) and other chronic diseases

WARNING: The following list of the known and/or suspected mechanisms by which exercise and diet reduce the risks of coronary artery disease CAD and other chronic diseases contains a lot of "50 dollar words" that don't have a whole lot of meaning to a majority of my audience. Fundamentally, exercise is very good for you and the most powerful preventive medicine known to man.

Diet and Exercise Improves Endothelial Function:

- Increases in endothelial NO synthase (NOS), Akt Phosphorylation, and endothelial NOS Ser[1177] phosphorylation by Akt which contribute to improved endothelial dependant vasodilation.

- Improvements in endo-thelium-dependent vasodilation in patients with CAD and chronic heart failure
- Reduction in mononuclear cell production of *harmful* atherogenic cytokines [interleukin (IL)-1α, tumor necrosis factor-α, and interferon-7] and CRP. "These fell by 58 and 35% respectively, after the exercise program"[194]
- Positive changes in transforming growth factor-β and cytokine production proportionate to the time subjects spend performing lower body exercise.
- Increase in mononuclear cell production of *protective* atheroprotective cytokines (IL-4, IL-10, and transforming growth factor-β_1) which rose by 36%.
- Improved processing of harmful Reactive Oxygen Species (ROS)
- Increased levels of the antioxidant enzymes superoxidase dismutase and glutathione peroxidase
- Decreased vascular inflammation

What we know is that exercise keeps the walls of our blood vessels healthy and pliable so as to support a healthy, dynamic, fluid communication and exchange across the walls between our blood and the cells of our body. When exchange between the blood and the cells is interrupted by damaged, stiffened, coated, hardened blood vessel walls, the health of every system and cell is compromised, and that gives disease a doorway or portal of access into the inner chamber. Exercise and proper diet keep the blood vessel walls porous and healthy in order to allow rapid, fluid and dynamic exchange. Of course, exercise and proper diet provide many other benefits as well!

Beyond this simple explanation it becomes difficult to explain simply and concisely. Exercise and proper diet stimulate protective physiological mechanisms that fortify the organism, making it more resilient to degeneration.

This explains why the human genome appears to possess a certain *expected level* of exertion in order to trigger-initiate its adaptive or maladaptive response to our behavioral inputs.

Healthy is as healthy does. The body's collective physiological mechanisms and cellular interactions are exquisitely complex, and science is only barely beginning to understand how it all operates. We do not know exactly how all the pieces come together, but there is overwhelming evidence that exercise and a healthy diet work very effectively to reverse current declines in health and slow the rate of future declines dramatically.

Mechanisms, interactions, processes, and physiological underpinnings of these scientific terms exceed the scope of this book. For more information, input the following key word searches:

- Endothelial Dependant Vasodilation
- Reactive Oxygen Species (ROS)
- Atheroprotective Cytokines
- Antioxidant Enzymes
- Atherogenic Cytokines
- CRP
- Vascular Inflammation

Mechanisms by which exercise and proper diet are thought to impart health benefits: (simplified)

- Improved endothelial-dependant vasodilation
- Reduction in *harmful* atherogenic cytokines
- Positive changes in transforming growth factor-β and cytokine production
- Increase in *protective* atheroprotective cytokines
- Improved processing of harmful Reactive Oxygen Species (ROS)
- Increased levels of antioxidant enzymes;
- Decreased CRP
- Decreased vascular inflammation

Diet and exercise improve plasma lipid profile, raise *healthy* HDL-C levels, and lower triglyceride levels and *unhealthy* LDL-C levels after just 7 days of 45-minutes daily walking or jogging.

Other ways in which exercise and diet reduce the risks of CAD and other chronic diseases:

- Improves insulin sensitivity
- Lowers blood pressure
- Decreases musculoskeletal inflammation
- Improves heart function
- Improves circulation
- Improves mobility
- Improves coordination and reaction times
- Improves oxygenation of the brain and body
- Improves mental clarity
- Improves peace of mind

Hypertension Trials And Studies

Several cohort and epidemiologic studies document that both physical activity and diet have blood pressure-lowering effects.

National High Blood Pressure Education Program

Research into the effects of diet and exercise on hypertension have resulted in recommendations for the primary prevention of hypertension from the National High Blood Pressure Education Program. They recommend engaging in moderate physical activity and consuming a diet rich in fruits, vegetables, and low-fat dairy products, as well as reducing both saturated fat and total fat in the diet.

Diet-Only Studies:

Seventh-Day Adventist vegetarians

A study of the effects of diet on hypertension (HTN) among Mormon and Seventh-Day Adventists found that Mormon omnivores had a prevalence of 10% having HTN, while Seventh-Day Adventist omnivores had a prevalence of 8.5% having HTN and Seventh-Day Adventist vegetarians had a prevalence of <2% having HTN. Analysis of the vegetarians' dietary records revealed that the vegetarians consumed significantly more dietary fiber, fruits, vegetables, polyunsaturated fat, magnesium, and potassium, and significantly less saturated and total fat than did the Mormon omnivores.

The DASH clinical trial

The DASH clinical trial tested a diet high in fruits and vegetables and reduced intake of red meat, sugar and refined carbohydrates for its effect on blood pressure. Significant reductions in blood pressure were noted within 2 weeks—and at 8 weeks, the diet reduced blood pressure in hypertensive patients by 11.4 and 5.5 mmHg respectively, with 70% of hypertensive patients exhibiting normalized blood pressure.

Exercise-Only Studies:

Coronary Artery Risk Development in Young Adults (CARDIA) Study

In the *Coronary Artery Risk Development in Young Adults (CARDIA) study*, individuals with low fitness had a relative risk of 2.59 for hypertension, compared with those with high fitness, as determined by duration on a maximal treadmill test.[194a]

Harvard Alumni Study

Harvard alumni who did not engage in vigorous sports play had a 35%

(or 2.86 times) greater risk of developing hypertension than those who engaged in vigorous sports play. These exercise studies indicate that there is clearly an inverse relationship between fitness (exercise tolerance) and blood pressure.

Combined Diet And Exercise Studies:

Pritikin combined lifestyle modification

Pritikin used combined lifestyle modification in an effort to lower blood pressure, the effects of which were measured in over 7 studies and 1,117 subjects. The 26 day intervention resulted in a significant reduction in blood pressure, with the great majority of patients having their blood pressure normalized, and resulting in being taken off blood pressure medication—and among those not taken off their medication, their dosages were reduced.

The Diet, Exercise, and Weight Loss Intervention Trial and The PREMIER trial, a Comprehensive Lifestyle Intervention

In these two comprehensive lifestyle intervention programs, participation in the program resulted in weight loss and significant reductions in both blood pressure and cholesterol levels.

All three comprehensive lifestyle modification programs implement, at their core, a strict diet consisting of a high intake of fruits and vegetables and a low intake of red meat, sugar and refined carbohydrates. Proper diet is combined with a *minimum* of 3 hours per week of moderate intensity exercise (consisting of both aerobic and strength training components).

Diabetes Trials And Studies

More "gene study" evidence:

Gene-environment interaction in the pathogenesis of diabetes is epitomized in studies comparing the Pima people of in rural Mexico with Pima living in Arizona. Despite the similarity of genetic background—the traditional lifestyle of the Pima living in Mexico (characterized by greater expenditures of physical energy in hunting and gathering and consisting of only complex (unprocessed) carbohydrates and the availability of far less animal fat) experienced markedly lower rates of obesity, insulin resistance and diabetes than their westernized counterparts living in Arizona, whose westernized lifestyle is sedentary and whose diet is both highly processed and high in fat. [195]

Nurses' Health Study

During a 16-year follow-up in the *Nurses Health Study*, 91% of diabetes cases were attributed to lifestyle factors—namely poor diet and physical inactivity.

Studies On The Effect Of Diet On Diabetes

In particular, the consumption of refined grain foods such as white bread, white rice, desserts, refined muffins, pancakes, and breakfast cereals were associated with an increased risk of diabetes. Diabetes *is not* something that "you get" or that "gets you"—Diabetes is largely something *you buy* every time you go shopping. All you have to do is buy enough of *diabetes-refined food precursors* and you get the whole enchilada!

Nurses' Health Study, The Health Professionals Follow-up Study, and The Seven Countries Study

Positive fat is where it's at! In both the *Nurses' Health Study* and the *Health Professional Follow-Up Study,* a link was determined between the incidence of diabetes and higher glycemic load. Also detected was an association between the concentration of long-chain omega-3 fatty acids in the phospholid membranes of skeletal muscles and insulin sensitivity. Further support for correlation was found by the Seven Countries Study that determined that fish consumption was shown to reduce the risk of glucose intolerance and inversely related to 2-hr postload glucose levels in a cohort of the Seven Countries Study.

On the other hand . . . *Negative fat kills the cat!* After performing 14 years of follow-up, the *Nurses Health Study* concluded that the consumption of trans-fatty acids is positively associated with an increased risk of diabetes.

Studies On The Effects Of Exercise On Diabetes

University of Pennsylvania Alumni Health Study

This study surveyed 5,990 men in whom "the amount of leisure-time physical activity was inversely related to the development of diabetes." The correlation was so clear that an exercise dose-dependant formulae could be established. They found that for every 500 kcal/week of physical activity there was an associated 6% reduction in the risk for diabetes.

The Physicians' Health Study

The *Physicians Health Study* followed 21,271 men who were free of diagnosed diabetes (between the ages of 40 – 84) for 5 years. This study determined that men who exercise at least once a week had an age-adjusted

0.64% *reduction in risk* for developing diabetes, compared to those who exercised less frequently.

British Regional Study

This study examined the effect of activity on insulin sensitivity. They concluded that "activity levels were inversely related to insulin sensitivity," which was associated with the development of diabetes.

Studies On The Combined Effects Of Diet And Exercise On Diabetes

Malmo Preventive Trial

The *Malmo Preventive Trial* conducted a health screening of 6,956 men at age 48. Out of those screened, 41 subjects with early stage diabetes and 181 subjects with impaired glucose tolerance were selected for a long-term lifestyle intervention. These patients were re-evaluated at 6 and 12 year follow-ups. At the 6-year follow-up, glucose tolerance was normalized in more than 50% of those who had been glucose intolerant, and more than 50% of the diabetic patients were in remission. At the 12-year follow-up, those who had been glucose intolerant at the beginning of the study had the same mortality rate as those with normal glucose tolerance at the beginning of the study, and their mortality rate was 50% lower than those with glucose intolerance at the beginning of the study who received routine treatment.[195]

The three leading predictors of diabetes are obesity, poor diet and physical inactivity. Those with a genetic predisposition toward diabetes usually do not develop diabetes unless that genetic predisposition is combined with (or prompted by) 1, 2 or all 3 of these risk factors. In other words, a genetic predisposition toward diabetes is a *dependent variable* that is not "initiated" unless or until it is "prompted" by obesity, poor diet and/or physical inactivity.

Finnish Diabetes Prevention Study, and The Diabetes Prevention Program Study

In two large randomized intervention trials—the *Finnish Diabetes Prevention Study* and the *Diabetes Prevention Program* in the United States—both studies independently demonstrated that "lifestyle change can significantly reduce the risk of developing diabetes in individuals with impaired glucose tolerance".

The *Finnish Diabetes Prevention Intervention* studied 522 subjects with impaired glucose tolerance, who were randomly assigned either to a control or lifestyle intervention group. The lifestyle intervention group was instructed and supported in maintaining adherence to a diet of increased dietary fiber and decreased fat intake via whole grains, vegetables, fruits, low-fat dairy, and meats. They were encouraged to lose weight and exercise daily, including a supervised progressive resistance training program as well as progressive endurance exercise. After a three-year follow-up, the risk of diabetes was reduced by 58% in the intervention group as compared to the control group, even though the intervention group experienced minimal weight loss.

The *Diabetes Prevention Program* randomized 3,234 individuals into three different intervention groups to monitor what each intervention's effect would be upon the participants' risk of diabetes. Subjects were placed in a placebo group, the insulin-sensitizing drug metformin group, or a lifestyle modification group. The lifestyle intervention group included more than 150 minutes a week of exercise, as well as a low-fat diet. At the 2.8 year follow-up evaluation, the metformin intervention group had reduced their risk of diabetes by 35%, and the lifestyle modification group reduced their risk of diabetes by 58%, as compared to the placebo group.

In closing the review of studies on diabetes I have included my review of the following study by Dr. Tuomilehto: "Nonpharmacologic Therapy and Exercise in the Prevention of Type 2 Diabetes" [196]

"Non Pharmacological Therapy and Exercise in the Prevention of Type 2 Diabetes."

Dr. Tuomilehto reviewed the research reports from several randomized controlled trials dealing with nonpharmacologic interventions aimed at preventing type 2 diabetes with early lifestyle interventions.

After reviewing these studies, Dr. Tuomilehto determined that the results of the randomized controlled trials show that the majority of people with impaired glucose tolerance who received enhanced lifestyle advice, direction, and support (and who were able to correct their lifestyle habits as recommended) had significantly lowered their incidence of type 2 diabetes (by more than 50%) as compared to those allocated to receive "usual care". He concluded, "Randomized controlled trials have unequivocally demonstrated that lifestyle management is highly efficient in the prevention and also in the early management of type 2 diabetes." [196]

Dr. Tuomilehto identifies several problems and potential solutions:

Problem #1:

There is little evidence indicating that drugs slow the progression of the early stages of diabetes. "It is not clear how much anti-diabetic drugs can help in preventing progression from Impaired Fasting Glucose (IFG) or Impaired Glucose Tolerance (IGT) to overt diabetes." [196]

Problem #2:

There is considerable evidence that antidiabetic drug treatment has a limited and deteriorating effect on glycemic control. "It is a well-known fact that anti-diabetic drug treatment in type 2 diabetes has only a limited effect on glycemic control, which deteriorates in diabetic patients despite intensive treatment, as demonstrated in newly diagnosed type 2 diabetic patients in the U.K. Prospective Diabetes Study." [196]

Problem #3:

The cost of treating diabetes far exceeds the cost of its prevention and/ or reversal. "Type 2 diabetes is also a very expensive disease; ~10–15% of the total health care costs in developed countries are spent treating type 2 diabetes and, in particular, its complications." [196b]

Problem #4:

There are very few programs available and far too little funding directed toward primary prevention/reversal of diabetes through comprehensive lifestyle transformation programs. "To avoid late complications of type 2 diabetes and related costs, primary prevention of type 2 diabetes itself and its early treatment are therefore necessary." [196]

Solution #1:

The superior effectiveness of Nonpharmacologic approaches on the prevention and early treatment of type 2 diabetes is overwhelming. "The efficacy of prevention in subjects with IGT has been tested, and currently there is unequivocal and strong evidence that we can prevent or delay the progression of hyperglycemia to type 2 diabetes." [196]

Solution #2:

Low cost long-term management of type 2 diabetes. "It is evident that long-term effects of lifestyle interventions are highly beneficial and that long-term costs are very low." [196]

Solution #3:

Cases of disease process reversal are well documented. "Can the situation be reversed by reversing these lifestyle changes? Yes, this has been demonstrated among Australian Aboriginals by O'Dea. In these studies, hyperglycemic subjects reverted to living naturally, in the traditional hunter-gatherer way of life. As a result, hyperglycemia was reversed." [196]

Solution #4:

Changes in social/economic policies are needed. Dr. Tuomilehto states: "In their analysis stress that the real answer to reductions in the incidence and prevalence of diabetes is in social policy, not in medical care." [196] "It is well known that obesity, unbalanced diet, and physical inactivity are the major risk factors for diabetes. In people genetically predisposed to the disease, the probability to develop type 2 diabetes is high once exposed to "unhealthy" lifestyles. In understanding the potential for prevention of type 2 diabetes, it is important to understand the enormity of a preventive lifestyle intervention." [196]

More On Gene-Environment Interaction . . .

The human genome was organized during a time when survival depended upon large expenditures of physical energy. To survive, a human needed to expend a great deal of energy hunting and gathering, and sheltering and protecting their clan. That is what humans are hard-wired to do. That order, or rule of survival, has been written (integrated) into our genetic code. To do otherwise meant we would rapidly disintegrate. To fall short of the high demands required to survive meant one did not survive.

Gene-Environment Interaction:

Humans were designed to interact with their environment in a dependant and adaptive way. The environmental demands (stimulus) defined the "rule" of our survival. That stimulus (*correctly* interpreted) assured continuing survival. If *incorrectly* interpreted, that stimulus forfeited our survival. Thus, survival depended upon intelligent gene-environment interaction. Sensitive, alert, quick, responsive interaction with the environment assured survival. Adapt well and live, or adapt poorly and die—that is the rule. Survival of the fittest was survival of those that adapted most effectively and quickly.

The reason that drugs do not work well with chronic diseases is that the real conversation is between our genes and the environment. Our genes respond to our interaction with our environment. Intelligent (self-preserving) interaction with our environment—that is, a healthy adaptation to our environment—is genetically coded for survival. Again, the reason that drugs do not work well with chronic diseases is that the problem is maladaptive-behavior, which is behavior that is inconsistent with survival. When human behavior is inconsistent with behaviors coded for survival, the genetic code within us is triggered to initiate self-extinction.

Also, the reason that drugs do not work well in many *lifestyle-induced conditions* (chronic diseases) is because we are genetically coded to behave (interact) with our environment in ways that optimize our survival. When we do not behave in ways that optimize our survival, we initiate genetic pre-programming for self-extinction. That is, we prompt our own self-extinction. During the era in which the human genome was being written, that is, hardwired (programmed) into our DNA, human survival depended upon the expenditure of tremendous amounts of energy in gathering food and fighting for survival. Humans' survival was dependent upon meeting those expectations, and that expectation is coded into our DNA. That is how humans are wired to survive. To do less negates our survival impulse or, stated differently, fails to initiate our drive for survival. Those individuals who expend considerable amounts of energy in exercise and consume the best nutrition available thrive!

Our Genes have not changed, but society has. Survival in modern society no longer requires expending tremendous amounts of energy (both mentally and physically) to survive. However, our genes still operate under those expectations, and *when we live in harmony with those genetic expectations* and exert ourselves (both mentally and physically), our survival is affirmed and encouraged—and *when we do not live in harmony with those genetic expectations* and do not exert ourselves (both mentally and physically) our survival is negated and discouraged.

Back in prehistoric times, when the human genome was designed, any digression from survival-optimizing behaviors encouraged self-extinction This genetic code is still in effect today.

Any time we use drugs
To offset symptoms
That unhealthy behaviors create
We avoid the real solution
And increase self-pollution

We cannot beat our genetic code
However, we can become aligned
With the way we were designed
And suddenly the genetic code
Begins
Working for us
To initiate and support our survival
Instead of working against us.

The genetic code (Mother Nature) pins your survival upon adaptation

Give your body a healthy stimulus to adapt to

And your body struggles to survive (adapt)
By rising to meet the challenge
Of the newly imposed healthy challenge

Give your body an unhealthy stimulus
And your body struggles to survive (adapt)
By rising to meet the challenge
Of the newly imposed unhealthy challenge

If a stimulus (challenge) is to become stronger, wiser, quicker
The body attempts to become stronger, wiser, quicker
If the stimulus is to become weaker, slower, soft and dependent
The body adapts to that stimulus as well
By becoming weaker, slower, dull and dependent

We become like the things we give ourselves to
To what you commit your love
You commit your life

Commit yourself to things that make you stronger
Your body will struggle to get you there
However, be advised
The opposite is also true

Contrary to modern medical emphasis, the control and reversal of chronic disease lies in the introduction and maintenance of a highly active and healthy lifestyle. Nothing, and I repeat nothing, works besides this!

Metabolic Syndrome Trials And Studies

NCEP's ATP III Criteria

As defined by *ATP III Criteria,* the diagnosis of metabolic syndrome is based on the presence of the following factors: abdominal obesity, hypertension, fasting hyperglycemia, and low HDL.

Third National Health and Nutrition Examination Survey

A multiethnic representative sample of 12,363 men and women from the US of age 20 years and older were evaluated in the *Third National Health and Nutrition Examination Survey.* The survey determined that metabolic syndrome was present in 22.8% of the men and 22.6% of the women. The survey classified individuals as either normal weight, overweight, or obese. The survey found that metabolic syndrome was present in 4.6%

of normal weight, 22.4% in overweight, and 59.6% obese individuals. Physical inactivity was also found to be associated with increased risk of metabolic syndrome.

CARDIA Study

In the *CARDIA Study,* low fitness was found to predict risk for metabolic syndrome just as powerfully as the other four conventional risk factors. Another significant discovery from this study was a significant exercise "dose-response" relationship between cardio-respiratory exercise-fitness level and mortality observed in men with the metabolic syndrome. This finding provides compelling evidence that indicates the protective effect of exercise against mortality for men with metabolic syndrome.

The Oslo Diet and Exercise Study

The Oslo Diet andExercise Study randomized 219 men and women to a one-year participation in one of four groups: 1) no treatment (control), 2) dietary changes alone—with increased fish and reduced fat intake, 3) exercise alone—aerobic exercise three times a week, or 4) a combination of the two treatments. Significant improvements in insulin sensitivity were noted in the three intervention groups, with the most significant improvements coming from the combination (diet & exercise) group.

Heritage Family Study

In the *Heritage Family Study,* Peter T. Katzmarzyk, investigated the efficacy of exercise training in treating the metabolic syndrome, using a sample population of 621 black and white participants The presence of the metabolic syndrome and its component risk factors were determined before and after the program and was prevalent in 16.9% of the subjects at the beginning. The program consisted of 20 weeks of supervised aerobic training 3 days/week (at 55%VO2 max for 30 minutes, then progressing up to 75% VO2 max for 50 minutes). Of the 105 participants determined to have the metabolic syndrome at baseline, 30.5% were no longer classified as having the metabolic syndrome after the exercise training.

In Summary: "The purpose of the Heritage Family Study was to determine the efficacy of exercise training in treating the metabolic syndrome. It concluded that, "Aerobic exercise training in patients with the metabolic syndrome can be useful as a treatment strategy and provides support for a role for physical activity in the prevention of chronic disease." The authors of the study went on to elaborate that: "Current recommendations for the treatment of the metabolic syndrome and the primary prevention of cardiovascular diseases encourage the use of therapeutic lifestyle changes such as increasing physical activity and reducing the dietary intake of saturated fat and cholesterol (21,27). Physical activity interventions, in the form of exercise training programs, have been shown to reduce individual heart disease risk factors such as high blood pressure (7), high plasma triglycerides (6), high blood glucose (14), and low HDL cholesterol (6,19). However, little is known about the effects of exercise training on the reduction of several risk factors simultaneously in individuals already at a high risk for metabolic diseases. Thus, the purpose of this study was to determine the efficacy of aerobic exercise training for treating the metabolic syndrome in participants in the HERITAGE Family Study." [196a]

This study has highlighted the extraordinary efficacy of exercise and especially aerobic exercise in reducing several risk factors of chronic disease simulataneously.

Effects of Exercise Training on Metabolic Syndrome

Two critical risk factors associated with metabolic syndrome are Endothelial dysfunction and inflammation. Endothelial dysfunction is known to be ameliorated by exercise independent of changes in body weight and/or blood pressure. Exercise has been shown to reduce the inflammatory levels of chemokines monocyte chemicals. Exercise has also been documented to lower blood pressure, reduce abdominal adipose, improve insulin sensitivity, and increase muscle size and glycogen depot areas, resulting in lower fasting blood sugar levels.

Heredity can play a role in whether a person develops the metabolic syndrome; however, its underlying causes are abdominal obesity—too large a waist—and physical inactivity. The metabolic syndrome is also related to a condition called "insulin resistance," which can lead to diabetes. Insulin is a hormone that helps your body convert the glucose (sugar) in the blood into energy. With insulin resistance, the body cannot properly use the insulin it produces. As more and more Americans have become obese in recent years, the problem of metabolic syndrome has become more widespread. Today, about one quarter of all adults in the United States have metabolic syndrome.

If you have three or more of the following factors, you have metabolic syndrome:

- Large waist measurement—35 inches or more for women, 40 inches or more for men (This is also one of the measurements that determine if you need to lose weight.)
- Triglceride level of 150 mg/dL or higher
- HDL cholesterol of less than 50 mg/dL in women, less than 40 mg/dL in men

- Blood Pressure of 130/85 mmHg or higher (either number counts as a raised blood pressure)
- Fasting blood sugar of 100 mg/dL or higher

For more information on protective lifestyle changes that can dramatically reduce your risk of developing metabolic syndrome, please see: http://www.nhlbi.nih.gov/health/public/heart/chol/chol_tlc.pdf

Cancer Trials And Studies

Seventh-Day Adventist

Study found that the consumption of foods such as lentils, beans, peas, and tomatoes was associated with a lower risk for prostate cancer. [197] The US's longest-lived community, the Seventh Day Adventists of Loma Linda, California, eat a largely vegetarian diet.

Burkitt's Observational Study

Avoid high fat, low fiber, refined carbohydrate diets, which increase circulating insulin levels and contribute to hyperinsulemia, a condition thought to play a role in the etiology of colorectal cancer.

Other Studies...

Reddy et al.

Studied the effect of diet and lifestyle modifications on cancer risk factors in eight women. The results showed the value and benefits of a High Fiber diet and exercise program— increasing stool bulk, decreasing stool transit time, and decreasing total stool bile acids; especially secondary bile acids deoxycholic and lithocholic acid, which are thought to be the most carcinogenic bile acids.

Slattery et al.

Avoid a "western" diet, which generates a high glycemic load on the metabolic system, and avoid red meat, which is correlated with increased mutations.

Steinmetz and Potter

Increased fruits and vegetables are also protective against colon cancer. The benefits may be independent of fiber, as *Steinmetz and Potter* have suggested that vegetables contain an "anticarcinogenic cocktail" of substances (i.e., carotenoids, vitamins C and E, selenium, dithiolthiones, glucosinolates and indoles, isothiocyanates, flavonoids, and plant sterols) that inhibit carcinogenesis by a variety of mechanisms. Increased vegetable consumption may also increase stool bulk and decrease transit time, thereby minimizing contact between the colon and potential carcinogens. [198]

SECTION 2: CORPORATE WELLNESS PROGRAMS

A Brief Review and Commentary on Corporate Wellness Programs: Their Effectiveness and Return on Investment [199]

Introduction: The human body is an amazing, self-healing organism that can reverse the progression of disease, restore loss of function, rebuild damaged organs, clear clogged circulatory pathways, strengthen trembling arms, and fortify tottering knees. The body has tremendous recuperative powers; however, we have to get out of its way. We have to stop our constant barrage of bodily insult: abuse and neglect, stress and exhaustion, consuming too much that fattens and too little that nourishes.

Regaining your health is simply going to take place. . . if . . . and it's a big if . . . *if* . . . you prioritize it over other things. Healing starts as we get our hearts in the right place.

"Wherefore do ye spend money for that which is not bread? And your labour for that which satisfieth not? Hearken diligently unto me, and eat ye that which is good, and let your soul delight itself in fatness. Incline your ear, and come unto me: hear, and your soul shall live..."
- King James Bible, Isaiah 55:2-3

Why expend your life pursuing a bigger house and a newer car when it is a far deeper form of wealth to obtain glowing health.

"Better it is to experience genuine awe and respect for the LORD and have little, than to have great treasure and the trouble that comes with it."
- King James Bible (Paraphase), Proverbs 15:16

Here is a further review in commentary on corporate wellness programs, discussed in the primary article "Prevention Makes Comment 'Cents' For Corporations."

Prevention Makes Common "Cents" For Corporations

As the population of the United States ages substantially over the next several decades, the prevalence of chronic diseases, and their impact on healthcare costs, will likely increase. Each individual's health is shaped by many factors, including medical care, social circumstances, and behavioral choices. Increasingly, there is clear evidence that the major chronic conditions that account for so much of the morbidity and mortality in the U.S., and the enormous direct and indirect costs associated with them, are in large part preventable—and that to a considerable degree, they stem from and are exacerbated by individual behaviors. In particular, overweight and obesity, lack of physical activity, and smoking greatly increase the risk of developing the most serious chronic disorders. Most of the dollars spent on health care in the United States, however, are for the direct care of medical conditions, while only a very small portion is targeted at preventing those conditions. [199]

By changing the way they live, individual Americans could change their personal health status and the health landscape of the Nation dramatically. "So many of our health problems can be avoided through diet, exercise and making sure we take care of ourselves. By promoting healthy lifestyles, we can improve the quality of life for all Americans, and reduce health care costs dramatically." *Tommy G. Thompson, Secretary, DHHS.*

Introduction to Specific Corporate Wellness Programs

Employers are becoming more aware that overweight and obesity, lack of physical activity, and tobacco use are adversely affecting the health and productivity of their employees and ultimately, the bottom line. As a result, innovative employers are providing their employees with a variety of worksite-based health promotion and disease prevention programs.

These programs have been shown to improve employee health, increase productivity, and yield a significant return on investment for the employer.

I contend that the same principle (with an even higher *return on investment*) can be achieved by major health insurers with regard to their most costly populations. The largest per capita savings (that can be made) *will be made* in applying strategic, focused, health-restoring interventions to the lives of the 1-5% most costly (most chronically ill) populations. This is the arena where the greatest amount of savings in healthcare can be realized.

The following is a review of several corporate wellness programs. A review of corporate health promotion and disease management programs found a significant return on investment for these programs, with benefit-to-cost ratios ranging from $1.49 to $4.91 (median of $3.14) in benefits for every dollar spent on the program. Many large employers have developed award-winning and cost-saving health promotion and disease management programs, and a few of those programs are reviewed.

- Motorola's wellness programs save the company $3.93 for every $1 invested.
- The Northeast Utilities WellAware Program reduced lifestyle and behavioral claims by $1,400,000 in its first 24 months.
- Caterpillar's Healthy Balance program is projected to result in long term savings of $700 million by 2015.
- Johnson & Johnson's Health and Wellness Program has produced average annual healthcare savings of $224.66 per employee.

Company: Union Pacific

Vision and Goals:

Union Pacific's vision is to be the healthiest company in America. Union Pacific is committed to long-term wellness, and well over 27,000 employees have participated in their Health Risk Assessment program and participated in follow-up programs when indicated. Union Pacific's goal is to continue to "decrease lifestyle related health claims, enhance employee productivity, improve employer relations and decrease injuries and absenteeism."[199]

Program/Components:

The Health Track Program provides routine health risk assessment surveys, and when indicated, also offers stage-based intervention programs. They also offer a smoking cessation program, access to fitness facilities at over 500 locations, and a healthy lifestyle incentive program tied to the company's incentive program, as well as opportunities to participate in research studies. They provide access to a network of occupational nurses, periodic health screenings, and the entire program is supported by local management and the executive staff of the company facilitating the program.

Benefits and Returns:

Evidence of The Health Track Programs cost-effectiveness include: "over a 10% decrease in Health Care Costs due to Lifestyle-Related Factors equating to a $53.6 million dollar difference in 2001." Smoking prevalence has been lowered significantly, and Union Pacific has won many national awards over the last several years for the quality and cost-effectiveness of its programs.

For more information see: www.up.com

Company: Caterpillar

Program & Components:

The goals of Caterpillar's Healthy Balance Program include the following: motivating positive change in modifiable health risk factors; "improve long term health status; promote self-efficacy and informed decision making; reduce health care and related expenses." The program seeks to maintain a high level of employee participation through providing strong incentives! As a result, the program has enjoyed exceptional participation from both employees and their spouses at 93% and 62% respectively. Key to the Healthy Balance Programs are its strong incentives, top-down management support, and inclusion of spouses in the program. The program includes both demand reduction and behavior change components; low cost health assessment; stratification based on low/high risk profile; interventions individually tailored based on risk factors and readiness to change; intensive interventions for high-risk behaviors and chronic conditions, including ongoing monitoring/adjustment of interventions as needed. Phone counseling and referral to community-based programs and interventions. Several educational resources are provided, including a self care book, quarterly newsletter, and website with links to scientifically validated information. Ongoing evaluation of healthcare claims, health assessments performed, and the summary of results are shared with employees.

Benefits and Returns:

Caterpillar is confident that the Healthy Balance Program is cost-effective and predicts that the program will lead to a long term savings of $700 million by 2015. "Participants who completed the high-risk program reduced their doctor office visits by 17%, and hospital days by 28%." [199]

Improvements in the major risk factors—physical activity, cigarette smoking, stress, high fat diet, and low fiber consumption—have reduced the aggregate health risk score by over 6% in the "low risk" population and by over 14% among the "high risk" subjects.

For more detailed information, see: www.caterpillar.com

Company: Northeast Utilities

Program & Components:

The goal of the Northeast Utilities WellAware program is to improve the health and wellbeing of its employees and their families, and to reduce healthcare costs. Northeast Utilities evaluated its healthcare claims and "found that almost 17% of those claims were attributable to modifiable lifestyle behaviors." As a result, Northeast Utilities developed targeted programs designed to address lifestyle-related health risks and assist participants in reducing those risks. Key features of the program include financial incentives to participate, with both employees and their spouses being eligible. The program is strongly supported by senior management and undergoes ongoing evaluation and re-design. A key component is the program's health risk assessment, which is the required "ticket" into the rest of the program. The health risk assessment serves as a light to guide which particular interventions ought to be recommended for each participant, including coordination and networking "with internal departments (health, safety and EAP) and external partners (health plan, local hospitals, etc.) accessible via on-site programs." The program provides telephonic interventions for high risk situations and a secondary coronary artery disease management program as well as telephonic smoking cessation counseling, including a rebate for purchasing smoking cessation aids. Participants are informed of community programs, guidebooks, videos, and telephonic intervention programs available via an internet site which can be accessed both at work and at home. There is also a toll-free hotline for materials and to have questions answered.

Benefits and Returns:

In its first 24 months, Northeast Utilities documented a 1.6 return on investment from the WellAware program, including a $1,400,000 reduction in lifestyle and behavioral claims and flat per capita costs for healthcare.[199] Evidence of the program's effectiveness can be seen in participants' reduction of health risk factors, such as a 31% decrease in smoking, a 29% decrease in the lack of exercise, a 16% decrease in mental health risk, a 5% reduction in stress, a 10% improvement in eating habits, and a 11% decrease in cholesterol levels.

To contact Northeast Utilities for more detailed information, see: www.nu.com

Company: Cigna

Program & Components:

The goal of CIGNA's Working Well Moms Program is to keep its 34,000 U.S. employees healthy and at work." [199] The Working Well Program has a budget of 2.5 million and is utilized at all 250 domestic offices. Working Well Moms has a broad range of programs for all employees, including the Working Well Triumph Program, which provides skill training and lifestyle support for its disabled employees to improve their health and adopt a healthy lifestyle. CIGNA has placed a special emphasis on supporting women, which make up 76% of their workforce, and of which over three-quarters are of childbearing age. The Working Well Moms Program encourages and supports breast-feeding.

Benefits and Returns:

As a result of the Working Well Moms Program, Cigna has decreased pharmacy costs, with 62% fewer prescriptions for breast-fed children. At the time of this research, the program had resulted in a savings of $240,000 in healthcare expenses and a savings of $60,000 in reduced time lost while away from work. CIGNA's smoking cessation program has helped 67% of its participants quit smoking after 12 months, which is a quit rate that is three times higher than that of comparable programs. CIGNA has estimated that it saves $949 in health care expenses for every participant that successfully quits, which is a 9.5 to 1 return on investment for every dollar spent on the program. To contact CIGNA for more detailed information, see: www.Cigna.com

Company: Johnson & Johnson

Program & Components:

Johnson and Johnson has provided a health promotion program since 1979, and spends millions on the program's evaluation and refinement. The Johnson & Johnson program integrates employee health, wellness, disability management, employee assistance, and occupational medicine programs, and places considerable emphasis on health promotion and disease prevention. [199]

Benefits and Returns:

The study reviewed up to 5 years of data on cost-effectiveness and determined that "Across all categories, total savings were $224.66 per employee per year." The study noted that a substantial portion of the savings were in years 3 and 4 and resulted from a decrease in inpatient hospital stays and outpatient and physician visits. [199]

Summary: Corporate Wellness Programs

While researchers caution that a "variety of methodological limitations make it difficult to definitively establish causality for the observed effects and savings, and to be certain about the exactness of the savings for each of the health outcome categories, they suggest that a more in-depth and comprehensive analysis would likely show that the total program savings were even greater." These studies demonstrate that well-conceived programs that focus upon identifying risk factors and providing interventions specifically designed to reduce those risk factors and instill healthier lifestyle patterns are highly cost effective.

Employers Report The Following Benefits:

- Improved employee health, work performance, and productivity
- Reduced absenteeism and medical claims

Demand Management Program:

- ROI ranging from $2.19 to $13 per dollar spent

Disease Management Programs:

- ROI from $7.33 to $10.38 per dollar spent

Return on Investment:

- Disease Management Programs: Highest ROI
- Demand Management Programs: Widely-Ranging ROI
- Health Education/Disease Prevention Programs: Lowest ROI

Evaluating Program Value: Which program components and in what proportions yield the greatest Return-On-Investment?

Prevention Makes Perfect "Cents"—A Further Review And Response

The benefit-to-cost ratio of the nine employer programs ranged from $1.49 to $4.91 per dollar spent on the program, with the average being $3.14. These returns-on-investment were the total ROI for each company's program—however, within each company's program, certain specific arenas yielded a wider range of benefit-to-cost ratios. Three of these specific arenas were: A) Demand Management Programs, B) Disease Management Programs, and C) Multiple Category Programs.[200]

Demand Management Programs help employees increase the use of self-care and decrease their use of medical care, often through self-care books, newsletters, telephone information lines, counseling, and other means. *Disease Management Programs* identify employees with specifically identified "high risk" profiles and custom-tailor programs to manage their risks, including education, counseling, and telephonic monitoring. *Multiple Category Programs* combine elements of different programs.

Looking at the ROI for five *Demand Management Programs*, they found a greater variation in the return on investment in these kinds of programs, ranging from $2.19 to $13 in benefits per dollar spent. They examined ROI for three *Disease Management Programs* and found a range in benefit-to-cost ratios from $7.33 to $10.38. They examined ROI in *Multiple Category Programs* and found a range of $5.47 to $6.47 in benefits per dollar spent.

Type of Program	Range of Return-On-Investment	Mean ROI
Demand Management Programs	$2.19 to $13	$7.59
Disease Management Programs	$7.33 to $10.38	$8.85
Multiple Category Programs	$5.47 to $6.47	$5.97

The Bottom Line

The studies revealed that, "For these employers, disease management programs resulted in the highest returns on investment, and the educational health promotion and disease prevention programs the lowest returns. Moreover, the more expensive programs resulted in lower returns on investment than some of the less expensive ones. The reviewers suggest the possibility that the higher costs may stem from the larger capital investments that go into on-site fitness centers or classroom-based education programs."[200]They also point out that, "the typical health promotion and disease prevention program provides health education to most or all employees but usually shows savings for only a small portion of the neediest employees, whereas disease management programs are targeted on a smaller selected group of employees."[200]

In reviewing the bottom line for the companies involved in this study, a few principles stand out. Specifically-focused programs addressing specific needs and vulnerabilities among specific high risk populations appear to bring the greatest ROI. Generalized programs and generalized health education yield the lowest ROI. Clearly identifying specific needs and high risk groups, and developing programs designed to specifically address and resolve those areas of vulnerability, appears to yield the greatest ROI. [201]

One weakness of the study was that a majority of the data—the costs, effects, and benefits of corporate health promotion and disease prevention programs—came from relatively short studies of two years or less. Relatively little data was available on long-term effects upon employee health and their utilization of healthcare services. However, the Johnson

& Johnson Health & Wellness Program examined long-term impact upon employee health, utilization of medical services and healthcare expenditures.[202]

Conclusion:

There is clear evidence that the costs of chronic conditions are enormous, as are the potential savings from preventing, managing, and reversing them effectively. "Since a large part of the root cause of chronic conditions involves attitudes and behavioral choices, the prospect of reducing their prevalence appears daunting and promising at the same time." [203]

"Attitudes and behaviors may be resistant to change, even when the desire to change is there. Moreover, people often encounter significant barriers in their social and physical environments. On the other hand, the actions that would eliminate much of the morbidity and mortality in our country are clear, and to a large extent these are practicable measures that the average person can take. By changing the way they live, Americans could change their personal health status and the health landscape of the nation dramatically." [203]

Public, Private And Personal Responsibility:

"Americans could save themselves, their employers, and the Nation substantial amounts of money if they took certain measures that are well-understood and relatively modest in scope. Even though some efforts over the last several decades to educate individuals about ways to improve their health and prevent disease have had limited influence on large proportions of our population, others have been very successful. Public and private policies need to focus on sustained efforts to encourage positive behaviors, building on proven, successful models." [203]

"The stakes are so great that the challenge must be met. It is ironic that in this day of high-tech, complex, and costly medical procedures and treatments, simple, inexpensive, easily-understood actions, such as increasing physical activity, controlling weight, and quitting smoking, could have such a huge impact on the quality of life and the cost of health care. While there always will be legitimate debate over the costs and benefits of particular health promotion and disease prevention endeavors, the Nation simply cannot afford not to step up efforts to reverse the growing prevalence of chronic disorders." [203]

Resources and energy need to be marshaled in all sectors and at all levels of society: federal, state, tribal, and local governments, as well as foundations, associations, healthcare providers and insurers, businesses, communities, schools, families, and individuals—to prevent, control, and reverse the chronic conditions that threaten the nation's physical and financial well-being.

Observations & Recommendations

Many of the usual drivers of healthcare costs are relatively fixed: inflation, large numbers of baby boomers retiring from the healthcare workforce, advancing age of baby boomers, increasing number of aging/chronically ill, increasing demand for healthcare workers relative to other sectors, advancing technologies, etc. These are all cost-driving factors that affect not only healthcare but all sectors; and which will proceed at relatively fixed rates.

However, there is one medical cost driver that can be greatly reduced, and that is the prevalence of chronic disease. The prevalence of chronic disease can be greatly reduced by adopting fiscal reimbursement strategies that reward both providers and patients for improving health. Those health improvement strategies fall under two categories: Medical Reimbursement Practices, and Patient Health Promotion Policies

A) Medical Reimbursement Practices:

Currently, medical reimbursement practices can be categorized as a fees-for-service delivery system, which is a polite way of saying it's a fees-for-disease delivery system. The current economic reimbursement practices actually encourage disease promotion as a means of income generation. However, economic reimbursement policy can be changed over time to reflect new understanding. If our nation is to turn around its growing epidemic of chronic disease, it must make chronic disease economically unappealing to both medical providers and individual patients. The introduction of a fees-for-recoveries delivery system, which rewards progressive wellness more than it rewards progressive illness, is a big part of the solution. This is the only way to stimulate large scale movement away from medicine's present era of disease promotion, and into medicine's next era of health promotion.

B) Patient Health Promotion Policies

Patient health promotion requires a multifaceted approach:

- Those whose poor health cost the system the most must be identified.
- Their return to a healthier condition must be fully supported and facilitated.
- Their return to a healthier condition must be encouraged with personal economic incentives.

This is the same approach used by Auto Insurers offering a "Good Driver Program." America is a free country. In America, no one can be forced to drive safely or to eat healthy, but people in all nations can and should be held responsible for their actions. Specifically, safe drivers cost auto insurers less money than unsafe drivers, and insurers have the right to pass those costs along to those consumers accordingly. Note that the savings passed along by insurers to good drivers is the result of those consumer's safe driving practices. Rewards given to safe drivers have actually made America's streets safer. I propose that similar incentives be created for those with "healthy lives". I believe that "Healthy Living" incentives will encourage patient wellness.

America is a free country. In America, no one can be forced to live a healthy life, but all people can and should be held responsible for their actions. Specifically, those leading Healthy lives cost health insurers less money than those leading unhealthy lives and insurers have the right to pass those costs along to those consumers accordingly. Note that the savings passed along by insurers to those leading healthy lives is the result of those consumers' healthy living "practices." Rewards given to those leading healthy lives will actually make America a healthier nation. I want to make it clear that for this to work, the unhealthy—that is, the 1% - 5% most chronically ill—will require access to all the resources they need in order to renew their commitment to healthier living, as well as the financial incentive to do so. Strong corporate incentives to keep the most chronically ill well and strong personal incentives for the chronically ill to get healthier must both be in place simultaneously for this to work.

This may sound complex or difficult to achieve but the concept is simple. Healthy Rewards is what it's all about.

- Hospital systems will be required to alert health insurers of patients meeting a pre-specified criterion for critical health declines (patient status).
- Health Insurers will be required to refer those patients meeting the criterion to the YMCA and other health and fitness centers for the comprehensive health promotion/chronic disease reversal program.
- Health & fitness centers like the YMCA will receive incentive fees (above and beyond their basic membership fees) to improve the health of the chronically ill.
- Patients who comply with the health recommendations and demonstrate structured measures of compliance will receive a health insurance discount.
- Patients who fail to comply with health-restoring practices will

receive an increase in health insurance premiums (commensurate with the increased acute care medical intervention costs associated with lifestyle-induced conditions).

To continue with the analogy of the Safe Driver Incentive Program, I would like to reiterate that America is a free country and no one can be forced to drive safely, but getting repeated driving tickets goes on your DMV driving record and consequently raises your insurance rates—and rightly so. Those living in a free country likewise cannot be forced to live healthfully, but repeatedly demonstrating negligence of one's health can be measured and the costs associated with unhealthy lifestyles can be passed along to those who refuse to take responsibility for their health.

At first, the chronically ill may resent being made financially responsible for taking care of themselves and living a healthy lifestyle, but as the long-term benefits of living healthfully overtake the immediate gratification of unhealthy choices, they will be renewed, refreshed, and made more whole.

MY CONCLUDING COMMENTS

Many American corporations have found ways to support their employees and dramatically decrease their healthcare costs through implementing targeted risk reduction and disease management programs. Why hasn't Medicare (the federal health insurance system) followed suit?

The reversal of chronic disease in America will only take place when managed by corporations and institutions for whom the reversal of chronic disease is *profitable*. Positively connecting increasing corporate/institutional wealth to improving patient's health should be the highest priority.

The real economic and social cancers are the forces and institutions which are directing the public's focus away from the real evidence, that is, scientifically demonstrable behavioral solutions to chronic disease, and directing the public and its care toward false, scientifically unfounded, and scientifically un-demonstrable chemical solutions to chronic disease. Those entities' interests and intentions are diametrically opposed to their patient's best interests. Those institutions take advantage of the great trust the public has been led to place in them, and sell as science that which is little more than cleverly concealed marketing. For such a trusted institution to direct the public toward the progressive treatment of largely preventable conditions is a breach of its client's trust, and is costing the nation billions of dollars.

In the previous section, I highlighted several examples of

corporations which have a vested interest in seeing the individuals under their care, direction, and supervision become progressively healthier. Those corporations are effectively improving health outcomes of their employees, and decreasing medical costs and medical claims dramatically. I have highlighted these programs as examples of the results that can take place when medical direction and medical care are placed in the hands of entities who stand to benefit financially from the improving health of the individuals under their care.

Improvement in the health of the chronically ill is highly achievable, but only if it is highly encouraged, supported, and monitored. Until corporate wealth is intimately connected to their patients' improving health, the necessary supports will not be provided. Likewise, until many patients have a vested interest in the costs of their health and/or its neglect. they will not become vested partners in remaining healthy. There should be economic incentives for rewarding individuals that take good care of themselves, and for corporations that promote health. I believe it is necessary to pay the fees associated with the progression of disease, but not to allow the loss of health to be a source of wealth for corporations treating progressive decline.

Although I have talked a lot about the economics of disease and how to turn around the nation's progressive descent into largely preventable decline, my greatest passion is for the restoration of health for those who are living with a chronic disease, or who are at risk of developing a chronic disease, or are caring for someone with a chronic disease. As a nurse, I have seen countless patients whose lives have been deeply discounted and compromised by following the standard medical recommendations and usual care.

In this book, the points of greatest importance to the chronically ill will be found in the sections on optimizing your personal health. Chronic disease is something that can be reversed in many cases and minimized in all cases *if* the steps of your life are very well ordered. Proceed gently, but stay with it!

If you are serious about reclaiming your health or assisting loved ones in regaining their health, I have created the following three challenges.

Choose the one that best suits your situation. *The 3 week challenge* is for those who are already healthy and want to take it to the next level, or who want to jump start a process of personal health transformation. This commitment is very challenging but short!. *The 5 week challenge* is directed at those who would like to help a spouse, parent, family member or friend in making the transition from "getting by" to a place where they "thrive while alive." This challenge is for those who want to help another along the path to self recovery. *The 8 week challenge* is a personal challenge that is conservative and sustainable. Both the other challenges can merge into this one and this one can be sustained indefinitely. This challenge is for those who wish to improve their health, but realize that competing challenges and demands must be taken into the equation. This challenge provides a practical "maintenance" plan that can fit into the midst of the rest of life's daily challenges, and keep you on track and living above the affliction zone.

The 3-Week Challenge:

Diet Component

Cut out all sugar, wheat (including all refined flour products), all breads (even healthy whole grain breads) and dairy products (except for a little butter, cream, and non fat yogurt). You may have "wheat-free" whole grains—just no bread/flour at all: Oatmeal, brown rice, quinoa, millet, etc. Sweeten foods with fruit. Eat plenty of fruits, vegetables, salads, legumes, whole grains

Exercise Component

Begin aerobic exercise, stretching, and core exercises—increase duration and intensity gradually as comfortably tolerated—perform this for 5 days a week for the entire 3 weeks. Vary the routine and aerobic activities enough to make the entire process enjoyable. Examples would be activities like walking, cycling or stationary bike, swimming or water aerobics, jogging or hiking, walking or elliptical machine, rowing or calisthenics. If you get progressively more fatigued from several days of exercise, take a day or two off and resume at a little easier pace. Be warned! This is a very demanding challenge! Giving up so much fun food and taking on a strong commitment to regain your fitness takes a lot of discipline and focus.

It may be very difficult at first, but the rewards of "coming clean" are far greater than the rewards of remaining firmly fixed in food and sugar addictions and a sedentary lifestyle. After 3 weeks, evaluate your results and see if you don't feel a lot healthier. Finish the 3 week challenge and then adjust your commitment level *after* completing the challenge. Sugar, flour, and dairy addictions are hard to kick! Be strong for 3 weeks, knowing that you can reevaluate the cost/benefit ratio and your commitment level *after* completing the challenge. On the bright side—it's only 3 weeks and the results may surprise you!

The 5-Week Challenge:

I am reminded of the lyrics of a song by Jason Gray, titled "With

Every Act of Love":

God put a million, million doors in the world
For His love to walk through
One of those doors is you

Helping a loved one who is chronically ill break through to a healthier lifestyle is a genuine act of love. What makes the effort even more difficult is the fact that the effort may not even be appreciated. You may have a parent, spouse, or child who needs a boost. This challenge requires that you commit 5 weeks to gently support a loved one toward a healthier lifestyle. You may realize that they need to adopt a healthier lifestyle, but the problem is that they may not realize it, or if they do, they may not have the chutzpah to make the difficult transition without significant support *every step of the way*. This challenge will involve time on your part to investigate the various opportunities for fitness in your area (but the 5 weeks don't actually begin until after you have collected a fair amount of information about available fitness facilities and programs, have presented it to your loved one, and they have decided to begin the journey to reclaim their life in earnest).

The YMCA of America has many locations and offers family-friendly and senior-friendly classes in a warm and supportive environment. Many senior centers and communities have recreation and community centers with exercise classes for those with health challenges. This challenge will require you to be very patient with your patient. Keep your eye on the goal of supporting them through a difficult "patch" or phase of personal transformation.

The greatest challenge will be working with people's deep-seated aversion to behavioral reform, even when they acknowledge that the change would do them good. Please understand that you cannot simply tell them about it. People do not care how much you know until they know how much you care. You are going to have to join *with them* in the process. Yes, actually engage in the activity and participate with them in the discovery process until they become comfortable with the new behavior and routine. This type of support often goes unappreciated at first, until the value of healthier habits become evident to them down the road. We cannot coerce people into change if they are not ready for it, but we can assist and support them in the process of discovering and embracing healthier choices.

Components of Behavioral Change

Positive behavioral changes are encouraged by helping your loved one (or client) to explore and resolve ambivalence. The following table explains various stages of change with a short description:

Precontemplation: Not ready to change

Contemplation: Thinking about change

Preparation: Getting ready to make a change, with planning and commitment

Action: Making the change, implementing the plan, taking the action

Maintenance: Sustaining behavioral change until integrated into lifestyle—healthy self-maintenance

Relapse/Recycling: Slipping back to previous behavior and re-entering the cycle of change

Termination: Leaving the cycle of change in order to sustain a healthier pattern

This approach *does not* involve:

- Arguing that the person has a problem and needs to change
- Offering direct advice or prescribing solutions to the problem without asking for the person's permission to make recommendations, or without actively encouraging the person to make his or her own choices
- Using an authoritative/expert stance—leaving the client in a passive role
- Doing most of the talking, or functioning simply as an information delivery system, or rather, as a "talking head"
- Imposing a label upon them
- Behaving in a punitive or coercive manner

It is difficult to tolerate peoples' passivity and ambivalence toward their own recovery. It requires a lot of patience to support a person through the stages of change, even when they are receptive. Becoming frustrated with them rarely bears positive results. Patience and mercy triumphs over judgment. Consider this an opportunity to share the gifts: the gift of words of personal affirmation and affirmation for positive steps taken, the gift of sharing quality time together—engaging in mutually healthy activities, the gift of acts of service to them and taking time out of your busy schedule to support their wellness, and the gift of physical touch, as you connect through exercise and recreation.

The 8-Week Challenge

This challenge involves a commitment to reclaiming the best years of your life. Look for an athletic event that you used to really enjoy in the past, or thought you might enjoy in the future. Nothing over the top, but something challenging (yet reasonable), based on your current level of fitness. If it's some sort of event, choose something that is about 8-12 weeks out and sign up for it. If it's a personal adventure, set it on the calendar 8-12 weeks away as well.

Now you've done it! Look at the hot water you've gotten yourself in! Now, *you have to get in better shape in order to complete it without embarrassment*! The size of the event makes no difference. It may not even be an event, it may be a goal instead; such as losing two dress sizes or getting in better shape so you can fully enjoy golfing on your next vacation, or getting in good enough shape to swim 40 laps in a pool or to go backpacking or to just stroll around the park. It doesn't matter what it is—just so long as you look *forward to it* and get excited about *getting in shape for it!*

Now the work begins. Now you begin "training" for it. You know—pull out the sneakers, or better, go buy a new pair and begin the journey of personal transformation. Commit yourself to getting in better shape than you have been in a long time. Visualize the shape you wish to achieve or the dress you wish to fit in when the big event arrives. Determine the level of commitment required to getting in shape for it, and begin! "Training" three days a week is a good introduction to get things started, is easier to maintain, and fits comfortably into most people's lives. The goal for which you are preparing should be a smart goal—that is, a S.M.A.R.T. (specific, measureable, achievable, realistic, timely) goal. And your training program for that goal should be S.M.A.R.T. as well. Write down a plan and include the following elements in your program: strength training, stretching, endurance, and heat/sweat therapy for cleansing your body of toxins. Choose the weapons of your ascendency: swimming, jogging, cycling, rowing, hiking, golf, or tennis. Hire an exercise coach for a few sessions if it will help you get off to a solid start. Develop a strategy and stick to the plan. Do a personal self evaluation at the beginning and end of the "training" program to measure your progress, and keep a journal to chronicle your "healthy insights" along the way. In the end, we each realize that it's not really so much about the event or goal for which we are preparing as it is about the journey of self empowerment that we follow to get there.

"All men dream, but not equally, those that dream by night in the dusty recesses of their minds, wake in the day to find that it was vanity; but the dreamers of the day are dangerous men, for they may act upon their dreams with open eyes, to make it possible."

- T.E. Lawrence, Seven Pillars Of Wisdom

"It is not the critic who counts, or the man who points out how the strong man stumbles or when the doer of deeds could have done them better. The credit belongs to the man who is actually in the arena, whose face is marred by dust and sweat and blood; who strives valiantly; who at best knows in the end the triumph of high achievement, and who, at the worst, if he fails, at least fails while daring greatly—so that his place shall never be with those cold and timid souls who know neither victory nor defeat . . . for those who have had to fight for it, life has truly a flavor the protected shall never know."

- Roosevelt

You must acknowledge to yourself that you're
Capable of discovering your dream in order to find it.
You don't have to be a genius, lucky, or rich.
You just need to believe it can happen.
"Becoming A Person Of Influence"
- John G. Maxwell

"Be not afraid of moving slowly, only of standing still."
- Chinese Proverb

Effort will be required to get in the best physical condition that you are capable of, but be assured: the effort required to climb out of the lethargy and disabling frailty of chronic disease is far less costly, painful, and demanding than that of managing progressive declines. If you don't apply yourself very diligently to becoming more fit, you will end up applying yourself very diligently in the management of further decline.

Discipline Or Suffer

This is my hearty recommendation: Choose life with every waking breath!

Make me broken
So I can be healed
'Cause I'm so calloused
And now I can't feel
I want to run to You
With heart wide open
Make me broken

Make me empty
So I can be filled
'Cause I'm still holding
Onto my will
And I'm completed
When you are with me
Make me empty

[Chorus:]
'Til You are my one desire
'Til You are my one true love
'Til You are my breath, my everything
Lord, please keep making me

Make me lonely
So I can be Yours
'Til I want no one
More than You, Lord
'Cause in the darkness
I know You will hold me
Make me lonely

- from "Keep Making Me," by Sidewalk Prophets

Last Confession...

I must confess, just like the lyric of a song by Mumford & Sons, "Man is a giddy thing," I have done let it happen to myself once again! I have let my health fall by the way side. Ironic, isn't it! The guy who's writing a book about optimizing health and fitness letting his health fall apart. Earlier this summer, however, I remember feeling strong and fit and one day, while cycling with a group of strong and fit riders, I was feeling that extra "sauce" that athletes sometimes feel and I (gently at first), began pushing the pace. Long story short, I gained some respect amongst my clan and became a legend in a circle just outside my inner circle of riders (who already know I have a few short circuits). I only say that to set the stage for what is happening to me now. I have been working like *a dog with a bone* on finishing this book. Writing, editing, . . . editing, writing and editing some more. It reminds me of those lyrics, "I smoke two joints before I smoke two joints, and then I smoke two more"—"I edit two times before I edit two times and then I edit two more!" All that to say, I sit for long hours at a time. Incidentally, I also had back surgery a number of years ago, and man, what a lifesaver that was! That was an example of medicine operating in its proper domain and saving lives!

But, as a result of the underlying vertebral compression and nerve damage at the L5/S1 vertebrae (that took place before the surgery) I have had unrelenting nerve *impairment* down my left leg, and this is felt in my left calf and especially in my left foot. The positive side is that this injury (minor disability) has given me a lot of insight into my own humanity. You see, the first couple of years after the surgery, I took very good care of myself—exercising conscientiously, stretching, and so on—but then a few years *after* the back surgery, work became very demanding and I started exercising less and sitting more, and the pain and numbness of the underlying disability gradually started to return.

I went back to my doctor and he wrote me a prescription for Neurontin (Gabopentin) for the nerve pain and numbness. At that time, I had been under tremendous work-related stress and had not been exercising *hardly at all* for six months. The underlying problem had gotten out of hand, resulting in left foot swelling, redness, numbness, and poor circulation and temperature control. My left foot was *always* a little hotter on hot days and colder on cold days than my right foot, but that condition is ten times worse *when I haven't been exercising for an extended period of time.*

This got very old, and as I said, I went to my doc and he did what docs do: he gave me some drugs. I went home and said to myself, "I feel like I'm a prisoner in my own body, but taking these meds, man, I'm not sure about that, that's just not me! I am going to do everything in my power to rise *above this affliction* (that I have let settle in over myself)." I did some serious introspection—which led to some serious lifestyle and life priority rearrangement (prompted by my relentless foot numbness) and *by virtue of that prompting*, I (reluctantly at first) resumed an aerobic exercise program. I gradually built my stamina, training distances and muscular power back up to legendary levels...as I was gloating above. Did I mention, I am a legend in my own little circle?

Then, however, we fast forward to today...I have, once again, become a dilapidated house. I have let myself slide for a good three months with hardly any exercise in order to pour my all, my life blood, my soul, into completing this book. Is this book a labor of love? Yes and no: it's more fitting to call it an obsessive-compulsive disorder.

So here I am! My body has settled, like un-homogenized peanut butter. I feel like my body's all stiff with my body's "oil" floating to the top. I just feel out of sorts and out of joint, like I can actually feel my lower back's individual vertebrae "stacking" on top of each other. My left foot's numbness is back *with a vengeance,* and my left foot's coordination is noticeably declined so that it is a shade slower than the right foot—plus, I have a slightly pasty complexion.

I start to think, "wow, this sucks...I mean getting older—it's not me of course, the body just gets old and gives out, and, what's a guy to do but..." and then I realize what I am saying to myself—on a very subtle level. I am buying into *the path of least resistance.* I am becoming the compromise I see in the world. I am slowly and subtly giving up. I am settling—because *excuses* are easier.

That's when *I have* to have a talk with myself, which I am having before you all. "Rich, you know you brought this on yourself. This is the result of neglecting your own body's needs for exercise for a looooooong, looooong time. Get a hold of yourself. You are not the victim of age and disc degenerative disease, you are the victim of sludge—that is, of slowing down to a standstill and allowing yourself to become stagnant, timid and weak—and you're allowing passivity and self-negation to settle in. What you are, Rich, is the victim of your own self neglect! You can break out of this cycle."

But I am actually a little scared that I cannot pull it off and pull myself out of it this time, that maybe I am not going to be able to get myself up and running again—in tight solid form. Then I say to myself, you won't have anyone fighting for you if you aren't fighting for yourself. The beginning of the climb out of this stronghold of self-limitation is taking hold of the reins once again and beginning to assert control over my own destiny. When I give up, I become prey. I may have stopped but whatever has been tracking me has not. What are my alternatives? To submit to the jaw of the lion? I have to invest in myself now or I will be carried out in a stretcher or wheelchair soon thereafter. If I don't give a damn about my body, my body certainly isn't going to give a damn about me. If I formulate a plan; a strategy; a means by which to redeem myself from the scrap heap I have relegated myself to, I can rise again! If I formulate a plan and I stick to it - it will serve me well. If I stick to the plan and work the plan, the plan will stick to me and work for me! If I invest in myself, damn it, I will find myself bearing the fruit of that love. If I love myself, and take care of myself, I will give myself - back to me.

If I return to faithfully caring for my body I am certain my body will return to faithfully caring for me. If I reclaim responsibility for my fitness, my fitness will reclaim responsibility for me. God, I love you, I mean, myself, I mean I am in love - again!

The following Bible verse has great meaning for me...

"If we [freely] admit that we have sinned and confess our sins, He is faithful and just (true to His own nature and promises) and will forgive our sins [dismiss our lawlessness] and [continuously] cleanse us from all unrighteousness [everything not in conformity to His will in purpose, thought, and action]."
- 1 John 1:9 Amplified Bible

And again another verse has brought me great comfort...

"And we know [with great confidence] that God [who is deeply concerned about us] causes all things to work together [as a plan] for good for those who love God, to those who are called according to His plan and purpose."
- Romans 8:28 The Amplified Bible

My Confession: I confess that I have slipped, I have drifted. I have neglected the physical harbor of my spiritual soul. It's time to begin the journey back.

I need to move from a place of thinking:
"Oh my, look what my body is doing to me."

To a place of thinking:
"Oh my, look what I have allowed my body to become."

And then, I must enter into the arena of my heart
and grapple with myself:
"What am I going to do about it?"

Life is not a dress rehearsal. I need to get "back into the game" and be all that I can be. The alternative is to be washed up on the shores of disrepair and languish there. That possibility is, however, entirely preventable. *That* outcome would be *a choice,* and a terribly unnecessary one.

These are the challenges and choices we must face every day.

"Listen to yourself and in that quietude you
might hear the voice of God."
– Maya Angelou

I will not be able to report back to you what happens this time around as I am finishing the book and putting down the pen; but I can assure you that I am putting my hand back unto the plow of cultivating physical fitness.

I can say, however, that previously in my life there have been seasons of balance, when my priorities were not askew, when I loved my body and my body in turn took good care of me. I spent time in nature and the peace of nature came to abide in me. I loved life and gave myself to the things that gave me life, and those things filled me up and I saw—and rested in—all that was good. There were other seasons of stress and overwork that resulted in distraction that overrode my instinct for healthy living, and I succumbed to months of sedentary ways. Inevitably, my left foot started to develop a pronounced numbness and get cold and swell, and my left toes got reddish and sensitive to pressure. When this painful feedback from my environment gets old enough—enough to say "enough is enough," by George, I will change my ways—I find that my change of behavior changes my experience, which is nature's way of discouraging unhealthy behavior and affirming healthy behavior.

When I begin exercising regularly, especially with aerobic exercise, I feel much better, my mood is elevated - and my circulation improves to the point where it seems to compensate for my left foot's permanently impaired nerve conduction, which is always running in the background. When I exercise regularly, my foot is never a problem. I am aware of it having a slight impairment, not perfect, but the constant drone of numbness, pain, swelling, and delayed responsiveness is swallowed up by the compensatory protective mechanisms stimulated by exercise. Fitness truly is the best medicine.

On the other hand, as a nurse, I have witnessed numerous patients who were put on the same nerve medication (Neurontin) that my doctor put me on, and then years later they were rapidly taken off that medication because of the damage that particular medication was doing to their kidneys. As for me and my house (my body), we shall serve a wiser, more loving God.

Another Day

This world is made with sweat and toil,
pushing muscle and elbow oil
We can't lie too long in the shade, 'cause
every day must be remade
Some days you fall some days you fly, but
in the end we all must die
Our rotting flesh and broken bone will feed
the ground that we call home

But a new sprout grows from a fallen tree,
my sons will go on after me
So lift your heart and dry your eye, it's
another day to live and die

I've run naked in the wild, seen the beauty
of a newborn child
Like the alchemists of old, I've tried to spin
my straw to gold
Most times a giver, sometimes a thief, so
full of hope but prone to grief
Between freedom and despair, I know that
truth is lying there
I've seen the truth, it's lying there

And a new sprout grows from a fallen tree,
this world will go on after me
So lift your heart and dry your eye, it's
another day to live and die

So go on now, don't you worry 'bout me,
you've miles to go and a world to see
My life's been long and full and good, I've
run this race the best I could

It's a short time here and long apart,
But the same song rings in both our hearts
So take my guitar when I'm gone, write your own rhymes, then pass it on
Just take your hit and then pass it on

Let a new sprout grow from a fallen tree, this song will go on after me
So lift your heart and dry your eye, it's another day to live and die
It's another day to live and die, just another day

- Timothy Page O'Brien and Darrell Scott

THE END

Chapter Notes

CHAPTER 1. OVERVIEW—AT THE CROSSROADS …

1] www.kpihp.org/kpihp/CMS/Files/tipping_points.pdf / *Tipping Points* / George Halvorson – Commentary (Healthcare Financial Management Association) March 2005

2] www.politico.com/news/stories/0409/21882_Page2.html / *Health Style Key to Controlling Costs*

3] "Health: Prevention is Worth the Money" by Dean Ornishwww. NewsWeek 4/23/2008

4] www.aspe.hhs.gov/health/prevention / *Executive Summary*

5] http://jap.physiology.org/content/98/1/3.full / *Effects of Exercise and Diet on Chronic Disease,* by Christian K. Roberts and R. James Barnard

6] www.nejm.org/doi/full/10.1056/NEJMp0708558 / *Does Preventive Care Save Money?*

7] For an exhaustive, comprehensive, long-term study, see "Effects of exercise and diet on chronic disease," by Christian K. Roberts and R. James Barnard, of the Department of Physiological Science, University of California, Los Angeles, California

CHAPTER 2. PROBLEM ONE—HOW DOES OUR "HEALTHCARE" SYSTEM REALLY WORK?

Who decided that those who profit off disease should be in charge of healthcare anyway?

8] "As a psychopathic creature, the corporation can neither recognize nor act upon moral reasons to refrain from harming others. Nothing in its legal makeup limits what it can do to others in pursuit of its selfish ends, and it is compelled to cause harm when the benefits of doing so outweigh the costs. Only pragmatic concern for its own interests and the laws of the land constrain the corporation's predatory instincts, and often that is not enough to stop it from destroying lives, damaging communities, and endangering the planet as a whole" (*The Corporation: The Pathological Pursuit of Profit and Power*, by Joel Bakan, Free Press: New York, NY: 2004. p. 60).

9] "The old business model was to develop drugs that would deal with specific sicknesses—take that drug three times a day for 10 days, and you're cured. The new model is: Take the drug two times a day for the rest of your life. ... From the drug companies' perspective, a drug you take every day for the rest of your life is a better business model than a drug you take every day for two weeks and then you're done." From "On the record: George Halvorson, Kaiser CEO, looks at the high cost of health care," *San Francisco Chronicle*, Sunday, November 16, 2003 (http://articles.sfgate.com/2003-11-16/business/17516964_1_prescription-drug-costs-drug-companies-care-costs).

10] See www.4therapy.com/news/also-news/obesity-fast-becoming-nations-number-one-health-threat-2536; Also: "In 2000, poor diet including obesity and physical inactivity caused 400,000 U.S. deaths — more than 16 percent of all deaths and the No. 2 killer," in http://www.pacifichealth.com/sitemap.htm.

11] "Critical examination of the effectiveness of prescription drugs reveals that there is (1) convincing data that most prescription drugs are not only ineffective but may worsen the condition being treated (yet are approved by the FDA), that (2) some of these medications appear to be designed to create life-long dependency upon the drug (drug withdrawal exacerbates symptoms), and that (3) some long-standing drugs that are the hallmarks of modern medicine have begun to lose their biological punch," Bill Sardi, in *When The Cure Is Worse Than The Disease*; http://www.lewrockwell.com/sardi/sardi90.html . See also: "Medicines that Cause Liver Damage," by Cicely A. Richard, at http://www.ehow.com/about_5364932_medicines-cause-liver-damage.html#ixzz1FeWCA2H0.

13] www.cdc.gov/nchs/healthy_people/hp2010/hp2010_final_review.htm

14] See http://jap.physiology.org/cgi/content/full/98/1/3#R240.

15] www.economist.com/node/18226821 / Feb 24th 2011 / *Citation on*

Alchemy, Alchemists, ancient and modern / from the print edition, Science and technology

16] www.economist.com/node/18226821 / Feb 24th 2011 / *Citation on Alchemy,* Alchemists, ancient and modern / from the print edition, Science and technology

17] "75% of all health care dollars are spent on patients with one or more chronic conditions, many of which can be prevented, including diabetes, obesity, heart disease, lung disease, high blood pressure, and cancer." Source: Health Affairs: www.healthpaconline.net/health-care-statistics-in-the-united-states.htm.

[17a] 1 Corinthians 10: 23 Amplified Bible

18] "Lobbyists spend millions to influence health care," by *Washington Post* reporter Dan Eggen, http://voices.washingtonpost.com/health-care-reform/2009/07/health_care_continues_its_inte.html?hpid=topnews?hpid=topnews.

19] "Most of our food supply has been processed and refined to the point that it has become more a drug and less a nutrient. Although alarming, it is no surprise to see our country moving toward more refined and processed foods. Whole aisles of food in the grocery store contain no whole foods. The poor quality of our food supply is causing an increase in obesity and other health-related issues. For food addicts, these highly refined foods act as mood-altering drugs with extensive negative health consequences. Refined food choices contribute to serious health issues—physical, mental and emotional—creating a health care crisis." From "The Science of Food Addiction," by Kay Sheppard, MA, LMHC, CEDS, found on http://www.counselormagazine.com/component/content/article/52-food-addiction/969-kay-sheppard-ma-lmhc-ceds.

20] Information taken directly form Healthy People 2020, Published by U.S. Department of Health and Human Services. http://www.healthypeople.gov/2020/topicsobjectives2020/default.aspx

21] For example, see http://www.naturalnews.com/033050_Gerson_Tapes_cancer_cure.html for the story of natural cancer cures moved to Mexico; or http://www.cancertutor.com/WarBetween/War_Fda.html for the backstory of why there is "no scientific evidence" for the majority of alternative treatments.

22] "The American Medical System is the Leading Cause of Death and Injury in the United States," By Gary Null PhD, Carolyn Dean MD ND, Martin Feldman MD, Debora Rasio MD, Dorothy Smith PhD, found on http://www.ourcivilisation.com/medicine/usamed.htm.

23] http://money.cnn.com/magazines/fortune/fortune500/2009/performers/industries/profits/.

24] "A mere 1 percent of the insured are consuming 30 percent of total costs, and the top 5 percent account for as much as two-thirds of all costs," George Halvorson, CEO of Kaiser Permanente, in commentary at the March 2005 Healthcare Financial Management Association.

25] "Healthy Lifestyle Key to Controlling Costs" / by Tommy G. Thompson / www.politico.com/news/stories/0409/21882.html / Politico, April 2009

CHAPTER 3. PROBLEM TWO—HOW DO WE PROMOTE "CHRONIC WELLNESS"?

26] "In a widely publicized study from the CDC and the German Institute of Human Nutrition, adult men and women who followed four healthy lifestyle factors—never smoking, healthy diet, physical activity, and body mass index (BMI) under 30—were 78 percent less likely to develop chronic conditions, such as cardiovascular disease, type 2 diabetes, cancer and stroke. Adults who adhered to just one of the four healthy behaviors lowered their chronic disease risk by nearly 50 percent, and their risk levels decreased progressively as their number of healthy behaviors increased." http://www.ada.org/3127.aspx, citing "Healthy Living is the Best Revenge," on http://archinte.ama-assn.org/cgi/reprint/169/15/1355.

27] See "Incidence of Adverse Drug Reaction in Hospitalized Patients," by Lazarou, et.al., found at http://online.statref.com/titleinfo/fxid-285.html. Also see: "Drug-Induced Diseases: Prevention, Detection, and Management," by James Tisdale and Douglas Miller, found at http://online.statref.com/titleinfo/fxid-285.html.

28] See http://www.worstpills.org/public/page.cfm?op_id=5#summary for a list.

29] ww.beckershospitalreview.com/news-analysis/us-hospital-stay-costs-outpace-other-countries-by-more-than-three-fold.html / Becker's Hopspital Review / *U.S. Hospital Stay Costs Outpace Other Countries by More Than Three Fold* by Sabrina Rodak, / Statistics from 2011 studies / March 2012

30] www.consumerhealthratings.com/index.

php?action=showSubCats&cat_id=207 / *Healthcare Cost and Utilization Project, AHRQ* / Published by Consumer Health Ratings.com / Oct. 2011.

31] www.streetdirectory.com/travel_guide/27212/medical_conditions/is_it_better_to_treat_the_symptoms_or_the_causes.html / *Is it Better to Treat the Symptoms or the Cause?* by conscioushealth, Dr. Loretta Mears / 2012

32] "What does chronic long term exposure to these substances cause? and as the potency of the "soup" builds, exposure at an earlier and earlier age may have more repercussions in development. and those born today will, over the course of their lives, be exposed at current levels or greater, and over a much longer period overall." From http://curezone.com/forums/fm.asp?i=587300.

33] "Besides my breath, researchers at Harvard's School of Public Health examined my blood, hair, urine, toenails and bones. It's all in the name of the emerging science of body burden, a concept referring to the amount of chemicals that accumulate in the human body. As it turns out, I am polluted. Everyone is to some degree. But as the list of toxic chemicals identified in people continues to grow, scientists are trying to figure out what the implications are for human health." From http://curezone.com/forums/fm.asp?i=587300.

34] "The most frequently cited evidence is a large clinical trial conducted by the Diabetes Prevention Program Research Group. It randomly assigned more than 3,000 pre-diabetic adults to one of three groups. One group received a placebo, another the oral diabetes drug metformin, which decreases glucose production, and the final group took part in an intensive lifestyle modification program of diet, exercise, and behavior modification counseling aimed at helping them lose 7 percent of their body weight. They were put on a low-fat, low-calorie diet, exercised 150 minutes a week, and sat down regularly with a case manager for one-on-one behavior modification sessions. The results, published in 2002, were impressive: Over nearly three years, people in the lifestyle intervention group were 58 percent less likely to develop diabetes, while those on metformin shaved their risk by just 31 percent." From http://health.usnews.com/health-news/diet-fitness/diabetes/articles/2008/10/10/battling-diabetes-with-diet-and-exercise.html.

35] See "Effects of exercise and diet on chronic disease," by Christian K. Roberts and R. James Barnard, of the Department of Physiological Science, University of California, Los Angeles, California. http://jap.

physiology.org/content/98/1/3.full (#sec-27)

CHAPTER 4. SOLUTION ONE—HEALTH IS THE NEW WEALTH

36] See http://www.naturalnews.com/024246_cancer_cures_natural_remedies.html, Monday, October 26, 2009. Also, see http://foodfreedom.wordpress.com/2010/06/04/fda-defeated-in-federal-court-over-censorship-of-truthful-health-claims/.

37] "Since 2006, the health sector has spent $1.7 billion lobbying Congress and federal agencies—more money than any other sector of the economy…Lobbyists for Genentech, a subsidiary of Roche, and two Washington law firms ghostwrote at least part of the statements issued by more than a dozen lawmakers; an estimated 42 House members—22 Republicans and 20 Democrats—used some of the talking points." *From* "Lobbying, Campaign Contributions, and Health Care Reform," by Robert Steinbrook, M.D., in *The New England Journal of Medicine*, December 3, 2009. Accessed at http://www.nejm.org/doi/full/10.1056/NEJMp0910879#t=article.

38] "The pharmaceutical industry has the largest lobby in Washington, DC — there are more pharmaceutical lobbyists there than members of Congress — and it gives copiously to political campaigns. As a result, the prescription drug legislation and policies that come out of Washington are usually made to order for the industry." in "Over and above: Excess in the pharmaceutical industry," by Marcia Angell, http://www.cmaj.ca/cgi/content/full/171/12/1451.

39] www.opensecrets.org/news/2010/02/federal-lobbying-soars-in-2009.html / *Federal Lobbying Climbs in 2009 as Lawmakers Execute Aggressive Congressional Agenda,* by Communications / February 12, 2010 - and -www.opensecrets.org/news/2010/02/federal-lobbying-soars-in-2009.html / *Efforts by Health Industries Help Push Influence Peddling to New Heights,* by Dave Levinthal / February 2010

40] "The American Project," by Ken Hambrick, *Contra Costa Times*, Dec. 31, 2006.

41] In outcomes [A and E] If payment (by insurer to medical provider) is denied due to providers not providing patients with a referral to facilities for: information, guidance, support and chronic disease reversal programs → Patients cannot be billed by medical provider (for fees not approved by health insurer).

42] http://www.undergroundhealth.com/fast-food-as-addictive-as-heroin-study-confirms/

43] *"Food Addiction: Could It Explain Why 70 Percent Of America Is Fat?"* Dr. Mark Hyman, http://drhyman.com/blog/2011/02/04/food-addiction-could-it-explain-why-70-percent-of-america-is-fat/

44] http://smoking-tobacco.whocanisue.com / *Smoking/Tobacco Attorneys,* Summary / 2012

45] "Pfizer, which had $48.3 billion in revenue last year, reported in January that it took a fourth-quarter charge of $2.3 billion to cover the preliminary agreement. The company said today it would have no additional charges from the case." In "Pfizer Agrees to Record Criminal Fine in Fraud Probe," by Cary O'Reilly and Tony Capaccio, http://www.bloomberg.com/apps/news?pid=newsarchive&sid=a4h7V5lc_xXM.

46] http://www.ncicdp.org/documents/2008%20Tipping_the_Scales.pdf *Tipping The Scales: How obesity and unhealthy lifestyles have become a weighty matter for the North Carolina economy* / Be Active North Carolina, Inc / June 2008

47] http://www.naturalhomefoods.com/other-articles.php?article=the-enormous-cost-of-not-living-a-healthy-lifestyle Service Foods */ The Enormous Cost of Not Living A Healthy Lifestyle,* By Dana Yarn, RDLD and Dr. Keith D. Kantor

48] www.aalatimes.com/2012/03/05/a-hospital-stay-costs-236-per-day-in-india-vs-3949-per-day-in-the-us-study/ *A hospital stay costs $236 per day in India Vs $3,949 per day in the US: Study* / ALALATimes, India / March 2012

49] www.beckershospitalreview.com/news-analysis/us-hospital-stay-costs-outpace-other-countries-by-more-than-three-fold.html / Becker Hospital Review / *U.S. Hospital Stay Costs Outpace Other Countries by More Than Three Fold,* by Sabrina Rodak / March 06, 2012

50] George Halvorson – Commentary *(Healthcare Financial Management Association)* March 2005. https://www.kpihp.org/wp-content/uploads/2012/12/tipping_points.pdf

51] www.aalatimes.com/2012/03/05/a-hospital-stay-costs-236-per-day-in-india-vs-3949-per-day-in-the-us-study/ *A hospital stay costs $236 per day in India Vs $3,949 per day in the US: Study* / ALALATimes, India / March 2012. www.beckershospitalreview.com/news-analysis/us-hospital-stay-costs-outpace-other-countries-by-more-than-three-fold.html / Becker Hospital Review / *U.S. Hospital Stay Costs Outpace Other Countries by More Than Three Fold,* by Sabrina Rodak / March 06, 2012

52] Mam·mon (măm′ən): 1. Bible Riches, avarice, and worldly gain personified as a false god in the New Testament.
2. often mammon Material wealth regarded as having an evil influence.

53] https://www.fda.gov/Drugs/DevelopmentApprovalProcess/DevelopmentResources/DrugInteractionsLabeling/ucm110632.htm

54] Committee on Quality of Health Care in America: Institute of Medicine. To err is human: building a safer health system. Washington, D.C.: *National Academy Press*; 2000.[2] Lazarou J, Pomeranz B, Corey PN. Incidence of adverse drug reactions in hospitalized patients: A meta-analysis of prospective studies. *JAMA* 1998;279:1200–1205.

55] Johnson JA, Bootman JL. Drug-related morbidity and mortality. A cost-of-illness model. *Arch Intern Med* 1995;155(18):1949–1956. Leape LL, Brennan TA Laird N, Lawthers AG ,Localio AR, Barnes BA et al. The nature of adverse events in hospitalized patients. Results of the Harvard Medical Practice Study II. *N Engl J Med* 1991;324(6):377–384. Classen DC , Pestotnik SL, Evans RS, Lloyd JF, Burke JP. Adverse drug events in hospitalized patients. Excess length of stay, extra costs, and attributable mortality. *JAMA* 1997;277(4):301–306.

CHAPTER 5. SOLUTION TWO—LIVING ABOVE THE AFFLICTION ZONE

56] http://www.ncbi.nlm.nih.gov/pubmed/22530749 *and* http://www.nejm.org/doi/full/10.1056/NEJMoa020245

CHAPTER 6. ESTABLISHING AN EFFECTIVE MEDICAL APPROACH

57] "BioBran: Strengthening the Immune System" 2008/2012 (www.biobran.org/overview/immune-system.html) and "Statins Impair Immune System Function," by Brian J. Richards, Director Wellness Resources, Inc. , 2012 (www.worldwidehealth.com/health-article-Statins-Impair-Immune-System-Function.html)

58] "Runners Connect: Ibuprofen and Running," 2011 (http://runnersconnect.net/ibuprofen-and-running)

59] "Live Strong: The Effects of Drugs on a Man's Reproductive System" by Carole Wegner, 2010 (www.livestrong.com/article/134524-the-effects-drugs-mans-reproductive-system)

60] "Greek Medicine: Understanding the Healing Crisis," 2007 (www.greekmedicine.net/Principles_of_Treatment/Understanding_the_Healing_Crisis.html)

61] AARP Magazine: When Medicine Makes You Sick," by Mary Fischer, 2010 (www.aarp.org/health/drugs-supplements/info-08-2010/toxic-drugs-when-medicine-makes-you-sick.html)

62] http://www.webdc.com/pdfs/deathbymedicine.pdf

63] See articles: "7 Benefits of Regular Physical Activity," by Mayo Clinic Staff, 2011 (www.mayoclinic.com/health/exercise/HQ01676); "USNews and Health: Mind Blowing Benefits of Exercise," by Deborah Kotz and Angela Haupt , 2012 (health.usnews.com/health-news/diet-fitness/slideshows/7-mind-blowing-benefits-of-exercise); "Georgia Sate University: Benefits of Aerobic Exercise and Strength Training ," by Department of Kinesiology and Health, 1997 (www2.gsu.edu/~wwwfit/benefits.html); "NutriStrategy: Health Benefits of Exercise," 2010 (www.nutristrategy.com/health.htm); "The Informed Patient: The Hidden Benefits of Exercise," by Laura Landro, 2010 (online.wsj.com/article/SB10001424052748704350304574638331243027174.html)

Also, see references in the Bibliogrphy, 38-43 for more articles and information.

64] There are a variety of organizations that promote Lifestyle Transformation. One such organization is LTC, Lifestyle Transformation Centre out of Jamaica, W.I. The Lifestyle Transformation Centre is a limited liability company established under the laws of Jamaica in October 2006 and commenced operations in November 2006. Lifestyle Transformation Centre is the expansion of Dr. L. Danovan Whyte's medical practice, which is designed to promote healthy lifestyle to local and overseas clients. Find them at: https://www.facebook.com/YourHealthMattersNaturally/.

65] http://en.wikipedia.org/wiki/Howard_Thurman / Gil Bailie's *Violence Unveiled*, p. xv, where he attributes the quotation to a conversation he had with Thurman.

66] www.healingdaily.com/colon-kidney-detoxification / Healing Daily, Mark Lacassa /2012

67] Group classes: Participation in group classes is encouraged on both guided and self-guided days. For our purposes they are not considered "guided" but simply as a "group class."

68] Initially, the chronically ill will not be able to participate in group classes without modification of the exercises. However, over time it is hoped that their progressive fitness will allow minimally-modified participation in regular group classes. (If there were enough chronically ill patients/clients enrolled at a health club, additional classes could be created to address their specific needs more directly.)

69] www.healingdaily.com/colon-kidney-detoxification / Healing Daily, Mark Lacassa /2012

70] Tipping Points / George Halvorson – Commentary (Healthcare Financial Management Association) March 2005: https://www.kpihp.org/wp-content/uploads/2012/12/tipping_points.pdf

71] SOURCE: http://www.beckershospitalreview.com/lists/average-cost-per-inpatient-day-across-50-states-in-2010.html / Written by Jaimie Oh, April 30, 2012 , *Average Cost Per Inpatient Day Across 50 States in 2010*

72] www.aalatimes.com/2012/03/05/a-hospital-stay-costs-236-per-day-in-india-vs-3949-per-day-in-the-us-study/ *A hospital stay costs $236 per day in India Vs $3,949 per day in the US: Study* / ALALATimes, India / March 2012

73] www.beckershospitalreview.com/news-analysis/us-hospital-stay-costs-outpace-other-countries-by-more-than-three-fold.html / Becker Hospital Review / *U.S. Hospital Stay Costs Outpace Other Countries by More Than Three Fold,* by Sabrina Rodak / March 06, 2012

74] www.nejm.org/doi/full/10.1056/NEJMp0708558

75] www.philadelphiadebtresource.com/files/2012/02/www.kaiseredu.org_health-care-costs.pdf

PRELUDE CHAPTER 7

76] Principal Data Source: *Overdosed America: The Broken Promise of American Medicine,* by John Abramson, Published June 14th 2005 by Harper Perennial, Published by Harper Collins in 2008, New

York, NY. (Chapter 13 and 14: From Osteoporosis to Heart Disease and Healing Our Ailing Healthcare System.) Used with permission.

CHAPTER 7. INFLUENCES OF THE AMERICAN MEDICAL SYSTEM ON ADULTHOOD AND AGING

The Evidence: What Caused the Problem with the American Medical System

77] John Abramson, *Overdosed America: The Broken Promise of American Medicine,*, (New York: Harper Collins Publishers, 2004), Page 220-221

78] *Ibid.*, Page 221

79] *Ibid.*, Page 221

80] *Ibid.*, Pages 222-223

81] *Ibid.*, Pages 94-95

82] *Ibid.*, Page 189

83] *Ibid.*, Page 210

84] *Ibid.*, Page 204

85] Dr. Donald Berwick is one of the nation's leading crusaders for improving quality in medicine and author of the Institute of Medicines report *Crossing the Quality Chasm*

86] U.S. Health-Care System Ranks as One of the Least-Efficient, https://www.bloomberg.com/news/articles/2016-09-29/u-s-health-care-system-ranks-as-one-of-the-least-efficient

87] John Abramson, *Overdosed America: The Broken Promise of American Medicine*, (New York: Harper Collins Publishers, 2004), Page 46

88] *Ibid.*, Page 184

89] *Ibid.*, Page 45

90] Rand Corporation, http://www.rand.org/content/dam/rand/pubs/research_reports/RR1200/RR1252/RAND_RR1252.pdf

91] John Abramson, *Overdosed America: The Broken Promise of American Medicine*, (New York: Harper Collins Publishers, 2004), Page 255

92] *Ibid.*, Page 252

93] *Ibid.*, Pages 96, 277

94] Melody Petersen, "Heart Device to Get More U.S. Support," *New York Times*, June 7, 2003.]

95] A. J. Moss, S. Wojciech, J. Hall, et al., "Prophylactic Implantation of a Defibrillator in Patients with Myocardial Infarction and Reduced Ejection Fraction," New England Journal of Medicine 346:877-883, 2002

96] John Abramson, *Overdosed America: The Broken Promise of American Medicine,,* (New York: Harper Collins Publishers, 2004), Page 100

97] *Ibid.*, Page 184

98] *Ibid.*, Page 256

99] D. M. Berwick, "A User's Manual for the IOM's 'Quality Chasm' Report," Health Affairs 21 (3):80-90, 2002

100] Selected quotes from this excellent summary of the weaknesses and dangers of unrestrained capitalism.

- http://www.governmentisgood.com/articles.php?aid=13&print=1
- *Government is Good,* An Unapologetic Defense of a Vital Institution
- A web project of Douglas J. Amy, Professor of Politics at Mount Holyoke College

101] John Abramson, *Overdosed America: The Broken Promise of American Medicine,*, (New York: Harper Collins Publishers, 2004), Page 256

102] *Ibid.*, Page 258

103] The Institute of Medicine (IOM) Report *To Err Is Human: Building a Safer Health System*

104] The Quality Solution (Page 69): The Stakeholder's Guide to Improving Health Care edited by David B. Nash, Neil I. Goldfar, / Cleary PD, Edgmann-Levitan S. Health care quality: Incorporating consumer perspectives. JAMA 1997;278(19):1608-12.

105] Leap LL, Berwick DM, Bates DW. What practices will most improve safety? Evidence-based medicine meets patient safety. JAMA. 2002;288(4):501-7

106] IOM Report: Kohn LT, Corrigan JM, Donaldson MS. To Err Is Human: Building a Safer Health System. Washington, DC: National Academy Press; 1999

107] Dr Barbara Starfield, AMERICAN MEDICAL ASSOCIATION (JAMA) Vol 284, No 4, July 26th 2000

108] Leape L. Unneccessary Surgery. Annu Rev Public Health. 1992; 13:363-383 / Lazarou J. Pomeranz B, Corey P. Incidence of adverse drug reactions in hospitalized patients. JAMA. 1998; 279:1200-1205

109] IOM Report: Kohn LT, Corrigan JM, Donaldson MS. To Err Is Human: Building a Safer Health System. Washington, DC: National Academy Press; 1999

110] Altman DE, Clancy C, Blendon RJ. Improving patient safety — five years after the IOM report. N Engl J Med 2004;351:2041-3.

111] IOM Report: Kohn LT, Corrigan JM, Donaldson MS. To Err Is Human: Building a Safer Health System. Washington, DC: National Academy Press; 1999 (Page 1)

112] John Abramson, *Overdosed America: The Broken Promise of American Medicine,*, (New York: Harper Collins Publishers, 2004), Page 256

113] *Ibid.*, Page 250

114] *Ibid.*, Page 250

115] Quoted in B. Sibbald, "U.S. Health System Needs Major Overhaul; Academy," Canadian Medical Association Journal 164:1197, 2001.

116] John Abramson, *Overdosed America: The Broken Promise of American Medicine,* (New York: Harper Collins Publishers, 2004), Page 258

117] *Ibid.*, Page 249

118] *Ibid.*, Page 250

119] *Ibid.*, Page 249

120] John Abramson, *Overdosed America: The Broken Promise of American Medicine,* (New York: Harper Collins Publishers, 2004) / Thomas Kuhn, The Structure of Scientific Revolutions, Chicago: University of Chicago Press, 1962, pp. 64—65.

121] Susan Haack, Evidence and Inquiry: Towards Reconstruction in Epistemology, Oxford: Blackwell Publishers, 1993, p. 206.

122] Quoted in Jan Golinski, Making Natural Knowledge: Constructivism and the History of Science, Cambridge, England: Cambridge University Press, 1998, p. 17.

123] "The Need for a New Medical Model: G. L. Engel, "The Need for a New Medical Model: A Challenge for Biomedicine," Science 196:129—136, 1977.

124] Medical Economics and Medical Ethics, http://healthblog.ncpa.org/medical-economics-and-medical-ethics/#sthash.PBYif082.dpbs For further research, please refer to: How Economic Incentives have Created our Dysfunctional US Medical Market, https://medium.com/@RosenthalHealth/how-economic-incentives-have-created-our-dysfunctional-us-medical-market-b681c51d6436 ; "Perverse Incentives" and the Triple Aim: Overcoming the Troubled Path to Economic Integration for Integrative Medicine and Health, https://pdfs.semanticscholar.org/ab25/2b36c55c9d7d7652034d9f5e59c426bea62d.pdf ; Division of Health Care Finance and Policy http://www.mass.gov/chia/docs/pc/final-report/final-report.pdf

125] John Abramson, *Overdosed America: The Broken Promise of American Medicine,* (New York: Harper Collins Publishers, 2004), Page 258

126] Principal Data Source for this chapter portion: "Prevention Makes Common "Cents,"" U.S. Department of Health and Human Services. http://aspe.hhs.gov/health/prevention/prevention.pdf

127] American Obesity Association/The Lewin Group. *Costs of Obesity*. September 13, 2000.

128] Permission for reference see Principal Data Source: "Prevention Makes Common "Cents,"" U.S. Department of Health and Human Services: http://aspe.hhs.gov/health/prevention/prevention.pdf /

129] Sturm R. The effects of obesity, smoking, and drinking on medical problems and costs. Health Affairs. 2002; 21(2):245-253.

130] Mokdad AH, Ford ES, Bowman BA, Dietz WH, Vinicor F, Bales VS, Marks, JS. Prevalence of obesity, diabetes, and obesity-related health risk factors, 2001. JAMA. 2003; 289(1):76-79.

- NHLBI/NIH. Clinical Guidelines on the Identification, Evaluation, and Treatment of Overweight and Obesity in Adults. 1998.
- Finkelstein EA, Fiebelkorn IA, Wang G. National medical spending attributable to overweight and obesity: how much, and who's paying? Health Affairs–Web Exclusive. 2003 Project Hope.
- The Surgeon General's call to action to prevent and decrease overweight and obesity

131] NIDDK. General Information and national estimates on diabetes in the United States, 2000 (Note: Similar information is found in the American Diabetes Association, "National Diabetes Fact Sheet").

132] NIH/NHLBI. Clinical Guidelines on the Identification, Evaluation, and Treatment of Overweight and Obesity in Adults. 1998.

133] Prevention Makes Common "Cents," U.S. Department of Health and Human Services. http://aspe.hhs.gov/health/prevention/prevention.pdf, Page 100

134] Prevention Makes Common "Cents," U.S. Department of Health and Human Services; September 2003

135] Preventing Heart Disease and Stroke: Addressing the Nation's Leading Killers. CDC: April 2002.

136] Cardiovascular Diseases. Stanford Health Library: 2002.

137] American Heart Association. Heart and Stroke Statistics–2003 Update.

138] Prevention Makes Common "Cents," U.S. Department of Health and Human Services; September 2003

139] Preventing Heart Disease and Stroke: Addressing the Nation's Leading Killers. CDC: April 2002.

140] Prevention Makes Common "Cents," U.S. Department of Health and Human Services; September 2003

141] Platts-Mills TA, Carter MC, Heyman PW. Specific and nonspecific obstructive lung disease in childhood: causes of changes in the prevalence of asthma. Environmental Health Perspectives 2000; 108 Suppl 4: 725-31.

142] Principal Data Source: Prevention Makes Common "Cents," U.S. Department of Health and Human Services. http://aspe.hhs.gov/health/prevention/prevention.pdf

143] Quotes found on this site. www.breathing.com/articles/prescription-drugs.htm

144] Heidi Stevenson, "Former Shill for Big Pharma Tells the Truth About Drug," Natural News, www.naturalnews.com/023127_drug_doctor_doctors.html Download 2014

145] http://healthimpactnews.com/2011/prescription-drugs-now-kill-more-people-than-illegal-drugs/

CHAPTER 8. INFLUENCES OF THE AMERICAN MEDICAL SYSTEM ON ADULTHOOD AND AGING

Part 2: The Solution: A Cause for Solution to the American Medical System Crisis

146] Booth FW, Chakravarthy MV, Spangenburg EE. "Exercise and gene expression: physiological regulation of the human genome through physical activity," PubMed.gov, http://www.ncbi.nlm.nih.gov/pubmed/12205177

147] Brain glycogen supercompensation following exhaustive exercise." By Matsui T, Ishikawa T, Ito H, Okamoto M, Inoue K, Lee MC, Fujikawa T, Ichitani Y, Kawanaka K, Soya H. / Laboratory of Exercise Biochemistry & Neuroendocrinology, Institute for Health and Sports Sciences, University of Tsukuba, 1-1-1 Tennoudai, Tsukuba 305-8574, Ibaraki, Japan.

148] www.humankinetics.com/excerpts/excerpts/defining-supercompensation-training

149] Booth FW, Charavarthy MV, Gordon SE, Spangenburg EE. Waging war on physical inactivity: using modern molecular ammunition against an ancient enemy. Journal of Applied Physiology.2002;93:3–30. www.ncbi.nlm.nih.gov/pubmed/12070181

150] *"Exercise and Gene Expression: Physiological Regulation of the Human Genome Through Physical Activity,"* authored by Frank Booth, Manu Chakravarthy and Espen Spangenburg. PubMed.gov, http://www.ncbi.nlm.nih.gov/pubmed/12205177

151] *"Exercise and Gene Expression: Physiological Regulation of the Human Genome Through Physical Activity,"* authored by Frank Booth, Manu Chakravarthy and Espen Spangenburg. PubMed.gov, http://www.ncbi.nlm.nih.gov/pubmed/12205177

151a] Journal of Applied Physiology by Christian K. Roberts , R. James Barnard, *Effects of Exercise and Diet on Chronic Disease* / January 2005, Vol. 98no. 3-30DOI: 10.1152/japplphysiol.00852.2004 / SOURCE: http://jap.physiology.org/content/98/1/3 Section 3 "Lifestyle Modification Can Mitigate Disease Progression and Reverse Existing Disease"

152] Journal of Applied Physiology by Christian K. Roberts and R. James Barnard entitled, *Effects of exercise and diet on chronic disease.* http://jap.physiology.org/content/98/1/3

153] Ames BN. Dietary carcinogens and anticarcinogens. Oxygen radicals and degenerative diseases. *Science* 221: 1256–1264, 1983 / Science 23 September 1983: Vol. 221 no. 4617 pp. 1256-1264 / DOI: 10.1126/science.6351251

154] Friedenreich CM and Orenstein MR. *Physical activity and cancer prevention: etiologic evidence and biological mechanisms.* J Nutr 132: 3456S-3464S, 2002.

155] Burkitt DP. *Related disease—related cause?* Lancet 2: 1229–1231, 1969.

156] "Effects of exercise and diet on chronic disease," by Christian Roberts and R. James Barnard / http://jap.physiology.org/content/98/1/3

157] Burkitt DP. *Related disease—related cause?* Lancet 2: 1229–1231, 1969.

158] Journal of Applied Physiology by Christian K. Roberts and R. James Barnard entitled, *Effects of exercise and diet on chronic disease.* http://jap.physiology.org/content/98/1/3.full%23R361%23R361

159] Journal of Applied Physiology by Christian K. Roberts and R. James Barnard entitled, *Effects of exercise and diet on chronic disease.* http://jap.physiology.org/content/98/1/3.full%23R361%23R361/ Hypothesized mechanisms by which physical activity and diet reduce the risk of coronary artery disease (CAD), hypertension, and diabetes.

160] David Perlmutter, "Grain Brain—The Surprising Truth About Wheat, Carbs, and Sugar—Your Brain's Silent Killers" / Culver, et al., "Statin Use and Risk of Diabetes Mellitus in Postmenopausal Women in the Women's Health Initiative" (see introduction, n. 2).

161] Mevacor Side Effects Center, http://www.rxlist.com/mevacor-side-effects-drug-center.htm ; Mevacor Side Effects, https://www.drugs.com/sfx/mevacor-side-effects.html

162] Seneff, Stephanie, APOE-4: The Clue to Why Low Fat Diet and Statins may Cause Alzheimer's, Dec. 15, 2009 (54, 53, 35) - Reference: Grain Brain

163] Uffe Ravnskov, Fat and Cholesterol are Good for You, Sweden, GB

Publishing, 2009,

164] There are numerous studies and support materials available dealing with high cholesteral and related topis, including the following:

- Kozarevic D et al. Serum cholesterol and mortality: the Yugoslavia Cardiovascular Disease Study. Am J Epidemiol. 1981 Jul;114(1):21-8.
- Rudman D et al et. Antecedents of death in the men of a Veterans Administration nursing home. J Am Geriatr Soc. 1987 Jun;35(6):496-502.
- Forette B et al. Cholesterol as risk factor for mortality in elderly women. Lancet. 1989 Apr 22;1(8643):868-70.
- Staessen J et al. Is a high serum cholesterol level associated with longer survival in elderly hypertensives? J Hypertens. 1990 Aug;8(8):755-61.
- Harris T et al.The low cholesterol-mortality association in a national cohort. J Clin Epidemiol. 1992 Jun;45(6):595-601.
- Casiglia E et al. Predictors of mortality in very old subjects aged 80 years or over. Eur J Epidemiol. 1993 Nov;9(6):577-86.
- Krumholz HM et al. Lack of association between cholesterol and coronary heart disease mortality and morbidity and all-cause mortality in persons older than 70 years. JAMA. 1994 Nov 2;272(17):1335-40.
- Weverling-Rijnsburger AW et al. High-density vs low-density lipoprotein cholesterol as the risk factor for coronary artery disease and stroke in old age. Arch Intern Med. 2003;163(13):1549-54.
- Jonsson A et al. Total cholesterol and mortality after age 80 years. Lancet. 1997 Dec 13;350(9093):1778-9
- Räihä I et al. Effect of serum lipids, lipoproteins, and apolipoproteins on vascular and nonvascular mortality in the elderly. Arterioscler Thromb Vasc Biol. 1997 Jul;17(7):1224-32.
- Behar S et al. Low total cholesterol is associated with high total mortality in patients with coronary heart disease. The Bezafibrate Infarction Prevention (BIP) Study Group. Eur Heart J. 1997 Jan;18(1):52-9.
- Fried LP et al. Risk factors for 5-year mortality in older adults: the Cardiovascular Health Study. JAMA. 1998 Feb 25;279(8):585-92.
- Chyou PH, Eaker ED. Serum cholesterol concentrations and all-cause mortality in older people. Age Ageing. 2000 Jan;29(1):69-74.

- Schatz IJ et al. Cholesterol and all-cause mortality in elderly people from the Honolulu Heart Program: a cohort study.Lancet. 2001 Aug 4;358(9279):351-5.
- Weverling-Rijnsburger AW et al. High-density vs low-density lipoprotein cholesterol as the risk factor for coronary artery disease and stroke in old age. Arch Intern Med. 2003;163(13):1549-54.
- Onder G et al. Serum cholesterol levels and in-hospital mortality in the elderly. Am J Med. 2003;115(4):265-71.
- Casiglia E et al. Total cholesterol and mortality in the elderly. J Intern Med. 2003 Oct;254(4):353-62.
- Psaty BM et al. The association between lipid levels and the risks of incident myocardial infarction, stroke, and total mortality: The Cardiovascular Health Study. J Am Geriatr Soc. 2004 Oct;52(10):1639-47.
- Ulmer H et al. Why Eve is not Adam: prospective follow-up in 149650 women and men of cholesterol and other risk factors related to cardiovascular and all-cause mortality. J Womens Health 2004 Jan-Feb;13(1):41-53.
- Schupf N et al. Relationship between plasma lipids and all-cause mortality in nondemented elderly. J Am Geriatr Soc. 2005 Feb;53(2):219-26
- Akerblom JL et al. Relation of plasma lipids to all-cause mortality in Caucasian, African-American and Hispanic elders. Age Ageing. 2008;37:207-13.
- Newson RS et al. Association between serum cholesterol and noncardiovascular mortality in older age. J Am Geriatr Soc.2011;59:1779-85.

165] http://www.greenmedinfo.com/blog/consumer-alert-300-health-problems-linked-statin-drugs

166] http://www.sciencedaily.com/releases/2009/02/090223221430.htm

167] David Perlmutter, *Grain Brain*, Little, Brown and Company, New York, NY, 2013, Page 93

168] "Dangers of Statin Drugs: What You Haven't Been Told About Popular Cholesterol-Lowering Medicines" by Sally Fallon and Mary G. Enig, Ph.D. http://www.westonaprice.org/cardiovascular-disease/dangers-of-statin-drugs ; for further information: Dr. Duane Graveline, *Lipitor, Thief of Memory: Statin Drugs and the Misguided War on Cholesterol*

169] https://drmalcolmkendrick.org/2013/11/18/you-need-a-statin-now-what-was-the-question/

170] http://www.cdc.gov/cholesterol/cholesterol_education_month.htm

171] Coenzyme Q10 (CoQ10): http://www.drweil.com/drw/u/ART03367/Coenzyme-Q10-CoQ10.html

172] *CoQ10 and Statins: The Vitamin C Connection*, by Owen R. Fonorow PhD, ND. Conduct the following word search in your preferred browser: "CoQ10 and Statins: The Vitamin C Connection by Owen R. Fonorow", or go to http://www.internetwks.com/owen/coq10.htm
Also of great interest and potential benefit is the Pauling Therapy: http://www.paulingtherapy.com/

173] For more information on the numerous benefits of CoQ10 please visit: http://www.epic4health.com/whatiscoq10.html

174] Statin drugs interfere with cellular production CoQ10 enzyme: http://www.epic4health.com/coqandstatdr.html

175] Statin drugs interfere with the synthesis of Vitamin D from cholesterol. http://www.naturalnews.com/027897_statin_drugs_vitamin_D.html#

176] Goldstein, D., *The epidemic of Vitamin D deficiency.* J Pediatr Nurs, 2009. 24(4): p. 345-6.

177] Dr. John Cannell, Executive Director, Vitamin D Council. http://www.vitamindcouncil.org/about-us/the-team-and-board/john-j-cannell-md-biography/

178] Grain Brain: The Surprising Truth about Wheat, Carbs, and Sugar—Your Brain's Silent Killers by David Perlmutter and Kristin Loberg / 2013

179] The following is a collection of support material relating to Vitamin D: Main Source: http://www.webmd.com/food-recipes/features/vitamin-d-vital-role-in-your-health

- *Demographic Differences and Trends of Vitamin D Insufficiency in the US Population*, 1988-2004, http://www.ncbi.nlm.nih.gov/pubmed/19307527
- The relationship of vitamin D deficiency to statin myopathy. http://www.ncbi.nlm.nih.gov/pubmed/21185021
- Severe myopathy associated with vitamin D deficiency in western New York. http://www.ncbi.nlm.nih.gov/pubmed/10789615

- Hypovitaminosis D myopathy without biochemical signs of osteomalacic bone involvement. http://www.ncbi.nlm.nih.gov/pubmed/10821877
- Vitamin, Mineral, & Nutrition Related Syndromes: http://neuromuscular.wustl.edu/nother/vitamin.htm
- Statin Effects on Blood Levels of Vitamin D: http://www.livestrong.com/article/510972-how-can-i-avoid-leg-cramps-when-taking-cholesterol-medicine/
- Statin Adverse Effects: A Review of the Literature and Evidence for a Mitochondrial Mechanism: http://www.ncbi.nlm.nih.gov/pmc/articles/PMC2849981/?tool=pubmed
- CoQ_{10} deficiency diseases in adults: http://www.ncbi.nlm.nih.gov/pmc/articles/PMC2001314/?tool=pubmed
- The Cancer-Causing Mistake 1 in 4 People Over 45 Make: http://articles.mercola.com/sites/articles/archive/2011/12/07/statin-increases-risk-of-prostate-cancer.aspx
- Vitamin D Helps Diabetic Neuropathy Pain: https://expertnutrition.com/store/
- Statins' Adverse Effects Documented on the website: http://www.sciencedaily.com/releases/2009/01/090127090735.htm

179a] "Cholesterol-Lowering Statin Drugs More Than Double Breast Cancer Risk," by David Brownstein, HealthImpactNews.com

180] http://www.webmd.com/diabetes/guide/type-1-diabetes)

181] (http://www.webmd.com/heart-disease/guide/heart-disease-heart-attacks)

182] (http://www.webmd.com/rheumatoid-arthritis/default.htm)

183] (http://www.webmd.com/multiple-sclerosis/default.htm)

184] For further information about Statins see; *Grain Brain: The Surprising Truth about Wheat, Carbs, and Sugar—Your Brain's Silent Killers* by David Perlmutter and Kristin Loberg / 2013, Pages 93-98, and John Abramson, *Overdosed America,* (New York: Harper Collins Publishers, 2004), Pages 13-22 and 142-148 and Duane Graveline, *Lipitor, Thief of Memory: Statin Drugs and the Misguided War on Cholesterol* (Duane Graveline, MD, 2006)

184a] SOURCE: http://www.fda.gov/forconsumers/consumerupdates/ucm293330.htm

184b] REFERENCE: Culver, et al., "Statin Use and Risk of Diabetes

Mellitus in Postmenopausal Women in the Women's Health Initiative"

184c] REFERENCE: Geiss LS, Cowie CC. Type 2 diabetes and persons at high risk of diabetes. In: Narayan KM, Williams D, Gregg EW, Cowie CC, eds. Diabetes and Public Health: From Data to Policy. New York, NY: Oxford University Press; 2011:15-32.

184d] Chart reflecting upon the influence of modern medicine on Adulthood and Aging.

Source: http://www.cdc.gov/diabetes/pubs/reportcard/diabetes-incidence.htm

185] *Guide for Nurses*, by April Hazard Vallerand PhD RN FAAN, Cynthia A. Sanoski BS PharmD FCCP BCPS and *Lippincott Nursing Drug Guide*, by Amy M. Karch, complied by professional hospital nursing staff.

186] Principal Data Source: "Effects of exercise and diet on chronic disease," by Christian K. Roberts and R. James Barnard

187] Quotes above are from the Principal Data Source: "Effects of exercise and diet on chronic disease,"by Christian K. Roberts and R. James Barnard

187a] Journal of Applied Physiology, "Effects of exercise and diet on chronic disease," by Christian K. Roberts , R. James Barnard / January 2005, Vol. 98 no. 3-30, DOI: 10.1152/japplphysiol.00852.2004 <http://jap.physiology.org/content/98/1/3#sec-3>

188] "Effects of exercise and diet on chronic disease," by Christian Roberts and R. James Barnard / http://jap.physiology.org/content/98/1/3#R281#R281 / #R282#R282

189] *Arteriosclerosis, Thrombosis, and Vascular Biology.* 1995; 15: 1079-1085doi: 10.1161/01.ATV.15.8.1079 / http://atvb.ahajournals.org/content/15/8/1079.full

190] "Efficacy of a National Cholesterol Education Program Step 2 Diet in Normolipidemic and Hypercholesterolemic Middle-Aged and Elderly Men and Women" By Ernst J. Schaefer, Alice H. Lichtenstein, Stefania Lamon-Fava, John H. Contois, Zhengling Li, Helen Rasmussen, Judith R. McNamara, José M. Ordovas.

191] "Effects of exercise and diet on chronic disease," by Christian Roberts and R. James Barnard / http://jap.physiology.org/

content/98/1/3#r121#R121

192] "Effects of exercise and diet on chronic disease," by Christian Roberts and R. James Barnard / http://jap.physiology.org/content/98/1/3#R389#R389

193] Some information and quotes from: http://www.sciencedirect.com/science/article/pii/S0026049503005110 / "Effect of diet and exercise intervention on inflammatory and adhesion molecules in postmenopausal women on hormone replacement therapy and at risk for coronary artery disease." / By Julia K. Wegge[a], Christian K. Roberts[a], Tung H. Ngo[a], an d R.James Barnard / Department of Physiological Science, University of California, Los Angeles, CA, USA

194] "Effects of exercise and diet on chronic disease," by Christian Roberts and R. James Barnard / January 2005, Vol. 98 no. 3-30 DOI: 10.1152/japplphysiol.00852.2004 / http://jap.physiology.org/content/98/1/3#sec-4

194a] "Effects of exercise and diet on chronic disease," by Christian Roberts and R. James Barnard / http://jap.physiology.org/content/98/1/3#R65#R65.

195] Principal Data Source: "Effects of exercise and diet on chronic disease," by Christian K. Roberts and R. James Barnard

196] http://care.diabetesjournals.org/content/32/suppl_2/S189.full: *Non-pharmacologic Therapy and Exercise in the Prevention of Type 2 Diabetes,* by Jaakko Tuomilehto, MD, MPOLSC, PHD

196a] "Targeting the metabolic syndrome with exercise: evidence from the HERITAGE Family Study." by Katzmarzyk PT1, Leon AS, Wilmore JH, Skinner JS, Rao DC, Rankinen T, Bouchard C. / http://journals.lww.com/acsm-msse/pages/articleviewer.aspx?year=2003&issue=10000&article=00013&type=abstract

196b] Willians R, Van Gaal L, Lucioni C : "Assessing the impact of complications on the costs of type II diabetes." *Diabetologia* 2002; 45: S13-S17

197] "Effects of exercise and diet on chronic disease," by Christian Roberts and R. James Barnard / http://jap.physiology.org/content/98/1/3#R260#R260

198] "Effects of exercise and diet on chronic disease," by Christian Roberts and R. James Barnard / http://jap.physiology.org/content/98/1/3.full#R361#R361 / #R360#R360

199] Principal Data Source: "Prevention Makes Common "Cents,"" U.S. Department of Health and Human Services. http://aspe.hhs.gov/health/prevention/prevention.pdf / 02/01/2014

200] "Prevention Makes Common "Cents,"" U.S. Department of Health and Human Services. http://aspe.hhs.gov/health/prevention/prevention.pdf / 02/01/2014, Pages 24-25

201] Goetzel RZ, Juday TR, Ozminkowski RJ. What's the ROI? A systematic review of return on-investment studies of corporate health and productivity management initiatives. AWHP's Worksite Health. 1999;6(3), Pages 12-21

202] Ozminkowski RJ, Ling D, Goetzel RZ, Bruno JA, Rutter KR, Isaac F, Wang S. Long-term impact of Johnson & Johnson's health & wellness program on health care utilization and expenditures. Journal of Occupational and Environmental Medicine. 2002; 44: Pages 21-29.

203] This is a public domain document belonging to the "People of the United States."

Principal Data Source: Prevention Makes Common "Cents," U.S. Department of Health and Human Services. http://aspe.hhs.gov/health/prevention/prevention.pdf, Pages 25-26

BIBLIOGRAPHY

I pray this book will go way beyond being informative and become transformative.

"These were more noble than those in Thessalonica, in that they received the word with all readiness of mind, and searched the scriptures daily, whether those things were so."
- Acts 17:11 (1611 King James Bible)

In order for the words of this book to be effectively transformative, it will require more of you than passive reflection. I heartily encourage you to do the research, with readiness of mind, to see if the points I am arguing are valid. I have compiled an annotated bibliography to help you review the information presented in this book.

These resources inform you about the issues at play in this battle of medical philosophies. Without knowledge (which imparts power), you will not be adequately equipped to go forward with evidence-based understanding and confidence into the exploration of a far more effective medical model. We have been led by a lie for so long that it will take serious effort to deprogram our immersion in the myth of the superiority of technology to nature. Please believe me; I am speaking from the earnest voice of a teacher. Do the research beyond these pages.

I have attempted to serve and support my readers insofar as directing you to evidence that demands a complete overhaul of the current medical system's failure-to-fortunes approach. However, the effort to become informed and demand justice is still the responsibility and duty of every individual citizen.

Do the research. Don't simply take my word for it. Begin or continue the process of becoming informed and then, having examined the evidence on your own, continue with my arguments for the establishment of a just and ethical medical approach that is not measured by the polish with which it is presented, but by the effectiveness with which it delivers its patients from the vortex of physical decline into the victory and vibrancy of renewed health.

For the unhealthy longing to be disease free
whose behaviors perpetually engrain them
in habits that perpetually drain them
we must physically sustain and retrain them
till they own the keys that will unchain them

1] *The Corporation: The Pathological Pursuit of Profit and Power*, by Joel Bakan, Free Press: New York, NY. 2004.

2] "Alchemy," found at http://en.wikipedia.org/wiki/Alchemy.

3] "The History of Medicine," found at www.mnwelldir.org/docs/history/history03.htm.

4] "Allopathic Medicine," found at http://en.wikipedia.org/wiki/Allopathic.

5] "What the American Medical Association Hopes You Never Learn about Its History," by Mike Adams, found at www.naturalnews.com/008845.html.

6] "Healthy People 2020," found at www.healthypeople.gov/2020/default.aspx.

7] "The Science of Refined Food Addiction," by Kay Sheppard, MA, LMHC, CEDS.

8] "Fast Food as Addictive as Heroin, Study Confirms," by Amber Greviskes,

9] "4 Signs of Fast Food Addiction, Are Your Kids Addicted Too?"

10] US Government Resource for Wellness found at www.healthypeople.gov/hp2020/Comments/CommentList.aspx?cmd=stc&Id=8.

11] "The American Medical System Is The Leading Cause Of Death And Injury In The United States," by Gary Null, PhD; Carolyn Dean, MD, ND; Martin Feldman, MD; Debora Rasio, MD; and Dorothy Smith, PhD," found at www.ourcivilisation.com/medicine/usamed.htm.

12] "Adverse Drug Reactions," found at www.worstpills.org/public/page.cfm?op_id=4.

13] "Drugs and Adverse Drug Reactions—How Worried Should We Be?" by David W. Bates, MD, MSC

14] "The Influence of the Pharmaceutical Industry on Healthcare Practitioners' Prescribing Habits," by James Rhee, PA-S, found at www.ispub.com/journal/the_internet_journal_of_academic_physician_assistants/volume_7_number_1_26/article/the-influence-of-the-pharmaceutical-industry-on-healthcare-practitioners-prescribing-habits.html.

15] "Top Industries: Most Profitable,"

16] "Paying your doctor in ancient China,"

17] "FTC Launches Operation False Cures to Suppress Natural Cancer Remedies,"

18] "FDA defeated in federal court over censorship of truthful health claims,"

19] "Over and above: Excess in the pharmaceutical industry," by Marcia Angell, found at www.cmaj.ca/cgi/content/full/171/12/1451.

20] "Pfizer Agrees to Record Criminal Fine in Fraud Probe,"

21] "Array of toxic chemicals in humans 'alarming'; I am polluted," found at http://curezone.com/forums/fm.asp?i=587299#i.

22] "Why Do Americans Take So Many Prescription Drugs?" by J. Douglas Bremner, MD, found at www.oftwominds.com/journal08/Prescription-Drugs.htm.

23] "Effects of exercise and diet on chronic disease," Christian K. Roberts and R. James Barnard, Department of Physiological Science, University of California, Los Angeles, California

24] "Overdosed America," by John Abramson, M.D. HarperCollins: New York, NY. 2004.

25] "Social Learning Theory: An Overview of Bandura's Social Learning Theory," by Kendra Cherry

26] Frankl, Viktor E. *Man's Search for Meaning.* Simon and Schuster: New York, NY. 1963.

27] "Healthy Living Is the Best Revenge: Findings From the European Prospective Investigation Into Cancer and Nutrition–Potsdam Study," by Earl S. Ford, MD, MPH, et. al.

28] "Battling Diabetes with Diet and Exercise," by Michelle Andrews

29] "Lobbying, Campaign Contributions, and Health Care Reform," by Robert Steinbrook, M.D., in *The New England Journal of Medicine*, December 3, 2009.

30] "In the Headlines: Poor Diet and Obesity a Major Problem in the U.S.,"

31] "Obesity is Fast Becoming the Nation's Number One Threat,"

32] "When The Cure Is Worse Than The Disease," by Bill Sardi

33] "Medicines that Cause Liver Damage," by Cicely A. Richard

34] "Incidence of Adverse Drug Reaction in Hospitalized Patients," by Lazarou, et.al.

35] "Drug-Induced Diseases: Prevention, Detection, and Management," by James Tisdale and Douglas Miller

36] "God's Principles of Healthful Living,"

APPENDIX

APPENDIX A: RECOMMENDED WEBSITES

Note: If a web link becomes broken, you can use your favorite search engine to find the following resources by typing in the article title.

1] Google search "Evidence of chemical burden catalyzing increased chronic disease"

2] Google search "sauna detox can be harmful—far infrared rays are safer"

3] Conversation on chemical burden: http://drclaudiamiller.com/tag/cumulative-exposures/

4] Drug – drug interactions: http://www.fda.gov/drugs/resourcesforyou/ucm163354.htm

5] how drug – drug interactions occur: http://www.medicinenet.com/drug_interactions/article.htm

6] Drug watch: http://www.drugwatch.com/

7] Drug conspiracy—rveloutionary voice: http://www.vaughns-1-pagers.com/medicine/prescription-drug-side-effects.htm#pharmaceutical-drug-classification-system

8] Google search "Beer's List to avoid polypharmacy"

9] Polypharmacy: What it is and how to avoid it. http://longevity.about.com/od/agingproblems/f/polypharmacy.htm

10] Armor Tool to prevent polypharmacy—EXPLANATION OF "PRESCRIBING CASCADE": http://www.annalsoflongtermcare.

com/content/armor-a-tool-evaluate-polypharmacy-elderly-persons

11] On the track: DRUG TOXICITY: http://www.aarp.org/health/drugs-supplements/info-08-2010/toxic-drugs-when-medicine-makes-you-sick.html

12] Google search "Drug induced liver disease (Hepatoxicity)"

13] What are the symptoms of liver disease / How do drugs induce liver disease ALSO What is drug induced liver disease? (see prior page of long web article): http://www.medicinenet.com/drug_induced_liver_disease/page2.htm

14] Classification of drug induced damages from medications: http://en.citizendium.org/wiki/Drug_toxicity

15] Adverse Drug Reactions: http://www.worstpills.org/public/page.cfm?op_id=4

16] Google search "Adverse Drug Reactions: WHO"

17] FDA and Adverse Drug Reactions: http://www.fda.gov/drugs/developmentapprovalprocess/developmentresources/druginteractionslabeling/ucm110632.htm#ADRs: Prevalence and Incidence

18] The Nutrition Institute of America mandated that every count in this indictment of American Medicine be verified by independent peer reviewed study: http://www.webdc.com/pdfs/deathbymedicine.pdf

19] Good Information / Contact info: http://www.bhagavandharma.org/pdf-documents/Death_by_Modern_Medicine.pdf

Legacy Tobacco Document Library (LTDL) UCSF.EDU
Tobacco Documents Library—American Legacy Foundation www.legacyforhealth.org/what-we.../tobacco.../tobacco-documents-library
Why is this website important? Because they are also investigating the BigPharma the way they pursued the tobacco industry!!! That's my baby!!!

Google search "Jack La Lanne—Why people are unhappy!"

Google search "Sugarholics"

APPENDIX B: Overview and Contrast of Two Competing Medical Approaches

Western medicine is very effective at addressing acute (rapid onset) medical conditions. However, it is very ineffective at managing chronic (slow onset) medical conditions. The best scientific evidence demonstrate superiority of comprehensive lifestyle modification for the treatment of lifestyle-induced chronic conditions. Lifestyle modification and exercise truly provide the best medicine for the majority of chronic diseases.

Two competing medical approaches:

A] Ineffective Non-Evidence Based Pharmaceutically Marketed Approaches to Chronic Disease:

Pharmaceutical Prescriptions for Symptom Management/ Progression of Chronic Diseases:

Ineffective Medical Approaches will: Compromise / Enfeeble / Enslave Patients

Disengage personal responsibility:

1] Rely upon diagnostic imaging and interpretation

2] Submit to lab testing, and defer to your doctor's interpretation of the results.

Weaken self reliance:

3] Defer to the advice of medical experts

4] Depend upon medical advances and technology

Indoctrinate dependency:

5] Take medications as ordered

6] When conditions worsen consult your physician

7] After medications destroy the kidneys, its time to begin lifelong dialysis treatment

In stark contrast with,

B] Effective Evidence Based Medical Approaches to Chronic Disease:

Whole Life Prescriptions for Optimal Management/Reversal of Chronic Diseases:

Effective Medical Approaches will: Optimize / Enable / Empower Patients to:

Engage in:

1] Water Aerobics / Lap Swimming / Cycling / Hiking

2] Tai Chi / Rhythm & Movement / Core Strengthening & Stability Exercises

Develop:

3] Strength / Stamina / Endurance

4] Stretching / Range of Motion / Flexibility

Employ:

5] Detoxification with Heat Therapy: Dry Sauna, Jacuzzi Pool, Steam Room

6] Good Nutrition / Healthy Hydration / Nutritional Supplementation

7] Group Support / Health Coaching / Health Measurement & Maintenance

The Downward Spiral of Chronic Disease:

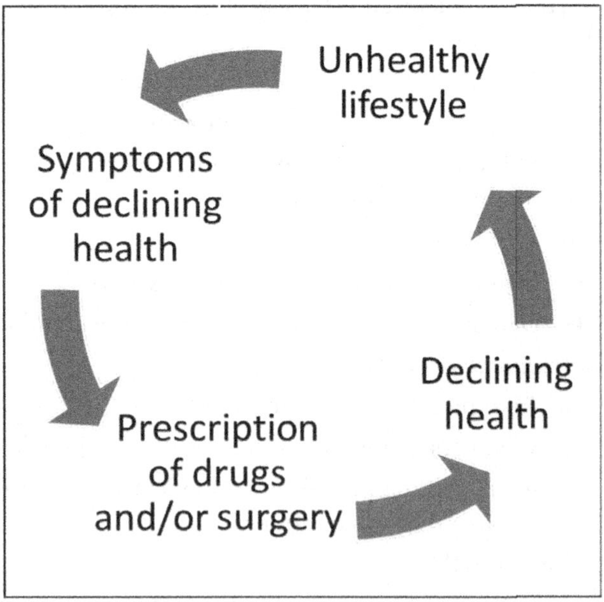

Patients enter the system with the lifestyle that produced their current symptoms. Patients continue to stagnate in the exercise-deficient and poor diet lifestyle that is causing their deconditioned/debilitated state of chronic illness. From this state, a deepening progression of symptoms inevitably erupts: for which more drugs are prescribed…(repeat).

Stairway to Disintegration

Pattern of Stairway to Disintegration:

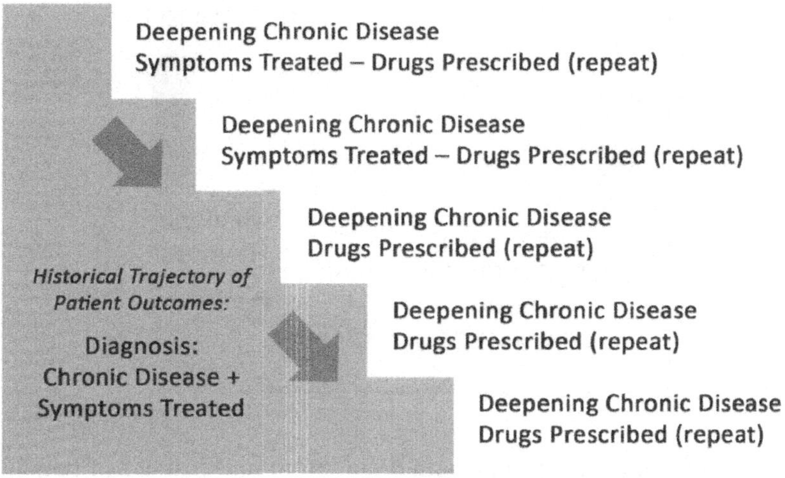

Stagnate → Decondition (repeat)

Patient enters the medical system with symptoms of chronic disease and are given (prescribed) an assorted array of chemicals to treat their symptoms. Patients are given various blood, urine, and other diagnostic tests to determine a definitive diagnosis. Patients are diagnosed, and sent home with chemicals.

The Upward Spiral of Health Renewal:

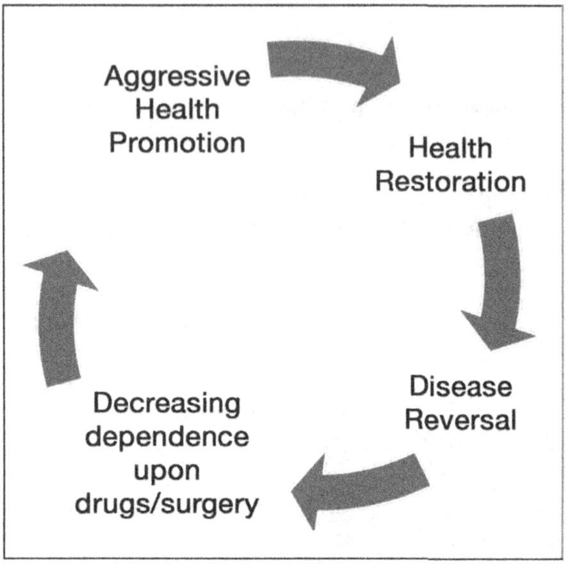

Patients enter the system with a symptom and instead of patient being assessed and tested to determine a definitive diagnosis and which drugs are most appropriate for treating patients chief complaints, that is their symptoms; the patient is given an extensive lifestyle questionnaire to determine how patient spends their day: exercise, diet, liquids, work, commute, time spent watching TV, recreational activities, alcohol, drugs, medications, hours spent being sedentary vs. hours spent being physically active; as well as questions about the home environment and situations causing stress, fear, depression, loneliness etc. Patient will also receive a basic physical fitness assessment to determine current fitness level.

The purpose of this extensive questionnaire and fitness assessment is to ascertain whether patient's condition, complaints and symptoms are the result of an absence of a healthy lifestyle, that is, a lifestyle induced condition or something best treated with drugs. If patients condition (chief complaint and symptoms) are largely due to the absence of a healthy lifestyle then the patient is referred to a comprehensive lifestyle transformation program. That referral would include information about local health club and fitness resources as well as chronic disease rehabilitation programs specifically designed to fully support every aspect of the patient's journey back to health through the gradual yet progressive adoption of a healthier lifestyle.

As patients come to understand and embrace the truth about how to get well and follow the guidance provided, they will gradually become more fit and healthy. As a result, their attitudes about exercise and diet with also change and the symptoms that daily afflicted them will gradually diminish and resolve of their own accord. Patients will become more and more progressively self-empowered and thus less and less dependent upon others for the management of their biology.

Stairway to Integration

Pattern of Stairway to Integration:

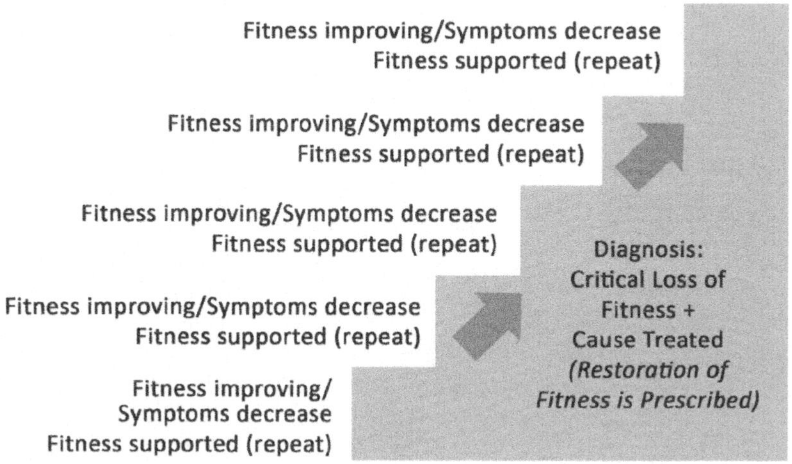

Patients enter the medical system with symptoms of chronic disease and are given an extensive lifestyle questionnaire and physical evaluation to ascertain the underlying causes of their decline in health. Patients are counseled on the long-range consequences of an unhealthy lifestyle that are obesity, diabetes, heart disease, back pain, degenerative joint disease, digestive disorders, fatigue, peripheral neuropathy, weakness, etc. Patients are asked to consider these facts seriously before making a decision about their course of treatment. Then on a secondary follow-up visit, the patient receives further examination of the underlying emotional blocks and motivational challenges/hurdles standing between them and their health restoration. Patients are asked on a medical form to be included in their medical record the following question:

1] Do you want to get well? Y or N

2] Or do you simply want the symptoms of your declining health and deepening state of disease to be treated? Y or N

Based on the response to this question and the patient's perceived readiness to embark on the journey of health renewal, the patient is recommended a life transformation program that supports all aspects (i.e. physical, environmental, and emotional layers) of transition to a healthier lifestyle. (See previous diagram.)

APPENDIX C. DRUGS IMPAIR VARIOUS ORGANS AND SYSTEMS WITHIN THE BODY

1] Drugs impair healthy immune function.

RESOURCE: www.worldwidehealth.com/health-article-Statins-Impair-Immune-System-Function.html

"The statin drug Zocor (simvastatin) has been shown to directly compromise the immune response to an opportunistic infection. This is not good news for any person taking any statin, as the type of impairment involved seriously compromises basic immune system function."

Many Antidepressants, Corticosteroids, cholesterol lowering agents (statins) and chemotherapy drugs have been shown to impair healthy immune function.

2] Drugs impair normal function of healthy organs.

a. http://www.ncbi.nlm.nih.gov/pmc/articles/PMC3181655/

3] Drugs impose a toxic burden on the eliminative organs.

a. http://www.ener-chi.com/why-we-need-to-constantly-cleanse-the-bodys-various-systems-and-eliminative-organs/
b. http://www.hepcnet.net/drugsandliverdamage.html
c. http://www.patient.co.uk/doctor/Drug-induced-Hepatitis.htm

4] Drug toxins are stored in organs and tissue and how to eliminate them.

a. http://www.able.org/studies/detox/drug_storage.pdf
b. http://www.ndhealthfacts.org/wiki/Elimination_of_Toxins
c. http://www.stuartwilde.com/2013/04/14-ways-to-cleanse-the-body-from-toxins/
d. http://www.huffingtonpost.com/dr-mark-hyman/detox-tips_b_1289488.html

5] Accumulated drug toxins damage bodily organs and systems.

RESOURCE 1: "Drug Induced Liver Disease" www.medicinenet.com/drug_induced_liver_disease/page3.htm#what_types_of_liver_disease_do_drugs_cause

What is drug-induced liver disease? Drug-induced liver diseases are diseases of the liver that are caused by physician-prescribed medications, over-the-counter medications, vitamins, hormones, herbs, illicit ("recreational") drugs, and environmental toxins.

What types of liver disease do drugs cause? Drugs and chemicals can cause a wide spectrum of liver injury. These include:

- Mild elevations in blood levels of liver enzymes without symptoms or signs of liver disease
- Hepatitis (inflammation of liver cells)
- Necrosis (death of liver cells) that often is caused by more severe hepatitis
- Cholestasis (decreased secretion and/or flow of bile)
- Steatosis (accumulation of fat in the liver)
- Cirrhosis (advanced scarring of the liver) as a result of chronic hepatitis, cholestasis, or fatty liver
- Mixed disease, for example both hepatitis and necrosis of liver cells, hepatitis and fat accumulation, or cholestasis and hepatitis.
- Fulminant hepatitis with severe, life threatening liver failure
- Blood clots in the veins of the liver

6] Adverse Drug Reactions increase in the elderly due to age related decreases in drug metabolism, excretion and counter-regulation.

RESOURCE 1: "When drug therapy gets old: pharmacokinetics and pharmacodynamics in the elderly" www.sciencedirect.com/science/article/Pii/s0531556503001335

Aside of these pharmacokinetic changes, one of the characteristics of old age is a progressive decline in counterregulatory (homeostatic) mechanisms. Therefore drug effects are mitigated less, the reactions are usually stronger than in younger subjects, the rate and intensity of adverse effects are higher. Examples of drug effects augmented is this manner are postural hypotension with agents that lower blood pressure, dehydration, hypovolemia, and electrolyte disturbances in response to diuretics, bleeding complications with oral anticoagulants, hypoglycemia with antidiabetics, and gastrointestinal irritation with non-steroidal anti-inflammatory drugs. The brain is an especially sensitive drug target in old age. Psychotropic drugs but also anticonvulsants and centrally acting antihypertensives may impede intellectual functions and motor coordination. The antimuscarinic effects of some antidepressants and neuroleptic drugs may be responsible for agitation, confusion, and delirium in elderly. Hence drugs should be used very restrictively in geriatric patients. If drug therapy is absolutely necessary, the dosage should be titrated to a clearly defined clinical or biochemical therapeutic goal starting from a low initial dose.

APPENDIX D. A SYSTEMATIC APPROACH TO GRADUAL DRUG REDUCTION

Thoughts on an approach for reducing medication dosage:

Disclaimer: This book is intended to provide information about medical issues in general, but not provide specific professional advice to any particular reader about his or her medical condition. Accordingly, any such information provided is not intended to replace or be a substitute for professional medical advice or to override the labeling recommendations of any given product. Readers are advised to seek out a physician whose approach and practice are consistent with their goals for treatment; and with whom they feel comfortable discussing individual health needs and concerns, in order to discuss specific medical advice and treatment. It is my hope that this publication will educate readers to the dangers of conventional medicine's prescriptive practices so that they can proceed more freely along their own path to positive health.

Before reducing medications seek the advice of a qualified physician/ pharmacist to support you in this process.

If your doctor or pharmacist does not support the gradual reduction of your medications, seek one who does.

Recommended Conservative Approach to Gradual Drug Reduction (6 months):

- Reduce dosage by ¼ (for 1 month)
- Further reduce dosage by ¼ (for 2 months)
- Further reduce dosage by ¼ (for 3 months)
- Further reduce dosage by ¼ (which eliminates dose).
- Many medications can be withdrawn according to this simple Gradual Drug Reduction (GDR) strategy.
- However, certain classes of medication require an even more refined strategy for their gradual systematic withdrawal (more on which medication classes require greater caution later).
- If withdrawal from a medication requires greater caution and a slower tapering process the following guideline is helpful:
- XR (Extended Release) tablets should not be cut in half. To reduce dosages of XR - Extended Release tablets first request the prescription be changed to a "single dose" formulation. Single dose tablets can be safely cut to smaller portions for gradual dose

reduction.

- If a medication is taken more than 1x per day. Start by reducing 1 dosage per day and do not reduce the other dosage (administration times) for that day. Then after the first dose for that day is reduced and tolerated well—say, for 1 week for example, then reduce the second dose for that day and when that is tolerated well, reduce the 3rd dose and so on. After all dosages (times per day a medication is taken) have been reduced (and are tolerated well); begin the next round of dosage reduction (by lowering 1st dose of day—while leaving other doses for day that at the current level) and repeat step above until all doses for that day have been reduced (and reduction is tolerated well) before proceeding with further reductions.
- If symptoms return for which medication was being taken: Consult your physician and speak of your concerns and request the lowest possible dosage be given and/or:
    - Restore dosage by ¼ (for 1 month) if symptoms require.
    - Restore dosage by ¼ (for 1 month) repeat as necessary up to original dosage.

A More Aggressive Approach To Gradual Drug Reduction (4 Months)

- Reduce dosage by ¼ (for 1 month)
- Further reduce dosage by ¼ (for 1 month)
- Further reduce dosage by ¼ (for 2 months)
- Further reduce dosage by ¼ (which eliminates dose).
- Many medications can be withdrawn according to this simple Gradual Drug Reduction (GDR) strategy.
- However, certain classes of medication require an even more refined strategy for their gradual systematic withdrawal (more on which medication classes require greater caution later).
- If withdrawal from a medication requires greater caution and a slower tapering process the following guideline is helpful:
- XR (Extended Release) tablets should not be cut in half. To reduce dosages of XR - Extended Release tablets first request the prescription be changed to a "single dose" formulation. Single dose tablets can be safely cut to smaller portions for gradual dose reduction.
- If a medication is taken more than 1x per day. Start by reducing 1

dosage per day and do not reduce the other dosage (administration times) for that day. Then after the first dose for that day is reduced and tolerated well—say, for 1 week for example, then reduce the second dose for that day and when that is tolerated well, reduce the 3rd dose and so on. After all dosages (times per day a medication is taken) have been reduced (and are tolerated well); begin the next round of dosage reduction (by lowering 1st dose of day—while leaving other doses for day that at the current level) and repeat step above until all doses for that day have been reduced (and reduction is tolerated well) before proceeding with further reductions.

- If symptoms return for which medication was being taken: Consult your physician and speak of your concerns and request the lowest possible dosage be given and/or:
    - Restore dosage by ¼ (for 1 month) if symptoms require:
    - Restore dosage by ¼ (for 1 month) repeat as necessary up to original dosage.

Exercise Is Medicine!

It is important to not simply reduce medications but to fully embrace a healthier lifestyle that supports healthier outcomes. Exercise is the best medicine. Do not simply take yourself off medications without establishing a healthy lifestyle.

Remember!

It wasn't medication that got you on medication it was largely the result of living an unhealthy lifestyle. Unless you begin a healthier lifestyle there is no reason to assume that you will be able to stay off medications.

The following medication classes require greater caution in withdrawal and hence, a slower tapering process: Antipsychotics, anti-anxiety, antidepressants, sedatives, hypnotics, opioids.

Gradual Drug Reduction (Gdr)

Sometimes, the decision about whether to continue a medication is clear; for example, recurrent seizures in which case the patient may need an anticonvulsant medication indefinitely. Often, however, the only way to know whether a medication is needed indefinitely and whether the dose remains appropriate is to try reducing the dose and to monitor the effect closely for improvement, stabilization, or decline.

The time frames and duration of attempts to taper any medication depend on factors including the coexisting medication regimen, the underlying causes of symptoms, individual risk factors, and pharmacologic characteristics of the medications. Some medications (e.g., antidepressants, sedative/hypnotics, opioids) require more gradual tapering so as to minimize or prevent withdrawal symptoms or other adverse consequences.

NOTE: If the patient's condition has not responded to treatment or has declined despite treatment, it is important to evaluate both the medication and the dose to determine whether the medication should be discontinued or the dosing should be altered.

Use caution in reducing medication dosages. To employ too rapid of a withdrawal from some medications—antipsychotics, for example can result in severe withdrawal symptoms. Keep a long-range perspective and proceed with patience. Devise a plan of gradual systematic dosage reduction and revise it if necessary but stick with it—to completion.

For more information on the dangers of taking antipsychotics and the challenges of being withdrawn from them please see:

manicmurses.wordpress.com, and in the search engine, type: "Is there now evidence withdrawal from antipsychotics can induce psychosis?"

Freedom From Pharmaceutical Enslavement

The following websites provide additional information and support to help you regain your freedom from pharmaceutical enslavement. Guard against narrowly focusing on the reduction of medications without giving ample attention to the introduction of healthier behaviors.

The following blog entry from the website below provides a practical plan for safely withdrawing from propanolol—and provides a *systematic approach to gradual drug reduction* that can be applied to any class of medication.

> *"Hi Leopoldbloom, and welcome. You are on a low dose of propranolol, but if you are on extended release, you can't cut the tablets, or capsules in half. I suggest you (if you are indeed on the extended release), get a script from your doctor of the regular propranolol, and start cutting down from there. Remember that you have to adjust the dosage from extended release to the regular medication. The way I wean myself off of medicine, is one dose at a time. So if you are taking 20mg 2X/day, I would cut ONE DOSE in half, and the second dose remains at 20mg, until you have no side effects. For me, this can take up to three weeks. Then I would cut the second dose in half, again, until no side effects. Never*

go too quickly, so wait at least a week until you cut the dose again. Then I would go to 5mg on one dose, then 21/2mg, and finally off. Remember start with just one dose."

- Anonymous

SOURCE: http://www.drugs.com/answers/you-safely-reduce-propranolol-dosage-negative-622093.html

Freeing Yourself From Chemical Dependency

The following websites provide additional information and support in successfully freeing yourself from chemical dependency.

- http://www.theroadback.org/antipsychotictaper.aspx

For very difficult cases of withdrawal from antipsychotic and anxiolytic (anti-anxiety) medications the following guidance and resource is provided: Please seek a qualified professional—committed to supporting safe and effective drug withdrawal—to assist you in the drug withdrawal process and especially when dealing with complications and failure in achieving safe and effective drug withdrawal.

The following article was written by Dr. Alice Lee and has been included by permission. Dr. Alice Lee is a psychiatrist and medical doctor who is concerned for the long-term health of patients taking antipsychotic medications. She has provided detailed recommendations on tapering off antipsychotic medications, which can be a very difficult process. For additional support, contact Dr. Lee directly through the web address provided.

SOURCE: http://holisticpsychiatrist.com/2010/05/06/five-easy-tips-on-how-to-withdraw-from-antipsychotics-safely/

Five Easy Tips on How to Withdraw from Antipsychotics Safely

Is it possible to withdraw from antipsychotic medications safely and successfully, without the "chronic" psychotic condition recurring? YES! Although psychosis is one of the most difficult conditions to treat in psychiatry, it is definitely possible to safely and effectively taper off of antipsychotic medications.

When an individual becomes psychotic, typically an antipsychotic medication is used to ameliorate symptoms. However, there are many side effects associated with the use of antipsychotics, and no clear way to ever come off the medication once symptoms are under control. In addition, withdrawal from an antipsychotic medication, after taking it for several years, will often result in withdrawal symptoms that mimic the original psychotic illness.

Over the years, I have learned how to overcome the difficulties and dangers associated with antipsychotic medication withdrawal. In the beginning, I was under the misconception that because all these medications treated psychosis, that they will have the same level of difficulty when it came to withdrawal. Not so. Consider Zyprexa—it affects no less than 17 different subtypes of receptors, while Haldol affects only two dopamine receptor subtypes. In between, we have Abilify, which affects 10 different receptor subtypes, to Seroquel which affects seven different receptor subtypes. When these medications are lowered, the body has to adjust to the changes in how receptors are affected during the taper. Which medication do you think would be the easiest for the body to adjust to, the medication that affects 17 receptor subtypes, or the one that only affects two? For most individuals, this would be a rhetorical question.

In the process of learning about medication withdrawal in general and antipsychotic withdrawal in particular, I have discovered that in addition to supporting the body with plenty of supplements and energy medicine techniques, there are some certain aspects of the medication withdrawal process that are critical for a smooth and safe withdrawal process. They are as follows:

1] Carefully follow sleep patterns: Do not reduce antipsychotic medications until sleep has increased through nutritional and energy medicine support to at least 9 hours per day; sleeping 10 hours per day would be preferable. Lowering antipsychotic medication when sleeping 8 hours or less would generally create a problem with insomnia.

2] Use liquid antipsychotics whenever available: It is easier to taper down in small amounts when using liquid antipsychotics. Of course, this principle applies to antidepressants or anxiolytics as well. If liquid antipsychotics are not available, they can be specially compounded through certain compounding pharmacies, especially through pharmacies that also sell nutritional supplements.

3] Antioxidant support: typically I use a combination of whole food powders such as acai, goji, and maqui powder to lower oxidative stress.

4] Strengthen the GABA neurotransmitter system: I prefer to use GABA rice (about half a cup twice daily), GABA drops by Deseret Biologicals (typically 10 drops three times daily), and/or GABA 500mg capsules (2-3 capsules a day) to help support the GABA nervous system. Supporting the GABA neurotransmitter system allows individuals to avoid insomnia during antipsychotic withdrawal, but just as importantly, it helps to decrease the risk for mania associated with unblocking serotonin receptors during withdrawal from those antipsychotics that block these receptors. Of the three, it is my clinical experience that GABA rice is the winner when it comes to efficacy during withdrawal. Zojirushi makes GABA rice cookers and can make GABA rice from organic, brown rice. Organic, germinated brown rice cooked in a regular rice cooker will also make GABA rice.

5] Most importantly, the "step-down process of withdrawal": when lowering an antipsychotic medication that affects many different neurotransmitter subtypes, such as Zyprexa, it is important to use a "step-down process," tapering down the antipsychotic through the use of another antipsychotic that affects fewer receptor sites. For example, when tapering down on Zyprexa, gradually increase the dosage of Seroquel. Once the individual is only on Seroquel and has safely and completely weaned off of Zyprexa, then gradually taper the dosage of Seroquel while gradually increasing the use of liquid Haldol. Once the individual has transitioned to Haldol and has completely been weaned off Seroquel, then very gradually lower Haldol. All the while, the individual should be using supplements and energy medicine to facilitate the recovery process. Tapering off Haldol, the last step of the "step-down process" will be a lot easier to accomplish successfully than coming directly off of Zyprexa.

Healing from psychotic episodes and getting off antipsychotic medications is possible. But a healthy respect for the withdrawal process will reward you with a safe and successful outcome. Otherwise, it would be easy to blame an unsuccessful withdrawal process as just another indicator that the patient has a "chronic" and severe psychiatric condition. I have come to understand "chronic" as another term for "failure in treatment." Don't let our traditional attitude towards psychotic conditions and our limited understanding of antipsychotic withdrawal be conveniently blamed on the disease process! You can get well if you are careful and have the right professional supports.

SOURCE: http://holisticpsychiatrist.com/2010/05/06/five-easy-tips-on-how-to-withdraw-from-antipsychotics-safely/. Use with permission.

The Reasons To Free Yourself From Chemical Dependency

The reasons for freeing yourself from chemical enslavement are many; among those reasons are the preservation of the organs damaged by chemical consumption. There is a major epidemic of *medication induced* kidney and liver failure in our nation. Yes, you heard that correctly, the American medical machine is causing an epidemic of kidney and liver failure in our nation. American medicines destruction of its patient's health only leads to its prescription of additional medications which further promotes the cycle of physical decline and billable episodes of medical care.

"For the love of money is a root of all evil; it is through this craving that some have been led astray and have wandered from the faith [and moral soundness] and pierced themselves through with many acute [mental] pangs."
- 1 Timothy 6:10 Amplified Bible

As a consumer, I strongly urge: Do not fall prey to marketing that is cleverly concealed as science. The evidence may be very thin upon which your doctors prescribe. Do you want the symptoms of your continually declining health being continually treated or do you want to achieve real health which will require real work. Do you want a quick fix or a long-term solution? Ah, but here's the rub! Real answers require real work. You cannot swallow better health but you can certainly *choose to* wallow in disease *with ease* by swallowing pills.

Your future is largely your own doing *or undoing*. Therefore invest in what is best for yourself. The kingdom of health is within you. You were created to be a habitation of God and to enjoy Him forever. Take care of your body which is the temple of the Holy Spirit.

"But those who wait for the Lord [who expect, look for, and hope in Him] shall change and renew their strength and power; they shall lift their wings and mount up [close to God] as eagles [mount up to the sun]; they shall run and not be weary, they shall walk and not faint or become tired."
- Isaiah 40:31 Amplified Bible

APPENDIX E. DIET FOR LIFE

The following is a review and commentary of an article in The Gaurdian that ran on June 19, 2013 by Michael Booth titled "The Okinawa diet—could it help you live to 100? The article can be viewed in its entirety at the following address: http://www.theguardian.com/lifeandstyle/2013/jun/19/japanese-diet-live-to-100

How can we extend our lives? There are a few vital substances, that is, super nutrient dense food sources that help to balance and fortify our bodies. These definitely help but there is no singular magic bullet or fountain of youth. Health is rather a constellation of good behaviors and habits that encourage the youth within our aging. There has been observed a few "communities of youth" and we can glean a few things from them as well. This is a brief review of the diets of the "longest living" peoples on Earth. Dr Craig Willcox, who has spent many years investigating Okinawan longevity and co-wrote a book, The Okinawa Program, recommends that we "Eat as low down the food chain as possible."

Added Perspectives And Commentary:

According to the theory of evolution we evolved out of the oceans to inhabit the land. Whether man is a product of slime or something more divine is a separate discussion but borrowing from the sciences presented here I agree that we should "eat as low down the food chain as possible" and that fish according to science are lower on the food chain than birds and all manner of four footed creatures. Even the Genesis account from the Bible tells the story of God having created the earth as a void; then separating the earth and waters; and then God created the creatures of the sea and then the birds of the air and then the creatures of the land and lastly man. Genesis 1: 9-12; 20-21; 24-25;29

So what do the longest living people have in common?

Some things vary among the longest-lived populations but some things are consistently the same. The longest-lived populations eat less meat and more plants than the rest of us. What all the longest-living people groups share in common is that they gather their foods from very low on the food chain. That is, a majority of their foods are directly from the plant kingdom with a minimum of processing. They also tend to gather a higher percentage of their proteins from lower on the food chain, that is from "the waters."

Long Live The Okinawan People

The Okinawan people are renowned for their long lives, and as such their diet and lifestyle has been studied extensively for insights into the sources of their longevity.

As for protein intake the Okinawan people average three servings of fish per week, including octopus and squid, plenty of whole grains, vegetables and soy products too—more tofu and more konbu seaweed than anyone else in the world. Okinawa's indigenous vegetables are also important: their purple sweet potatoes are rich in flavonoids, carotenoids, vitamin E and lycopene and the local bitter cucumbers, or "goya," have been shown to lower blood sugar in diabetics. Willcox was asked which elements of the Okinawan diet he had introduced into his life and he said, turmeric and jasmine tea; because they both potentially ward off cancer.

The Okinawans eat small portions, practicing "hara hachi bu" which means they eat only till they are 80% full. Many now believe that eating 10% - 40% below the average dietary consumption levels can add up to 10 years to your life. The longest lived Americans are the Seventh Day Adventist of Loma Linda, California which eat a predominately vegetarian diet. The people of Costa Rica's Nicoya peninsula are also known for their longevity and also eat a predominately vegetarian diet which includes consuming large quantities of beans. So which diet is the best? According to Professor John Mather, a director of the Institute for Aging and Health at Newcastle University says that the prevailing scientific evidence weighs more heavily in favour of the Mediterranean diet. "There is not enough research on people who adopt the Japanese diet in non-Japanese settings." This is not an argument against the Japanese diet, only that there is less evidence available supporting its value in non-Japanese settings. Whereas there is a growing body of evidence supporting the value of the Mediterranean diet in non-Mediterranean settings.

In May, "The Guardian" newspaper published a story on the robust long lived people of Ikaria—a Greek island in the Mediterranean. The article reported that "one out of every three people live beyond 90." The dietary factors cited for the high percentage of long lived adults on the Greek island of Ikaria are herbal teas rich in antioxidants (including wild mint, good for digestion, and artemisia for blood circulation), gallons of olive oil, plenty of fresh vegetables and eating very little meat or dairy. "All of these diets work on similar mechanisms," Mather tells me. "One hypothesis is that the secret about aging is to avoid accumulating molecular damage, and eating fish, beans, nuts, seeds, legumes, whole grains, and not so much red meat, dairy or sugar may help us to reduce that kind of cellular damage."

APPENDIX F. 4 SIMPLE RULES TO SHAPE UP YOUR BRAIN

The latest research shows that all of us can pump up our brainpower by exercising regularly.

by Margery D. Rosen, AARP, May 8, 2013 Reprinted by permission.

Rarely do you find neuroscientist, psychologist and physicians agreeing unequivocally on anything. But here's an exception: They all say that exercise is hands down the single best thing you can do for your brain.

"If we had a pill that could do what exercise does, its sales would put Viagra's to shame," says Laura L. Carstensen, director of the Stanford Center on Longevity and author of *A Long Bright Future.*

Aerobic exercise "keeps cognitive abilities sharp and slashes your lifetime risk of Alzheimer's in half," says John Medina, an affiliate professor of bioengineering at the University of Washington School of Medicine and author of Brain Rules.

How is this possible? Scientists think exercise boosts the flow of blood to certain parts of the brain, spurring the release of brain-derived neurotrophic factor (BDNF), a brain chemical scientists have dubbed Miracle-Gro for the mind. BDNF stimulates the formation of new neurons in the hippocampus, the area involved in memory, learning and the ability to plan and make decisions. At the same time, the substance repairs cell damage and strengthens synapses, or the connections between brain cells.

Exercise also dials down stress, reduces the risk of stroke, helps control blood sugar and reduces the chances of falling by improving balance and coordination.

So if you're worried that your memory is fading as fast as your tennis game, it's time to get moving. For the greatest brain benefit, follow these four simple rules.

1: Start Now

It's never too late to start exercising for brain health, says Laura DeFina, M.D., medical director of research at the Cooper Institute and lead author of the study. "People always say, 'I'm 55 and I've never exercised. Does starting now really make a difference?' I tell them this: 'The answer is simple — yes, it absolutely matters.' "

In a pivotal study at the University of Illinois at Urbana-Champaign, researchers found that seniors 60- to 79-years-old who completed a six-month program of walking briskly on a regular basis showed an increase in the size of the hippocampus, as well as an increase in levels of BDNF comparable to those found in people almost two years younger. (The hippocampus typically shrinks by 0.5 percent each year, starting in some people as early as their 40s.) Two control groups in the study — one did stretching and toning exercises, another did nothing — showed no brain changes at all.

"This was the first time that we were able to demonstrate that you can actually increase the size of the hippocampus," says Kirk Erickson, a neuroscientist at the University of Pittsburgh and one of the study's lead authors.

"It was as if we'd rolled back the clock," he adds. "It proves that exercising even in late adulthood, even if you've not been active before, is not futile. People need to know that dementia is not inevitable.

Tips:

- If your doctor says you're healthy enough for exercise, find something that feels good to you. "The best exercise to do is the one you'll keep doing," says Carstensen. "It should be something you love, not something you dread."
- Recruit a friend or coworker to take a fitness class with you. Being with others can motivate you to keep going.
- Lay out your workout clothes the night before so you see them first thing in the morning. Athletes call this a "prime" — your personal signal to get moving.
- Plug in your iPod. Studies show that those who work out while listening to music exercise harder, and longer — without even realizing it.

2: Aim For 150 Minutes Of Moderate Exercise Per Week

Do the math — that's just 2-1/2 hours a week. "To get the brain benefit of exercise, the gold standard is 150 minutes of aerobic exercise, such as walking briskly, spread over the course of a week," says Medina. (Be sure to warm up before and cool down after with gentle stretches for five minutes.)

Nor do you have to train for a marathon to reap brain benefits. In a recent Canadian study, researchers followed a large group of elderly adults for 2-5 years. None were fitness fanatics; their daily activities included walking, cooking, gardening and cleaning house. The results were stunning: Year after year, 90 percent of those who were consistently active showed no decline in their ability to think and remember.

Anything that gets your heart beating faster works. "You want to break a light sweat and feel like you're huffing and puffing," says Majid Fotuhi, M.D., medical director of the Neurology Institute for Brain Health and Fitness in Lutherville, Md., "but you should still be able to speak."

Does it still count if you break up those 150 minutes into lots of smaller spurts? "That's the million-dollar question," says Erickson. "These figures have been largely based on studies of cardiovascular disease. While it's true that what's good for the heart is good for the brain, we can't say for sure that the figures also apply to brain fitness."

Tips:

- Go green. In a study from Ohio State University, people were more likely to stick with an exercise regimen when they were exercising outdoors. And researchers in Britain found that people who strolled through a park or other outdoor environment, as opposed to exercising indoors, had a measurable boost in focus, energy and well-being.
- Sneak it in. Park your car at the far end of the mall lot. Get off the bus several stops before home, or walk up and down the field during your grandchild's soccer game.
- If joints are stiff and muscles weak, try a low-impact workout like walking in the pool or taking a spin on a stationary bike. Pilates, yoga and tai-chi also place minimal stress on the body but still strengthen core muscles and improve balance. Never done any of that? All the better! As you'll read in our article on mental workouts, learning something new is another important pillar of brain health.

3: Add Strength Training

Strength or resistance training — using free weights, bands or machines — does more than bulk up your biceps. A study published in the Archives of Internal Medicine last year found that when women 70- to 80-years-old, who already had symptoms of mild cognitive impairment, did one to two hours of weight training two days a week for six months, they had better focus and decision-making skills than those in a control group who did only balance and toning exercises. They also were able to resolve conflicts more readily. The benefits went beyond simply stemming memory loss, researchers said, to actual improvements.

Tips:

- Especially if you have limited mobility or haven't lifted weights in more decades than you'd care to count, go easy, at least to start. Stretch before and after your workout.

- Aim for at least 30 minutes twice a week, and work all the major muscle groups — arms, shoulders and chest; abdomen and back; hips and legs.
- If you don't want to pay for a gym membership, buy your own hand weights and resistance bands. Then stow them next to the couch so you can squeeze in reps while you watch the news or catch up on Mad Men.
- If you're thinking "There's got to be an app for that," you're right! Look for inexpensive watches, earbuds and bracelets with sensors that sync to your smartphone and record data about your weight, sleep habits, vital signs and how many steps you take each day. Log on to your computer for graphs and charts that show how much you've accomplished and how far you have to go. Think of your smartphone as your personal trainer, cajoling you to stick with the program even when you're convinced you can't.

4: Dance Like Nobody Is Watching

"A colleague once told me, 'The problem with older people is they just don't dance anymore!'" says Carstensen. "He's right. Dancing is terrific exercise; it's fun and something most people can easily do."

Besides giving you a great cardio boost, dance improves balance, coordination and flexibility. It's also a weight-bearing exercise like jogging, walking, skiing, climbing stairs or skipping rope. These impact-producing activities all help you build bones and slow bone loss, expercially in the legs, hips and lower spine. Ballroom dances (think waltz, tango, foxtrot, salsa, cha-cha and swing) also work all the major muscle groups and build stamina.

Recent studies also have found that dancing helps forestall memory loss and dementia. A 2011 study in the Journal of Sports Science and Medicine found that older adults who met twice weekly for six months to dance the cha-cha improved their memory and cognitive performance on a variety of tests.

A 2005 study by researchers at McGill University in Montreal compared two groups of older adults — one group danced the tango twice a week, the other simply walked. After 10 weeks, both groups did better on several cognitive tests. But the dancers outperformed the walkers on multitasking tests and saw additional gains in their coordination and balance.

The next time you have friends over, shove the coffee table aside, put on some music and just move it. No one's judging you, so park your ego at the door.

Feeling rusty? Check out dance classes at your local Y or senior center; you'll be surprised at the variety. Learning new moves, or refreshing old ones, challenges your brain and builds new connections.

Too shy? YouTube offers thousands of videos that can get you up to speed before you put on your dancing shoes.

DOCTOR'S ORDERS

There's no one-size-fits-all exercise strategy, but we can all make simple lifestyle changes that go a long way toward boosting brain fitness. In his new book, *Boost Your Brain: The New Art and Science Behind Enhanced Brain Performance*, Majid Fotuhi, medical director of the Neurology Institute for Brain Health and Fitness in Lutherville, Md., outlines three fitness plans — one for couch potatoes who never exercise; a second for weekend warriors or those who only work out occasionally; and a third for people who want to bump up their fitness to the optimal level.

"The more fit your body gets, the stronger will be your 'memory muscle' — the hippocampus," says Fotuhi. "For the best brain boost, I recommend 30 minutes of vigorous aerobic activity, plus 15 minutes of resistance training, 5 days a week."

Who said an old dog can't learn new tricks? (Always get your doctor's OK before starting any exercise program.)

If you don't exercise at all:

Week 1: Start by walking for 5 to 10 minutes at a time, three days a week.

Week 2: Increase your walking time to 15 minutes, three days a week.

Week 3: Increase your walking time to 20 minutes, three days a week. In addition to your scheduled time, find ways to be active throughout the day.

If you exercise occasionally:

Week 1: Walk or jog for 20 minutes without interruption, three times a week.

Week 2: Increase your walking or jogging time to 30 minutes, four days a week. If you're walking, try to jog at least some of the time gradually increasing your jogging time if possible. Increase the amount of time you jog as the week goes on.

Week 3: Increase your walking or jogging to 30 minutes, five days a week. Gradually increase the intensity of your workout. If you'd like, you can substitute stationary bike, swimming or another aerobic activity, or you can substitute a one-hour game of tennis (or another intense activity) for two of your 30-minute sessions.

If you've been exercising regularly for years:

Week 1: Do 30 minutes of uninterrupted aerobic activity, five days a week, plus five extra minutes of weight lifting, push-ups or another muscle building activity, three days a week.

Week 2: Continue with 30 minutes of uninterrupted aerobic activity, five days a week. Bump up your muscle-building to 10 minutes, three days a week.

Week 3: Continue with 30 minutes of uninterrupted aerobic activity, five days a week. Bump up your weight lifting to 15 minutes, five days a week. Increase the intensity of your workout as needed so that you're improving your physical fitness.

APPENDIX G: GETTING STARTED

What you plant today will always harvest later.

This book contains a great deal of very valuable information about living a healthier life. However, large amounts of information can be overwhelming. It's easy to get lost in the details. People often need a simple place from which to begin, and simple, straight-forward, easy-to-follow instructions to get started. The following are practical, straight-forward steps to take today.

Beginning is half the journey.

I have found the following to be the simplest, easiest, and most effective way to eat healthy and lose weight naturally without a lot of willpower or have the sensation that you are enduring continual self-deprivation.

Let me start by saying that fasting is a very healthy activity for the body when done properly. Fasting stimulates the body's self-healing mechanism. Fasting for extended periods of time (3-21 days) is an age-old practice with many scientifically-proven health-restoring benefits.

Fasting (done properly) can be an awesome way to jump-start your health renewal. Seek a qualified source of guidance and authoritive book on the subject before beginning. If you have existing medical conditions, you may want to work with a doctor who is supportive and knowledgeable about the benefits of fasting.

Whether you choose to begin your health renewal with a fast or not is up to you. The nutritional plan that I recommend optimizes the value of our bodies' short-term natural fast (between dinner and breakfast) and also follows rules for combining foods at meals in ways that optimize digestion and minimize digestive burden.

Even a short fast for just half a day (12 hours) provides the body enough rest from the work of digesting food to begin the work of detoxification and self-healing. The nutritional plan that I recommend builds upon and optimizes our bodies natural fast (between dinner and breakfast) that is, literally, between dinner and when we "break fast".

This nutritional plan also follows rules for food combining which combines food groups together in ways that minimize digestive burden for the body. Stated negatively, rules for food combining restrict the combination of foods in ways that increase digestive burden. This is based upon strong scientific evidence that indicates that certain food groups digest well (easily and completely) together while other food group combinations digest poorly (with difficulty and incompletely) together. Simply put, the body secretes specific acids and specific enzymes to enable its digestion (breakdown) of specific food groups. Close examination of digestive processes indicates that the digestion of proteins requires a very different order and combination of hydrochloric acid and digestive enzymes than the digestion of starches and that the very different ways in which proteins and starches are digested do not complement one another; in fact they interfere with one another, impairing digestion and create digestive burden.

The nutritional approach that I recommend (and follow) combines the food groups together that digest well together and avoids combining food groups that digest poorly together, that is, the approach avoids combining foods together that require different and opposing digestive processes that interfere with one another and make digestion more difficult.

In essence, it is a matter of understanding how the process of human digestion operates and respecting my own body enough and loving my own body enough to follow an eating plan that makes the difficult work of digesting food as easy as possible. In return for loving myself enough to follow an eating plan that works with the body instead of against it, my body operates more efficiently. I experience less digestive burden and less physical fatigue after meals and I have found weight loss to be far less challenging.

Food combining is a complex enough subject to fill an entire chapter and becomes too restrictive to be sustainable for most people (myself included). However, the most important concepts of food combining are easily enough practiced as part of a "normal" diet and greatly ease the body's difficult work of digesting food. The following are the simplest and most important rules of food combining. For a complete examination of the subject and the scientific rationales for each rule read, "Food Combining Made Easy" by Herbert M. Shelton. Also many "Food Combining" charts can be printed out to make sense of the Do's and Don't's of food combining. I personally do not take Food Combining so seriously as to make my diet impractical and completely inconvenient; but I do follow the following rules most of the time, except for holiday gatherings when it becomes impractical. It is not the way you eat or do once in a while that will hurt you. It is living out of concert with your own best interests on a daily basis that sinks you down into the "affliction zone" of chronic disease.

These are the simplest and most beneficial "Food Combining" rules to follow:

- Do Not combine fruit with any other food except milk products, yogurt, cottage cheese or cheese.
- Do Not eat proteins and starches at the same meal.
- Limit fluids consumed with meals.
- Observe adequate digestion time between meals: 2.5 hrs for fruit/cultured milk meals; 3 hours for starch based meals; 4 hours for protein based meals.
- Limit food and fluid consumption during times required for normal digestion.
- An exception to the rule is eating enough food and drinking enough fluids during periods of extended physical/mental exertion.

Here is how I plan my meals in a way that optimizes my daily fast (between dinner and "break-fast"):

Upon awaking: Water or carrot juice mixed with Kylea "Total Living Drink: Greens" (Whole Food Dietary Supplement Powder)

30 mins. – 1 hr. later: Strong coffee mixed a little honey and coconut oil (used as a much healthier pseudo-creamer and to slow the absorption rate of the coffees caffeine into my system)

30 mins. – 1 hr. later: Fruit mixed with plain yogurt or low fat cottage cheese.

2.5 – 3 hrs. later: LUNCH - Starch or protein combined with living (raw) salad and/or cooked (preferably steamed) vegetables.

3 – 4 hrs. Later: DINNER - (depending on whether lunch was a protein or starch based meal) I have the other food group base. Example: If I had a starch with lunch I will have a protein based dinner or visa-versa.

Comments: I may have a little red wine with or after dinner. For daily hydration: I consume a majority of my fluids either after meals have fully digested and/or at least 30 minutes before next meal. If I am still hungry or feel a little low blood sugar 4 hours after dinner I may have a glass of carrot juice with Kylea Total Living Drink or a small portion of dessert or fruit and yogurt.

Commentary: My first real meal (with heavier foods) isn't until lunch usually between 12 – 2 pm. This pattern allows me to extend my body's natural fast between dinner and breakfast and consume large amounts of salad and vegetables with both lunch and dinner. By avoiding the consumption of starches and proteins at the same meal there doesn't leave much to eat except large raw salads and/or cooked or raw vegetables.

Let me repeat: By avoiding the consumption of protein and starches at the same meal (a basic staple of the American diet) I create the space for the consumption of a far more healthy alternative; which is having a large salad and vegetables with both lunch and dinner. I have found this dietary strategy to be an easy way to extend the benefits of my body's natural night time fast, reduce the amount of heavy foods I eat, and increase consumption of large amounts of fruit (early in the day) and vegetables/ salad that I eat (at both lunch and dinner).

It's All About Balance: I Follow the 70/30 Principle

70% of the time, I live well and eat well, but 30% of the time I allow myself the liberty and convenience of going with the flow. I follow these food-combining rules and this dietary regimen most of the time, but I do not hesitate to break them when they do not serve me well. If the demands of my day require I eat heavier foods earlier in the day, I do so. If the demands of my day do not allow me the option of having a salad and/or vegetables with my starch- or protein-based lunch or dinner, then I will combine protein and starches together for a meal. For example, a hamburger and bun or sandwich. I eat simply and healthfully a majority of the time, but I enjoy my freedom all of the time.

Getting Started on an Exercise Program

This whole book speaks about the benefit of exercise as your first and primary means to health recovery. But what type and how much? If you are not familiar with exercise for its own sake. It can be daunting to know where to begin.

Just do it! Beginning is half the journey. Start with walking daily, or if that is hard on the joints. Start with a water aerobics class or on a recumbent (stationary) bike. Start out very gradually and build up the distance, time and intensity. It is important not to increase the volume of exercise (either time, distance, or intensity) by more than ten percent per week.

Variety and companionship helps keep exercise interesting. Allow for a period of warming up and a period of stretching afterwards to cool down and to prevent muscular stiffness and improve flexibility. Add some resistance exercises, and explore different exercises and combinations of exercise and gradually increase the time and intensity of the exercises you enjoy most. Stay the course. Commit yourself to sticking with it for 3 months and then re-evaluate how you feel. Give it at least 3 months of dedicated follow through before making an evaluation of whether the benefits are worth the effort. My hope is that you will have made exercise your friend and its benefits your life long companion.

Appendix H

Premise and supporting evidence:

A Healthy Lifestyle Decreases Hospital Utilization and Medical Costs

Below you will find excerpts from seminal articles on the topic at hand. For a more complete review please access these articles in their entirety.

The Healthcare Challenge

Article 1

Effects of exercise and diet on chronic disease

Christian K. Roberts, R. James Barnard

Journal of Applied Physiology Published 1 January 2005 Vol. 98 no. 1, 3-30 DOI: 10.1152/japplphysiol.00852.2004

http://jap.physiology.org/content/98/1/3

Abstract

Currently, modern chronic diseases, including cardiovascular diseases, Type 2 diabetes, metabolic syndrome, and cancer, are the leading killers in Westernized society and are increasing rampantly in developing nations. In fact, obesity, diabetes, and hypertension are now even commonplace in children. Clearly, however, there is a solution to this epidemic of metabolic disease that is inundating today's societies worldwide: exercise and diet. Overwhelming evidence from a variety of sources, including epidemiological, prospective cohort, and intervention studies, links most chronic diseases seen in the world today to physical inactivity and inappropriate diet consumption. The purpose of this review is to 1) discuss the effects of exercise and diet in the prevention of chronic disease, 2) highlight the effects of lifestyle modification for both mitigating disease progression and reversing existing disease, and 3) suggest potential mechanisms for beneficial effects.

Article 2

Do Prevention Or Treatment Services Save Money? The Wrong Debate

http://content.healthaffairs.org/content/28/1/37.full

Abstract

Health improvements and cost savings are achievable by providing targeted, evidence-based, and cost-effective health promotion and disease prevention programs that reduce modifiable risk factors, often the cause of costly chronic diseases. Adopting commonsense health practices does not require expensive technology, medication, specialty training, or elaborate treatment facilities. Instituting environmental, policy, and normative interventions, in addition to individual behavior change programs, can shift our thinking about how we pay for health. Employers' efforts in providing health promotion programs to their workers offer a microcosm of how prevention can lead to population wide risk reduction and cost savings.

Instead of debating whether prevention or treatment saves money, we should determine the most cost-effective ways to improve population health.

Article 3

Decline In Utilization Rates Signals A Change In The Inpatient Business Model

Mark Grube, Kenneth Kaufman, and Robert York; March 8, 2013

http://healthaffairs.org/blog/2013/03/08/decline-in-utilization-rates-signals-a-change-in-the-inpatient-business-model/

Use rates for inpatient and certain hospital outpatient services are declining in many areas of the country, reflecting fundamental change brought by the new business model. Importantly, as evidenced by trends in Chicago and Minnesota, there also appears to be a correlation between the level and pace of a market's shift toward value-based care and the level and pace of utilization decline.

We believe this trend is here to stay and that it has significant strategic and financial implications for health care providers. Specifically, providers that embrace the migration to value-based care will need to work aggressively to eliminate unnecessary and/or ineffective activities in order to thrive under risk contracts. This requires a fundamental change in mindset, culture, and attitude about volume and activity. It also requires providers to rethink the organization and structure of their delivery networks to avoid supporting unnecessary capacity, and to drive patients into the lowest-possible cost setting in which quality care can be delivered.

The goal will be to manage a population's health across the care continuum, keeping patients healthy through preventive and primary care services, and out of acute care facilities whenever possible. The right place to provide the right care at the right time with the right quality, cost, and access increasingly will be a setting other than a hospital. By eliminating waste and redirecting patients to ambulatory centers, physician offices, clinics, and online and/or telephonic interactions, less work will be done in the hospital.

Article 4

Health Literacy and Health Outcomes

https://health.gov/communication/literacy/quickguide/factsliteracy.htm

Choosing a healthy lifestyle, knowing how to seek medical care, and taking advantage of preventive measures require that people understand and use health information. The ability to obtain, process, and understand health information needed to make informed health decisions is known as health literacy.

Choosing a healthy lifestyle, knowing how to seek medical care, and taking advantage of preventive measures require that people understand and use health information. The ability to obtain, process, and understand health information needed to make informed health decisions is known as health literacy.

Given the complexity of the healthcare system, it is not surprising that limited health literacy is associated with poor health. This fact sheet summarizes key research study findings on the relationship between health literacy and health outcomes.

Use of preventive services

According to research studies, persons with limited health literacy skills are more likely to skip important preventive measures such as mammograms, Pap smears, and flu shots.1 When compared to those with adequate health literacy skills, studies have shown that patients with limited health literacy skills enter the healthcare system when they are sicker.2

Knowledge about medical conditions and treatment

Persons with limited health literacy skills are more likely to have chronic conditions and are less able to manage them effectively. Studies have found that patients with high blood pressure,3 diabetes,3-5 asthma,6 or HIV/AIDS7-9 who have limited health literacy skills have less knowledge of their illness and its management.

Rates of hospitalization

Limited health literacy skills are associated with an increase in preventable hospital visits and admissions.10-13 Studies have demonstrated a higher rate of hospitalization and use of emergency services among patients with limited literacy skills.12

Healthcare costs

Persons with limited health literacy skills make greater use of services designed to treat complications of disease and less use of services designed to preventcomplications.1, 11-13 Studies demonstrate a higher rate of hospitalization and use of emergency services among patients with limited health literacy skills.10-13This higher use is associated with higher healthcare costs.15 16,

Article 5

Reducing Hospital Readmissions With Enhanced Patient Education

http://www.bu.edu/fammed/projectred/publications/news/krames_dec_final.pdf

At least 20 percent of all patients who are admitted to a U.S. hospital make a repeat visit within 30 days of discharge, according to Medicare and others who've studied the pervasive problem of hospital readmissions.1 Medicare alone currently spends $15 billion a year on re-hospitalizations, and in 2004 estimated the total cost to be $17.4 billion. These tallies do not account for the intangible strain high readmissions put on hospitals or the distress and dissatisfaction caused to patients who repeatedly find themselves back in the hospital. But a whopping three-quarters of readmissions could likely be avoided with better care, reported a 2007 congressional report by the Medicare Payment Advisory Commission. And hospitals, insurance companies, and the US Congress have taken notice. Specifically, under the new federal healthcare law, the Centers for Medicare & Medicaid (CMS) services will use a 30-day cutoff to start penalizing hospitals with higher than expected rates of readmissions, starting in 2012, and may ultimately refuse payment for selected diagnoses that occur within this timeframe. Health reform legislation also initiates a closer look at global payment systems, with a number of pilot projects planned that would include reimbursement per diagnosis as opposed to each service, including readmissions, related to a diagnosis.

Patients who have a clear understanding of their after-hospital care instructions, including how to take their medicines and when to make follow up appointments, are 30 percent less likely to be readmitted or visit the emergency department than patients who lack this information.

Making patient education work

While the pattern is clear that patients who have a better understanding of their medications, signs and symptoms of disease, diet and lifestyle requirements and upcoming physician appointments and tests have exponentially better success staying healthy outside the hospital, not all patient education programs are created equal. Across the dozens of completed studies and initiatives underway, organizations with the best results have the following traits in common: • Teaching efforts are consistently targeted to the appropriate key learner • Educators consistently evaluate patients' understanding of the information provided • Organizational culture supports efforts to prioritize patient education • Strategies and technologies are adopted to make patient education activities fit easily, if not automatically, into hospital employees' work flow • Education materials are designed thoughtfully with the patient in mind

1] Identify the key learner
2] Evaluate learning
3] Create a culture supporting education
4] Adopt systems to make it seamless
5] Provide patients with well-developed materials

Author Summary:

Improving patient education programs will greatly help in reducing rates of hospitalization and re-hospitalization. However, I believe that the most effective use of limited financial resources will be the promotion of aggressive, targeted comprehensive lifestyle transformation programs committed to supporting the 5% - 10% most chronically ill in adopting a lifestyle pattern that optimizes their health and wellness at every age.

Train the mind and the body will follow…

Human personality and behavior respond well to nurturing and positive reinforcement.

To effectively reduce the medical costs of our nation, it will require more effort and energy be applied to training up our patients in the ways of healthy self-maintenance.

The effects of legislative efforts to mandate more effective patient education programs and rapid follow up of patients in the home health setting has led to significant reductions in the costs associated with frequent re-hospitalizations.

But what is still needed is federal funding to support our patients adoption of a health promoting lifestyle. Once patients begin to participate in healthier habits and reap the benefits of an improving sense of well-being, they will become increasingly convinced of those habits enduring value and strive to maintain their newly acquired habits and lifestyle in order to continue to enjoy improving health. Both wisdom and health are their own greatest reward and once partaken of they are not easily forsaken.

Article 6

What kinds of health problems are linked to overweight and obesity?

https://www.niddk.nih.gov/health-information/weight-management/health-risks-overweight

Excess weight may increase the risk for many health problems, including

- type 2 diabetes
- high blood pressure
- heart disease and strokes
- certain types of cancer
- sleep apnea
- osteoarthritis
- fatty liver disease
- kidney disease
- pregnancy problems, such as high blood sugar during pregnancy, high blood pressure, and increased risk for cesarean delivery (C-section)

Article 7

How Health Care Costs Lower With Healthy Diet & Exercise

by VAN THOMPSON Last Updated: Sep 11, 2017

http://www.livestrong.com/article/302080-how-health-care-costs-lower-with-healthy-diet-exercise/

With the advent of the Affordable Care Act, health insurers can no longer deny coverage or increase rates based upon pre-existing medical conditions. While the overall costs of health care will go down, you'll still have to pay some health care costs out of pocket. A good diet and regular exercise can reduce your risk of falling prey to the common conditions that drive up the costs of health care.

Better Cardiovascular Health

Both diet and exercise can affect your cardiovascular health. A high-fat diet can result in obesity, high cholesterol, heart attacks, high blood pressure, diabetes and other costly maladies. Regular exercise improves your heart's health and can lower blood pressure and cholesterol over time. Those with chronic heart problems can also benefit from exercise. A 2013 study published in the Canadian Journal of Cardiology found that regular physical exercise can improve symptoms in patients with atrial fibrillation. If your heart health improves, you'll likely avoid spending money on cardiologists, heart medications and regular heart checkups.

Reduced Risk of Chronic Illnesses

According to the U.S. Centers for Disease Control and Prevention (CDC), regular exercise can reduce your risk of diabetes, osteoarthritis and obesity. The CDC reports that obesity alone costs $147 billion a year. Diabetes, a common result of obesity, often necessitates medication, regular checkups, massive diet changes and even surgery. Obesity puts you at risk of a wide variety of costly conditions. By exercising regularly and eating a healthful diet, you can significantly decrease your health care costs and avoid being a part of the group who drives up the overall cost of health care.

Improved Emotional Well-Being

According to the CDC, regular exercise can reduce the risk of depression and improve sleep quality. According to the National Alliance on Mental Illness, mental illness costs $34 billion each year in health care costs, in workplace inefficiency and other costs. By reducing your susceptibility to mental health problems, you will save money on the costs associated with those problems, like therapy and medication. You'll also likely be more productive and more content with your life.

Preventing Cancer

According to the Physicians Committee for Responsible Medicine, a high-fat diet increases the risk of cancer. A diet rich in vegetables and whole grains lowers the risk of cancer. Similarly, the CDC reports that regular exercise can decrease the risk of some cancers, such as lung and endometrial cancers. A healthful diet and regular exercise can help reduce your risk of cancer and save you the exorbitant costs and hardships associated with a cancer diagnosis, such as chemotherapy, regular hospital visits, surgery, prescription drugs and palliative care.

Article 8: Case Study (Research in Action, Issue 9)

Reducing Costs in the Health Care System: Learning From What Has Been

This synthesis describes evidence-based research demonstrating what strategies reduce health care costs and what strategies have only mixed results.

By Mark W. Stanton, M.A.

SOURCE: https://archive.ahrq.gov/research/findings/factsheets/costs/costria/costria.html

Introduction of a State mental health parity mandate [Author's Note: Generally speaking, parity means equality. The term parity for mental health and chemical dependency means that insurance benefits for any group of mental health diagnoses are the same as insurance benefits for medical/surgical diagnoses including cost sharing, service limits, and lifetime or annual spending limits. This essentially means one would receive equal coverage for mental health and physical health.] for severe mental disorders was expected to lead to significant increases in health care costs for a large employer group and its insurers. One insurer responded to this concern by introducing a managed behavioral health care carve-out. In a carve-out, an organization separate from the principal health insurer is selected to manage health care needs in a specific area (e.g., behavioral health) for the employees of the group.

One particular program proved very cost effective. The Managed Behavioral Health Carve-Out program lowered costs dramatically.

To learn how the managed behavioral health care carve-out affected use and costs of care, researchers from AHRQ and the National Institute of Mental Health studied 75,000 enrollees over a 4-year period before and after the carve-out went into effect.10

After the carve-out had been in effect for 3 years:

- Per-member plan costs for mental health/substance abuse services declined by almost 40 percent.
- Per-member plan costs for children and adolescents declined even more steeply—by 64 percent.

Almost the entire drop in mental health/substance abuse costs was attributable to a decline in the number of inpatient hospital days for children and adolescents.

Examples of: Lifestyle Transformation Programs

Sisters Together Program:

- https://www.niddk.nih.gov/health-information/weight-management/sisters-together-program-guide

Weight Management Resources:

- https://www.niddk.nih.gov/health-information/weight-management/adult-overweight-obesity

Pritikin Longevity Center:

- https://www.pritikin.com/

YMCA Diabetes Prevention Program:

- http://www.ymca.net/diabetes-prevention/

Neuro Yoga Resources:

- https://neuroyoga.zone/
- https://www.northeastrehab.com/services/healthy-lifestyles/